D0998500

DEATH IN ANCIENT ROME

DEATH IN ANCIENT ROME

CATHARINE EDWARDS

YALE UNIVERSITY PRESS
NEW HAVEN AND LONDON

Copyright © 2007 Catharine Edwards

All rights reserved. This book may not be reproduced in whole or in part, in any form
(beyond that copying permitted by Sections 107 and 108 of the U.S. Copyright Law
and except by reviewers for the public press), without written permission from the
publishers.

For information about this and other Yale University Press publications please contact:
U.S. Office: sales.press@yale.edu   yalebooks.com
Europe Office: sales@yaleup.co.uk   www.yalebooks.co.uk

Set in Minion and Trump Medieval by Carnegie Book Production, Lancaster

Printed in Great Britain by St Edmundsbury Press Ltd, Bury St Edmunds

Library of Congress Cataloging-in-Publication Data
Edwards, Catharine.
Death in ancient Rome / Catharine Edwards.
    p. cm.
Includes bibliographical references and index.
ISBN 978-0-300-11208-5
1. Death--Social aspects—Rome.   2. Rome—History.   3. Rome—Social life and
customs.   4. Civilization, Ancient.   I. Title.
HQ1073.5.R66E38 2007
306.90937—dc22

A catalogue record for this book is available from the British Library

10 9 8 7 6 5 4 3 2 1

For Bernard

CONTENTS

List of illustrations   ix

Acknowledgements   xi

Introduction: Dying a Roman death   1

1   Dying for Rome? The glorious death of a commander   19

2   Death as spectacle: looking at death in the arena   46

3   Fighting the fear of death   78

4   Defiance, complicity and the politics of self-destruction   113

5   Dying in character: Stoicism and the Roman death scene   144

6   Tasting death   161

7   A feminine ending?   179

8   Laughing at death? Christian martyrdom   207

Notes   221

Abbreviations   264

Bibliography   268

Index   283

ILLUSTRATIONS

1 Pottery oil lamp, first century CE   48
  (Lü 663; Römisch-Germanisches Museum, Cologne)

2 Pottery oil lamp, Italy, late first century BCE   56
  (Q761; © The Trustees of the British Museum)

3 Pottery oil lamp made in Roman Britain or Gaul, first century CE 57
  (RES1469A; © The Trustees of the British Museum)

4 Relief of gladiators   65
  (GL 364; Staatliche Antikensammlungen und Glyptothek,
  Munich)

5 Mosaic of skeleton butler from Pompeii, probably first half of
  first century CE   165
  (Museo Nazionale, Naples, Bridgman/Alinari Archives, Florence)

6 Silver goblet from Boscoreale   166
  (Paris, Musée du Louvre, Photo RMN/© Hervé Lewandowski)

ACKNOWLEDGEMENTS

I owe a particular debt to Mary Beard for her encouragement over the years, as well as for her acute and thought-provoking criticism of earlier versions of this project. Altan Walker has induced me to think about death more generally in new and (sometimes uncomfortably) challenging ways, in particular helping me to understand something of death's potential appeal. Thomas Osborne and Daniel Pick, too, have helped me to clarify some important conceptual issues. Important intellectual and moral support has also been provided by Denis Feeney, Robin Osborne and Susanna Morton Braund. Responding to earlier versions of individual chapters, seminar participants and lecture audiences at the universities of Bristol, Cambridge, Exeter, London, Oxford, Nottingham, St Andrews and Washington (Seattle) have asked testing questions and offered valuable suggestions and insights. I am also grateful to William Fitzgerald and to David Wray for allowing me to see unpublished work, which has, in both cases, significantly influenced my argument. Lucy Grig, Shelley Hales, Caroline Humfress, Matthew Innes and Denis Blandford have provided vital bibliographic help. Malcolm Gerratt at Yale University Press has been a very supportive editor and I am most grateful to Vanessa Mitchell for scrupulous copy-editing. Thanks also go to Paul Taylor for helping me to find the cover illustration.

The School of History, Classics and Archaeology at Birkbeck has been a wonderful environment in which to work. In particular I have benefited immensely from the support of my colleagues Christy Constantakopoulou and, especially, Emma Dench, who in suggesting I teach a course on death in antiquity prompted me to conceive of this book. The enthusiastic interest and critical acuity of Birkbeck students have also played a key role in helping my ideas develop over recent years. The project's completion was made possible by financial support from the AHRC and from Birkbeck. Thanks go to CUP for permission to publish a revised version of Chapter 5. Parts of this originally appeared as 'Acting and self-actualisation in ancient Rome'

377–94 in P. Easterling and E. Hall (eds) *Greek and Roman Actors: Aspects of an Ancient Profession* (Cambridge 2002).

During the time I was writing this book, my step-father Robert Weevers (who died in May 2006), my mother Elinor Edwards and my father John Edwards have shown inspiring courage in the face of grave illness and bereavement, a set of circumstances which has given this project a particular poignancy for its author. My husband Bernard Rafferty and our daughters Isabel and Miranda have been sources of life-affirming distraction and sustaining love, without which I could not have embarked on or completed such a sober work.

INTRODUCTION
DYING A ROMAN DEATH

An epigram of Martial written in the late first century CE praises the 'Roman death' – *Romana mors* – of a man called Festus, who kills himself rather than suffer a long-drawn-out death from cancer. For Romans killing oneself was often an act of heroism, something to be celebrated. Festus did not choose starvation to end his life, as the terminally ill in ancient Rome often seem to have done; an allusion to Cato makes it abundantly clear that Festus has taken his life with a blade.[1] Cato's suicide, a century before Martial was writing, had come to constitute the archetypal Roman death. His particular act of self-destruction – painful, bloody, inflicted with a sword – would be seen as the inspiration or point of comparison for a host of other deaths.

Cato's death was an iconic event. Marcus Porcius Cato came from a distinguished aristocratic family. Most eminent among his forefathers was another Marcus Porcius Cato, celebrated for his severity as censor (a role involving the regulation of aristocratic morals) in the second century BCE. The Younger Cato, noted for his adherence to Stoicism and for his own austere morals, was a long-term critic of Julius Caesar's ambitions. Once civil war had broken out he sided with Pompey (reluctantly, historians relate) in an attempt to contain Caesar. He was celebrated as a fearless general; even after Pompey's defeat at Pharsalus, Cato was noted for his leadership of the remaining republican forces.

The most detailed version of his death to have survived is that of Plutarch (*Cato minor* 66–73), who wrote his biography in Greek more than a century after Cato's death. News of another defeat in the civil war, making the prospect of Caesar's tyranny inevitable, is brought to Cato at Utica, on the North African coast.[2] Though Caesar offers to spare Cato (and is known for his clemency toward his defeated enemies), Cato asserts that allowing Caesar the opportunity to spare him would serve to acknowledge and legitimate Caesar's rule. Cato resolves to die rather than live under Caesar, first making arrangements to ensure the safety of those with him in Utica.

The night before his death Cato is calm and discusses Stoic philosophy over dinner with his companions. He is, however, roused in offering a defence of the Stoic proposition that 'only the good man is free, while the bad are all slaves'; his companions perceive from this that he has made up his mind to kill himself. On retiring to bed he takes with him Plato's dialogue on the immortality of the soul (usually identified with the *Phaedo* which recounts the death of Socrates, condemned by an Athenian court to die by drinking hemlock). When his companions express concern, he offers them reasoned arguments for his suicide. Later that night he tries to kill himself with his own sword – but because his hand is injured, the blow is not quite powerful enough. His companions come to his rescue and his wound is sewn up by a surgeon. But such is Cato's determination that he tears open the wound again with his bare hands and eventually succeeds in taking his life. The original suicide attempt – the plunging in of the sword – is one without witnesses. His companions are, however, present for the tearing open of the wound and for Cato's final, agonising moments.

Cato's bravery and determination in taking his own life brought him immediate glory. A few months later, in July 46 BCE, Cicero wrote to Papirius Paetus: *ceteri quidem, Pompeius, Lentulus tuus, Scipio, Afranius foede perierunt. At Cato praeclare.* 'The others indeed, Pompey, your Lentulus, Scipio, Afranius died wretchedly. But Cato with distinction' (*Fam.* 9.18.2).[3] Other leading Romans also took their own lives during the civil war years.[4] Besides Scipio, there were, most notably, Cassius and Brutus, the leading assassins of Julius Caesar who both committed suicide in 42 BCE, following defeats in battle by Mark Antony and Octavian at Philippi.[5]

Cato's nephew Brutus, celebrated in another of Plutarch's biographies, was also known for his commitment to philosophy.[6] It was Cato's opposition to Caesar, however, which seemed most principled and consistent, Cato's death which seemed most resolute. Cicero in a letter to Atticus (written around May 46 BCE) stresses Cato's *gravitas* and *constantia* (his 'seriousness' and 'endurance'), then continues:

Sed vere laudari ille vir non potest nisi haec ornata sint, quod ille ea quae nunc sunt et futura viderit et ne fierent contenderit et facta ne videret vitam reliquerit.

But true praise of that man must make clear that he anticipated our present situation and struggled to avert it and killed himself rather than see it come to pass.

(*Att.* 12.4.2)

Cato's death confirms the value, and marks the end, of all that the republic stood for. Cicero himself wrote a pamphlet celebrating Cato. Shortly afterwards in 45 BCE Cato's nephew Brutus, apparently dissatisfied with Cicero's attempt, wrote his own eulogy of his uncle (around this time he married Cato's daughter).[7] But Cato's controversial life and death provoked heated criticism as well as praise.[8] Responding to these works (which no doubt at least implied criticism of Caesar) Caesar himself wrote an *Anticato*.[9]

Almost immediately, then, versions of Cato's death were written up and in circulation (though little of these early versions has survived).[10] Cato's death was rapidly taken as emblematic of Roman striving to place liberty above life – a death which marked the end of the republic yet also served as a testament to the value some Romans at least placed on its ideals. Lucan's celebration of Cato in his epic poem on the civil war (composed a century later and usually referred to as *Bellum civile*) is among the most striking treatments of this theme.[11] But the resonance of Cato's death went beyond the specifically political. In some respects, the death of Cato may be seen as modelled on the death of Socrates, as celebrated in the work of Plato and Xenophon (this is clearly signalled by Plutarch's reference to Cato's reading the night before he died). For the philosopher Seneca, Cato's protracted and laborious end offered a perfect example of specifically Stoic endurance of suffering. All these aspects of Cato's end will be explored further in what follows. Cato's death, as represented by his contemporaries and by later Romans (as well as by the Greek Plutarch), constitutes a key episode in the development of Roman attitudes to death and dying. Indeed this event may be seen as precipitating the Roman obsession with aristocratic death – or at least taking it to a new level of intensity.[12]

For writers in later periods, too, Cato's death has often been treated as emblematic of a specifically Roman approach to investing the end of life with meaning – or using one's death to convey a potent message.[13] Writing in the late sixteenth century Montaigne (who was deeply immersed in Greek and Latin literature, most particularly the works of Seneca) returned again and again to Roman attitudes to death, particularly but not exclusively in relation to the death of Cato.[14] For him the exploration of such topics could constitute a kind of death meditation, a resource to enable him to face the prospect of his own death, whenever it should come.[15] Let us consider his treatment of another Roman death, one motivated by illness rather than politics.[16] Indeed suicide motivated by illness is another Roman paradigm (as Martial's epigram on Festus suggests). Ill and in pain, Titus Pomponius Atticus (close friend and correspondent of Cicero) summoned his friends and family and announced that he intended to end his own life by starving himself to death. Yet his chosen means of self-destruction within days seemed to cure his disease. Despite this, Atticus continued to refuse food. His reason, according to Montaigne? He would have to die some time: 'Having got thus far, he wanted to rid himself of the trouble of starting all over again on another occasion.' Montaigne's version of the death of Atticus, included in an essay 'On judging someone else's death', is adapted from Cornelius Nepos' biography of Atticus (21–2). The comment on Atticus' motive, we might note, is Montaigne's own addition.[17] Recounting a number of Roman deaths, Montaigne observes: 'It is to go far beyond having no fear of death actually to want to taste it, to savour it.'[18] To him this seems to be a notable characteristic of the most distinguished Roman deaths. It is this extended contemplation of death's imminence which shows true resolution and constancy. At the same time, Montaigne appears to suggest also that for some at least there is a kind of pleasure to be had in experiencing fully one's own end. His account stresses the self-consciousness of the dying subject who can appreciate the beauty of his own death.[19]

Montaigne's essay draws almost exclusively on examples from the Greek but especially the Roman worlds. Despite his Christian beliefs, which entailed a condemnation of suicide and a commitment to the grace and salvation Stoic virtues on their own could never secure, Montaigne is full of wonder and admiration at the capacity of these ancient exemplars to confront their deaths so bravely.[20] Pride of place in Montaigne's essay goes to the death of Cato. Montaigne repeatedly touches on aspects of Cato's life, but it is particularly Cato's death which compels his attention.

> But so that Cato alone should furnish a complete model of virtue it seems that his good destiny gave him some trouble in the arm with which he dealt himself the blow, in order to afford him leisure to confront Death and to fall about its neck, strengthening his courage in that peril, not weakening it.[21]

Montaigne draws heavily here (as often elsewhere) on Seneca, in particular *De providentia* 2.12, which we shall consider later.[22] But Montaigne goes further than Seneca in having Cato embrace death. Here, too, Montaigne traces, without seeming to stigmatise, a kind of desire for death on the part of his Roman heroes.

The aesthetic dimension to his treatment of Roman death scenes finds striking expression in the concluding sentences of 'On judging someone else's death', where Montaigne imagines Cato's death as the subject of a work of sculpture.[23] This image may be seen as a response to the strongly visual nature of ancient descriptions – most notably those of Seneca. In the later eighteenth century, when the vogue for history painting took on a new urgency in the context of revolutionary France, the death of Cato formed the subject of numerous paintings, such as that of Pierre Narcisse Guérin, dating from 1797.[24]

Why should the narrative of Cato's death hold such strong appeal in Roman antiquity and beyond? How should we explain the Roman preoccupation with the specific detail of Cato's death scene – and those of others too? By what means did these deaths come to be invested with such intense political and philosophical resonance? The strategies by which death is represented, the extent to which Romans may be seen as aestheticising death, fascinated as well as repelled by the limit of life, all these issues lie at the heart of my project. The exploration of such questions will serve, I hope, to generate insights into Roman culture more generally. But perhaps, too, it may highlight matters of broader significance, for in every culture we must develop strategies to confront death.

Approaching Roman death

Commemoration and mortuary ritual in the Roman world – practices which leave extensive material traces – have received considerable attention in recent studies.[25] Important work has also been carried out on questions such as the relation between demography and attitudes to death.[26] Did lower life expectancy, for instance, mean death was more of a preoccupation? Should the Romans (and the Greeks) be seen as making a more limited emotional investment in young children, given that any child ran a significant risk of dying in the first year of life? The specific determinants of the distinctive Roman attitude to self-killing have also been the subject of a number of studies in the last few decades.[27] But these accounts of Roman conceptions of self-killing have not been fully integrated into an exploration of Roman attitudes to death more generally. Other facets of Roman discussions of death have been suggestively discussed in the work of Keith Hopkins, Carlin Barton and Paul Plass.[28] Yet the significance Romans attached to the act of dying has yet to be fully explored.

The act of dying as it is represented in some key Latin literary texts is the central concern of this book. Dying is fundamentally an active rather than a passive process for these Roman writers. In particular we shall explore the nexus of preoccupations which centre on dying as an act of communication with the living. Almost all the writers we look at share a perception of death as a privileged moment which has the capacity to reveal the true character of the dying subject. In this respect, the death of Cato remains a key *exemplum*. But a huge number of other deaths, as they are described by a wide variety of different authors, show similar characteristics. Poetic texts will be discussed (Virgil and Lucan in particular) but the emphasis is rather on prose literature, above all the works of Seneca and Tacitus, whose writings seem particularly preoccupied with a certain type of morally and politically resonant death. These authors have also played a key role in transmitting a very specific notion of Roman death to later cultures. For all their idiosyncrasies, their preoccupations are, as I hope to show, in tune with the treatment of death on the part of many other Roman writers.

This literature was read by only a small proportion of the Roman empire's population – those with a high level of literary education. It was produced by an even narrower circle. Such texts, then, can give us little help with questions such as whether the average Roman believed in an afterlife, though there are moments when we may glimpse something of the multifarious nature of such beliefs. At times Romans thinking with death may seem primarily engaged in the pursuit of complex literary and philosophical games. Nevertheless, as I shall argue, the circulation of such literature clearly affected how some at least thought about death and their expectations of how people should die.

Undoubtedly the advent of Christianity made an enormous difference to attitudes to death (and some aspects of this will be discussed briefly in the concluding chapter). Yet the culture represented by the non-Christian texts examined here remains fundamentally imbricated in the culture of the modern west. At certain times, ancient Rome has functioned as a source of immense cultural authority, an enabling counterweight to the doctrines of the church. This may be less true now than in some earlier periods. Nevertheless many of the most influential thinkers of the last century return to the literature of Roman antiquity. In writing about the inexpressibility of death, for instance, Derrida draws on Seneca's treatise on the brevity of life *De brevitate vitae*. Seneca's intense engagement with death Derrida finds particularly good to think with – to contemplate the 'rear-view mirror of a waiting-for-death at every moment'.[29]

The purpose of my book is to explore this Roman death discourse in a way which will demonstrate the degree to which it is rooted in other aspects of Roman culture – anxieties about gender difference, social differentiation, personal identity, national identity, political change. The language Romans use to talk about death is of fundamental importance here.[30] We shall explore, for instance, the idea of death as a particularly testing form of combat for the soldier-subject; death as an aesthetic artefact wrought by a self-conscious artist; death as a brutal act of rape. Roman writers compare human life to a play or a banquet, a structured process with an inevitable conclusion (the implications of these analogies are teased out in Chapters 5 and 6). Conversely death itself functions as metaphor – for religious initiation, for instance, or poetic inspiration (as we shall see below), while suicide might be invoked as a metaphor for civil war. Finally, a brief concluding discussion will touch on some key respects in which Roman explorations of death anticipate concerns of Christian texts – while remaining profoundly different.

It is commonplace in the modern western world to see a sudden death as a desirable way to go. A similar view is occasionally articulated in Roman texts. The Elder Pliny, in Book 7 of his *Natural Histories* (a work in which he aims to give an exhaustive account of the wonders of the natural world), discusses at length aspects of the human condition. In relation to death he comments that 'sudden deaths', *mortes repentinae*, are 'life's supreme happiness', *summa vitae felicitas*, and goes on to list many individuals who have been so blessed (*NH* 7.180). According to the biographer Suetonius, Julius Caesar shared this view: *pridie quam occideretur, in sermone nato super cenam apud Marcum Lepidum, quisnam esset finis vitae commodissimus, repentinum inopinatumque praetulerat*, 'The day before he died, a discussion had arisen over dinner at Marcus Lepidus' house as to what was the best way to finish one's life, in which Caesar voiced his preference for a death that was quick and unexpected'. For Suetonius' sources, Caesar's dramatic end, assassination at the hands of the conspirators, was *talem ei mortem paene ex sententia obtigisse*, 'of pretty much the kind of which he approved' (Suet. *Iul.* 87). There is perhaps an implication that Caesar's preference is unusual.[31] At any rate the particular 'fit' between Caesar's wishes and the circumstances of his death is thought worthy of record. Suetonius places considerable emphasis on the manner in which each of the twelve Caesars dies and devotes much space to a narrative of each death. Indeed his accounts of the deaths of Julius Caesar (*Iul.* 81–2) and of Nero (*Nero* 40–9) are among the most gripping chapters in his writing.[32]

Even when a death was relatively quick it might still disclose much about the dying subject. More often Roman texts focus on deaths which are long drawn out and self-conscious. Despite the militaristic nature of Roman society, death in war, as we shall see in Chapter 1, receives only limited attention in Roman discussions of death. Yet, as Roman aristocrats are increasingly excluded from high-profile military campaigns under the principate, the process of dying seems to become a new arena for the exercise of a kind of quasi-martial virtue (as we shall see in Chapters 2 and 3). Martial virtue was considered an exclusively masculine preserve; dying could scarcely be so circumscribed. To what degree was it possible for a woman to die a properly Roman death? Women's deaths will be the focus of Chapter 7 but the relationship between death and gender more generally will also be a particular preoccupation of this study.

Death marked the organisation of life in countless ways in ancient Rome (as, of course, in other societies). The revelatory character of an individual's death was thought to be mirrored, for instance, in the sincerity of his or her will. Will making, too, was a moment of truth, when one's real sentiments towards friends and family would be set down, to be revealed after one's death. The Younger Pliny reports a popular saying: *creditur vulgo testamenta hominum speculum esse morum*, 'it is commonly believed that a will is a true reflection of man's character' (*Ep.* 8.18.1). The provisions made in the wills of deceased Roman aristocrats were subject to intense scrutiny by their relatives – and also by their friends, each of whom expected to receive a legacy reflecting the esteem in which he or she had truly been held by the deceased. The ways in which the prospects offered by a wealthy individual's will might condition his or her relations with others are often the target of Roman satirists, attacking the practice of legacy hunting.[33] The Roman aristocratic funeral was a complex ritual which struck the Greek visitor Polybius in the second century BCE as bizarre and fascinating but also as a crucial mechanism for the transmission of Roman values (6.53–4) (aspects of this ritual will be discussed briefly in Chapter 1).[34] Funerals and commemoration more generally may be seen as primarily concerned with negotiating a relationship between the living and the dead; my chief concern in this study is rather with the ways in which Romans negotiate a relationship with death itself. For this reason, too, the important topics of bereavement and consolation will receive only cursory discussion.[35] What of the relationship between love and death? In the elegies of Propertius, for instance, the self-abandonment of sexual pleasure prefigures the self-abandonment of death.[36] Erotic aspects of Roman treatments of death are touched on at several key points in what follows. However, the role of death in configuring representations (and indeed experiences) of sexual desire more generally is a large and complex topic to which full justice cannot be done within the compass of this book.[37]

The systematic engagement with death to be traced in the work of some Roman authors in particular may offer more than historical interest. It is worth considering what gains and losses may have been entailed for this culture which seems, at certain times at least, unusually preoccupied with the process of dying. For some critics, the Roman obsession with death appears pathological. Yet one might also see this preoccupation rather as in part at least reflecting a concern with the preservation of an intact narrative of self-identity, something which recent sociological studies have posited as the key to a good death.[38] In the context of a new focus in twenty-first-century western culture on different ways of dying, this Roman preoccupation may particularly repay our attention.[39]

The mortal condition

Death is of course a universal phenomenon. It is a truism that the consciousness of death is what renders us specifically human. Martin Heidegger's *Being and Time*, for instance, articulates a distinction between *verenden* 'perishing' – what animals do – and *sterben* 'dying' – what humans do, which underlies his characterisation of human existence.[40] Schopenhauer termed death 'the muse of philosophy'.[41] For some critics much of what might be termed culture is precisely a response to the fact of death. Different cultures have developed radically different ways of making sense of death.[42] Philippe Ariès' ambitious and wide-ranging study *L'Homme devant la mort* (1976), translated as *The Hour of Our Death*, sought to articulate a number of different phases, some overlapping with others, in western attitudes to death from the middle ages to the late twentieth century.[43] Thus for Ariès, peasant communities up until the nineteenth century generally accepted death, trusting in the Christian church's promise of resurrection. For such people death was 'tame'. Alongside this, however, the more individualistic attitudes of the educated came to be characterised by a new fear of death.[44] Enlightenment debates contributed in turn to a move to deny death, a development which Ariès saw as lying behind the unhealthy refusal to acknowledge death characteristic of twentieth-century western culture. The detail of Ariès' schema has been much disputed; he has been criticised for using different criteria to identify different phases and for focusing too closely on the elite.[45] Nevertheless his work vividly highlights the diversity of ways in which the approach of death has been viewed even within ostensibly Christian western cultures.

A particular type of death can also evoke significantly different responses in different cultural contexts. Attempts to interpret the self-inflicted death of Cato in terms of Durkheim's late nineteenth-century categorisation of suicides (a scheme which has been hugely influential in subsequent sociology and beyond) offer a clear illustration of this.[46] For Durkheim suicide is the result of the individual's maladaptive level of integration with his or her social group. One category of suicides is those resulting from a lack of integration with society. Such suicides may be 'anomic' (consequent on a lack of social norms with which the individual can engage) or 'egotistical' (stemming from a refusal to abide by such norms). A second category of suicides is those who go too far in surrendering their own desires to those of the group. These may be 'altruistic', when the individual kills him or herself for the community's greater good. Or they may be 'fatalistic', when the individual sees his or her own desires as incompatible with the norms of the community. These categories continue to govern much modern discussion of suicide, discussion which tends to see suicide as inherently pathological.[47] On one level, Cato could be classed in the last category as a 'fatalistic' suicide. But the parallels which Romans repeatedly drew between Cato and other individuals who had been forced to kill themselves as a judicial or quasi-judicial punishment make clear that Durkheim's categories cannot accommodate Roman attitudes to self-killing.[48] Indeed there is no Roman term exactly equivalent to the modern notion of suicide.[49] Tim Hill's recent analysis of the representation of self-killing in Latin literature rightly stresses the importance of honour over agency; who carries out the killing is significantly less important than how the individual dies.[50] For aristocratic Romans there is a strong sense that life without honour is not worth living.[51] A death accepted, indeed chosen, under critical circumstances, may play a positive role in self-definition, in bearing witness to a system of values.[52] This is an issue we shall return to particularly in Chapter 4.

In the western world, recent decades have seen a new focus on attitudes to death, stemming in part from a perception that the twentieth century's medicalisation of death, alongside other social changes associated particularly with the two world wars, led to a marginalisation, indeed repression, of death and bereavement. A ground-breaking study by Geoffrey Gorer, published in 1965, argued that death and mourning were treated with much the same prudery as the sexual impulses had been a century previously.[53] This is part of the context for the genesis of Ariès' work on past attitudes to death. A parallel perception lies behind the development of the Hospice movement, whose establishments specifically aim to explore and to meet the needs of the dying and their families, so that each individual may have the best possible death.[54] At the same time, in part at least a response to the spread of Aids, terminal illness in relation to dying individuals and those who survive them has been the focus of an increasing number of sociological studies.[55]

While such works may focus on the death of the self in relation to the terminally ill, as regards attitudes to death more generally they tend to be concerned with issues such as mortuary ritual and bereavement.[56] Similar concerns dominate in anthropological studies of attitudes to death.[57] On the whole, the contemplation of death is the preserve of the dying. Studies with a more literary and psychoanalytic approach, such as Jonathan Dollimore's *Death, Desire and Loss in Western Culture*, have explored attitudes to death from a broader perspective, interrogating the relationship between death and the constitution of the self, as well as love and bereavement.[58] Another strand in recent criticism, exemplified in the work of Elisabeth Bronfen and Sarah Goodwin, focuses more specifically on gender in relation to discourses about death.[59] For these scholars the language used to discuss death is of crucial significance. Aspects of these latter approaches most immediately inform my study. We cannot assume that models generated in relation to later cultures will fit Roman concerns (as the problem in applying Durkheim clearly shows) but some models can offer suggestive ways into understanding how Roman representations of and responses to death are conditioned.

Seeing death

If the death of Cato offers one archetype for Roman death, the death of a gladiator in the arena offers another. Here we come up against a peculiarly Roman configuration of death but one which will have been familiar to many well beyond the confines of the literary few. Gladiatorial spectacles, staged in permanent and temporary amphitheatres all over the Roman empire, constituted a key marker of Roman identity (and a phenomenon which continues to evoke fascination and horror). Here, death is a process which takes place under the eyes of thousands of spectators. Chapter 2 explores the place of death in the Roman amphitheatre and, particularly, the role gladiatorial deaths come to play in the meditations on death of a number of elite authors.

Elias Canetti argues that to witness another's corpse assures the survivors that they are still alive: 'The moment of survival is the moment of power.'[60] The murderous games staged in the arena may have served in part to reassure their spectators, to allow them to vindicate their own continuing claim to life. As the Christian Tertullian famously commented: *ita mortem homicidiis consolabantur*, 'Thus they find comfort for death in murder' (*Spect.* 12).[61] While such reassurance might be especially welcome in a society with very limited life expectancy, it cannot of course provide an adequate explanation for the popularity of the arena. And it is not just in discussions of the amphitheatre that Romans were made to engage with the question of how to look at death. Visual representations of gladiators facing death were evidently very popular in Roman antiquity. At the same time, Roman descriptions of deaths more generally often invite the reader or listener to imagine the scene, to visualise the dying subject, engaged in a final act of self-fashioning – and sometimes, too, to visualise the dead body. Canetti's insight may readily be extended to the experience of the represented corpse.[62]

The idea of death as something to be observed, as an edifying spectacle, is an important one in many Roman texts. Yet it raises some very disconcerting issues. What is at stake in looking at the death of another, whether real or represented? Drawing on psychoanalysis, feminist critics persuasively highlight the eroticised manner in which the dead female is often objectified in more recent literary texts (as well as the visual arts). In Freud's work, femininity and death constitute western culture's two principal tropes for the enigma. Death as the limit of cultural representation is readily associated with the multiply coded feminine body, which itself defies understanding.[63] To the male viewer or reader, literary representations of the dead female body may offer a version of death which is the more reassuringly 'other'. 'Because the feminine body is culturally constructed as the superlative site of alterity, culture uses art to dream the deaths of beautiful women,' writes Elisabeth Bronfen in analysing representations of women's deaths in later periods.[64] The written texts and visual representations which present the female dead body as an object of aesthetic beauty can be read as a means of repressing and articulating culture's unconscious knowledge of death.[65]

The relationship between death, gender and the visual in ancient Rome is of crucial significance. Livy's description of the death of Lucretia or Virgil's account of the death of Dido (which will be discussed in more detail below) seem to invite the reader to assume the position of male spectator. The dying woman is objectified. By a variety of means, Livy and Virgil emphasise the spectacle these deaths offer. Presenting the female character as the object of the male gaze these texts can be read as working to constitute the reader's masculinity. Visualising the suffering and death of a beautiful woman, the reader becomes a sadistic voyeur, whose masculinity is reinforced or even constructed through this experience.[66]

Yet it is hard to avoid the sense that the dead (and dying) male is also, at least sometimes, objectified or aestheticised in Latin literature. We have already noted elements of aestheticising in ancient and later accounts of the death of Cato and this is a theme we shall return to repeatedly. In some cases, we may feel that the wounded, dying man is perhaps himself being presented in a feminised role. As the victim of violence he is perhaps in the role of surrogate female, while the reader identifies with the victor, thus reinforcing his own masculinity. Yet there are numerous Roman texts where the reader seems invited to identify rather with the victim of violence, with the dying man. Should we detect an element of masochistic pleasure in such treatments?[67] A response of this kind seems to be evoked by the figure of Vulteius in Lucan's account of the spectacular mutual suicide of some of Caesar's men, stranded on a raft at sea (an episode from his epic treatment of the civil war between Caesar and Pompey).[68] Vulteius embraces violent death with disconcerting intensity. Not only this but he is adamant his death must have an audience – part of the pleasure is precisely in being observed. We shall return to Vulteius in a discussion of death in civil war in Chapter 1.

Lucan's account of the death scene of Vulteius and his men is couched in explicitly gladiatorial terms. Chapter 2's discussion of gladiatorial combat will explore the interrelationship of power, identification and death in the Roman arena itself. Here the experience of the spectator is not mediated by authorial control, as it is in Lucan's epic. And yet the particular circumstances of the arena, as well as the particular structures of Roman society, might be thought to dispose viewers to identify with the winning gladiator. To what extent, though, do members of the audience identify with the victor? Is the dying gladiator indeed objectified? Here, too, issues of identification may be less straightforward than they at first appear.

The complex strategies that narratives of death use to shape the reader's perspective will be a particular concern in what follows. Some texts seem to construct the reader as witness to the honourable nature of the death described. The reader of Tacitus' *Annals*, for instance, has a vital part to play, it seems, in vindicating the honour of Nero's victims by bearing witness to the nobility of their deaths (this responsibility itself constructs the reader as a person of dignity, honour and status). But the role of the witness may go further than this. These exemplary deaths are intended to inspire others to emulation – that is a significant part of their value. We, as readers, are perhaps also invited to figure our own deaths on the model of the examples offered. As Freud observes, it is impossible for us to conceive of our own deaths. Whenever we try to do so, we find ourselves in the position of spectator – and consequently survivor – of the very death we are seeking to imagine.[69] How far can we see these Roman death texts as inviting the reader to rehearse his (or indeed her) own end? Or does the death of a surrogate spare the regarding subject, serving to evoke precisely that sense of reassurance identified by Canetti? One means for the mortal reader to transcend death – at least for a while.

Transcending death

Ideas of the afterlife might seem to have a significant bearing on any culture's responses to death. Yet Roman attitudes to the question of whether humans may expect any kind of post-mortem survival and what any such afterlife might be like are notoriously difficult to determine.[70] Traditional Roman cult included a number of festivals in which worshippers honoured and made offerings to the dead, such as the Parentalia, when families met at the tombs of dead relatives.[71] But there seems to have been little emphasis on the fate of the individual after death. Prose texts rarely offer any kind of speculation on this topic (with some significant exceptions, discussed below). For one commentator, the Elder Pliny, the idea of the afterlife, seductive though it may seem, is to be abhorred for spoiling nature's greatest good, death: *perdit profecto ista dulcedo credulitasque praecipuum naturae bonum, mortem* (*NH* 7.190). Epitaphs on Roman tombstones suggest a wide range of attitudes to post-mortem survival.[72] It is striking that many explicitly reject the possibility of any kind of life after death.[73]

Undeniably, the underworld was a potent poetic presence in Greco-Roman antiquity. In the eleventh book of Homer's *Odyssey*, Odysseus goes down to a bleak and sombre underworld and encounters the shades of the dead, including many who had fought with him at Troy, as well as his own mother. The fate of the shades in Homer's underworld is largely undifferentiated (though the Isles of the Blessed seem in some passages to offer a kind of paradise for the select few, while eternal torments are reserved for a handful of cosmic offenders).[74] Homer's epic had (and continues to have) a long literary afterlife. But what might have been the relationship between this vision of the fate of the soul after death and people's expectations in relation to their own individual experience?

Some Greco-Roman religious rituals do appear to have a bearing on beliefs about the fate of the soul after death. The Eleusinian mysteries, which took place in the sanctuary of Demeter at Eleusis, near Athens, seem to have promised a privileged afterlife for the initiated – though tantalisingly little is known about them. There are references to this as early as the Homeric hymn to Demeter dating from around the seventh century BCE but the association continues well into the Roman period (and numerous distinguished Romans are known to have been initiates).[75] According to one of the characters in Cicero's dialogue *De legibus*, from the rites at Eleusis, *principia vitae cognovimus; neque solum cum laetitia vivendi rationem accepimus, sed etiam cum spe meliore moriendi*, 'we have learned the beginnings of life, and have gained the power not only to live happily, but also to die with a better hope' (*Leg.* 2.36). Other mystery cults, such as that associated with Bacchus, also appear to have offered access to a better afterlife. At the same time the initiation rituals of these cults seem in some cases to have invoked elements associated with a mythical descent to the underworld (*katabasis*).[76] The secret nature of these cults, however, means that evidence about them is particularly scarce and problematic. Beginning around the fifth century BCE, Pythagoreanism and Orphism also asserted the immortality of the soul; indeed their adherents seem to have been committed to a belief in reincarnation.[77] Centuries later, Plutarch comments, in relation to the fear of death, that many believe 'that some sort of initiations and purifications will help: once purified, they believe, they will go on playing and dancing in Hades in places full of brightness, pure air and light' (*That Epicurus actually makes a pleasant life impossible*

1105b). Yet it is very hard to ascertain how widespread such views may have been in the Greek world or the Roman.

Plato's philosophical dialogues draw on a number of elements associated with these different cults, and articulate several distinct versions of an afterlife, all associated with post-mortem judgement. In Plato's writing, most notably *Phaedo*, *Gorgias* and *Republic*, myths of the afterlife serve a particular philosophical purpose, working to reinforce ideas which are also articulated in more logical form. In particular, the soul's journey to the realm of the dead functions as an analogy for the philosopher's quest for understanding in relation to the transcendent realm of ideas. In the *Republic* (382d), Plato makes Socrates describe such myths as useful falsehoods – 'we make the false as like the truth as possible'. The very fact of variation between the dialogues underlines the point explicitly made here by Socrates that the reader is not being asked to believe every detail.[78]

Cicero, a keen admirer of Plato, set himself the project of providing an introduction to philosophy for his fellow Romans. He engages with the question of what happens to the soul after death at several points in his voluminous philosophical writings. The account of a dream put in the mouth of Scipio Aemilianus (a prominent Roman of the mid second century BCE) constitutes what is generally recognised as the final part of Cicero's fragmentary *De republica*, a treatise on the ideal state, partly based on Plato's *Republic* and written around 51 BCE. In this dream, Scipio is addressed by his adoptive grandfather, Scipio Africanus, who tells him of the blessed afterlife which awaits all those *qui patriam conservaverint, adiuverint, auxerint*, 'who have preserved, helped or enlarged the fatherland' (6.13).[79] Such souls escape from the prison which is the body to enjoy the only true life, life after death. These heavenly rewards are far superior to the earthly rewards offered to virtue. In important respects, this dream is parallel to the myth of Er recounted at the end of Plato's *Republic*.[80] It serves to reinforce the arguments for a virtuous life found in the preface and introduction to Book 1 of the *De republica*. *Suis te oportet inlecebris ipsa virtus trahat ad verum decus*, 'Virtue herself through her own attractions should lead you on to true glory', Scipio Africanus is made to comment (6.25). Although the *De republica* depreciates the value of embodied existence (in terms often reminiscent of Plato), its project as set out in the (fragmentary) preface is to demonstrate that Nature has implanted in humankind ... *tantam necessitatem virtutis ... tantumque amorem ad communem salutem defendendam datum, ut ea vis omnia blandimenta voluptatis otiique vicerit*, 'such a devotion to virtue, such a love of defending the common good, that the strength of it has overcome all the attractions of pleasure and of idleness' (*Rep.* 1.1).[81] As with Plato, it remains unclear how far Cicero is committing himself to a specific claim about the actual fate of the soul after death.

Writing a century after Cicero, the Stoic philosopher Seneca on occasion celebrates the transcendent calm that philosophy can bring through contemplation of the universe.[82] In Letter 102 he describes his own meditation on the fate of the soul after death (a topic which dominates this lengthy letter) as like a pleasant dream, *iucundum somnium*. In terms familiar from Plato's *Republic* its pleasure is characterised as *falsam effectum tamen verae habentem*, 'false but with the weight of truth' (102.1).[83] In thinking of the better life the soul has in prospect, a life transfused with light, we may let go our already useless limbs and dispense with our bodies (102.27). This vision of the soul going on to enjoy communion with the cosmos can have a vital role to play in freeing us from the fear of death – a key concern in Seneca's philosophical writing as we shall see in Chapter 3. Yet belief in the immortality of the soul is explicitly acknowledged as offering the same deceptive pleasure as a dream does (102.1–2).

A much more elaborate vision of the afterlife is articulated in the sixth book of Virgil's *Aeneid*, written a few decades earlier. The poem's hero Aeneas descends to the underworld to see his father. Here the dead are judged and disposed according to their deserts, with misery in store for many, who have erred during their lives (6.426–627). Anchises is made to describe to his son what happens to the soul after death: a process of purification and reincarnation (6.713–51). Once purified of their sins, the souls are sent to Elysium, some to return from there to new bodies.[84] Among the spirits who are to return to earth are some of Rome's most distinguished leaders, many of them Aeneas' own descendants, who file past in a procession, culminating with the emperor Augustus. Anchises explains what each will achieve when he comes to take his place in the land of the living (this scene bears a notable resemblance to the Roman aristocratic funeral described in Chapter 1 below).[85]

Aeneas' departure from the underworld may provide a clue as to how to read this account of the afterlife. There are two gates, the gate of ivory and the gate of horn, the former associated with *falsa ... insomnia* 'false dreams', the latter with *veris ... umbris* 'true shades'; Aeneas leaves through the gate of ivory, the gate of false dreams. Virgil's underworld, then, can perhaps be seen as a counterpart to the stories offered by Plato concerning the fate of the soul after death; Virgil's account evokes the dream of Scipio, itself explicitly modelled on the myth of Er in Plato's *Republic*.[86] In the *Republic*, as we have seen, Plato makes Socrates describe such myths as useful falsehoods. Further Platonic resonances underline the significance of this connection; the Sibyl, Aeneas' guide, insists that he should take with him the golden bough. Only thus can his return to the land of the living be guaranteed. This talismanic object is perhaps an allusion to the golden bough the poet Meleager had associated with Plato in an earlier epigram.[87] Virgil's underworld is offered as a useful fiction following a specifically Platonic model.

The conception of the afterlife offered in the *Aeneid* is in negotiation with a complex literary and philosophical tradition.[88] Cicero, Plato and, of course, Homer are all evoked but also Lucretius' great didactic poem *De rerum natura*, which aimed to set out Epicurean philosophy in Latin verse and systematically attacked traditional mythological stories about the afterlife (this work will be discussed further in Chapter 3).[89] Virgil's underworld articulates a rich, complex but teleologically driven account of Rome's history, underpinned by allusions mythical, religious, philosophical and literary.[90] At the same time the poignancy of Aeneas' encounters with his dead father, his one-time love Dido, as well as lost comrades from the fall of Troy and the perilous voyage to Italy, invest the episode with an emotional potency which authenticates the carefully wrought teleology and cosmology.

The region of the dead is figured here (as often elsewhere) as a medium for accessing privileged knowledge, a place of revelation; Aeneas is offered understanding of the workings of the cosmos and also of the Roman future. Other texts deploy the motif of descent to the underworld as a figure for the experience of more specifically poetic inspiration.[91] Virgil's earlier work, the *Georgics*, had also invoked, though more briefly, a vision of the underworld. Eurydice, killed by a snake, descends to the regions of the dead. The loss of his wife inspires Orpheus to sing a mesmerising song (*Geo.* 4.464–6). He, too, descends to the realm of Hades. The beauty of his singing moves even the gods of the underworld to relent; Eurydice is allowed to return, following behind Orpheus, on condition that he does not look back (*Geo.* 4.467–84). Human frailty supervenes, with tragic consequences, and ultimately death triumphs. Yet Orpheus' beautiful song does, for a while at least, overcome death – a metaphor for the power of poetry. Love, creativity and death are inextricably linked.[92]

Metaphors of transcendence have power and vitality in the sphere of poetry or philosophical analogy. Indeed, paradoxically, death, encountered through the medium of poetry or philosophy, can often seem to have an energising effect, intensifying creativity. Only rarely, however, do we find ideas of the afterlife invoked in the context of the physical imminence of death for a particular individual. Those who confront their own ends, at least in the works of Seneca, the Younger Pliny or Tacitus, seem to take no comfort from the prospect of a life to come. The afterlife they contemplate is in the hearts and minds of those who survive them – and perhaps, for the fortunate, a more enduring place in a literary tradition in which their last moments, masterfully reconfigured, still make compelling reading. Paradoxically the contemplation of one's own finitude might even be thought to offer the means for a mortal to transcend human limitations – in Seneca's view at any rate. In one of the last of his philosophical letters to survive, Seneca comments that the human heart *numquam magis divinum est, quam ubi mortalitatem suam cogitat*, 'is never more divine than when it reflects on its mortality' (120.14).

CHAPTER 1

DYING FOR ROME?

THE GLORIOUS DEATH OF A COMMANDER

The Greek historian Polybius, writing in the middle of the second century BCE, sought to analyse the phenomenal success of the expanding Roman empire. He presents the Roman aristocratic funeral, an essentially public event, as a key mechanism in the transmission of martial values from one generation to the next. The funeral procession included not only the body of the deceased and the mourners, but also other family members wearing masks (and the appropriate clothing), each impersonating a distinguished ancestor of the man who had died.[1] These dead ancestors took their seats on the platform, while the individual chosen to deliver the funeral oration recounted the achievements of the dead man.

> When he has finished the eulogy of him, he begins praising the others who are present, starting with the oldest and recounting the successes and achievements of each. In consequence of this, since the reputation for virtue of good men is being perpetually renewed, the renown of those who have achieved some noble deed is undying and the glory of those who have rendered service to their country becomes familiar to the many and a legacy for later generations. But the greatest result is that young men are encouraged to undertake anything for the common good, spurred on by the hope of securing the good reputation which follows men's brave deeds. This is confirmed by the following consideration. For many Romans have willingly entered single combat to decide an entire battle. A number have also chosen certain death, some of them in war to promote the safety of others, and some in peace for the state's security.
>
> (6.54.1–4)

The glory given to the dead spurs on the living to emulate them in their martial valour. This is the afterlife the ambitious young Roman yearns for – to secure the place of his own *imago* in the funeral pageant of his descendants, to come to life again each time one of them is laid to rest.

Cicero, in a speech of 56 BCE emphasising his own readiness to face death for Rome, celebrates willingness to meet death in battle as a distinctively Roman characteristic. This is a city 'from which countless men, partly to gain glory, partly to avoid disgrace had met death in various wars with the greatest calmness', *ex qua innumerabiles alii partim adipiscendae laudis, partim vitandae turpitudinis causa mortem in variis bellis aequissimis animis oppetissent* (*Pro Sestio* 48).[2] True manhood, he asserts, lies in the readiness to die for one's country. In a later speech, against Mark Antony, Cicero comments 'It is not a man's part – and least of all that of a Roman – to hesitate to surrender to the republic that breath of life which he owes to nature', *non est viri minimeque Romani dubitare eum spiritum, quem naturae debeat, patriae reddere* (*Phil.* 10.20). Another of his *Philippics* includes a funeral oration for the dead of the legion of Mars, killed in civil war fighting with the forces of Mark Antony (14.25–35). Cicero proposes the erection of a monument to promote 'the perpetual glory of most valiant men', *ad virorum fortissimorum gloriam sempiternam* (14.31).

For Cicero, deaths in battle were an ideal subject for history-writing; he advises his friend Lucceius in a letter of 55 BCE:

> Quem enim nostrum ille moriens apud Mantineam Epaminondas non cum quadam miseratione delectat? Qui tum denique sibi evelli iubet spiculum postea quam ei percontanti dictum est clipeum esse salvum, ut enim in vulneris dolore aequo animo cum laude moreretur. Cuius studium in legendo non erectum Themistocli fuga ±redituque± retinetur?

> Which of us does not feel pleasure as well as a certain pity at the scene of Epaminondas dying at Mantinea? He only ordered the spear to be removed once he had asked if his shield was safe and been assured it was, so that despite the pain of the wound, he could die honourably with his mind at rest. Whose attention is not aroused and gripped by reading about Themistocles' exile and death?

> (*Fam.* 5.12.5)

Though the examples are Greek, the imagined readership is Roman. Writing history some time later, Tacitus, too, with an ironic apology for what he presents as the very different content of his own *Annals*, describes the proper subject of history as follows: 'What interests and stimulates readers is a geographical description, the changing fortunes of a battle, the glorious death of a commander', *Nam situs gentium, varietates proeliorum, clari ducum exitus retinent ac redintegrant legentium animum* (*Ann.* 4.33.3).[3] Such deaths make arresting and inspirational reading. As in Cicero's observation, the issue of the reader's pleasure is raised. Comments of this kind might be taken to suggest that Romans placed a great value on death in battle. Ancient Rome was a highly militaristic society. Huge numbers of deaths in war must have been a consequence of the vast military campaigns which characterised long periods in the middle and late republic.[4] We might expect considerable energy to be devoted to celebrating death on the field of battle.

Death in battle was certainly celebrated as a privileged end in the Greek world. The ancient Greek preoccupation with death in war finds its earliest and perhaps most arresting expression in the *Iliad*, which has indeed been termed 'the poem of death'.[5] For the Homeric warrior it is a heroic death in battle that offers the best guarantee of undying glory (*Iliad* 9.497–504). 'Through a beautiful death, excellence no longer has to be measured against someone else or to be tested in combat. Rather excellence is actualised all at once and forever after in the deed that puts an end to the hero's life,' in the words of Jean-Pierre Vernant.[6] Greek lyric and elegiac poets of later centuries also celebrate warriors who die in the flower of youth; for Tyrtaeus, 'It is a fine thing for a brave man to die when he has fallen among the front ranks, while fighting for his homeland.'[7] In Athens, from some time in the early to mid fifth century BCE, it became customary to celebrate an elaborate public funeral for those who had died in war in the course of a year's campaigning.[8] According to the historian Thucydides, the man most distinguished for his wisdom and public standing was chosen to deliver a funeral oration (2.34.6). The speech he puts in the mouth of Pericles honours both the city and also those whose deaths have brought her glory (throughout the speech the city is figured as feminine). It is precisely in dying that they have served their community; by this means they have 'become good' (2.35.1).[9] A public monument was erected to perpetuate the memory of those who had died on campaign.[10]

Polybius' account of the Roman funeral and Cicero's comments on death in battle might lead us to see the Romans as equally inclined to celebrate the war dead. But other texts from the late republic provide only limited confirmation of this. Cicero's fourteenth *Philippic* can best be seen as a pastiche based on the Greek model of a funeral oration for the war dead but serving a very different purpose, part of an attempt to secure a particular *senatus consultum* (senatorial decree), which would have brought benefits to the surviving soldiers.[11] In a letter to Brutus, Cicero, at that time a supporter of Octavian (who was later to become Augustus), confesses one of his motives in making the proposal was the desire to set up a permanent reminder of the impious behaviour of Antony and his supporters (*Brut.* 1.15.9). The monument itself was never built, as Antony and Octavian were reconciled shortly after – at least for a while.[12] Moreover Cicero's speech suggests that normal Roman practice was to leave the war dead unburied (*Phil.* 14.34), in contrast to Greek practice.[13]

Another aspect of the contrast between Athens and Rome in their treatment of the war dead is explicitly articulated by a Greek writing in the time of the emperor Augustus. Dionysius of Halicarnassus gives an account of the death in war centuries earlier of Rome's first consul Brutus; Brutus and Arruns, leader of the Etruscan forces, have killed one another in single combat. The Romans are disconsolate at the death of their leader but are spurred on to ultimate victory by a divine voice. They then return to their city, with the body of Brutus, to celebrate a triumph and conduct their leader's funeral. According to Dionysius, this is the origin of the practice of making an oration at the funeral of a great man (the practice so admired by Polybius in the passage discussed above).[14] Dionysius concludes this episode by drawing a contrast between Greek and Roman practice in delivering funeral orations:

> If anyone ... would like to learn about the custom itself and in which nation it is practised best, he will find that it is observed more wisely among the Romans than among the Athenians. For the Athenians seem to have decreed that these orations should be delivered at the funerals of those only who have died in war, on the grounds that one should judge men to be good solely on the basis of their bravery in death, even when in other respects they are unworthy. The Romans, however, determined this honour for all their illustrious men, whether they served as commanders in war or have offered wise advice and performed nobly as political leaders, not only for those who have died in war but also for others, however they ended their lives, for they believe that good men should be praised for the virtues they have shown throughout their lives and not merely for the glory of their deaths.
>
> (5.17.5–6)

Dionysius elides the fact that the Roman funeral oration is reserved for the elite, choosing rather to emphasise the Romans' relative lack of concern with the particular manner of an individual's death. A death in war, even for a military leader, is by no means the only determinant of a man's value.[15] The passage from Polybius, quoted above, certainly stresses the inspiring effect of the funeral but also mentions self-sacrifice in a civil context, alongside death in war. The men whose *imagines* appear in the funeral processions of their descendants are men who have achieved senior magistracies, as praetors and consuls. These are not men killed in battle in the flower of their youth.

Elsewhere, Roman responses to death in war can seem closer to those articulated in earlier Greek literature. Virgil's *Aeneid*, composed around the time Dionysius was writing, appears to offer a more positive evaluation of death in battle (the influence of Homer's *Iliad* is of course a significant factor here). In the underworld visited by Aeneas in Book 6, the war dead have an honourable place, alongside other benefactors of humanity (*Aeneid* 6.660). As the poem's narrative unfolds, there are beautiful young men who die in battle. Evander's son Pallas chooses to fight alongside Aeneas against Turnus and his Rutulians. Facing Turnus, he boasts: *Aut spoliis ego iam raptis laudabor opimi/aut leto insigni*, 'soon I shall be praised either for seizing a commander's spoils or else for a noble death' (*Aen.* 10.449–50). Perhaps closest to the Homeric ethos of a beautiful death in war come the ends of Nisus and Euryalus, two young Trojan warriors who die in Book 9. They attempt a daredevil raid on the Rutulian camp. Euryalus is captured. Nisus considers *an sese medios moriturus in enses/inferat et pulchram properet per vulnera mortem?*, 'if he should hurl himself in the midst of the swords to certain death and seize a beautiful death through wounds?' (9.400–01). He flings forth his weapon, killing the warrior Sulmo. Enraged the Rutulians retaliate, killing Euryalus. Euryalus' unsurpassed beauty has already been highlighted (179–80). In his death he is compared to a flower mown down in the field (432–7) – a *pulchra mors*, very much in the style of the *Iliad*.[16] Nisus then hurls himself on the enemy. He kills several of them, but is then cut down.

> Fortunati ambo! Si quid mea carmina possunt,
> Nulla dies umquam memori vos eximet aevo.

> Fortunate pair! If my poem has any power, the day will never come when you are erased from memory.

> (9.446–7)

These two are to be eternally remembered. Yet the *Aeneid*, despite the many deaths it recounts, is not ultimately a 'poem of death' on the Homeric model.[17] In some ways Nisus and Euryalus are throwbacks to a different, simpler age. They are not the central characters of this epic. In his first speech, Aeneas, a refugee exhausted by his long-drawn-out, storm-racked journey, exclaims in envy at those of his fellow Trojans who had died on the battlefield and wishes himself dead:

'O terque quaterque beati,
Quis ante ora patrum Troiae sub moenibus altis
Contigit oppetere! O Danaum fortissime gentis
Tydide! Mene Iliacis occumbere campis
Non potuisse tuaque animam hanc effundere dextra ...'

'O three and four times blessed those whose luck it was to fall before the
eyes of your fathers, beneath the walls of Troy! O Diomedes, bravest of the
race of Greeks! Could I not have fallen on the fields of Ilium and poured
out my spirit at your right hand?'

(*Aen.* 1.94–8)

His lament echoes that of Homer's Odysseus, a hero who survives many
perils to reach home and die as an old man (*Odyssey* 5.306). During the
course of the last desperate battle amid the smoking ruins of Troy, a younger
Aeneas had felt the urge to die in battle (2.317). But Romans do not generally
serve Rome best by dying. Aeneas himself will fight again. He survives,
grows older. The death of his opponent Turnus in the poem's concluding
lines is not a beautiful death but one which raises problems, provokes deep
discomfort – even if it is necessary to the foundation of Rome.

This chapter will explore a number of aspects of Roman responses to war
deaths, in particular the deaths of leaders. Historians such as Polybius and
Livy certainly offer some dramatic death narratives associated with military
campaigns against Rome's enemies. There are contexts in which a self-sacrificing death in war evokes admiration. Yet for Polybius and Dionysius of
Halicarnassus, as we have seen, part of the explanation for Rome's success is
that Romans do not privilege death in battle over other ways of serving the
state. At the same time it will, I think, become clear that it is more particularly death in civil war which exerts a fascination for Roman writers, Sallust,
Lucan and Tacitus, most notably. Why might this be? And how should we
see the context of civil war as changing the evaluation of a 'good' death
in combat? The final part of this chapter considers a scene of spectacular
mutual suicide from Lucan's epic. Even self-sacrifice might have a sinister
dimension in civil war. There is an explicit emphasis here on the capacity
of such dramatic deaths to offer a kind of entertainment to observers. We
might remember the edifying pleasure associated with reading of noble
deaths in battle by both Cicero and Tacitus. The question of how to look at
death is posed by Lucan in an especially disconcerting manner.

One for all

A number of self-sacrificing deaths in wars with external enemies are certainly held up for particular admiration in the works of epic poets and historians. Perhaps the most extreme instance of this self-sacrifice is what is termed the *devotio* of a military leader.[18] Decius Mus gives a speech in which he offers himself as a sacrifice on behalf of the Roman army at the battle of Sentinum in 295 BCE in one of the surviving fragments of Ennius' *Annals*, an epic poem of the early second century BCE (*Annals* 200–02).[19] Livy, too, tells the story not only of this Decius Mus but also of his father (another Decius Mus) who also vowed his life to the gods to secure a Roman victory during Latin war 340–338 BCE (Livy 8.9 and 10.28).[20] In Livy's narrative of the battle of Sentinum, the young and impetuous Decius overstretches his troops. Then, when they turn to flee, he stems the rout by making an offering of himself:

> 'Quid ultra moror' inquit 'familiare fatum? Datum hoc nostro generi est ut luendis periculis publicis piacula simus. Iam ego mecum hostium legiones mactandas Telluri ac Dis Manibus dabo.'

> 'Why do I longer delay', he cried, 'our family destiny? Our house was granted the privilege of being sacrificed to ward off dangers from our country. Now it is my turn to offer the legions of the enemy together with myself as victims to Earth and the gods of the Underworld.'

> (10.28.13)

Ritual prayers are said by a priest to offer both Decius and the enemy soldiers to save the army of the Romans. Then Decius:

> haec exsecratus in se hostesque, qua confertissimam cernebat Gallorum aciem concitat equum inferensque se ipse infestis telis est interfectus.

> with these imprecations upon himself and the enemy, galloped his horse into the Gallic lines where he saw they were thickest, and hurled himself on the enemy's weapons to meet his death.

> (10.28.18)

This act causes terror and consternation in the enemy lines and inspires the Romans to win through. The act of *devotio* was constituted by a formal ritual. However, accounts of references to the Decii often focus rather on the hero's intense desire to save the state and the abandon with which the devoted man and his horse fly toward the enemy lines.[21] The frantic horse galloping forward conveys the *furor*, ectasy and rapture of the moment, here as often in such episodes.[22]

The effectiveness of the *devotio* depends on its being witnessed; the spectactors play a crucial role in the narrative. Such spectacles, comments Andrew Feldherr, 'become the means through which the collective power of the state operates on the spectators, devastating the enemy and drawing the Romans closer to the sources of their own strength.'[23] Livy's history frequently invokes the visual component of rituals and public acts. The term *spectaculum* is sometimes used explicitly in Livy's treatment of Roman public occasions (for instance at 42.49.1–6 describing the ritual departure of the general Publius Licinius) without apparently carrying the negative associations with artificiality or with the passivity of the spectators often implied by the modern term spectacle (the ambiguities of the Roman term *spectaculum* will be explored further in Chapter 2). Livy's vivid treatment allows his readers, too, to become spectators of the events described. In places Livy contrasts opposing models of the spectacular, such as in his account of the duel between Torquatus and his Gallic opponent, a little later in Book 7 (7.9–10). While the experience of the Romans – combatant and onlookers – seems an expression of social cohesion, that of the Gauls is presented as incoherent and meaningless.[24] The Roman spectators draw energy from witnessing this spectacle. They know how to look, they identify with their champion, who understands his responsibilities as the representative of his nation. The positive value sometimes placed on the term *spectaculum* is worth bearing in mind, as we see different ways in which other writers deploy the notion of the spectacular in relation to deaths in battle.

Devotio, as constructed in the writings of Livy, Cicero and others, was undeniably a powerful ritual. Even in Cicero's treatise *De natura deorum* the character Cotta is uncomfortable with the idea of gods who take pleasure in the destruction of good men, but sees the *devotio*, exemplified by the sacrifice of the Decii, as a:

> consilium illud imperatorium ..., sed eorum imperatorum qui patriae consulerent vitae non parcerent; rebantur enim fore ut exercitus impera-torem quo incitato se in hostem inmittentem persequeretur, id quod evenit.

> a device of generalship ..., though a device for generals who were ready to give their lives in their country's service; their notion was that if a commander rode full gallop against the foe his troops would follow him and so it proved.

> (*Nat. deor.* 3.15)

Self-sacrifice here can be read as a self-conscious, if desperate, move to inspire a flagging army.[25] The Decii are invoked as resonant symbolic figures in a wide range of texts; Cicero places them amongst the most notable examples of men who have died for Rome in *Pro Sestio* 48.[26] The Decii become paradigms of Roman patriotism.[27] Whatever their basis in historical fact, they are a potent imaginary construct.

In the case of Decius Mus father and son, Roman victory naturally ensues. Other instances of commanders dying in battle show some similar characteristics. But, outside the context of *devotio*, death in battle tends to be associated not with victory but with defeat. Cicero in the *Pro Sestio* commented on heroic death in battle as a means to avoid disgrace, *vitandae turpitudinis causa* (48). Even Decius in Livy's Book 10 can be read as offering his life in compensation for his own earlier error. Accounts of the general Gaius Flaminius' final hours fighting Hannibal in 217 BCE offer another good example of this. In Livy's version he struggles courageously in the thick of the battle, ceaselessly fighting wherever the action is most intense until he is cut down in single combat (Livy 22.6.2–4). By contrast, in Polybius' earlier version Flaminius is altogether less impressive. This may indicate a more specifically Roman ideological drive to celebrate military courage.[28] Indeed, generals actually died in battle with sufficient frequency in the last two and a half centuries of the republic to indicate that in a time of crisis commanders might often expose themselves to danger deliberately.[29] It was particularly embarrassing for a general to survive a military catastrophe, particularly as a prisoner of war; few are recorded as having permitted themselves to be captured alive.[30] In a number of Roman stories, then, we find individuals courting death as a mechanism for securing glory once defeat was pretty well inevitable and survival was likely to bring dishonour.[31] Under some circumstances, death in battle was, it seems, a reliable means of achieving a kind of distinction which Romans appear to have valued and one which seems to have been made use of frequently in the middle and late republic.

In most of the stories of honourable war deaths related by Livy, Polybius and others the emphasis is on the example set by Roman military leaders.[32] Dionysius of Halicarnassus, referring to the events of 494 BCE, has the Roman dictator Postumius inspire his troops with a speech emphasising the readiness of their leaders to risk death in combat (6.9.1). This highlighting of the significance of the death of a commander reflects the essentially aristocratic nature of Roman society. When the willingness to risk death on the part of the troops themselves is mentioned it is often as the consequence of effective military discipline. At least on some occasions, regular soldiers, if they failed to show adequate bravery in combat, might face death at the hands of military authorities.[33] For Polybius, the severity of military discipline played a key part in Roman military success (6.37.6).[34] The brave performance of soldiers might also be highlighted as a consequence of the desire to impress an effective commander. Julius Caesar records that he placed in command of three legions a quaestor and two legates, his most senior officers, as *testes virtutis*, 'witnesses to bravery' (*De bello Gallico* 1.52). Elsewhere he several times comments that soldiers perform better when Caesar himself is watching them, *in conspectu Caesaris* (*BG* 2.25; 3.14).[35] Caesar, as observer, inspires his men; to die with the commander looking on is to know that one's bravery will be properly esteemed (or at least that was the view of Rome's foremost general).

The death of a leader in war could serve as compensation for earlier errors, and as inspiration to his troops. Yet it remains the case that for Romans death in war seems not of particular value in itself. The war dead are not honoured as a category. The deaths of the Decii offer a supremely efficient example of death in war – the life of one man secures the victory of the entire Roman army. Nevertheless, despite the comments of Cicero and Tacitus, the historiographical tradition of Rome (and Greece, too) does not seem much preoccupied with recording how individuals die in wars with foreign enemies.[36] Roman historians, especially under the principate, are more often inclined to stress how few casualties have resulted from a campaign; this can serve as a significant index of its success. Tacitus, for instance, celebrating his father-in-law Agricola's victory at Mons Graupius in the far north of Britain, stresses that he shed no Roman blood (*Agr.* 35.2).[37]

Dying in civil war

An increasingly intense interest in war deaths of a rather different kind appears in other texts. The Roman literary preoccupation with war, at least as manifested in writing of the late republic and principate, comes to be characterised by a distinctive twist. A great deal of the fighting described – perhaps even most of it – takes place in the context of civil war – Romans fighting Romans. As John Henderson comments: 'Classical Roman culture ... invested heavily in the valour, conquest and triumph of ancestral militarism for its self-conception; yet a large proportion of the fighting and killing by Roman soldiers represented nothing but a conquest *of* Rome *by* Rome.'[38] Indeed civil war can be seen as a Roman obsession. It is a theme intrinsic to the story chosen by Romans to symbolise the foundation of their city, that of the fratricidal Romulus.[39] For some writers, Roman history can be seen as a perpetual cycle of civil war, each phase sowing the seeds of its successor.[40] The most extreme instance of this is surely Lucan's epic poem, *Bellum civile*.[41] Written in the time of Nero and focusing on the conflict between

Caesar and Pompey 49–48 BCE, the poem emphasises that civil war is a Roman tradition. Rome is fated to civil war:

> Nec gentibus ullis
> Credite, nec longe fatorum exempla petantur:
> Fraterno primi maduerunt sanguine muri.

Search not the history of foreign nations for proof, nor look far for an instance of fate's decree. The rising city walls were wetted with a brother's blood.

(1.93–5)

Episodes of civil slaughter from earlier in the first century BCE are also invoked. An anonymous figure in Book 2 gives a gruesome account of the proscriptions (effectively licensed killings) under Sulla, which serve as a foretaste of the horrors to come (2.118–93) – part of civil war's genealogy.[42]

Sallust's account (written in the 40s BCE) of the conspiracy of Catiline in 63 BCE, *Bellum Catilinae*, can be read as an early text in what could be characterised as a developing tradition of civil war literature. Catiline, as Sallust represents him, is an aristocratic Roman with many strengths but also many vices, who twice tries and fails to be elected consul (for the year 63, when he is defeated by Cicero, and for 62), incurring, as so many candidates did, massive debts in the attempt. He then becomes a champion of the dispossessed, both humble and elite, advocating the redistribution of land and the abolition of debts. This provokes serious disorder and is interpreted as a conspiracy by Cicero and others. Forced out of Rome by Cicero, Catiline leads a body of Sullan veterans, who are eventually defeated by an army led by the consul Gaius Antonius in January 62.

Some readers have seen Catiline as quite straightforwardly the villain of Sallust's account. But for others Sallust's Catiline is an altogether more ambiguous figure.[43] Catiline shows significant positive qualities as a leader. He makes inspiring speeches at Chapter 20 and again much later in the narrative, when his cause is essentially lost but he decides to engage in battle with the consul Antonius. Most notably at 58.21, he urges his soldiers not to die 'like cattle', *sicuti pecora*, but 'fighting like heroes', *virorum more pugnantes*, an exhortation which offers an intriguing parallel with the opening sentence of the *Catiline*, where Sallust asserts that we must not pass our lives in silence, *veluti pecora*, 'like cattle' (Catiline and his men will at least escape that most dreadful fate). Battle ensues:

Interea Catilina cum expeditis in prima acie vorsari, laborantibus succurrere, integros pro sauciis arcessere, omnia providere, multum ipse pugnare, saepe hostem ferire; strenui militis et boni imperatoris simul exsequebatur.

Catiline with his light armed troops was busy in the front-line, aided those who were hard-pressed, summoned fresh troops to replace the wounded, had an eye for everything and at the same time fought hard himself, often striking down the enemy – thus performing at once the duties of a valiant soldier and a good leader.

(Sall. Cat. 60.4)

Omnia providere is a phrase which recurs both in Sallust's history of the war against Jugurtha (Bellum Jugurthinum 100.3) and in Livy (3.63.3), used of more unproblematically heroic leaders. And Catiline himself strikes at the enemy (60.4) in terms reminiscent of Sallust's own description of the noble Romans of old: in earlier times 'Each man strove to be the first to strike down the foe, to scale a wall, to be seen while doing such a deed': se quisque hostem ferire, murum ascendere, conspici dum tale facinus faceret, properabat (7.6). Catiline has made good the promise offered to his supporters at 20.16, where he urged them specifically to make use of him as either a soldier or a leader.

The death of Catiline is of crucial importance to the assessment of his character.

Catilina postquam fusas copias seque cum paucis relictum videt, memor generis atque pristinae suae dignitatis in confertissumos hostis incurrit ibique pugnans confoditur.

When Catiline saw that his army was routed and that he was left with only a handful of men, taking thought for his birth and former rank he plunged into the thickest of the enemy and there fell fighting, his body run through.

(60.7)

His body is found far ahead of his men, along with a heap of enemy slain. Strikingly the words Sallust uses of Catiline here are very similar to Livy's descriptions of the elder Decius at war with the Latins (8.10.10) and the younger Decius Mus at Sentinum, who 'galloped his horse into the Gallic lines where he saw they were thickest, and hurled himself on the enemy's weapons to meet his death', <i>qua confertissimam cernebat Gallorum aciem ... inferensque se ipse infestis telis est interfectus</i> (10.28.18).[44] Was Livy perhaps responding to the heroic flavour of Sallust's earlier narrative?[45]

Once the battle is over and Catiline defeated, the bravery of those fighting with him is also commented on – all held their ground (Sall. *Cat.* 61.1–2). A notable display of their *audacia* and *vis animi*.[46] And none of citizen birth survived the battle. This was a painful victory for the forces of the state. Not only had many brave fighters been lost but 'many who had gone from the camp to visit the field or to pillage, when they turned over the bodies of the rebels found here a friend, there a guest or relative', *Multi autem, qui e castris visundi aut spoliandi gratia processerant, volventes hostilia cadavera amicum alii pars hospitem aut cognatum reperiebant* (61.8). The concluding words of the monograph are especially striking: 'The whole army was variously affected with happiness and grief, lamentation and rejoicing', *Laetitia, maeror, luctus atque gaudia*.[47] The motif of friend and foe confused will become a recurring feature of later civil war narrative.[48]

The account of Catiline's conspiracy might initially seem to be a clear-cut story of good and evil. Corrupt aristocrats, resentful veterans and a city mob, all profligates, are defeated by the forces of order. But who is the hero? The figures of Cato, Caesar and Cicero are all compromised.[49] And the man who might seem to be the obvious villain ultimately shows greatest courage. He and his followers display bravery, virtue and the desire for liberty (see 58.8). In civil war, one might argue, no-one can be straightforwardly a hero. Or rather, killing the 'enemy' who is a fellow citizen can always be described as an act of impiety. At the same time, dying for one's cause can perhaps remain a privileged means of displaying *virtus*. Thus those who are defeated are paradoxically in a better position to claim heroic status. As Lucan comments in an authorial address to Pompey: 'It was worse to win': *vincere peius erat* (*BC* 7.706).[50]

A short poem usually dated to the second half of the first century CE (thus about a century after Sallust was writing) and ascribed to the younger Seneca explores some of these same issues.[51] Here the outcome is suicide. A reference to Antony situates the incident described in the civil war between Antony and Octavian which culminated in the latter's victory at Actium in 31. This poem, too, highlights the paradox of *virtus* in civil war.

Sicine componis populos, Fortuna, furentis
    Ut vinci levius, vincere sit gravius?

Is it thus, O Fortune, that you reconcile frenzied people, so that it is easier to be conquered, worse to be the conqueror?
        ([Sen.] *Anth. Lat.* vol. I frag. 461, ed. Shackleton-Bailey, 1–2)

Here, again, it is worse to win. A soldier, Maevius, is pleased to have killed one of the enemy but, in despoiling him, finds the man is his own brother: *Et scelus et fratrem pariter cognovit*, 'At one moment he recognised both his crime and his brother' (l.7). Come, he says to himself, 'a greater task awaits you': *Vincere victorem debes, defendere fratrem*, 'You must defeat the victor, defend your brother' (l.9). Yet the victor is himself. Only one course of action lies open:

> Eripuit virtus pietatem, reddere virtus
>   Debet: qua rapuit, hac reparanda via est.
> Quid moror absolvi?' dixit, gladioque cruento
>   Incubuit, iungens fratris ad ora sua.
> Sic, Fortuna, regas semper civilia bella
>   Ut victor victo non superesse velit.

Courage has taken loyalty, courage must return it. Let it be restored by the same route. Why do I delay in absolving my guilt?' he said and fell upon his bloody sword, his face lying beside his brother's. Thus it is, Fortune, that you direct civil wars, so that the victor has no wish to survive his victim.

(15–20)

Maevius' recognition of his brother forces him to recognise the essence of civil war in which *pietas* and *virtus* are necessarily in profound tension.[52] The only means by which they can be reconciled is through the killer's suicide, an act which constitutes both a recognition of guilt and also its absolution. In civil war, the only life one may legitimately take is one's own. Only in annihilating oneself may one display *virtus* in killing.

Suicide was by no means foreign to Roman military tradition. In particular it was an option which had always been available to unsuccessful military leaders.[53] Rome had a tradition of suicidal generals, men who might be seen as preferring death to capture at the hands of the enemy. When Cicero refers in the *Pro Sestio* to men who braved their lives for Rome, he names not only Mucius Scaevola (whose attempt to kill Lars Porsenna, the Etruscan king, is described in Livy 2.12) and the Decii but also Publius Licinius Crassus, consul in 97 BCE, who, *ne videret victorem vivus inimicum, eadem sibi manu vitam exhausisse, qua mortem saepe hostibus obtulisset*, 'to avoid living to see his enemy victorious, took his own life with that same hand with which he had often brought death to his foes' (*Sest.* 48). A death bravely chosen might do much to compensate for lethal incompetence in military leadership, particularly in civil war (as we have already seen, suicides of leaders are particularly associated with civil conflict).[54] There is some considerable slippage here between the leader who dies fighting for a lost cause and the leader who takes his own life once he sees his cause is lost.

Epic civil war

Lucan's *Bellum civile* announces its topic in the opening lines, as *bella plus quam civilia*, 'wars worse than civil'. This was war not just within the state but within the family. Caesar and Pompey, leaders of the opposing factions, are father-in-law and son-in-law.[55] As often in civil war narratives there is a repeated emphasis on killing kinsmen.[56] What can constitute bravery *virtus* in such a battle as this? Henderson comments that Lucan's take on epic tarnishes 'that commemoration of manliness – "andreia" or *virtus* – which it must enact'.[57] In Book 1 the religious authority Figulus predicts: 'atrocious crime shall be called heroism', *Scelerique nefando / nomen erit virtus* (667–8). This emerges most graphically from Lucan's description of Scaeva, an associate of Caesar whose bravery is spectacular, but who fails to realise 'how great a crime courage is in civil conflict', *in armis / quam magnum virtus crimen civilibus esset* (Lucan *BC* 6.147–8).[58] Even Cato is made guilty by shedding citizen blood (2.264–6).

If the act of killing is inevitably tarnished, how does Lucan handle dying? Some deaths in his epic might seem to correspond to the traditional epic criteria for a heroic death. One instance might be the death of Domitius at the battle of Pharsalus:

> Hic patriae perit omne decus: iacet aggere magno
> Patricium campis non mixta plebe cadaver.
> Mors tamen eminuit clarorum in strage virorum
> Pugnacis Domiti, quem clades fata per omnes
> Ducebant: nusquam Magni fortuna sine illo
> Succubuit. Victus totiens a Caesare salva
> Libertate perit; tunc mille in volnera laetus
> Labitur ac venia gaudet caruisse secunda.

All the glory of our country fell there: the corpses of patricians lay in a great heap upon the field, with no plebeians among them. Yet one death was most noticeable in that carnage of famous men – the death of that stubborn warrior Domitius. Fate led him from defeat to defeat; never was he absent when Pompey's cause was worsted. Though conquered so often by Caesar, he died without losing his freedom. Now he fell gladly under a thousand wounds, and rejoiced not to be pardoned a second time.

(7.597–604)[59]

Domitius meets his end with utmost bravery (unusually for Lucan the description of his injuries is far from graphic). Though he dies, his freedom, *libertas*, is unscathed. This is a significant passage in part since it describes the death of Nero's ancestor but also because Julius Caesar himself offered a rather different account of Domitius' death in his own *Bellum civile* – where he records that Domitius had fled from the Pompeian camp to the mountains where he was killed by some cavalry (3.99.5), a coward's death. Lucan's version is usually seen as governed by a particular Homeric pattern, a pattern exemplified in the deaths of both Patroclus (*Iliad* 16.818–61) and Hector (*Iliad* 22.247–366). However, while Lucan may allow his readers to be impressed with this heroic death he also points up the delusion behind it. Domitius dies predicting – or at least hoping for – Caesar's punishment (something which turns out to be far from imminent).[60]

More often Lucan's accounts of deaths on the battlefield focus not on glory but on violation and dismemberment. Books 3, 6, 7 and 9 in particular parade a succession of dramatically gruesome deaths. Limbs are lopped off, eyes gouged out. Trunkless heads are hurled through the air. The focus is not on the dying individual but on his body – a body dehumanised. The mutilated body of the citizen offers an uncomfortable parallel with the mutilated body of the state.[61] The death of Domitius is one of the very few individual deaths described in the battle of Pharsalus itself. Rather, especially in Book 7, Lucan presents us with a list of typical deaths, whose culmination is, perhaps inevitably, parricide (7.617–30). The dead are not named. 'But no death deserves a lament to itself, and we have no leisure to mourn any individual': *Mors nulla querella / Digna sua est, nullos hominum lugere vacamus* (7.630–1). This constitutes a striking negation of the traditional role of epic articulated not only by Homer's *Iliad* but also, as we have seen, by Virgil's *Aeneid*; in these works poetry has the power to confer an undying glory which can compensate the brave warrior for the loss of his life. Lucan thus denies glory not only to those inflicting death but even to most of those dying in battle.[62]

At the same time, however, some significant elements of earlier Roman treatments of death in battle do remain. The sacrifice of the one for the many is a topic explored with particular insistence in Lucan's epic.[63] His Cato expresses the desire to opt for *devotio* on the model of Decius (2.306–11) – to be the only target of both Roman and barbarian weapons, so that he may, as a scapegoat, ensure the safety of Rome. He exclaims at an early stage in the conflict:

'Excipiam medius totius volnera belli.
Hic redimat sanguis populos, hac caede luatur,
Quidquid Romani meruerunt pendere mores.'

'Place me in the middle that I may receive the wounds of the whole war. Let my blood redeem the nations and my death pay the whole penalty incurred by the corruption of Rome.'

(2.311–13)

Here Cato seems to articulate a model of the highest *virtus*.[64] Yet this is not quite how Cato dies, as we have seen. We shall return later to the treatment of Cato's actual death in Lucan's epic.

Lucan has Pompey make an offer rather similar to Cato's:

'Parcite' ait 'superi, cunctas prosternere gentes
Stante potest mundo Romaque superstite Magnus
Esse miser. Si plura iuvant mea volnera, coniunx
Est mihi, sunt nati; dedimus tot pignora fatis.
Civilene parum est bello, si meque meosque
Obruit? Exiguae clades sumus orbe remoto?

'Stop here, ye gods,' he said, 'and refrain from destroying all nations. The world may remain and Rome survive, though Magnus is doomed. If you desire to add to my afflictions, I have a wife, I have sons; all these hostages have I given to fortune. Is civil war still unsatisfied if it destroy me and mine? Is our overthrow not enough, unless the world be added? ...'

(7.659–64)

Asking his troops not to lose their lives on his behalf, he pleads that he is not worth it. Is this another offer of *devotio*?[65] Pompey's gesture is significantly undercut by his decision shortly afterwards to withdraw from battle (7.669–75).[66] His concern that fighting will continue for ever in the event of his death is proved wrong in Book 9 – though a case could also be made for seeing all subsequent Roman history as a version of civil war, as Lucan himself seems to suggest (*BC* 1.72–82).

Suicide as conflict resolution

After the battle of Actium in 31 BCE (where the forces of Augustus finally defeated those of Mark Antony and Cleopatra) there was peace of a kind until the reign of Augustus' descendant Nero. Tacitus' *Histories* (published around 109 CE) survives only in part (the manuscript breaks off part way through Book 5). The first three books relate the period of civil war, following Nero's death, from 69 to 70 CE (it is usually supposed the rest of the text must have covered the rest of Vespasian's reign and those of Titus

and Domitian, ending with Domitian's death in 96). After Nero's flight, first
Galba was declared emperor, with the support of the praetorian guard and
the senate. He was challenged by Otho and murdered in the heart of the city
of Rome by Otho's supporters. Otho in his turn was challenged by Vitellius,
who claimed to be Nero's chosen successor. After a number of military
encounters, Otho, in Tacitus' account, decides to commit suicide in order to
avert further losses to his troops. Vitellius is supreme for only a short time,
however, and is soon deposed by the supporters of Vespasian, on his way
back from campaigning in the east to be acclaimed emperor.

Tacitus' preface lists at length the many disasters afflicting Rome during
the period to be described but also praises the examples of heroism: *non
tamen adeo sterile saeculum ut non et bona exempla prodiderit*, 'This period
was not so barren as not to offer at least some fine examples' (1.31). This
– much shorter – list culminates with noble deaths: *supremae clarorum
virorum necessitates fortiter toleratae et laudatis antiquorum mortibus
pares exitus*, 'Distinguished men bravely facing the utmost straits and
matching in their ends the famous deaths of older times.' Rome might be in
chaos but at least at least Romans still know how to die. The ironies of civil
war are biting – but rather more low key in Tacitus than in Lucan, even if
Tacitus' account of the wars of 69 consciously evokes the Roman tradition of
civil war literature, Lucan above all.[67] In some ways, Tacitus can be seen as
taking on the challenge of exceeding Lucan. In this new phase four leaders
meet death by the sword and there are three civil wars, he emphasises (1.2.1).
Here, as in earlier accounts of civil wars, we encounter the motifs of sons
killing fathers and brothers killing one another (at 3.25; 3.51).[68] And Tacitus
too engages with the issue of what can constitute *virtus* in the circumstances of civil war. Sometimes it seems that only those lacking in moral
sensibility can sustain civil conflict with real energy. Interestingly Tacitus'
characterisation of Antonius Primus, one of Vespasian's supporters, who is
described as the most enthusiastic instigator of war (3.2), echoes aspects of
Sallust's description of Catiline.[69]

In Tacitus, too, the association between civil war and suicide is significant. Of special interest here is one particular death, that of the emperor
Otho. For, in significant respects, the death of Otho can be seen as reflecting
on that paradigmatic civil war death, the suicide of Cato. After the emperor
Otho's forces are defeated at Bedriacum in 69, his supporters urge him to
continue. But Otho himself, though still with a chance of victory, resolves
to short-circuit continued civil war by killing himself.

'Hunc' inquit, 'animum, hanc virtutem vestram ultra periculis obicere
nimis grande vitae meae pretium puto ... Mihi non ultione neque solaciis

opus est. alii diutius imperium tenuerint, nemo tam fortiter reliquerit. An ego tantum Romanae pubis, tot egregios exercitus sterni rursus et rei publicae eripi patiar? ... Plura de extremis loqui pars ignaviae est. Quod de nemine queror; nam incusare deos vel homines eius est qui vivere velit.'

'Am I to expose all your splendid courage and valour to further risks?' he said. 'That would, I think, be too high a price to pay for my life. ... I do not want revenge or consolation. Others may have ruled the empire longer, but no-one can ever have relinquished it so bravely. Am I the man to allow all the youth of Rome in all these famous armies to be mown down once again and lost to the country? ... It is a kind of cowardice to keep talking about the end. I complain of no-one. To blame gods or men is the mark of one who desires to live.'

(Tac. Hist. 2.47)

Otho goes on to make arrangements for his supporters to leave. He destroys compromising documents, distributes money and offers comfort to his nephew. He then calms a disturbance, which has arisen when his supporters, spotted leaving, are suspected of desertion.

Vesperascente die sitim haustu gelidae aquae sedavit. Tum adlatis pugionibus duobus, cum utrumque pertemptasset, alterum capiti subdidit ... luce prima in ferrum pectore incubuit. Ad gemitum morientis ingressi liberti servique et Plotius Firmus praetorii praefectus unum vulnus invenere.

As night was falling he quenched his thirst with a drink of ice-cold water. Then two daggers were brought to him, and after trying them both, he put one under his pillow ... At dawn he fell upon his dagger. Hearing his dying groan, his slaves and freedmen entered with Plotius Firmus, the prefect of the Guards, and found a single wound.

(2.49)

Otho's choice of a dagger could be read as recalling the death of Cato, as could a number of other elements in the narrative, in particular the provision Otho makes for his associates and his decision to wait until morning to kill himself.[70] Certainly Otho himself will have been familiar with the details of Cato's death (as indeed will Tacitus). There is, however, no reference to philosophical abstractions here – indeed Otho explicitly labels 'talking about death' as a cowardly deferral. The <i>pugio</i>, we might note, while echoing the weapon used by Cato, is also significant as

the weapon carried by emperors to symbolise their power of life and
death.[71]

Once dead, the Tacitean Otho is much mourned by his supporters:

Tulere corpus praetoriae cohortes cum laudibus et lacrimis, vulnus
manusque eius exosculantes. Quidam militum iuxta rogum interfecere se,
non noxa neque ob metum, sed aemulatione decoris et caritate principis.
Ac postea promisce Bedriaci, Placentiae aliisque in castris celebratum id
genus mortis.

The guard carried the body, with praises and lamentations, and covering
his hands and wounded breast with kisses. Some of the soldiers killed
themselves beside the pyre, not through servility or fear, but from love
of their emperor, and to follow his noble example. Such suicides became
common afterwards at Bedriacum and Placentia and other camps.

(2.49)

Tacitus has numerous negative comments to offer about Otho's earlier
behaviour – or at least reports many such comments.[72] Indeed Tacitus
is sometimes read as more critical of Otho's career than is Suetonius or
Plutarch.[73] However, Tacitus presents Otho's suicide as wholly admirable.
'By two acts, one highly criminal and the other heroic, he earned in equal
measure the praise and criticism of posterity', *Duobus facinoribus, altero
flagitiosissimo, altero egregio, tantundem apud posteros meruit bonae famae
quantum malae* (2.50).[74] For Tacitus, Otho's suicide is a rational means to
limit further bloodshed. This act too can be seen in the tradition of *devotio*.[75]
By a characteristically Tacitean twist, however, at least some bloodshed is a
direct outcome of Otho's suicide, insofar as he inspires a host of imitators,
celebratum id genus mortis.[76]

Tacitus' contemporary Martial explicitly compares the suicides of Otho
and Cato:

Cum dubitaret adhuc belli civilis Enyo,
    Forsitan et posset vincere mollis Otho,
Damnavit multo staturum sanguine Martem
    Et fodit certa pectora tota manu.
Sit Cato, dum vivit, sane vel Caesare maior:
    Dum moritur, numquid maior Othone fuit?

While the goddess of civil war remained in doubt still, and soft Otho
could yet have won the war, he cursed the conflict whose resolution
demanded so much blood and stabbed his breast right through with

certain hand. In life, let Cato be greater even than Caesar. In his death could he surpass Otho?

(Martial, Epigram 6.32)

For Martial, Otho's death is nobler than Cato's – not least in that he manages to kill himself efficiently on the first attempt.[77] Moreover Otho still had a chance of victory, while Cato had been decisively defeated. Otho's end serves to terminate civil war (or at least one phase of it), while Cato's could be read as serving to save his own face. On this reading, Otho's death is a genuine instance of self-sacrifice – and one which serves to problematise the death of Cato.[78]

Still, within the logic of Roman civil war narrative, suicide may ultimately be the only means of achieving a heroic death. In a way, suicide takes civil war to its logical conclusion. But with the highly significant point of contrast that no-one is made guilty by this death. Rather one death saves many lives by bringing civil war to an instant conclusion (or at least this particular phase of the civil war). At the same time, one could argue that this reaction to suicide is only really possible in the context of Roman society where an individual's decision to take his or her own life is regularly celebrated as a positive, almost life-affirming choice.[79] While taking the life of a fellow citizen might be impious, to kill oneself is not seen as intrinsically wrong.[80]

A suicidal state

In Lucan's treatment of civil war the idea of suicide is invoked repeatedly – almost incessantly. Charles Martindale, for instance, describes the *Bellum civile* as 'a poem which might well be read under the sign of self-slaughter, both individual and collective'.[81] Lucan insistently describes civil war itself as suicide.[82] The opening of the poem proclaims: 'I sing of', *populumque potentem/in sua victrici conversum viscera dextra*, 'how an imperial people turned its victorious right hand against its own vitals' (1.2–3). A few lines later he exclaims:

> Tum si tantus amor belli tibi, Roma, nefandi,
> Totum sub Latias leges cum miseris orbem,
> In te verte manus.

O Rome, if your desire for impious war is so great, then first subdue the whole earth to your law and then commit self-slaughter.

(BC 1.21–3)

In Lucan's writing, suicide can be seen not just as a metaphor for civil war but rather as its *reductio ad absurdum*. The Roman state disembowels itself.

Yet one might well argue that in using suicide as a metaphor for civil war, Lucan has effectively devalued it as an act, emphasising suicide's negative, self-destructive dimension (more in line with most modern perceptions of suicide).[83] A crucial issue here is that in metaphorical as opposed to actual suicide, the guilt of killing is not dispensed with but rather made universal. Lucan's preoccupation with the all-encompassing guilt of civil war is explored in detail in the debate between Brutus and Cato in Book 2 of his poem, where Brutus argues and Cato concedes that participation in civil conflict will make even Cato guilty (249–87).

One episode in which suicide might seem to be positively valued is the mutual suicide of Vulteius and his men in Book 4.[84] The mutual suicide of soldiers otherwise faced with capture or death at the hands of the enemy is a practice occasionally recorded in relation to other conflicts. Crassus' troops, defeated at Carrhae, are alleged to have killed one another (Dio 40.25.2), similarly Caesar's troops, facing the prospect of capture by Ambiorix (Caesar *BG* 5.37). The practice seems to have been particularly associated with civil war, however, where examples include the deaths of Pompey's soldiers after the fall of Corfinum (Caesar *BC* 1.21.6) and those of Caesar after Coructae (Dio 41.40.2), while Petreius and Juba allegedly sought death in hand-to-hand combat after Caesar's victory at Thapsus (Dio 43.8.4).[85]

In Lucan's Book 4, some troops under the command of one of Caesar's supporters attempt to escape from an island off the Illyrian coast where they are cut off by crossing over to the mainland in a series of rafts. Three of these, carrying around 600 men commanded by Vulteius, are trapped at sea by the Cilicians associated with Pompey. Vulteius recognises that there is no escape and first orders his men to fight, despite the huge disparity in numbers. Thousands surround them. Once night falls, however, he exhorts his men not to fight on but rather to kill themselves.

> 'Libera non ultra parva quam nocte iuventus,
> consulite extremis angusto in tempore rebus.
> Vita brevis nulli superest, qui tempus in illa
> Quaerendae sibi mortis habet; nec gloria leti
> Inferior, iuvenes, admoto occurrere fato.'

'Soldiers, free for no more than the brief space of a night, use the short time to decide upon your course in this extremity. No life is short that gives a man time to kill himself; nor does it lessen the glory of suicide to come to meet a death already close.'

(*BC* 4.476–80)

One might read Vulteius' exhortation as a strategy to induce terrifying courage in his troops. These desperate men will inspire the enemy with dread (4.505–6). There is clearly a parallel with *devotio* here; indeed Vulteius' men are described as *devota iuventus* (4.533). They are *ferox* precisely because they have despaired of life (534). Similarly in the episode described just prior to this one, a group of Pompeians under the command of Afranius, cut off and with no prospect of rescue, rush upon the enemy meaning to die (*ad certam devotos tendere mortem*, 272). Caesar, ever prudent, refuses to engage them in battle (not wishing to lose any of his own men), instead besieging them without supplies. Their ardour flags and eventually they surrender, accepting Caesar's *clementia*. Once these men no longer think of themselves as *morituri*, they are, it seems, less willing to take chances in battle.

To return to the raft: when day breaks, Vulteius' men do fight with the enemy for a while but killing the enemy is by no means Vulteius' primary objective. 'When they decided enough blood had been shed in battle, they turned their fury away from the enemy', *utque satis bello visum est fluxisse cruoris/versus ab hoste furor* (539–40). Now they turn upon each other. While the battle scenes are scarcely described by Lucan, the mutual suicide is presented in great detail. Vulteius himself is first to bare his neck and call for death:

> Primus dux ipse carinae
> Vulteius iugulo poscens iam fata retecto
> 'Ecquis' ait 'iuvenum est, cuius sit dextra cruore
> digna meo certaque fide per volnera nostra
> testetur se velle mori?'

First the leader of the raft himself, baring his neck, demands his death. 'Is any soldier here', he cried, 'whose right arm is worthy of my blood, who will prove his wish to die beyond all doubt by slaying me?'

(4.540–4)

These deaths might seem to have something in common with the death of Maevius in the poem attributed to Seneca, where suicide is the only remaining means of displaying *virtus*. Vulteius' *virtus* is certainly spectacular. Yet it is also profoundly compromised, firstly through its association with *furor* and secondly through Vulteius' blind devotion to Caesar.[86] Vulteius exhorts his men to think of freedom. This bears a resemblance to the kind of argument for suicide as the road to freedom, *libertas*, which also occurs in the philosophical writings of Lucan's uncle, Seneca. Seneca's Letters 70 and 77 in particular (as well as a striking passage from *De ira*, 3.15.3–4) repeatedly emphasise the possibility of killing oneself as a source of freedom for anyone, no matter what their circumstances.[87] And Seneca too can be found arguing that it may make sense to take one's life even when death by some other means is very close.[88] Later on Lucan comments:

> Non tamen ignavae post haec exempla virorum
> Percipient gentes, quam sit non ardua virtus
> Servitium fugisse manu.

> Yet even after the example set by these heroes cowardly nations will not understand how simple a feat it is to escape slavery by suicide.
>
> (*BC* 4.575–7)

The deaths of these men then might look like a kind of Stoic suicide. Yet they are fighting for Caesar – whose will to power has, throughout the *Bellum civile*, been presented as incompatible with *libertas*. Vulteius' men are told to demonstrate their *pietas* and *fides*, their 'loyalty' and 'good faith', towards their commander. Indeed, when their men gather up the dead bodies afterwards, the Pompeian leaders marvel that any man should prize his leader so highly (572–3). This kind of death would surely earn criticism rather than praise from Seneca.[89] Martindale terms this episode 'a parody of a Stoic sage seeking *libertas* through suicide'.[90]

Vulteius himself comments: 'By our death fortune designs some mighty and memorable example for posterity', *nescio quod nostris magnum et memorabile fatis/exemplum, Fortuna, paras* (4.496–7). These deaths certainly constitute a conspicuous *exemplum* – but of what? Fighting on would surely have enabled them to kill more of the enemy.[91] But deaths in the vast mêlée would have been far less visible.

> Conferta iacent cum corpora campo,
> In medium mors omnis abit, perit obruta virtus.

> When the dead lie crowded upon the field, each death is lost in the mass, and courage disappears submerged.
>
> (4.490–1)

Lucan himself complains later in his epic (7.630–1) that the profusion of slaughter on the battlefield leaves him no space to dwell on individual deaths, as we saw. Vulteius cannot bear this anonymity. Yet as critics have noted, of all those who die on the raft, only Vulteius himself is actually named in Lucan's poem.[92] He secures epic fame of a kind. But at what cost?

Vulteius is obsessed with having an audience. He urges his men to kill themselves; their conspicuous position offers an unparalleled opportunity:

> Nos in conspicua sociis hostique carina
> Constituere dei. Praebebunt aequora testes;
> Praebebunt terrae, summis dant insula saxis,
> Spectabunt geminae diverso litore partes.

> Us the gods have placed on a craft on view to friends and enemies. Witnesses will be offered by the sea, offered by the land, granted by the high cliffs of the island. Two parties from two opposed shores will look on.

> (4.492–5)

Vulteius thinks of death as a performance. Spectators are thus essential if the performance is to have meaning.[93] Those witnessing the spectacle are numerous but Vulteius' ideal spectator is one man, Caesar himself. Vulteius' ultimate wish is to die with Caesar as his witness (4.500). This spectacle is in a sense created for Caesar – although he is not actually present.

Lucan's text seems to invite the reader to look on this scene through Caesar's eyes. Katherine Eldred reads the episode as 'an illustration of Vulteius's deliberate objectification of himself in a power matrix, at the head of which is his (absent) commander Caesar'. The reader, identifying with Caesar, would thus take on the role of the masculinised spectator, whose fear of castration is allayed by the experience of looking at the feminised object on display.[94] Yet the reader's identification with Caesar is also subverted by the elements in the poem which invite the reader to identify rather with Vulteius himself, thus finding pleasure in taking on the role of victim. The reader oscillates between the positions of Caesar and of Vulteius, taking pleasure in changing perspective from one moment to the next.[95]

The instability generated by Lucan's treatment may be seen as ethical as well as libidinal. We might remember that Caesar himself, in his commentary on the Gallic wars, asserts that soldiers fight most bravely when he himself is looking on. Caesar as observer inspires and validates the *virtus* of his men, a *virtus* whose value is unambiguously positive. Even when he is not present, his soldiers may draw strength from the thought of him: *illum adesse et haec coram cernere existimate*, 'Imagine he is present and is watching', a well-trained subordinate officer exhorts his troops (Caesar *BG*

6.8.4). Vulteius, too, has been well trained. In the very different moral world of Lucan's epic, though, Caesar cannot function as arbiter of any of Rome's traditional values. He cannot function as moral witness.

The *devotio* of Decius in Livy's history is, as we saw earlier, a spectacle which demands witnesses to be effective – to activate the esprit de corps of the Roman soldiers, to inspire them to victory over their foreign enemies. But the moral status of the witnesses is crucial.[96] So too is the goal for which they fight. While the Decii fight for the legions or for the Roman people, Vulteius fights only for Caesar, *pro te* (4.500).[97] Vulteius, too, yearns to be exemplary. The deaths of Vulteius and his men also constitute a spectacle. But this is a spectacle with no tangible effect. All they achieve is show, the ultimate extravagant gesture – closer in significance to the show put on by Livy's Gallic champion but far more reprehensible. Though Vulteius sees these spectators as *testes*, 'witnesses' to the *virtus* of his men, they can be no more than an audience. The terms in which Lucan presents the mutual slaughter on the raft, highlighting display and effect, evoke the shows of the Roman theatre and especially the amphitheatre, where large audiences assembled to watch men kill their fellows with whom they had trained to fight.[98] A little later in Book 4, the commander Curio is made to exhort his men to fight, regardless of the rights and wrongs of each side:

'Qua stetit, inde favet; veluti fatalis harenae
Muneribus non ira vetus concurrere cogit
Productos, odere pares.'

'Each man supports the side on which he stands. Just so in the spectacle of the fatal arena those who are brought out are not driven to fight by long-held anger; they hate whoever's on the other side.'

(4.708–10)

All that is left is the spectacle of killing. Vulteius, too, is on one level merely a master of ceremonies, complicit with the pleasures of his audience. Indeed on one view even the pleasure of reading about civil war may be no more edifying than the uneasily visceral pleasure of watching gladiatorial combat.[99] In the end this ghastly spectacle of mutual suicide constitutes nothing more than an emblem of civil war in which citizens kill each other.[100] 'Others met in combat; and there the horrors of the civil war were enacted in full by one faction alone', *Concurrunt alii totumque in partibus unis / bellorum facere nefas* (4.548–9). The most the reader can do is to recognise that, despite the delusions of Vulteius, this is not Roman *virtus*. Yet none of the witnesses within the text has, it seems, sufficient moral grasp to see beyond the delusion.

Lucan goes on to set out at length the legendary story of the Spartai, the Theban warriors who sprang up from seeds sown from Cadmus only to kill one another – a dismal omen for Thebes (*dirum ... omen*, 551), a city whose later history was to be characterised by fratricidal strife.[101] This is hardly an endorsement for mutual suicide. Moreoever Lucan's comment at 580–1 might well be read as a claim that suicide is not in itself virtuous.[102] *Mors, utinam pavidos vitae subducere nolles, / sed virtus te sola daret!* 'O that death were the reward of the brave only, and would not let the coward from life!' One might well argue that the only truly heroic death of Lucan's *Bellum civile* is one escape that takes place outside the text: the suicide of Cato, which occurred in the aftermath of Caesar's victory.[103] To make this point does not, of course, require the claim that the *Bellum civile* is unfinished.[104] Rather it may be that the repeated exploitation of suicide as metaphor in Lucan's poem made it impossible for him to describe the actual suicide of Cato in positive terms.[105] Cato's suicide, then, is promised as the ultimate expression of true Stoic *virtus* but must for ever remain beyond the text.

Unlike the Athenian war dead, Romans did not necessarily 'become good' through dying in war. Some war deaths, most spectacularly those of the Decii, could be taken as exemplary, instances of what seemed a characteristically Roman willingness to place the needs of the state before those of the individual. But in general Roman soldiers appear to have aspired to conquer and survive. It is the experience of civil war which problematises and intensifies the focus on death in war. It is in this context that we find the celebration of ever more extreme instances of suicide on the field of battle. The pleasure of reading about deaths in battle as a highlight of historical works is commented on, as we saw earlier, by both Cicero and Tacitus. In the context of civil war we find an increasingly pathologised focus on such deaths as acts which seek not witnesses, perhaps, but rather an audience, a transformation most graphically highlighted by Lucan.

CHAPTER 2

DEATH AS SPECTACLE
LOOKING AT DEATH IN THE ARENA

Lord Byron's poetic travelogue, *Childe Harold's Pilgrimage*, in its treatment of Rome (first published in 1818), famously evokes the death of a gladiator in the Colosseum:

> He leans upon his hand – his manly brow
> Consents to death, but conquers agony.
>
> (Canto IV, stanzas 140–1)

The 'inhuman shout' of the Roman spectators hails the victor; the dying man thinks rather of his wife and children far away in barbarian Dacia, 'He, their sire, / butcher'd to make a Roman holiday.' The poet identifies with the dying gladiator and exhorts his fellow barbarians, the Goths, to avenge the gladiator's slaughter by turning on Rome. These lines, quoted by innumerable visitors to Rome in later years, were made to articulate northern European and American Christian horror at the pleasure ancient pagan Romans took in killing for sport.[1] While the civilised modern reader feels for the dying man, the arena's imagined crowd side with his killer.[2]

The obsession with gladiatorial combat has often been seen as an index of ancient Roman barbarity. Scholars have sought explanations for the Roman preoccupation with the arena in terms of mass psychology, in terms of Roman militarism, in terms of changing political circumstances.[3] Certainly in the spectacles of the Roman amphitheatre the death of a gladiator was not incidental but often the entertainment's climax. Even if the defeated gladiator survived the conflict, it was only because the provider of the games had made the decision to spare him. The manner in which the defeated gladiator met death was crucial. Gladiators were celebrated in Roman culture not only because they knew how to kill, but also because they knew how to die. One aim of this chapter will be to explore some ways in which Romans may have found meanings in the bloody deaths of gladiators, which had a bearing on their own mortal condition.[4] I want to argue that the experience of watching these games crucially conditions and is conditioned by both attitudes to dying and representations of death in Roman antiquity. In particular, the phenomenon of the arena has an important bearing on the idea of death as an edifying subject for display.

The imagery of gladiatorial combat is invoked in a wide range of literary and philosophical texts. Despite the profound ambivalence Roman elite writers feel towards gladiators (often regarded as the lowest of the low), the model of gladiatorial combat leaves its traces even in the high genres of history and epic; Lucan's treatment of the civil war between Pompey and Caesar, as we saw, repeatedly configures the conflict in terms which recall Roman spectacular entertainments generally but the arena in particular.[5] Philosophically inclined writers, most notably Seneca, invoke the dying gladiator as a model for facing death in the right frame of mind. This figure raises some complex issues concerning the relationship of the reader to the 'spectacle' described.

Part of the essence of gladiatorial combat was not just the fight to the death between two armed men but also the presence of an audience, and the host of complex and contradictory responses felt by that audience. Invocations of gladiatorial combat, whether in epic poetry or philosophical or historical prose, may well prompt us to think about who is to play the role of audience and how that audience should respond. The role of the viewer has in recent decades been the subject of searching analysis in Roman literary texts.[6] Though the arena can be seen as a key site of visual pleasure in Roman culture, this issue has received only limited attention in analyses of the arena itself. While the experience of the spectator at the arena was not itself mediated through a representation created by an authorial subject, nevertheless the texts (and images) through which we now have access to the games are so mediated. How do these texts construct the reader's response to this 'spectacle' of death?

The gift of death

Before examining representations of the gladiator's death in more detail we need to bear in mind its context. Under the republic, gladiatorial shows were generally given to mark an aristocratic funeral.[7] The first instance recorded dates to 264 BCE at the funeral games given in honour of Junius Brutus Pera by his two sons.[8] Three pairs of gladiators fought. In 216 BCE the three sons of the ex-consul Marcus Aemilius Lepidus gave funeral games in his honour, lasting three days and involving forty-four gladiators (Livy 23.30). The number of gladiators provided seems to have increased (though historians tended to record only the more spectacular contests). 320 pairs of gladiators, according to Pliny, fought at the funeral games Julius Caesar organised in honour of his long-dead father in 65 BCE (*NH* 33.53).[9] These shows generally took place in the Roman Forum, in the political centre of the city. Only in the time of Augustus was a permanent amphitheatre constructed (the arena of Statilius Taurus). Gladiatorial games were not an everyday occurrence in ancient Rome.[10] Nevertheless even by the second century BCE, when such games were given at infrequent intervals, they seem to have acquired a distinctive symbolic resonance. The *munera* given by noble families to mark the funerals of their members under the republic were scarcely private

1. Pottery oil lamp, first century CE.

occasions.[11] The individuals honoured were public figures and one aim of such spectacles was to raise the public profile of the family whose living members were usually involved in the often intense competition for public office.[12]

Under the autocracy established by Augustus, the provision of *munera* within the city of Rome appears to have been rigidly controlled; the praetors (senior magistrates) were to give no more than two spectacles a year and with no more than 120 men, according to a law of 22 BCE (Dio 54.2.2).[13] Games provided by the emperor himself were not subject to such restrictions. Augustus, in his record of his achievements, boasted that he had provided three sets of games in his own name, and two in the name of his grandsons, in the course of which 10,000 gladiators fought (*Res gestae* 22.1). Gradually the sponsoring of gladiatorial games seems to have become a prerogative of the imperial family, in particular serving to mark accessions, birthdays and triumphs.[14] This development in itself is an index of the influence of gladiatorial games over the Roman populace.

Gladiatorial imagery was all-pervasive in the Roman world. A character in Tacitus' *Dialogue on Oratory* (written in the late first century CE) complains that the topic dominates conversation in people's homes and in lecture halls (*Dialogus* 29). Depictions of gladiatorial fights are often to be found on wall-paintings, mosaics, terracotta lamps, graffiti and elsewhere (see, e.g., fig. 1).[15] A phase of the fight often represented is the moment when the defeated man has conceded – and waits to hear his fate from the provider of the games. This moment of supreme tension and its immediate aftermath – the release or death of the defeated gladiator – will be the particular focus of what follows.

Degraded heroes

Gladiators were heroes but they were regarded with profound ambivalence, reviled and subjected to a wide range of legal disabilities.[16] In some ways they were the lowest of the low, men who, even if free, nevertheless undertook to allow their bodies to be 'burnt, bound, beaten and slain by the sword' according to the terms of the gladiator's oath (Sen. *Ep.* 37.1). Yet they were also stars, incarnations of a potent masculinity, skilled fighters, above all, and men whose courage was such that they could look death in the face without flinching. 'In the powerful, erotically charged figure of the gladiator, the Roman romance with death, unendurably intensified and concentrated, met its ultimate and its limits,' comments Carlin Barton.[17]

The term gladiator is sometimes used loosely by modern scholars – and indeed by some ancient texts, generally Christians attacking the games (for instance Tert. *Spect.* 21, quoted below). Pagan authors usually distinguish carefully between trained gladiators on the one hand (a category which includes individuals condemned *ad ludos*) and prisoners condemned to death in the arena, *noxii*, who might also be forced to fight, though without training – and sometimes without weapons.[18] Since my concern is with preparation for facing death, the focus of this chapter will be on gladiators who were trained in the gladiatorial school (*ludus*). *Noxii* were not expected to meet death as gladiators did (a later chapter will consider some Christian martyrs who fall into the category of *noxii*).[19]

Some, perhaps most, trained gladiators were condemned criminals or slaves.[20] The routes by which men (and occasionally women) might end up fighting in the arena were diverse.[21] Under the republic many slaves fighting in the arena will have been prisoners of war.[22] Domestic slaves, however, might also find themselves condemned to gladiatorial training and performance.[23] Even if they survived long enough to win their freedom, such men, lacking other means to earn a living, often continued to fight in the arena.[24] The status of the gladiators who were to participate is sometimes specified in the advertisements for shows and was clearly perceived to be a matter of interest to spectators.[25]

Some gladiators were free men who volunteered for the arena. Professional gladiators of free status seem to have been found in Rome from the third century BCE.[26] These latter, in return for their pay, swore the oath under whose terms they surrendered their bodies to indignities normally experienced only by slaves.[27] Seneca describes this oath as 'most shameful', *turpissimi* (*Ep.* 37.1). It is impossible to determine what proportion of gladiators were volunteers.[28] These certainly included Roman citizens. If they were Roman citizens, those who were gladiators by profession were classed as *infames*, that is to say they were subject to a wide range of legal disabilities which, while for the most part relatively minor, marked them out as degraded.[29] These disabilities were, it seems, regarded as a consequence of the public nature of the spectacles they provided and the fact that they received payment for them (parallel measures applied to actors).[30] The kind of pleasure associated with these entertainments – a pleasure regarded as all too accessible – rendered those who provided them deeply suspect. We shall return later to the particular nature of the pleasure associated with the arena.

Gladiators were often regarded as low brutes. 'Gladiator' regularly appears as a term of abuse, for instance in the speeches of Cicero.[31] Volunteer gladiators are sometimes presented as driven to their profession by indigence. In other texts however they are motivated by a desire to fight.[32] Emperors sometimes chose to humiliate members of the elite by forcing them to fight as gladiators.[33] But sometimes members of the elite (and even the occasional emperor) themselves chose to fight in the arena.[34] As early as 122 BCE, a law of Gaius Gracchus excluded from the courts equestrians who had hired themselves out as gladiators.[35] Numerous pieces of legislation (passed between 38 BCE and 69 CE) attempted to restrict or eliminate the participation of members of the elite in the arena. These laws may be seen as an index of the arena's allure for the performer. This was a place in which glamour and danger were inextricably intertwined.[36]

It is difficult to gauge with accuracy what proportion of those gladiators who fought in the arena in Rome (and elsewhere in the empire) met their deaths there.[37] Condemned criminals, it seems, had almost no chance of surviving (those not killed in the arena were finished off in the *spoliarium*).[38] Slaves might retire after three years of fighting – if they managed to live that long. Those who were volunteers, especially once they had acquired skill and reputation, probably faced somewhat better odds. Yet a recent study suggests even for relatively successful gladiators the chances of dying early were very high. One set of graffiti from Pompeii implies that of those gladiators whose names are known, over three-quarters had died before completing ten fights. About one gladiator in six, then, would meet death in each show.[39] The sheer number of gladiators fighting in spectacles in Rome (Augustus *Res gestae* 22.1, as noted earlier, mentions 5000 pairs fighting in eight *munera*) meant that deaths in the arena were frequently to be observed by the vast throngs of people gathered in the audience.

Exemplary entertainment?

Gladiators were armed in a variety of different ways. The types known as Thraex, Myrmillo and Hoplomachus were all heavily armed, it seems, the *retiarius* was lightly armed with a net and trident, while the *essedarius* fought from a chariot.[40] Some of these had exotic associations. Indeed they can be seen as figuring for Rome's toughest adversaries, the Thraex representing the barbarians of Thracia, the *essedarius* fighting from the kind of chariot used by Gallo-British warriors. Their presence in the heart of the metropolis might thus work to advertise the need for continuing vigilance on the empire's margins.[41] Yet on a more fundamental level gladiators, as exemplars of martial *virtus*, that most quintessentially Roman characteristic, might seem profoundly Roman.[42] Gladiators fought in single combat, a mode of fighting associated with early Rome (as well as the world of Homer's *Iliad*) rather than the Roman armies of the late republic and principate.[43] Nevertheless, for many Romans, the gladiator set an example of how to do battle.[44] Cicero presents gladiators as providing models of military skill in action (*Phil.* 2.74). Livy describes the effect of King Antiochus' introduction of Roman-style gladiatorial combats on the Syrians of Antioch in 175 BCE (the king had spent many years as a hostage in Rome): *armorum studium plerisque iuvenum incendit*, 'He inspired many of the young men with the zest for warfare' (Livy 41.20.12). Gladiatorial spectacles were regularly provided for soldiers of the Roman army; the remains of amphitheatres have been found in association with military encampments from all over the empire.[45] Indeed there are some references to the use of gladiators to provide training for Roman soldiers.[46] At the same time, particularly in the city of Rome itself where the most lavish and spectacular displays were put on, the opportunity to watch gladiators has plausibly been seen as a substitute for the direct experience of battle – an experience that was often constructed as central to Roman identity but which many of the inhabitants of the metropolis will never have participated in directly.[47]

Pliny, in a speech in praise of the emperor Trajan (praise which is often articulated in terms of contrast with earlier less laudable emperors such as Nero and Domitian), offers the following comment on the emperor's provision of gladiatorial games:

> Visum est spectaculum inde non enerve nec fluxum, nec quod animos virorum molliret et frangeret, sed quod ad pulchra vulnera contemptumque mortis accenderet, cum in servorum etiam noxiorumque corporibus amor laudis et cupido victoriae cerneretur.

> A public entertainment was next seen – nothing spineless or dissolute to weaken and undermine the men's spirits, but one to inspire them to face honourable wounds and despise death, by exhibiting love of glory and desire for victory even in the bodies of slaves and criminals.

> (*Paneg.* 33.1)

Trajan was regularly represented as a soldier emperor (Pliny earlier emphasises his kinship with his troops, *Paneg.* 13). His choice of public spectacle appears as wholly in keeping with his military image. While other kinds of entertainment are deemed corrupting, watching gladiators could be seen as something edifying, even beautiful. At the same time, Pliny presents the gladiators themselves as despicable. But this merely sharpens the point. The gladiator functions as a symbol of *virtus* stripped down, with all the trappings of status pared away. The *virtus* of the gladiator was absolutely central to the institution of gladiatorial games.[48] Although in most contexts, particularly martial contexts, the term *virtus* is especially associated with men, women too fought as gladiators.[49] Their demonstrations of *virtus* may well have been read as form of burlesque.[50]

Gladiators provided entertainment, yet they also offered models for how a man should behave in fighting, killing – and dying. 'The Roman people came to see a *professional performance* of male self-control, *virtus*, in the face of death', as Bettina Bergmann comments.[51] Pliny praised Trajan's gladiators for showing the spectators 'how to face honourable wounds and despise death'. But Roman spectators watched men (and occasionally women) die in a context which disposed them to treat this sight as entertainment offered for their pleasure. There was a significant tension between the fight as *spectaculum* and the fight as *exemplum*.[52] Within what Eric Gunderson terms 'the apparatus of the arena', real deaths 'become fictive ones, and real blood is always also stage blood'.[53]

The politics of the arena

The emperor, as provider of the most splendid gladiatorial contests, could be said to dominate the arena under the principate.[54] As *editor*, provider of the games, it was he who decided whether a defeated gladiator should live or die – a vivid reminder of his power over the lives of other citizens, of his status as father of his country (the Roman *pater familias* had the right of life and death over those in his power – even if this power was rarely exercised).[55] Other aristocrats may sometimes in their capacity as magistrates have presided as *editores* over a set of games in the city of Rome but such games seem to have been relatively modest. It appears, as we saw, that at least by the time of Tiberius, aristocrats were effectively prevented from providing *munera* in their capacity as private citizens. The most lavish gladiatorial games were always those provided by the emperor or a member of his family. The emperor's command over the resources of the empire was thus graphically demonstrated.

A notable feature of the arena, to an even greater extent than the circus or theatre, was the fact that the spectators, too, were on display. Individuals might attend – most obviously members of the elite, seated in the front rows, hoping to attract attention. Ovid, in his mock didactic poem on the art of love, comments in relation to women at the games: 'they come to see the show, they come to be on show themselves', *spectatum veniunt, veniunt spectentur ut ipsae* (*Ars amatoria* 1.99).[56] We shall return later to the erotic dynamics of the arena. The very multifariousness of the audience, containing people drawn from all over the empire (and beyond), variously dressed, speaking in different languages, might function as an index of the empire's vast extent – a complement to the exotic origins of the performers, human and animal.[57]

Above all, those attending the amphitheatre saw an image of Roman society in the structured disposition of the audience, with separate seating for the elite, for women, for soldiers.[58] The individual spectator could not avoid being aware of his or her own position in this hierarchy. The image projected itself played a dynamic role in constituting that volatile social order.[59]

The emperor, seated in his box, was the most visible of all the spectators; the conduct of emperors at the games is itself the object of considerable critical comment, most notably in Suetonius' *Lives*. Augustus, for instance, won popular approval by attending the games and seeming to enjoy them, in striking contrast to Julius Caesar, who was criticised for dealing with his correspondence instead of concentrating on the fight (Suet. *Aug.* 45.1). At the games, above all, the emperor was rendered legible to his subjects.[60]

The emperor's authority was on display in the arena, but it was also subject to scrutiny and at times a degree of contestation.[61] Even under the republic, gladiatorial combats were recognised as providing one of the contexts in which the Roman people's views might find clearest expression (Cic. *Sest.* 106).[62] Under the autocracy of the emperors, when popular assemblies had become an irrelevance, requests about matters such as taxation seem to have been voiced at the games, where, faced with a noisy crowd, the emperor might find it hard to avoid giving a conciliatory response. Above all, emperors could make a display of their deference to the people's wishes by allowing the shouts of the crowd to determine a gladiator's fate. Such concessions might be ultimately trivial – even if not for the individual gladiator – but served as persuasive demonstrations of the degree to which emperor and people were at one.[63] In such moments above all we might glimpse the 'magic identification with a leader' characteristic of what Guy Debord terms the 'concentrated spectacle'.[64]

The relation between emperors and performers was also complex and uneasy. If a gladiator disappointed his audience, perhaps failing to die with a brave face, this was a reflection on the giver of the games, a source of embarrassment. Yet if a gladiator did especially well there was a sense in which his very achievement, his display of bravery without limit, might itself put the emperor in a poor light by comparison. Caligula, according to Suetonius, felt undermined by the warm applause given to an *essedarius*. The emperor left the arena in such haste that 'he fell down the steps in a state of fury shouting that the people who ruled the world gave more honour to a gladiator for the smallest act than to their deified emperors or to himself, their present one', *ita proripuit se spectaculis, ut calcata lacinia togae praeceps per gradus iret, indignabundus et clamitans dominum gentium populum ex re levissima plus honoris gladiatori tribuentem quam consecratis principibus aut praesenti sibi* (*Calig.* 35.3).

Hence, perhaps, one reason for the phenomenon of aristocrats who chose to fight as gladiators in the arena. On one level to fight in the arena was to reject the carefully policed social hierarchy, at whose apogee sat the emperor – a hierarchy most graphically manifest in the disposition of spectators in that same arena. At the same time, to fight in the arena was to offer the starkest possible demonstration of the degree to which one was dependent on the emperor's whim, an embracing of abject powerlessness.[65] Yet it was also an assertion of the individual's essential bravery, a profound contempt for death. Only a few aristocrats entered the arena.[66] But others too seem to have been drawn to identify with gladiators, as we shall see. Under the early principate above all, the gladiator as metaphor seems to have gained a particular potency.[67]

Waiting for death

A *munus* often extended over several days – of which the last was the most prestigious. The gladiatorial games given by the emperor Titus to mark the completion of the Colosseum apparently lasted 100 days (with 3000 gladiators competing on one day alone) (Dio 66.25). The emperor Trajan is said to have celebrated the conquest of Dacia with 123 days of games from 108 to 109 CE, in which 10,000 gladiators fought (Dio 68.15).[68] The number of gladiatorial pairs involved was staggering. The almost unending succession of combats in a show on this scale must have had a terrifying cumulative impact (though perhaps most of the spectators will not have been present for every day of the event). My concern here, however, is rather with the death of the individual gladiator. It is thus of crucial importance to appreciate the structure of the individual fight, insofar as we can reconstruct it from literary and visual evidence. Curiously, only one ancient text offers a description of an individual bout – a poem of Martial which details a combat between Priscus and Verus, a pair so evenly matched that the audience finally demanded their honourable discharge from gladiatorial service (*Spectacula* 29).[69] This was not, it seems from other sources such as Pompeian graffiti, by any means a typical outcome. The model set out in what follows, tentative though it is, does, I think, help to make sense of the particular ways in which Roman writers configure the gladiator's relationship with death.

The first part of the combat will have had similarities to combat sports familiar in the modern world – with fencing or boxing, for instance. But fatalities in these modern sports, though not unknown, are relatively rare. By contrast fatal wounds might be and often were inflicted during the course of gladiatorial combat. On some occasions a fight might be explicitly designated non-fatal. Combat which is simply *vulneribus tenus*, 'as far as wounding', is sometimes mentioned (as in Livy 41.20).[70] More often the fight continued until one gladiator conceded defeat, making a request for his *missio* – that is, to be let off, living to fight another day.[71]

The defeated gladiator would indicate his submission; often he will have been physically unable to continue fighting. Among visual representations of gladiatorial combat, particularly those on lamps, scenes depicting the moment when the defeated gladiator requests *missio* predominate (see figs 2 and 3).[72] Occasionally the defeated man is shown lying on the ground; more often he is raised on one elbow. Some scenes represent him kneeling or sitting.

2. Pottery oil lamp made in Italy, late first century BCE.

A gladiator might indicate himself beaten by raising a finger (again, a gesture often depicted). After this point, his opponent was obliged to stop fighting.

The victorious gladiator would then pause.[73] Now it was up to the provider of the games, the *editor*, to indicate the fate of the defeated gladiator – whether he should live, leaving the arena by the gate of the living, or die.[74] The pause, with the defeated gladiator poised on the brink of life, must for many of those watching have been the climax of the game. The audience waited. The *editor* either granted the defeated gladiator his *missio* or else gave the order that he should accept death.[75] The term *ferrum recipere*,

3. Pottery oil lamp, made in Roman Britain or Gaul, first century CE.

'receive the blade', occurs in a number of texts.[76] The most common means of dispatching the condemned gladiator was stabbing him in the neck – or at least this is how the term *iugulari* is most commonly understood.[77] Visual representations sometimes show the defeated gladiator bent over with his back toward his opponent. The bodies of dead gladiators were carried off on biers through the *porta libitinaria*, 'the funeral gate'.[78] Careful differentials seem to have been maintained in the disposal of their bodies.[79]

Gladiatorial combat, as Georges Ville emphasises, was concerned not only with the physical domination of one gladiator by another but also with a kind of psychological domination which led to a gladiator himself requesting that his own fate be decided.[80] The gladiator might not even be wounded. It sufficed that he was demoralised, his will broken. As Ville comments: 'Gladiatorial combat was not fencing taken a little too far, a fight whose unfortunate outcome was determined by the objective decision of armed combat. It was a tragedy focused on its epilogue, a putting-to-death on the physical level and certainly on the moral level, which obliged a man to agree to the sentence of his own possible slaughter.'[81] Yet some defeated gladiators managed to take possession of the role of the dying gladiator, to achieve a kind of redemption through making death their own.[82]

The disjunction between the fight and the kill played a major part in giving gladiatorial combat its highly distinctive character. Some texts explicitly designate the *editor* of the games, rather than the victorious gladiator, as the killer. Juvenal, for instance, writes in the *Satires* of those who 'now provide games and, when the people give the order with a turn of the thumb, inflict death to popular acclaim', *Munera nunc edunt et, verso pollice vulgus/Cum iubet, occidunt populariter* (3.36–7).[83] This power of life and death conferred on the *editor* an almost supernatural power (it is hardly surprising that emperors were cautious about letting other aristocrats assume such a position). As Juvenal's comment also indicates, however, the provider of the games might well bow to pressure from the audience in making his decision. The audience, too, then were often complicit in the decision to kill. The act of watching is sometimes itself elided with the act of killing. The Christian critic Lactantius attacks the games in the context of an account of the dangers attendant on the pleasures of the senses, insisting:

Nam qui hominem quamvis ob merita damnatum in conspectu suo iugulari pro voluptate computat conscientiam suam polluit, tam scilicet quam si homicidii quod fit spectator et particeps fiat.

Anyone thinking his pleasure is served by the spectacle of someone being put to death, however deservedly condemned, pollutes his own conscience, as much as if he were also taking part in the killing of which he is spectator.

(*Div. inst.* 6.20.10 trs. Bowen and Garnsey)[84]

Thus the Roman people, momentarily assimilated to the emperor himself, might experience the potent thrill of deciding whether a man should live or die – even if he was only a gladiator.

A lesson in dying

The Roman term generally used for set of gladiatorial games is a *munus*, or 'offering', implicitly to the gods of the underworld – though also, of course, a gift to the spectators from the *editor*. Under the republic at least, spectacles of gladiatorial combat, given to mark the funeral of a notable, were closely linked with death in terms of context as well as content. The Christian Tertullian, writing in the second century CE, offers this account of the early development of gladiatorial games:

> Officium autem mortuis hoc spectaculo facere se veteres arbitrabantur, posteaquam illud humaniore atrocitate temperaverunt. Nam olim, quoniam animas defunctorum humano sanguine propitiari creditum erat, captivos vel mali status servos mercati in exequiis immolabant. Postea placuit impietatem voluptate adumbrare. Itaque quos paraverant, armis quibus tunc et qualiter poterant eruditos, tantum ut occidi discerent, mox edicto die inferiarum apud tumulos erogabant. Ita mortem homicidiis consolabantur.

> The men of old, however, thought that by means of this spectacle they were making an offering to the dead, after they had tempered their practice with a more humane form of atrocity. For earlier, since it was believed that the spirits of the dead could be appeased with human blood, they used at funerals to sacrifice prisoners of war or slaves of poor quality whom they bought. Later they chose to dress up this impiety as entertainment. And so on the day of the funeral, at the tomb they would expose to death the men they had acquired, who had been trained in what arms they had then and as best they could – at least so they would learn to die. Thus they found comfort for death in murder.

(Tert. *Spect.* 12)

For Tertullian the horrific entertainment offered in the arena is simply a rather more sophisticated form of the human sacrifice, which, he contends, was earlier associated with aristocratic funerals. Other Christian critics, too, chose to represent gladiatorial combat as a form of human sacrifice.[85] This was one of a range of strategies to alienate Christians from the continuing allure of the pagan games.[86] It is important, however, to be aware of the Christians' agenda.[87] Any reference to human sacrifice served to colour the games still more strongly as an alien abomination, as well as tarnishing by association the pagan gods.

The case for seeing the gladiatorial games as precisely a form of human sacrifice has been made by a number of scholars over the years.[88] These public rituals of combat so often culminating in death might constitute sacrifice according to some models. But pagan Romans themselves, for whom sacrifice was a central part of their religious system, do not seem to have conceived of gladiatorial combat in these terms. And even on the rare occasions where an analogy is drawn this does not constitute a simple equation. There is a crucial difference between the certain death of sacrifice and the risk of death associated with gladiatorial combat.[89] Nevertheless the possibility of death was always present in the arena.

The fascination these spectacles exercised over their audiences stems to a significant degree from the desire to see how gladiators will behave in the face of death. Audiences often favoured a man who was perceived to have fought bravely. Cicero makes use of a gladiatorial analogy in defending his associate Milo, on trial for the murder of the aristocrat Clodius in a street fight:

Etenim si in gladiatoriis pugnis et infimi generis hominum condicione atque fortuna timidos atque supplices et ut vivere liceat obsecrantis etiam odisse solemus, fortis atque animosos et se acriter ipsos morti offerentis servare cupimus, eorumque nos magis miseret, qui nostram misericordiam non requirunt, quam qui illam efflagitant, quanto hoc magis in fortissimis civibus facere debemus?

For if in fights between gladiators where the fate of the lowest sort of men is at stake, we tend to loathe the ones who are timid and cringing and beg to be allowed to live and long to preserve those who are brave and spirited and hurl themselves ferociously at death, so that we feel for those who do not ask for it rather than those who demand our mercy, how much more should we do this when it is for our most brave citizens?

(*Mil.* 92)

Loathing for the timid may be read not simply as a function of their failure to provide good entertainment but as a reflection of the awareness they generated of the games' profound cruelty.[90] At the same time, the spectators rewarded with glory those gladiators who had paid them the honour of dying willingly for their pleasure.[91]

For Romans, the idea of the gladiator's death as something to be observed, indeed savoured, is a distinctive feature of contests between trained fighters. In gladiatorial combat (in contrast with the killing of *noxii*), the moment of death was artificially prolonged by the pause, after the defeated gladiator was brought down, while the victor waited for the provider of the games to indicate if the loser was to be killed or let go. At this moment, all eyes were focused on the bearing and – where his face was visible – the facial expression of the defeated man.[92]

A steady gaze could be associated with invincibility; the Elder Pliny comments that of the 20,000 gladiators in the *ludus*, training school, of Caligula, only the two who could refrain from blinking when threatened were unbeatable (*NH* 11.144). A significant part of the gladiator's training was a matter of learning how to look when looking death in the face. This aspect of his performance was from some points of view the most important. Many of the Roman texts which celebrate the gladiator as a model focus particularly on that pause as the defeated gladiator waits to be killed. He holds out his neck. It was very clear what was expected of him. Seneca commends the bravery of the defeated gladiator who guides the sword to his own throat (*Ep.* 30.8, quoted below). Gladiators who showed themselves unwilling to die were reviled by the audience (or so Seneca suggests, *De ira* 1.2.4–5).[93] For Cicero this was one of the key differences between the trained gladiator and the *noxius* (*Mil.* 92). A good death would earn the gladiator respect and admiration. Being seen to die in the right way might bring the only kind of afterlife that really mattered.[94]

Certainly it is true that the *editor*'s decision (frequently influenced by the audience) to have the defeated gladiator killed might well be motivated by the man's failure to perform well, to display adequate *virtus*, during the course of the fight.[95] The man who fought bravely, even if defeated, might thus escape having to confront death – for now. Nevertheless, once the decision to kill was made, the defeated gladiator did have a spectacular opportunity to redeem himself. As Thomas Wiedemann observes: 'though the gladiator was *infamis*, he would die by the sword, the death of a citizen on the field of battle. He was expected to take the *coup de grace* without protest, and the ritualised way in which it was carried out will have helped many gladiators fulfil this expectation. In that sense, even the gladiator who died in the arena had overcome death.'[96] Indeed perhaps one might say especially the gladiator who had died. As Paul Plass puts it, 'The purpose of the pain and carnage lay in tapping vital power by provoking, appropriating and finally "taming" death.'[97]

Most gladiators wore helmets; their facial expressions would not have been visible. The *retiarius* however did not have his head covered.[98] Those in the audience close enough would have been able to assess his facial expression as he encountered his imminent end. Roman texts express some ambivalence about how one should respond to this sight. The biographer Suetonius generally approves of emperors taking an interest in the games (and is also known to have written a separate treatise on the subject). However his *Life of Claudius* includes as evidence of that emperor's cruel and blood-thirsty character (*saevum et sanguinarium natura*) the pleasure he took in observing the faces of dying gladiators: 'Whenever he was watching gladiatorial games, whether he himself or someone else was providing them, if any fighters fell to the ground, even by accident he would give order for them to be killed, particularly in the case of net-fighters, so that he could see their faces as they died', *Quocumque gladiatorio munere vel suo vel alieno etiam forte prolapsos iugulari iubebat, maxime retiarios, ut expirantium facies videret* (Suet. *Claud.* 34.1).[99] This anecdote provides a nice illustration of the degree to which those watching (the emperor most particularly) were themselves on show. Yet if there was something perverse in scrutinising the face of a dying man, a passage from Cicero's *Tusculans* (quoted below, pp. 70–1) exhorts his reader to consider the ordinary gladiator's ability to maintain an unchanging expression in the face of death. The man's face, up to a certain point at least, is a proper focus of the audience's attention.

Tertullian attacks the contradictory nature of pagan attitudes to the spectacle of death:

Qui ad cadaver hominis communi lege defuncti exhorret, idem in amphitheatro derosa et dissipata et in suo sanguine squalentia corpora patientissimis oculis desuper incumbat, immo qui propter homicidae poenam probandam ad spectaculum veniat, idem gladiatorem ad homicidium flagellis et virgis compellat invitum, et qui ... gladiatori atroci petat rudem et pilleum praemium conferat, illum vero confectum etiam oris spectaculo repetat, libentius recognoscens de proximo quem voluit occidere de longinquo.

The man who recoils with horror from the corpse of someone who has died a natural death, that same man gazes at length in the amphitheatre on bodies savaged, torn apart and weltering in their own blood. Worse still is the kind of man who comes to the games to look on approving at the punishment of a murderer and forces the unwilling gladiator to homicide with rods and whips – and the one who ... demands the wooden sword for the murdering gladiator and gives him the cap of liberty, then when a man has been killed before his eyes in the games, has him brought back so he may gratify his wish to see close up the man he wanted to kill at a distance.

(*Spect.* 21)

On the one hand, murder is thought to deserve punishment – thus the man is condemned to the arena. Yet, at the same time, murder is deemed something to enjoy. The murderer is punished by being made to kill again. Interestingly when Tertullian criticises those who enjoy the spectacle of death he focuses on the preoccupation with looking at one who is already dead rather than observing someone dying. Thus he avoids any engagement with the dying gladiator as subject.

The texts considered here have already suggested something of the complexity of responses to the spectacle of gladiatorial combat. To look on as a man is killed – to have some part in the decision to kill him perhaps – is terrifying, edifying, thrilling, awesome. I now wish to pursue further two related issues which lie at the heart of responses to the death of the gladiator: identification and pleasure.

Pleasure, identification and the look

The term *voluptas*, 'pleasure', used more generally of the pleasures of the senses, is repeatedly associated with the gladiatorial games in ancient texts; Livy, for instance, writes of the pleasure of watching gladiators in the arena (41.20). Tertullian, attacking the spectacles in general, inveighs against the potency of the pleasure they offer: 'so great is the power of pleasures', *tanta est ... voluptatium vis* (*Spect.* 1). It is clear that more is at stake here than the pleasure one might take in watching the fighter's skilful deployment of his weapons. The phenomenon of physiological arousal in response to spectacles of violence is a well-attested one.[100] For the Christian writer Lactantius, as we saw, it is in identifying with the killer that the audience experiences a pleasure which is assimilated to the erotic. The witnessing of pain provoked a sexual thrill in the arena's audience.[101]

Gladiators themselves often served as emblems of an aggressive masculinity. The figure of the gladiator was frequently associated with overwhelming sexual prowess. Tertullian (as so often) expresses this with particular pungency: *arenarios illos amantissimos, quibus viri animas, feminae autem illis etiam corpora sua substernunt*, 'gladiators, whose appetite for love outdoes all others, to whom men surrender their souls and women their bodies, too' (Tert. *Spect.* 22). The satirist Juvenal describes a senator's wife who abandons her family to follow a gladiator (6.103–12); his epigrammatic conclusion: *ferrum est quod amant,* 'the sword is what they love' (112). The gladiator, it seems, is all sword.[102] Another Christian critic, Prudentius, presents as paradoxical the idea that the Vestal Virgins, though never deflowered, should come to watch gladiators killing and being killed. Describing a Vestal's experience, he continues:

> Consurgit ad ictus
> Et quotiens victor ferrum iugulo inserit, illa
> Delicias ait esse suas, pectusque iacentis
> Virgo modesta iubet converso pollice rumpi,
> Ne lateat pars ulla animae vitalibus imis,
> Altius inpresso dum palpitat ense secutor.

> She rises up as the blows fall and whenever the victor plunges his sword into the neck, she calls him her darling and, modest virgin that she is, she orders with her turned thumb for the chest of the fallen man to be torn open, lest there be any life left in the depths of his entrails, while the gladiator quivers as the sword probes deeper.
>
> (*Contra Symm.* 2.1096–1101)

Prudentius' language is heavily eroticised; the Roman priestess delights in the spectacle of lacerated flesh, revels in exercising the power of life and death.[103]

Augustine, in a well-known passage from the *Confessions,* writes of his friend Alypius who is ultimately overcome by a passion for gladiatorial combat. Initially unwilling to attend the games, Alypius does so only under pressure from his companions. At first he cannot bear to look at the spectacle and closes his eyes. But on hearing a great cry from the crowd he is overcome by curiosity (*curiositate victus*) and opens them: *et percussus est graviore vulnere in anima quam ille in corpore,* 'he sustained a worse wound in his soul than had the other [the gladiator] in his flesh.' The sight of the gladiator's blood was Alypius' undoing:

> Ut enim vidit illum sanguinem, inmanitatem simul ebibit et non se avertit, sed fixit aspectum, et hauriebat furias et nesciebat, et delectabatur scelere certaminis et cruenta voluptate inebriebatur.

> For as soon as he saw the blood, he drank in the cruelty and did not turn himself away but kept his eyes fixed and, unknowingly, absorbed the frenzy and took pleasure in that criminal contest and was made drunk by the bloody pleasure.
>
> (*Confessions* 6.8)

From that time, he became an avid fan of the games, returning again and again to drink in the ghastly sights. Only much later, Augustine writes, did the Lord rescue him from this madness.

Cicero emphasises the importance of the eyes as the medium through which we apprehend the lessons the arena has to teach. *Oculis ... nulla poterat esse fortior contra dolorem et mortem disciplina*, 'for the eyes there can be no more powerful lesson in how to face pain and death' (*Tusc.* 2.41). For Augustine the terrifying pull of the arena works above all through

4. Relief of gladiators.

the medium of the eyes. Alypius' gaze is fixed on the horrific spectacle of slaughter. Like Tertullian, Augustine focuses on the irresistible attraction exercised by the sight of human blood. Christian texts often foreground the moment after the fatal blow has been inflicted, probing the spectators' responses to the sight of a man in his death throes, the sight of a mangled corpse.

How might this characterisation of the pleasure which was thought to be aroused by the spectacle of pain and death relate to the performance, the production of *virtus* in the arena? We might well suppose that spectators derived a thrill from identifying with the victorious gladiator. Peculiar to the arena was the extended moment of death, that pause, that exchange of looks between the victorious gladiator and the *editor*, between the *editor* and the audience (fig. 4).[104] The spectators, shouting their verdicts, are assimilated to the *editor* – and through him to the victorious gladiator who carries out his command. We might be tempted to read the defeated fighter as objectified – metaphorically castrated, effeminised. Once the sign has been given, he is literally penetrated by his opponent's sword. The victor's prowess in combat has asserted his *virtus*, his bravery, but also his masculinity. Thus the manliness of victor, *editor* and audience is simultaneously confirmed (with the female spectators, such as Prudentius' Vestal, allowed a tantalisingly brief moment of identification with a hyperbolically masculine role). This sadistic pleasure in inflicting pain, in watching pain inflicted on another, seems to be the particular focus of Christian complaints. This might seem a classic instance of 'sadistic voyeurism'.[105] It is this experience, in which his own masculinity, as well as his own survival, is vindicated, that generates the male (or masculinised) spectator's pleasure, it might seem.

Yet there are important ways in which Roman discussions of the arena do not conform to a model of sadistic voyeurism. For numerous texts (among those by non-Christian authors at least) encourage their readers to identify with the defeated gladiator rather than the victor, focusing particularly, as we saw earlier, on that moment after the defeated gladiator has conceded but before the *editor* has signalled if he is to live or die. Cicero, in a passage from *Tusculans* (pp.70–1), invites his reader to compare himself with the gladiator accepting death manfully. Seneca, discussing how the would-be wise man should face death, also asks his reader to imagine himself as the defeated gladiator guiding the sword to his own neck.

Puto fortiorem esse eum, qui in ipsa morte est quam qui circa mortem. Mors enim admota etiam inperitis animum dedit non vitandi inevitabilia. Sic gladiator tota pugna timidissimus iugulum adversario praestat et errantem gladium sibi adtemperat.

I consider that one is braver at the very moment of death than when one is approaching death. For death, when it stands near us, gives even to inexperienced men the courage not to seek to avoid the inevitable. So the gladiator, no matter how faint-hearted he has been throughout the fight, offers his throat to his opponent and directs the wavering blade to the vital spot.

(*Ep.* 30.8)

The gladiator co-operates in his own slaughter, thus redeeming himself in the eyes of the massed onlookers.

It is, of course, unclear how far such texts reflect the experiences of spectators in the arena more generally. Indeed, the move to identify with the defeated may in part function as a strategy of social differentiation to distinguish the philosophically refined from the vulgar crowd, the latter perhaps thought more inclined to identify with the winner. Nevertheless we may suspect that viewers responded in a range of different ways to a gladiatorial pair. Some spectators in the arena may have identified firmly with one gladiator or another throughout the course of the fight, perhaps on the basis of what 'type' of fighter he was; the emperor Titus, Suetonius suggests, always backed those in Thracian armour.[106] Others, temperamentally inclined to favour the underdog, or the dominant fighter, may have shifted their identification over the course of a fight.

This 'game', then, like so many other spectator sports, enabled its observers to rehearse for themselves the role of the victor *and* the role of his defeated opponent.[107] We might compare here the comment made by the Spanish critic José Bergamín on the response of the spectator to a bull-fight in modern Spain: he is 'a suicidal masochist and a sadistic assassin both at once: both things are only imagined of course, and unknown to himself, as he feels pleasure and pain in the frustrated manner of an unconscious phantasmagorical onanism'.[108] A similar oscillation may be traced in Lucan's Vulteius episode, where the arena is invoked to characterise the spectacular mutual suicides of Vulteius and his followers. There the reader's imaginary gaze is profoundly unstable, sliding between masochistic identification with the victims and sadistic identification with the *editor*/victor.[109]

There can be a kind of pleasure, then, in identifying with the victim.[110] Indeed the defeated gladiator may be found serving as a figure for masochistic desire. Ovid, identifying the arena as especially conducive to erotic encounters, advises that often: *et qui spectavit vulnera, vulnus habet*, 'he who watched wounds being inflicted is wounded himself' (*Ars amatoria* 1.166). The experience of desire is compared to that of being stabbed with the gladiator's sword. The assimilation of pain and sexual pleasure articulates a disturbing connection between them. Prudentius' Vestal Virgin urges the victorious gladiator on but perhaps derives sexual pleasure from identifying with the violated body of his defeated opponent.

The gladiator who perversely desires to be hurt could on one level be read as an effeminised figure.[111] A few images do indeed hint at a loss of masculinity associated with the defeated gladiator.[112] Yet most of the texts we have examined focus on the defeated gladiator as exemplifying a manly capacity to endure pain, a masculine fortitude in the face of death. Masculinity is very much at issue in gladiatorial combat but it is entirely possible for both combatants to enhance their masculinity in the course of a fight. The model of the defeated gladiator facing death offered Romans an image of defeat and dispossession that need not involve any loss of manhood (even if some may also have experienced a certain pleasure in experiencing the role of the defeated as a passive one). We may imagine that this figure exercised considerable appeal to a range of different social groups. The defeated gladiator facing death was a powerfully attractive model for those members of the Roman elite who felt marginalised, indeed persecuted, under the Julio-Claudian emperors, most notably Nero.[113] This phenomenon would not however adequately explain the enormous appeal of gladiatorial combat earlier, under the Roman republic. Many no doubt thrilled to play a part in deciding another man's fate. But it is worth considering that poorer Romans, too, the vast majority of inhabitants of the teeming city, who experienced deprivation and defeat as part of their daily lives, may also have derived consolation from identification with the defeated gladiator, a figure who might, even in the face of death, remain a manly hero.

The noble gladiator

In the modern western world, to witness a death deliberately inflicted is usually considered taboo (though deaths feigned – and with an astonishing realism – are a commonplace sight on film and television). The spectacle of death – at least if it is a 'real' death – is something from which we are supposed to turn away.[114] Public exhibitions of death have been a feature of many other cultures besides that of ancient Rome (though generally without the element of game-playing).[115] In eighteenth-century Britain, public executions might be justified not only as a spectacular means of demonstrating the power of the law to avenge itself but also as a lesson in how to meet death. James Boswell, writing in 1768, characterises watching executions as an edifying experience:

Dying publicly at Tyburn, and dying privately in one's own bed, are only two different modes of the same thing. They are both death; they are both that wonderous, that alarming scene of quitting all that we have ever seen, heard, or known and at once passing into a state of being totally unknown to us, and in which we cannot tell what may be our situation. Therefore it is that I feel an irresistible impulse to be present at every execution, as I there behold the various effects of the near approach of death, according to the various tempers of the unhappy sufferers, and by studying them I learn to quiet and fortify my own mind.[116]

Such comments are disingenuous, perhaps; Boswell resists acknowledging any element of voyeurism in his own fascination with public executions. At the same time, though, his description captures a significant strand in responses to death as spectacle, one which resonates suggestively with some of the texts we shall be considering here.

Tertullian comments that spectators 'found comfort for death in murder', *ita mortem homicidiis consolabantur* (*Spect.* 12). If the pleasure one experiences in reading an account of someone else's death stems from the recognition that this death is not one's own death, this might hold good all the more strongly for those actually witnessing another's death.[117] Sociologist Clive Seale comments: 'The killing of other people both in actuality and in acts of symbolic violence, exclusion and stigma, is also a means for sustaining personal security about being in the world, ontological security.'[118] At the same time, the capacity of that other to meet death unflinchingly – even though he is otherwise morally inferior – can function as a source of comfort as one contemplates one's own mortality.

Roman philosophical literature pays particular attention to the question of how one should face the prospect of death. Philosophers, otherwise disdainful of the entertainments of the common people, nevertheless sometimes invoked the gladiator as an inspirational model in this context. Almost all metaphorical invocations of the gladiator invite readers to identify not with the gladiator as killer but with the gladiator as he meets death. The gladiator serves as a figure for a kind of pared-down humanity, denuded of the trappings of possessions, status.[119] And yet on some level the point of the gladiator's bravery is to give pleasure to his audience. To what extent, we might ask, can a Roman senator, for instance, comfortably accommodate himself to this aspect of the role?

Sometimes, as we have seen, Cicero does use 'gladiator' as a term of abuse. Yet elsewhere in his speeches, the gladiator serves as a positive model for bravery, as in the passage from his defence of Milo quoted above (p. 60, *Mil.* 92). Here the focus is on the staunch manner in which Milo conducts

himself under the scrutiny of the court as he faces the prospect of condemnation – or at least how Cicero imagines he would have conducted himself,
since this speech was never actually delivered but circulated in written form.
The comparison perhaps also serves implicitly to legitimise Milo's killing
of Clodius. Similarly in one of his speeches against Mark Antony, Cicero
exhorts his listeners:

> Quodsi iam... fatum extremum rei publicae venit, quod gladiatores
> nobiles faciunt, ut honeste decumbant, faciamus quod principes orbis
> terrarum gentiumque omnium, ut cum dignitate potius cadamus, quam
> cum ignominia serviamus.

> If the state... has come to its moment of truth, let us do as worthy
> gladiators do to die with honour, let us, the leaders of the world, of all
> peoples, fall with dignity rather than submit with shame.
>
> (*Phil.* 3.35)

The adjective *nobilis* is paradoxical. In terms of status, who could be
further from *nobilitas* than the gladiator? Yet when it comes to braving
all, to meeting death with glory, the gladiator has a special distinction. In
this passage, Cicero himself identifies with the gladiator. There is a telling
irony in his use of the gladiator, a man who, if not a slave, was still severely
circumscribed by the conditions of the oath he had sworn, as a figure for
libertas, freedom. Yet there was a kind of freedom in preferring death to
slavery (*quam... serviamus*).[120] And, as we have seen, the gladiator was an
especially apt metaphor in the context of civil war.[121]

Cicero's identification with the gladiator is not simply a bid to enlist
popular sympathy in speech aimed at winning over Romans of every social
condition. His philosophical writing too offers a sustained exploration of
the gladiator as model. Book 2 of the *Tusculans* examines at length the
endurance of pain. One of Cicero's interlocutors identifies practice and
discipline as playing a key role in enhancing an individual's ability to endure
physical suffering. Among his examples, which include the wounded soldier
and the boxer, the speaker lays particular emphasis on the gladiator, as an
exemplar of the power of *consuetudo disciplinae*, 'the habit which comes
from training':

> Gladiatores, aut perditi homines aut barbari, quas plagas perferunt! Quo
> modo illi, qui bene instituti sunt, accipere plagam malunt quam turpiter
> vitare! Quam saepe apparet nihil eos malle quam vel domino satis facere
> vel populo! Mittunt etiam vulneribus confecti ad dominos qui quaerant

quid velint: si satis iis factum sit se velle decumbere. Quis mediocris gladiator ingemuit, quis vultum mutavit umquam? Quis non modo stetit, verum etiam decubuit turpiter? Quis cum decubuisset, ferrum recipere iussus collum contraxit? Tantum exercitatio, meditatio, consuetudo valet. Ergo hoc poterit Samnis ... vir natus ad gloriam ullam partem animi tam mollem habebit quam non meditatione et ratione corroboret?

Gladiators, men who are either ruined or barbarians, what blows they endure! See, how men who have been well trained prefer to take a blow rather than shamefully avoid it! How frequently it becomes clear that they place nothing higher than giving satisfaction to their master or to the people! Even when done in with wounds they send messages to their masters to find out their wishes: happy to fall, if they have given satisfaction. What ordinary gladiator has ever groaned or changed his expression? Which of them has disgraced himself, let alone on his feet, but even in his fall? Who once fallen has drawn back his neck when ordered to accept the blade? So great is the force of practice, of training, of habit. Shall then the Samnite ... be capable of this, and shall a man born for glory have any part of his spirit so weak that it cannot be strengthened by training and reason?

(Cic. *Tusc.* 2.41)

While there is a significant contrast between the gladiator and the man of distinction (who will be sustained by *ratio* and *sapientia*, reason and wisdom, *Tusc.* 2.40), yet the qualities of the gladiator are not to be dismissed altogether. Possessing no other virtues but bravery, the gladiators can be a supreme showcase for that quality, as we have seen. At the same time, this bravery is conditioned above all by the demands of the provider of the games and the audience. The gladiator's dearest wish, we are told, is to satisfy his master and the *populus*. This audience will only be satisfied if he holds out his neck unflinchingly to receive the death blow.

In 43 BCE, Cicero himself, according to Livy, knowing that the soldiers of the triumvirs would catch up with him sooner or later, resigned himself to meeting the death to which Mark Antony, by including his name on the list of the proscribed, had condemned him. He ordered his slaves to set down the litter in which he was travelling from the city to his villa. 'He leaned out of the litter and offered his neck, unwavering, and his head was cut off': *Prominenti ex lectica praebentique inmotam cervicem caput praecisum est* (quoted from Livy by Seneca *Suasoriae* 6.17).[122] For Barton, this scene recalls 'the gladiator's gesture of defiant complicity'.[123] In place of an arena of spectators Cicero is rewarded with the more lasting honour accorded by generations of readers of Livy (at least up until the time this part of Livy's works was lost).

In Seneca's writing, a hundred-odd years later, the gladiator as role model for the philosopher appears with what might seem disturbing frequency.[124] For Seneca, the gladiator becomes an especially suggestive figure, whose employment can enable the exploration of a number of key issues. Some invocations of the gladiator might seem relatively circumscribed. In Letter 22, for instance, Seneca asserts that one cannot follow a set pattern in one's life but rather, like the gladiator in the course of a fight, who decides on his strategy in response to his opponent's moves, one should take one's cues from events as they unfold.[125] Yet here, too, if only implicitly, the analogy of the gladiator highlights the glaring imminence of death. The issue with which the letter opens, whether or not Lucilius should withdraw from public life, foreshadows the discussions, which dominate so many of the later letters (most obviously 70, 77), as to when might be the right time to withdraw from life itself.

The prospect of death which looms over the gladiator is more explicitly at issue in Letter 37. The letter begins by comparing the *proficiens*, the would-be philosopher, to a soldier who has enlisted under oath, *sacramentum*. Yet Seneca slides rapidly from this into another analogy, that of the gladiator, who also fights under a rather different oath.

> Ab illis qui manus harenae locant et edunt ac bibunt, quae per sanguinem reddant, cavetur, ut ista vel inviti patiantur; a te, ut volens libensque patiaris. Illis licet arma summittere, misericordiam populi temptare; tu neque summittes nec vitam rogabis. Recto tibi invictoque moriendum est. Quid porro prodest paucos dies aut annos lucrificare? Sine missione nascimur.

> From the men who hire out their fighting-strength for the arena, who pay for what they eat and drink with their blood, security is taken, to ensure they will suffer those things, if unwillingly, from you, that you suffer them willingly and voluntarily. They are permitted to lower their weapons, to see if the people will grant them mercy. It is for you to die upright and unconquered. And what use is it to gain a few days or years? There is no release from the condition to which we are born.

> (*Ep.* 37.2)

Life is a gladiatorial combat *sine missione* (37.2). There is no possibility of avoiding death in this contest. Seneca concedes that gladiators sometimes fail, meeting death unwillingly. The would-be philosopher must do better. As we have seen, in another letter (*Ep.* 30.8), which takes as its point of departure the failing health of a friend, Aufidius Bassus, Seneca again invokes the gladiator as a model for facing death. It is especially striking to find such a model being invoked in discussion of an elderly man succumbing to illness. For Seneca even an invalid can make himself a heroic figure, if he confronts death in the right frame of mind.[126]

Seneca's treatise on tranquillity of mind focuses on the fear of death as a profoundly destabilising emotion. Unless brought under control, it can subvert one's entire life. 'The man will live badly who does not know how to die well', he argues, *male vivet quisquis nesciet bene mori* (11.4). He goes on to cite with approval Cicero's observation in *Pro Milone* (see p. 60) that we feel hostility to gladiators who beg to be allowed to live and admire those who display contempt for death.

> Fortuna illa quae ludos sibi facit: 'quo' inquit, 'te reservem, malum et trepidum animal? Eo magis convulneraberis et confodieris, quia nescis praebere iugulum. At tu et vives diutius et morieris expeditius, qui ferrum non subducta cervice nec manibus oppositis sed animose recipis.' Qui mortem timebit, nihil umquam pro homine vivo faciet. At qui sciet hoc sibi cum conciperetur statim condictum, vivet ad formulam et simul illud quoque eodem animi robore praestabit, ne quid ex iis, quae eveniunt, subitum sit.

> This is Fortune who puts on games for herself. 'What are you holding yourself back for, low and fearful creature? You will suffer more wounds and sustain more blows, because you do not know how to hold forth your throat. But you will both live longer and die more easily, who accept the blade neither with bowed neck nor hands held up but with spirit. One who fears death will never do anything worthy of a living man. But the one who knows that from the moment when he was conceived he was subject to this condition will live according to the rules and at the same time will also with that same strength of mind guarantee that nothing which happens to him is unforeseen.'
>
> (*Tranqu. an.* 11.5–6)

The fear of death is crippling and must be thrown off. We can only embrace life by embracing the prospect of death. To acknowledge the imminence of death – as gladiators must – is to free oneself of the fear of death. Here, as in Letter 37, it is the gladiator's acceptance of death which is for Seneca so entrancing.[127] Like the gladiator bound by his contract, the would-be wise man, under contract to god, must surrender life and limb without hesitation.[128]

Thus the proximity of death for all gladiators is, for Seneca, not different in kind from the situation facing all of humanity:

Numquid feliciorem iudicas eum, qui summo die muneris, quam eum qui medio occiditur? Numquid aliquem tam stulte cupidum esse vitae putas, ut iugulari in spoliario quam in harena malit? Non maiore spatio alter alterum praecedimus. Mors per omnes it; qui occidit, consequitur occisum.

Do you really think that the man who is killed on the final day of the show is better off than the one who is killed on the middle day? Do you really think that anyone is so stupidly greedy for life that he would rather be killed in the disrobing room than in the arena? It is by no greater interval than this that we precede one another. Death comes to all. The one who kills follows the one who is killed.

(*Ep.* 93.12)

A glorious death in the arena – in front of a large audience – is infinitely preferable to an inconspicuous death only a few minutes later. To live a long time is of no greater significance than dying on the last day of the *munus* rather than in the middle. The gladiator's publicly exposed fate provides an extreme example of a life whose meaning is conferred by its conclusion, a conclusion which must be witnessed, if its meaning is to be fully realised.

Seneca's preoccupation with the gladiator confronting death is perhaps not typical and yet his insistent return to the topic resonates with other invocations of the arena. The identification between members of the Roman elite and gladiators even extended to the appearance in the arena of some equestrians and senators, as we saw earlier. For many others, this identification, though merely an imaginative one, was still seductive. This fascination with public and glorious self-destruction, this identification with the abject yet potent figure of the gladiator, has been read as a response to the changed position of the Roman elite under autocracy.[129] If political survival depended on collusion, the gladiator offered a compelling paradigm. Barton comments: 'The gladiator was, thus, *both* a version of the Stoic *sapiens*, offering a metaphor of apathy, independence, and contempt for the opinions of society, *and* an expression of intense interaction with, and acceptance of, others, a longing for esteem and appreciation, in other words, glory.'[130]

Yet, as we have seen, elements of this identification may be traced back to the late republic, if not earlier. The scrutiny under which the gladiator played his role might in some sense be construed as parallel to the regard which was fixed on the Roman magistrate or general competing for public honours. The gladiator could be seen as a mirror image of the aristocrat in this society of spectacle.[131] This is perhaps one implication of the passage from Cicero's *Pro Milone* cited earlier; Rome's leading citizens, like gladiators, must perform in accordance with the expectations of their audience. Their identity, like that of those same gladiators, is contingent on the recognition afforded them by that audience.

At the same time, this discourse serves to create an acceptable space for the gladiator even within high culture. Seneca is often seen as one of the few non-Christian Romans to offer criticism of the gladiatorial games (this view relies on an extended misconstrual of Letter 7, a letter which discusses the execution of *noxii* rather than gladiatorial combat).[132] His writings work rather to render the gladiator useful to the philosopher. 'In playing with the spatial/ontological taxonomies of the arena, he reinscribes the institution on a broader level, setting himself and his readers in a new set of stands ringing the arena,' comments Gunderson.[133] It should be noted that the gladiatorial model did not appeal to all philosophers. Marcus Aurelius, for instance, merely expresses his boredom at the arena (*To Himself* 6.46). But then, if he himself as emperor could not avoid assuming the role of *editor*, he may well have found the arena's paradoxes altogether less seductive.[134]

Dying for an audience

Seneca's treatise on providence, *De providentia*, engages with the benefits which the would-be philosopher may gain from the process of struggling with adversity.[135] The image of the gladiator is central to this text. Fortune, here playing the role of combatant, draws back from engaging with cowards. Instead she chooses as adversary one who will be a proper match for her. Similarly *ignominiam iudicat gladiator cum inferiore componi et scit eum sine gloria vinci, qui sine periculo vincitur*, 'The gladiator thinks it a source of shame to be matched with an inferior and knows that the man who is defeated without danger is defeated without glory' (*Prov.* 3.4). One of Seneca's most revealing invocations of the arena is in his treatment of the death of the Younger Cato in Book 2 of the treatise.

The topic of Cato's death is one Seneca revisits numerous times in his philosophical work.[136] The way Seneca presents his case here at once highlights and problematises the spectacular aspect of Cato's suicide:

Miraris tu, si deus ille bonorum amantissimus, qui illos quam optimos esse atque excellentissimus vult, fortunam illis cum qua exerceantur adsignat? Ego vero non miror, si aliquando impetum capiunt spectandi magnos viros conluctantis cum aliqua calamitate.

Are you surprised if that god who loves good men most dearly, who wants them to reach their greatest potential, assigns to them a fortune that will make them struggle? I am not surprised if the gods sometimes feel the urge to look on while great men struggle with some misfortune.

(*Prov.* 2.7)

Seneca argues here from the human desire to be a spectator at the games. We, Seneca confesses, take pleasure (*voluptas*) in watching a man fighting a wild beast. This pleasure is the sharper, the more distinguished the man: *Tantoque hoc spectaculum est gratius, quanto id honestior fecit* (*Prov.* 2.8). So who would top the bill for the divine spectator but that sublime exponent of virtue, Cato?

Ecce spectaculum dignum ad quod respiciat, intentus operi suo, deus! Ecce par deo dignum, vir fortis cum mala fortuna compositus! Utique si et provocavit. Non video, inquam, quid habeat in terris Jupiter pulchrius, si convertere animum velit, quam ut spectet Catonem, iam partibus non semel fractis, stantem nihilominus inter ruinas publicas rectum.

Behold! Here is a spectacle worthy god's attention as he contemplates his works; behold, here a contest worthy of god – a brave man matched against misfortune – especially if he called it upon himself. I do not know, I say, what fairer sight Jupiter would find on earth, should he wish to turn his attention there, than the spectacle of Cato, after his cause had already been destroyed more than once, nevertheless standing erect amid the ruins of the state.

(*Prov.* 2.9)

Seneca goes on to evoke Cato's last hours and especially his death allusively but with vivid detail. The suspenseful build-up, the long-drawn-out nature of Cato's death can themselves be seen as mirroring aspects of arena spectacles – especially since the account of Cato's actions is prefaced by Seneca's further emphasis on the gods as audience: *Liquet mihi cum magno spectasse gaudio deos*, 'I am sure the gods looked on with great joy' (*Prov.* 2.11).[137]

Drawing attention to the story that Cato only succeeded in killing himself by re-opening his initial wound (which had been sewn up by a doctor), Seneca concludes his consideration of Cato's death with the following declaration:

Inde crediderim fuisse parum certum et efficax vulnus; non fuit diis
immortalibus satis spectare Catonem semel. Retenta ac revocata virtus
est, ut in difficiliore parte se ostenderet; non enim tam magno animo
mors initur quam repetitur. Quidni libenter spectarent alumnum suum
tam claro ac memorabili exitu evadentem?

I should like to believe that this is why the wound was not well placed
and telling – it was not enough for the immortal gods to look only once
on Cato. His virtue was restrained and called back so that it might show
itself in a more demanding role; for seeking death does not require so
great a spirit as seeking it again. Surely the gods looked willingly upon
their pupil as he made his escape by so splendid and memorable an end.

(*Prov.* 2.12)

The gods, Seneca asserts, watch the deaths of good men gladly.[138] The
repetition of the verb *spectare* underlines the visual impact of this scene.
The repetition of the action also makes clear that this is a performance. At
the same time, the divine spectator – and only the divine spectator – has
no need of the lesson in dying offered by Cato's suicide. On this, Seneca
comments elsewhere: *Est aliquid, quo sapiens antecedat deum: ille naturae
beneficio non timet, suo sapiens*, 'There is one sense in which the wise man
is superior to the god; the latter fears nothing thanks to the good offices of
nature, the former thanks to his own good offices' (*Ep.* 53.11).[139] It is in his
very mortality that the wise man can go beyond the divine.

Seneca's gripping deployment of the figure of the arena to evoke the gods,
looking on as Cato kills himself, might be read as transcending the horror
of the scenes one might actually witness in the Roman amphitheatre. Yet at
the same time it is hard for the modern reader not to be alienated by the
idea that the sight of a man struggling against the pain of a fatal wound can
constitute a source of edification and indeed visual enjoyment. In Seneca's
ideal arena, these divine spectators are, it seems, free from base motives.
They experience not pleasure, *voluptas*, but joy, *gaudium*. But can his readers
rise above their baser impulses? Can their pleasure, too, be alchemised into
something pure?[140] From the bloody violence, cruel pleasure and urge to
glory of the arena, Seneca has forged a scene of sublimity, an iconic moment.
Yet it is hard to resist the feeling that the sublime joy of contemplating this
vision of Cato's virtue must ultimately have had its roots in the more visceral
pleasure of looking at death in the real Roman arena.

CHAPTER 3

FIGHTING THE FEAR OF DEATH

The excruciating agony of Cato's dying is highlighted rather than minimised in Seneca's description. His persistence in taking his own life made clear that Cato for one had succeeded in conquering the fear of death – the greatest of human challenges. How could others hope to rise to this challenge? Seneca's brand of Stoic philosophy concerns itself with this as an issue central to human existence. This chapter will examine the importance attached to the fear of death and strategies to overcome that fear in Roman philosophical writing of the late republic and early principate. While the principal focus is on Seneca, the distinctive characteristics of Seneca's approach emerge most clearly when we see his work against the background of earlier philosophical discussions of death, especially that of Lucretius, whose work also treats the fear of death as the central challenge of human life.

Cato's exit from life offers the inspirational example of a *virtus*, bravery, which, while bearing a resemblance to that of the gladiator meeting death in the arena, operates on an altogether higher plane. Yet for Seneca, in particular, the qualities needed to overcome the fear of death more generally – a fear which blights human life – are in important ways parallel to (as well as forming an aspect of) the qualities needed by the gladiator and, to an even greater degree, by the soldier. In traditional Roman historical writing, as well as treatments of the arena, *virtus* generally has the sense of bravery, both physical and mental. Even in philosophical contexts, although *virtus* has the sense of ethical 'virtue', the more general associations of the term can condition its use in significant ways. Thus the arena but also warfare are often invoked as image and analogy in Seneca's writing. The bravery of the philosopher, his *virtus*, does not, however, show itself in violent actions against others but, Seneca argues, the would-be philosopher's victory over the fear of death will sometimes manifest itself most effectively, will express itself, in extreme violence against his own person. It is, above all, in choosing death that he can show it holds no fear for him – though, as we shall see, there are significant tensions in Seneca's treatment of suicide. As Seneca probably expected, the circumstances of his own death tested to the full his preparations. His philosophical writing is inevitably read against the background of his own enforced suicide as described by the historian Tacitus.

Lucretius and the nature of death

The profoundly disturbing effects of the fear of death on human behaviour and the urgent need to overcome this fear are also central preoccupations of an earlier philosophical enterprise, Lucretius' *De rerum natura*, 'On the nature of the universe', which undertakes to offer an account of Epicurean philosophy in Latin hexameter verse (and was written probably in the early 50s BCE).[1] Lucretius engages at length with the technicalities of Epicurean physics, describing the role of atoms in structuring the world and everything in it. But this is essentially a preliminary to the primary focus of the poem on ethics. The attainment of peace of mind should be humankind's fundamental goal. One of the great benefits of Epicureanism, he asserts, is that it offers a cure for the greatest evil to afflict humanity, the fear of death.

The writings of Epicurus himself (only a small portion of which survives) also suggest a preoccupation with the fear of death. For Epicurus, most people fear death as 'the most terrifying of evils' (*Letter to Menoeceus* 125). Yet death is, he claims, no such thing. 'The correct understanding that death is nothing to us makes the mortal nature of life enjoyable, not by adding infinite time to life but by taking away the desire for immortality' (*L. Men.* 124).[2] The third book of Lucretius' *De rerum natura* is most explicitly concerned to address the fear of death, an issue approached through an account of the structure of the human body. Thus Lucretius, in Book 3, undertakes to provide a correct understanding of the kind advocated by Epicurus:

Et metus ille foras praeceps Acheruntis agendus,
Funditus humanam qui vitam turbat ab imo,
Omnia suffundens mortis nigrore, neque ullam
Esse voluptatem liquidam puramque relinquit.

And to be driven headlong out is that fear of Acheron which profoundly disturbs human life through and through, polluting all with the blackness of death and leaving no pleasure clear and pure.

(*DRN* 3.37–40)

Pleasure, *voluptas*, is a central term in Epicurean philosophy. Correctly understood, the impulse toward simple pleasures (such as those of satisfying pangs of hunger or thirst) can offer the key to a happy life. But, as Lucretius asserts here, such pleasures will be subverted, spoilt if the fear of death is not brought under control.

Most people, he concedes, do not admit to being afraid of death (*DRN* 3.41–58). Nevertheless Lucretius' ambitious claim is that the fear of death is the source of virtually all human unhappiness. Lucretius seeks to identify patterns of behaviour or conditions which appear to lack an adequate explanation and posits the fear of death as their underlying cause.[3]

> Denique avarities et honorum caeca cupido,
> Quae miseros homines cogunt transcendere fines
> Iuris et interdum socios scelerum atque ministros
> Noctes atque dies niti praestante labore
> Ad summas emergere opes, haec vulnera vitae
> Non minimam partem mortis formidine aluntur.

Then avarice and the blind desire for honours which force wretched humans to break the bounds of law and, as frequent associates and agents of crime, to struggle night and day with supreme effort to achieve the highest positions, these afflictions to life are in no small part nourished by the dread of death.

(3.59–64)

Resistance to the natural limit imposed by death renders people unable to accept any limits on their desires.[4] Thus it is the fear of death which goads people to amass wealth through civil bloodshed and family conflict. Paradoxically, the fear of death even drives people to suicide:

> Et saepe usque adeo, mortis formidine, vitae
> Percipit humanos odium lucisque videndae,
> Ut sibi consciscant maerenti pectore letum
> Obliti fontem curarum hunc esse timorem.

And often so extreme is it that, through terror of death, such hatred of life and of seeing the light takes hold of people that they contrive their own deaths in their miserable hearts, forgetting that this was the original source of their woes.

(3.79–82)

This phenomenon sums up the futility of human life, lived in the shadow of the fear of death.[5] There is no activity which can gratify people's desire for immortal life (3.1003–10).

Lucretius tackles the fear of death from a number of perspectives. Four separate but related elements in the fear of death can be distinguished: the fear of being dead; the fear that one will die, that one's life is going to end; the fear of premature death; fear of the process of dying.[6] Epicurean arguments can be shown to address all of these fears, he argues. Nevertheless Lucretius' principal argument is an elaboration of a central claim of Epicurus that 'death is nothing to us'. Death cannot be bad for the individual who dies because, for something to be bad for someone, that someone must exist as a subject of experience. It is a fundamental claim of Epicurean philosophy that a person has no existence after his or her death. It follows from this, according to the Epicurean argument, that being dead cannot be bad for that person. Therefore it is irrational to fear death. Lucretius devotes considerable space to arguing that people are no longer the subjects of experience after death.[7] He also underlines the illogicality of people who, although they claim not to believe in the afterlife, nevertheless imagine a surviving subject who feels deprivation at losing the pleasures of life.

Other arguments are deployed by Lucretius to reinforce this central one. Time after death is equated with the time before we were born. Since we feel no concern that we did not exist before, why should we mind about not existing afterwards (3.830–42)?[8] Another argument is put in the mouth of a personified nature (931–49). Life is compared to a banquet. It has a structure and a conclusion. To prolong it beyond this brings no pleasure.[9] Nature is also made to claim that death is necessary to avoid intolerable over-population (963–71).[10] The horrors ascribed to the underworld are, Lucretius argues, merely projections of the mental torments people experience in earthly life (3.978–1023).[11]

Sisyphus in vita quoque nobis ante oculos est,
Qui petere a populo fasces saevasque secures
Imbibit et semper victus tristisque recedit.
Nam petere imperium quod inane est nec datur umquam,
Atque in eo semper durum sufferre laborem,
Hoc est adverso nixantem trudere monte
Saxum quod tamen e summo iam vertice rursum
Volvitur et plani raptim petit aequora campi.

Sisyphus, too, is before our eyes in life, the man who strives to seek the lictor's rods and cruel axes from the people and, always defeated, draws back in wretchedness. For to seek power, an empty thing, which is never granted, and to that end always to endure hard labour, this is to push, struggling, a stone up an opposing mountain, that still rolls down again from the summit and with speed regains the level of the open plain.

(3.995–1002)

This is yet another instance of human insatiability.[12] Those who seek power can never gain stable possession of it.[13] Humans fashion their own under-world through their failure to grasp what their goals should properly be.

Part of the power of Lucretius' poem lies in the vividness with which he evokes the ways people articulate their fears of death. Even as Lucretius expresses his disapproval of those who lament what a man leaves behind at death, there is a poignancy in the words they are made to utter (3.894–9). This is a fear which must be taken seriously. Lucretius' main focus in treating this fear, however, seems to be on anxieties about what happens after death. The experience of dying, the suffering which may be involved in this process, is less directly a concern for most of the poem.[14] Nevertheless with his treatment of the plague in the final section of the last book the physical experience of dying is for once explored in harrowing detail.

Most of the deaths Roman texts concern themselves with are violent ones – death in battle, execution, suicide. The prospect of a lingering and painful death from disease could also, of course, arouse intense anxiety. Chapter 1 considered briefly the funeral oration which Thucydides puts in the mouth of Pericles near the beginning of the Peloponnesian war. Praising those who have died fighting for Athens, he is made to offer a model of death at its most meaningful.[15] This section of his history is immediately followed by an account of the terrible effects of a plague which, according to Thucydides, struck the city in 430 BCE (2.47–54). He describes in graphic detail the physical symptoms of this disease (scholars still argue over its precise identification). His account, for one critic at least, 'dramatically and ironi-cally overturns everything of which Thucydides made Pericles boast'.[16] The celebration of Athens and Athenian values is juxtaposed with a shocking account of the city's bleakest hour.

This same plague plays a crucial role as the concluding episode in Lucretius' De rerum natura. Lucretius rewrites Thucydides' account to highlight more particularly the damaging effects of the fear of death.[17] This later version detaches the plague from its historical context and exacerbates its impact, downplaying, for instance, Thucydides' reference to survivors. Lucretius describes at length the instances of self-mutilation to which the disease drives its victims:

Quorum si quis, ut est, vitarat funera leti,
Ulceribus taetris et nigra proluvie alvi
Posterius tamen hunc tabes letumque manebat,
Aut etiam multus capitis cum saepe dolore
Corruptus sanguis expletis naribus ibat:
Huc hominis totae vires corpusque fluebat.
Profluvium porro qui taetri sanguinis acre
Exierat, tamen in nervos huic morbus et artus
Ibat et in partis genitalis corporis ipsas.
Et graviter partim metuentes limina leti
Vivebant ferro privati parte virili,
Et manibus sine nonnulli pedibusque manebant
In vita tamen, perdebant lumina partim:
Usque adeo mortis metus his incesserat acer.

Of these, if any, as happens, escaped a deadly end, the wasting and death would still linger on with foul ulcers and black discharge of the bowels or often there would be a headache and much poisoned blood would fill the nostrils and flow forth. With this a person's reserves of strength and substance would drain away. And if some survived the painful flow of foul blood, yet into their muscles and limbs the disease would go and into the very organs of procreation. And some, with great fear of death's approach, would castrate themselves with a knife and thus live on. And some would remain without their hands and feet but still alive, while others lost their sight. So heavily did the fear of death lie on these people.

(6.1199–1214)

This passage is characteristically vivid in its treatment of the symptoms – and their brutal remedy. Some misguided people will do anything to cling to life, however diminished their existence might be.[18] These references to self-mutilation have no precedent in Thucydides.[19] For Lucretius, plague is a physical disaster but also – much more than for Thucydides – a moral calamity.[20] The worst aspect of the disease is not the physical pain people experience but the crippling depression which afflicts those who know they are going to die (6.1230–5). Social structures are undermined, moral values and ritual practices abandoned.

The plague's impact on Athens (the city which would later produce Epicurus, as Lucretius reminds his reader in the opening lines of Book 6) makes all too clear people's need for the enlightenment only philosophy can offer. The powerlessness of religion (whose inefficacy is repeatedly highlighted in the poem)[21] is thrown into sharp relief. The plague brings the poem to an abrupt conclusion.[22] Its concern with the fear of death mirrors the Epicurean arguments against the fear of death with which the first half of the poem concluded in the final sections of Book 3. Lucretius implies in Book 3 that the approach of death may offer the final test of a person's character.

> Quo magis in dubiis hominem spectare periclis
> Convenit adversisque in rebus noscere qui sit;
> Nam verae voces tum demum pectore ab imo
> Eliciuntur et eripitur persona, manet res.

> So it is more helpful to examine someone in dangerous peril and to learn in harsh circumstances what kind of person they are; for only then are true words drawn from the depths of the heart. The mask is pulled off, the reality remains.

> (3.55–8)

Here, the true face lies beneath the concealing mask (this theatrical analogy, we might note, is in strong contrast to those later deployed by Seneca, discussed in Chapter 5 below). Nevertheless in his treatment of death throughout the poem, Lucretius seems not to view it as part of an individual's life story.[23] Bad deaths are certainly shown in terrifying detail in Lucretius' plague narrative but they are hardly particularised.

What advice then does Lucretius offer as to how to approach one's own death? The would-be philosopher, by acquiring knowledge of the nature of things, is able to achieve a god-like detachment, claims Lucretius (for instance at 1.72–7; 2.4–6). A model for death consonant with this ideal life might seem to be offered when Lucretius writes of the deaths of Democritus and Epicurus:

> Denique Democritum postquam matura vetustas
> Admonuit memores motus languescere mentis,
> Sponte sua leto caput obvius obtulit ipse.
> Ipse Epicurus obit decurso lumine vitae.

> Democritus, then, when ripe old age warned him that the movements of his mind were slowing down, himself of his own free will offered his head to death. And Epicurus himself died, when the light of his life had run its course.

> (3.1039–42)

These deaths could be assimilated to the Socratic tradition (and other accounts of Epicurus' death certainly stress his serenity in the face of agonising pain).[24] Yet their treatment is so brief in Lucretius' poem they can scarcely be held to offer an inspiring model.[25] Rather they function as the culmination of a list of great and famous persons who have already gone to their deaths, an illustration that all men must die. For Lucretius, the fear of death offers the philosopher the greatest challenge. But he does not look to the heroic deaths of individuals for ways to rise to this challenge. The approach of death may strip off pretensions to reveal the human reality beneath but Lucretius makes no sustained attempt to exploit the force of these instances of reality to offer help to his readers.

Beyond the grave?

Epicurean approaches to the fear of death also receive some consideration in the philosophical writings of Lucretius' contemporary, Cicero. This series of works (composed in 45 and 44 BCE after he had lost his beloved daughter Tullia and was playing little part in Roman political life) also reflect a concern with death, though for him the fear of death seems not to be the driving force it is for Lucretius. His *Tusculans*, a philosophical dialogue in five books, which Cicero himself locates at the centre of his philosophical project, are presented as offering a form of therapy, *levatio* (5.121), oriented toward securing practical results.[26] The first book engages with the fear of death, its arguments, according to Cicero himself, generating *magna mortis ... contemptio*, 'a great contempt for death' (*Tusc*. 2.2).[27] The debate opens with the assertion by a character referred to as 'A' that 'death seems to me to be an evil, *malum*' (*Tusc*. 1.9). The interlocutors tackle both the issue of whether the dead are wretched or not and also the fact the one must face dying (1.14), issues central, as we have seen, to Lucretius' project in *De rerum natura*.

'M' interrogates 'A', at one point asking, *Num te illa terrent, triceps apud inferos Cerberus, Cocyti fremitus, travectio Acherontis ...?* 'You are not terrified are you by the stories of three-headed Cerberus in the lower world, the roar of Cocytus, the passage of Acheron ...?' To this A responds, 'You do not think I am so crazy (*delirare*) as to believe those tales?' (*Tusc*. 1.10).[28] The energy devoted by philosophers (among whom Lucretius could of course be numbered) to tackling people's fears of the afterlife is misplaced, he contends (1.11). Other aspects of the Epicurean position receive more serious attention. Indeed Cicero's 'A' offers a telling criticism of the core Epicurean argument, asserting that the evil of death, for those who have once existed, is precisely non-existence (*Tusc*. 1.13), though this observation is not fully developed.[29] As regards the fate of the soul after death, 'M', the dominant interlocutor, offers two and only two options: either the soul experiences total extinction at death or it passes to a higher level of blessedness. Since, he claims, it is not our natural instinct to believe the first proposition, the second must be true. Both speakers go on to praise the essentially Platonic view that the souls of the virtuous end up in a blissful afterlife, though 'A' invites 'M' to offer further arguments in support of this vision (*Tusc.* 1.24). 'M' goes on to reproduce long sections from Plato's *Apology* and *Phaedrus*.[30] Yet hope of a blissful afterlife is never the sole inducement to virtuous behaviour. The wise man, even if he believes the soul to be mortal, 'M' asserts, will be induced by the desire for virtue *cupiditate ... virtutis* to undertake deeds which may benefit the state even if they involve risking death (*Tusc.* 1.91).

Neither Lucretius nor Cicero seems especially concerned with the actual moment of death.[31] Indeed the lack of concern they express with the moment of death is quite striking.[32] Cicero, in the *Tusculans*, has 'M' comment at one point that dying often takes place without sensation, or even with a sensation of pleasure. Indeed he continues, 'the whole matter is trivial, whatever turns out to be the case, since it is over so quickly', *totumque hoc leve est, qualecumque est: fit enim ad punctum temporis* (*Tusc.* 1.82). However, as we have already seen in earlier chapters, perhaps in response to civil war and changing political circumstances, dying was coming to be re-evaluated as an experience whose symbolic significance could far outweigh its duration.

Learning to die

Writing a century after Cicero, Seneca, though he does discuss what happens after death is, as we have already noted, far more concerned with the process of dying. This concern with dying is particularly evident in the *Epistulae morales*, the collection of 124 letters addressed to his equestrian friend Lucilius (there were originally two further books which have not survived). Seneca appears to have written these letters in the final years of his life, after he had fallen out with Nero and had withdrawn from Rome.[33] Death forms a predominant theme in a significant number from the outset and is mentioned in over half the letters. The first letter in the collection stresses the need to understand *se cotidie mori*, 'that one is dying every day' (1.2).[34] Letter 4 asserts than one cannot achieve a composed mind unless one has overcome the fear of death (4.3). Letter 12 advises that death should be looked in the face by young and old equally (12.6). Subsequent letters develop these concerns at length. Throughout the letters, Seneca strives to engage with death as offering the possibility of philosophical progress and achievement, a supreme opportunity to actualise his long life's philosophical work. Seneca was, by Roman standards, an old man when he wrote these letters. Out of favour with an emperor already notorious for doing away with those close to him, Seneca will have been expecting the delivery of a lethal communication from Nero at any time. No surprise, then, that death was on his mind.

It is in Seneca that we find articulated most explicitly a view, which can also be found in the writings of other authors of the principate, that the moment of death, above all, expresses an individual's true value. *Mors de te pronuntiatura est*, 'death will pronounce judgement on you' (26.6). This chapter focuses on a small number of letters, particularly 24, 70, 71, 77, 78 and 82. My project here is in part to explore how Seneca makes this claim work as a means of countering the fear of death. It is because dying is such a significant experience that one must prepare oneself with particular care to face death: *egregia res est mortem condiscere*, 'It is a great thing to learn thoroughly how to die' (26.9).[35] The learning consists above all in overcoming the fear of death. We shall also consider how these concerns relate to Seneca's complex position on when it may be right to kill oneself.

In addressing the fear of death Seneca is especially concerned to address the fear of pain associated with death. This pain is rarely (as it sometimes seems to be in Lucretius or Cicero) minimised.[36] Rather it is imagined in shocking detail – dramatised even. As we saw in Chapter 2 with his treatment of Cato's death in *De providentia*, Seneca's strategy is to invest pain with meaning. Cato acquires heroic status through his demonstration of *constantia*, his persistence in seeking death, once he had decided death was the appropriate course, despite the agony he suffered in so doing. Letter 24 starts out from the concern Lucilius has allegedly expressed at a forthcoming lawsuit. Seneca works to put Lucilius' anxiety in perspective by setting it alongside the greatest of all fears – the fear of death.[37] As he comments in Letter 70, while all the other evils we prepare ourselves for may not happen, death certainly will (70.18).[38] A range of strategies is deployed in Letter 24 to steel the mind of the would-be philosopher against the fear of death but above all Seneca invokes stirring examples of brave individuals who have shown their contempt for the pain of dying.[39]

Socrates serves as the first example of endurance. His conversation with his friends as he awaited judicial execution is presented as serving *ut duarum rerum gravissimarum hominibus metum demeret, mortis et carceris*, 'to put aside the fear of two things which weigh most heavily on humankind, death and imprisonment' (24.4).[40] Seneca's other examples in this letter (as generally) are Roman. An example of the endurance of pain developed at length is that of Mucius Scaevola. This was a story associated with the late sixth century BCE and familiar to many Roman readers from

Livy's history.[41] Mucius had made a sortie to the camp of the Etruscan leader, Lars Porsenna. Having failed to assassinate the enemy leader, he gives an astonishing example of his bravery by holding his own right hand in a brazier until it is consumed by the flames – to the amazement of the Etruscan spectators.

> Mucius ignibus manum inposuit. Acerbum est uri; quanto acerbius, si id te faciente patiaris! Vides hominem non eruditum nec ullis praeceptis contra mortem aut dolorem subornatum, militari tantum robore instructum, poenas a se inriti conatus exigentem; spectator destillantis in hostili foculo dexterae stetit.

> Mucius put his hand on the fire. It is painful to be burned; how much more painful to suffer this when you are yourself the agent! You may see a man, lacking education and equipped with no philosophy against death and pain, armed only with his military valour, exacting from himself the penalty for his failed undertaking. He stood watching his own hand as it dripped into the enemy's brazier.

> (*Ep.* 24.5)

Seneca condenses a longer narrative into this one scene, which Lucilius (and other readers) is invited to picture for himself. Mucius lacked a philosophical education. How much the more will one who has devoted himself to philosophy be able to withstand suffering, Seneca argues.

Mucius is a beguiling figure for Seneca, reappearing several times in the letters.[42] The Younger Cato, however, is the key example in this letter, combining Greek philosophy with Roman valour.[43] Cato chooses to kill himself, thus spurning Caesar's offer of clemency. Seneca then moves on to the less exalted but more attainable example of another civil war commander Scipio who, defeated, also chose to take his own life in 46 BCE. This man's life lacked particular distinction. In death, however, he surpassed his noble ancestors (those conquerors of Africa who hold the stage in the final section of Cicero's *De republica*). Seneca comments, comparing him with his illustrious ancestor, Scipio Africanus: *multum fuit Carthaginem vincere, sed amplius mortem*, 'it was a great deed to conquer Carthage, but a greater deed to conquer death' (24.10). Death and pain, he continues, should be recognised as familiar presences, encountered daily even by the most ordinary of persons – including of course slaves.

Early on in the letters, Seneca stresses the potency of examples:

> Plus tamen tibi et viva vox et convictus quam oratio proderit. In rem

praesentem venias oportet, primum quia homines amplius oculis quam auribus credunt; deinde, quia longum iter est per praecepta, breve et efficax per exempla.

For the living voice and shared life will be of greater use to you than formal discourse. You should go to the scene of the action, firstly because people believe their eyes rather than their ears, and then because the journey is long through precepts, but short and direct through examples.

(*Ep.* 6.5)

Seneca is drawing here on an established Roman tradition of invoking great individuals of the past.[44] In acknowledging the danger that such examples may seem hackneyed, he highlights the brilliance of his own evocations of these men.[45] Through a kind of necromancy, these living presences are conjured up.[46] We should note here particularly Seneca's emphasis on seeing. *Exempla* even when communicated verbally have a visual impact – they appeal to our *oculis*, 'eyes', he asserts (we might also note his use of *vides*, 'you may see', in describing the scene of Mucius' self-mutilation in Letter 24 quoted above).[47] Such examples may sometimes be reduced to an iconic phrase: *truncam illam et retorridam manum Mucii*, 'the maimed and shrivelled hand of Mucius' (66.51). Similarly, Cato's wound is made to stand for Cato's virtue: a *vita honesta*, Seneca comments, may comprise, among other things, *Catonis scissum manu sua vulnus*, 'the wound of Cato ripped open by Cato's own hand' (67.7).[48] Visualising that wound, Mucius' hand can fortify the lowliest aspirant philosopher.[49]

While for Lucretius self-mutilation is pathological, a symptom of the way in which the fear of death blights life, for Seneca such an act can serve as a manifestation of supreme virtue. Mucius and Cato are notable examples of the ability to withstand pain.[50] In both cases that pain is self-inflicted. Part of the point of their actions in Seneca's account is precisely to make a statement, to communicate their powers of endurance. Mucius in particular is a showman who can turn a practical defeat into a symbolic victory, through a shocking and unforgettable act of self-mutilation. They both offer self-conscious examples of virtue as an edifying spectacle.[51]

Though some individuals – most obviously Cato and Socrates – might seem beyond imitation, yet other examples of virtuous behaviour may be found among lesser men. And any reader with sufficient motivation may rise to join their number:

Dic tibi: 'ex istis, quae terribilia videntur, nihil est invictum. Singula vicere iam multi: ignem Mucius, crucem Regulus, venenum Socrates, exilium

Rutilius, mortem ferro adactam Cato; et nos vincamus aliquid.' ... Nos quoque aliquid et ipsi faciamus animose; simus inter exempla.

Say to yourself: 'Of those things which seem terrible there is none which has not been overcome. Indeed many have overcome them individually: Mucius fire, Regulus the cross, Socrates poison, Rutilius exile, Cato death brought by the sword. Let us too overcome something... Let us too do something bravely; let us be among the examples.'

(*Ep.* 98.12–13)

It is through rehearsing in our minds the deeds of these great individuals of the past that we may summon up the strength to act with equal bravery.[52] Thus we too may feature among the *exempla*. Certainly Seneca accords prime importance to historical instantiations of the Stoic sage – which must include Cato, if anyone – in the process of concept formation;[53] they serve to generate our *imago virtutis*, the ideal of *virtus* (120.5–8). Yet they also have a crucial role as direct models for imitation. Even if it is only in extreme circumstances that lesser mortals can aspire to imitate them,[54] it is at such moments above all that we must labour to conjure up these *imagines*, for it is then that they can do most to help us.

Death and *virtus*

For Stoics, the only true good is *virtus*. In Roman philosophical discourse generally, the term *virtus* is used as translation of, or equivalent to, the Greek term 'arête', a concept of crucial importance in the academic tradition of Plato and his followers as well as for the stoics. However, to understand the weight the term *virtus* bears in Roman philosophical discourse, we need to appreciate the other associations of this term in Roman culture. Traditionally the term *virtus* had been most often linked to performance in battle. The epitaph of Lucius Cornelius Scipio Barbatus, for instance, composed around the middle of the third century BCE, celebrates his *virtus*, manifested in his magistracies and his conquests of Samnite and Lucanian territories (*CIL* I 2 7).[55] The term's military connotations are apparent in fragments of Ennius and in Livy's history, where most occurrences of *virtus* apply specifically to soldiers' bravery or steadfastness or to the activities of a magistrate, as military leader or in the domestic sphere.[56] Cicero, in one of his speeches against Verres, can be found praising Lucius Paulus for defeating Perses *vi et virtute*, 'with might and courage' (*Verr.* 2.1.55). Throughout the republican period and perhaps into the principate too, it seems that physical courage and prowess, particularly in the context of war, remained a key element in conceptions of manliness.[57] This is certainly the notion of *virtus* which Sallust associates with, for instance, Julius Caesar (*Cat.* 54.4). As Sallust comments, Caesar's *virtus* required a war to show itself to best advantage. Looking back to the early days of the Roman republic, Plutarch, in the opening chapter of his *Life of Coriolanus*, equates earlier Roman notions of *virtus* with *andreia*, 'courage'. Thus constructed, *virtus* is community-oriented, a social rather than an ethical quality.

Nevertheless one may also detect a different discourse of *virtus*, in tension with this military one, from early on.[58] Sallust also writes of the *virtus* of the younger Cato. Here *virtus* has an obviously ethical dimension: *esse quam videri bonum malebat*, 'he preferred to be rather than to seem good' (54.5–6). Writing after Cato's death, Cicero terms him *omnium gentium virtute princeps*, 'the leader of all peoples in virtue' (*Phil.* 13.30). Cicero in his philosophical works can be found using *virtus* as an all-embracing ethical term, where it often stands in opposition to *vitia*, 'vices', as for instance at *De officiis* 3.13. Cicero can also be found attempting to conflate the traditional notion of *virtus* with the philosophical. In the *Tusculans* 'M' is made to sum up a universally agreed position:

Vide ne, cum omnes rectae animi adfectationes virtutes appellentur, non sit hoc proprium nomen omnium, sed ab ea quae una ceteris excellebat omnes nominatae sint. Appellata est enim ex viro virtus; viri autem propria maxime est fortitudo, cuius munera duo sunt maxima: mortis dolorisque contemptio. Utendum est igitur his, si virtutis compotes vel potius si viri volumus esse, quoniam a viris virtus nomen est mutuata.

Observe that, while all good dispositions of the spirit are called virtues, this is not the name proper to them but they all took that name from the one which stood above the rest. For *virtus*, 'virtue', takes its name from *vir*, 'man'; and the proper virtue of a man is above all courage, whose particular functions are contempt for death and for pain. Therefore we must exercise these qualities, if we wish to be virtuous, indeed, if we wish to be men, since the term virtue is borrowed from the term for men.

(*Tusc.* 2.43)

Cicero stresses the etymological connection with man, *vir*.[59] Leaving the military associations of the term implicit, Cicero chooses to articulate the essence of *virtus* as contempt for death and pain. It is particularly courage, then, a quality associated above all with military endeavour, which lies at the heart of this conception of *virtus*.

It is hardly surprising then that *virtus*, for Cicero, is of greatest value when displayed in action. The preface to his earlier work *De re publica* offers the following comment:

> Virtus in usu sui tota posita est; usus autem eius est maximus civitatis gubernatio et earum ipsarum rerum quas isti in angulis personant, reapse, non oratione perfectio.

> The existence of virtue depends entirely on its use. And its greatest use is in the government of the state and the bringing to fruition in actions not in words the very things which those people [philosophers] sound off about in their corners.

> (*Rep.* 1.2)

There is a tension here between a purely philosophical notion of *virtus* and what Cicero presents as the superior manifestation of *virtus* in action.[60] In line with this, it is the *virtus* of those who have made contributions to the state which will be rewarded in the afterlife, according to the elder Scipio Africanus as he appears in his grandson's dream, at the conclusion of this dialogue.[61]

In Seneca's writing, by contrast, the philosophical use of *virtus* has, in some respects, supplanted the military. Seneca's Cato is no less an exemplar of *virtus* when he is conquered at Pharsalia than if he had won the battle (71.8). In the same letter, Seneca goes on to claim that: *Haec ubicumque apparuit, omnia eiusdem mensurae ac pretii sunt*, 'all acts in which *virtus* has revealed itself are of the same measure and value'. Most strikingly, for him: *paria bona esse eius, qui triumphat, et eius, qui ante currum vehitur invictus animo*, 'there is an equivalence between the goods of one who celebrates a triumph, and of one who, unconquered in spirit, is carried before the victor's chariot' (71.22).[62] Indeed, it often seems Seneca is only interested in battle when there is no chance of victory.[63]

The Stoics distinguished between the *summum bonum* – virtue – and *indifferentia* – all other perceived goods and ills.[64] Virtue is exercised in activities which involve choosing preferred indifferents. Usually these are understood as those things necessary to support human life but also those things conducive to life in a well-ordered community.[65] Yet Seneca lets slip that in some respects what might be described as ill fortune is more to be wished for than good fortune, since it is under circumstances of this kind that *virtus* can truly shine. This is expressed in the strongest form in Letter 66: *si ulla bona maiora esse aliis possent, haec ego, quae tristia videntur, mollibus illis et delicatis praetulissem*, 'If any good should seem greater than others, I would prefer those that seem harsh to those which are pleasurable and luxurious' (66.49).[66]

Here, though, we may sense the military associations of *virtus* coming back into play. Indeed military imagery repeatedly colours Seneca's characterisation of the true philosopher. In Letter 67, the Stoic Attalus, for instance, is made to assert *malo me fortuna in castris suis quam in deliciis habeat*, 'I would rather fortune kept me in her camp than in the lap of luxury' (67.15). Elsewhere Seneca exhorts his reader to receive the blows of fortune like a soldier (*Ep.* 99.32; 104.22). He comments that the training of the philosopher requires *disciplina* on the analogy of military training (for instance, *Ep.* 18.6).[67] Just as a soldier needs war to prove himself (only thus may the *virtus* of Sallust's Caesar shine forth), so a philosopher needs adversity. Seneca comments: *virtutem enim intellego animosam et excelsam, quam incitat quicquid infestat*, 'For I understand virtue to be something high-spirited and noble, such that it is aroused by whatever vexes it' (71.18). He goes on to assert:

> Beatus vero et virtutis exactae tunc se maxime amat, cum fortisimme expertus est, et metuenda ceteris, si alicuius honesti officii pretia sunt, non tantum fert, sed amplexatur multoque audire mavult 'tanto melior' quam 'tanto felicior'.

> But the happy man whose virtue is fulfilled loves himself most of all when he has been tested to the highest degree and when he not only tolerates but embraces those things which other men fear, if that is the price to be paid for performing an honourable duty. And he far prefers to hear said 'How much more noble!' than 'How much more lucky!'

> (*Ep.* 71.28)

At one point in the letter, Seneca does concede that those who have not attained the composure of the wise man may find themselves bowed down by adverse circumstances (71.26). And he comments later that he himself should be seen as a *proficiens*, a would-be philosopher (rather than a *sapiens*) in this respect (71.30). Nevertheless it is hard to imagine Seneca's *sapiens* manifesting himself under any other than adverse circumstances.

Seneca is an idiosyncratic writer whose often compelling vision of how to achieve philosophical perfection must in part have been conditioned by his own unusual career.[68] Yet there are significant resonances between his reconceptualisation of *virtus* and the reworking of Roman values in, particularly, Tacitus (as we shall see in the next chapters). A case has been made for connecting this shift in aspirations with the changing circumstances of the Roman elite more generally under the early principate. Roman senators, above all those from the most aristocratic families, were coming to be effectively excluded from the highest positions of military command.[69] The link between military achievement and high social status, so strong under the republic, was weakened. In this context Seneca's selection and deployment of examples has a particular significance. His exemplars of *virtus* make clear that (in accordance with Stoic teaching) moral virtue is not contingent on the success or failure of military operations.[70] As Matthew Roller comments, for Seneca: 'The proper arena for exercising *virtus* is now not warfare, but the endurance of ill fortune.'[71]

Battle then is on one level no longer the sphere in which aristocrats should seek distinction. And yet there is still scope for the exercise of a kind of *virtus* which, though mediated through philosophy, in crucial ways resembles that which distinguished earlier generations of Romans. Let us reconsider Seneca's use of Mucius Scaevola in Letter 24. A familiarity with the story in its context – in particular Livy's version of the story – adds another dimension to Seneca's arresting picture.[72] For Livy's account lays particular emphasis on the distinctively Roman nature of Scaevola's bravery. When he is captured Mucius exclaims: 'I can die as bravely as I can kill; both to do and to suffer valiantly is the Roman way!' *nec ad mortem minus animi est quam fuit ad caedem: et facere et pati fortia Romanum est* (2.12.9). In Seneca the specifically Roman quality of Mucius' virtue is elided; he is presented as an example to all. And yet in taking Mucius as our model (even if our philosophical training renders us in some respects superior to him) we are also aligning ourselves with a particularly Roman kind of virtue, that death-defying courage which could terrorise neighbouring peoples and serve to bring them under Roman domination.

The all-pervasive nature of battle imagery in Seneca's prose is striking.[73] We might note particularly the conclusion of Letter 71:

Quando continget contemnere utramque fortunam, quam continget omnibus oppressis adfectibus et sub arbitrium suum adductis hanc vocem emittere 'vici'? Quem vicerim quaeris? Non Persas nec extrema Medorum nec si quid ultra Dahas bellicosum iacet, sed avaritiam, sed ambitionem, sed metum mortis, qui victores gentium vicit.

When will it fall to our lot, once all the passions have been subdued and brought under our own control, to speak the words 'I have conquered'? Are you asking me whom I have conquered? Not the Persians, not the distant Medes, nor any warmongering people that lives beyond the

Dahae; not these but greed, ambition and the fear of death that has
conquered the conquerors of the world.

(*Ep.* 71.37)

The passions – in particular the fear of death – are figured as the enemy.[74]
This battle overshadows in importance any other one may undertake. Seneca
compares those who foolishly seek to conquer the world with those whose
goal is far superior – to attain dominion over themselves: *imperare sibi
maximum imperium est* (113.31).[75] Only in this conflict is victory or defeat
of the slightest significance.[76] There is perhaps a link here with the complex
of motivations analysed by Lucretius.[77] One implication of *De rerum natura*
(3.59–64) is that it is fear of death (as well as the more predictable *avaritia*
and *ambitio*, greed and lust for power) which motivates people to undertake
military conquest.

Yet while victory over human enemies may be irrelevant, for Seneca, the
kind of courage required of soldiers for whom death is imminent remains
one of the greatest sources of inspiration. In Letter 82 Seneca again returns
to the fear of death as something philosophy must vanquish.[78] Here Seneca
is particularly concerned to stress the inefficacy of the strategies offered by
some philosophers, described as *ineptias Graecas*, 'the foolishness of the
Greeks' (82.8).

Zenon noster hac collectione utitur: 'nullum malum gloriosum est; mors
autem gloriosa est; mors ergo non est malum.' Profecisti! Liberatus sum
metu! Post hoc non dubitabo porrigere cervicem. Non vis severius loqui
nec morituro risum movere?

Our Zeno used to use this syllogism: 'No evil is glorious, yet death is
glorious, therefore death is no evil.' You've done it! I am set free from fear!
After this I shall not hesitate to offer my neck. Won't you say something
more serious rather than provoking the dying man to laughter?

(*Ep.* 82.9)

Seneca regularly attacks the preoccupation of other philosophers with logic.[79]
In Letter 82 he shows himself quite at home with such reasoning, attacking
the false premise of Zeno's syllogism (death itself is not glorious; it is dying
bravely which is glorious, 82.10).[80] Death is indifferent, in Stoic terms. Yet,
as Seneca goes on to emphasise, it is not something easy to ignore: *magna
exercitatione durandus est animus, ut conspectum eius accessumque patiatur*,
'The spirit must be hardened by much practice to enable it to endure the
sight and the approach of death' (82.16). Practical exercises – particularly

regular attempts to visualise the most terrible experiences borne bravely – will be far more effective than quibbling over the meanings of words or the technicalities of argument.

But other strategies too are invoked. It is in this letter that Seneca addresses at greatest length concerns about what happens after death. He observes reprovingly: *multorum ingeniis certatum est ad augendam eius infamiam*, 'Many great minds have competed to increase its bad reputation' (82.16).[81] He goes on to quote some lines of verse, a composite of two passages in Virgil's *Aeneid* (6.400–1 and 8.296–7). The epic poet's description of the underworld seems a prime offender here. Yet Book 6 with its account of Aeneas' descent into the underworld is invoked in a number of other ways in this letter. Rousing his reader, Seneca exhorts: *nunc animis opus, Aenea, nunc pectore firmo*, 'Now you need your courage, Aeneas, now your stout heart!' (*Aen.* 6.261 quoted at 82.7). Seneca is not, it seems, especially concerned to attack poetic pictures of the underworld (though their authors are certainly reproached).[82] Even if fear of these horrors is overcome, one may still fear the prospect of nothing after death.[83] Virtue, asserts Seneca, must overcome fear entirely: *nihil honeste fit, nisi cui totus animus incubuit atque adfuit, cui nulla parte sui repugnavit*, 'No deed that a man does is honourable, unless he has devoted himself to it and committed himself to it entirely, with no part of himself resisting' (82.18). Here once again (at 82.18) the sixth book of the *Aeneid* is brought into play. The sibyl advises Aeneas:

> Tu ne cede malis, sed contra audentior ito
> Qua tua te fortuna sinet.

> You – do not give in to troubles but go forth more bravely where your fortune permits you.

> (*Aen.* 6.95–6)

Seneca harnesses the potency of Virgil's familiar lines – the would-be wise man must imagine himself as an epic hero braving the horrors of the underworld; for Seneca, too, this fiction can be a useful one. All the resources of poetry as well as history must be drawn on to attain a goal so important and so hard to reach.[84]

There is, we may feel, a significant tension here. Seneca presents fear as pathological. It must be rooted out. The wise man must be impassive. Yet the impassive wise man is with difficulty compared to the soldier, to the epic hero, whose bravery lies precisely in his continuing struggle to maintain control over his fears.[85] We might ask whether there can be virtue in this sense without fear (or some other emotion) to do battle against. Only mortality, we may suspect, gives true scope to *virtus*.[86] Indeed, while the reader is invited to aspire to the Stoic ideal of freedom from perturbation, Seneca often seems more interested in the act of self-assertion involved in preserving it than in the state itself.[87] *Noster sapiens vincit quidem incommodum omne*: 'Our wise man vanquishes every vexation' (9.3).[88]

The final part of the letter pursues at greater length the model of soldiers facing battle. 'When a leader is about to take into battle an army prepared to meet death for their wives and children, how will he urge them on?' Seneca alludes to the Fabii, to Leonidas and his Spartans at Thermopylae: *Nec victoriam sperant, nec reditum. Ille locus illis sepulchrum futurus est*, 'They have no hope of victory, no hope of returning home. Where they stand will be their tomb' (82.20).[89] Under these circumstances, no leader would offer a dry syllogism. Instead, Seneca offers the brief and rousing words traditionally attributed to these great generals. These are the examples we should seek to follow. *Magnis telis magna portenta feriuntur*, 'Great monsters are struck down by great weapons' (82.23).[90] Philosophical *virtus* is here not merely coloured but in a sense taken over by the military association of the term. For it is the supreme instance of courage evoked by the imminence of death which functions as the privileged moment for the display of *virtus*. As Seneca makes the Stoic adviser to his friend Marcellinus comment: *non est res magna vivere ... magnum est honeste mori, prudenter, fortiter*, 'It is not important whether you live ... but it is important to die honestly, with self-control and bravely' (77.6).

Brave endurance of death, claims Seneca, is glorious and fit to rank among the greatest accomplishments (*Ep.* 82.17). This claim in itself might not seem at variance with the notions of *virtus* entertained by much earlier generations of Romans. The Stoics of the principate had at least one way to show they could live up to traditional ideals of manly distinction. But Seneca's celebration of self-inflicted death as the supreme demonstration that the fear of death has been vanquished seems the product of a more recent sensibility. Cicero, in one of his speeches against Catiline, comments on a particular feature of Roman *virtus*:

Fuit, fuit ista quondam in hac re publica virtus ut viri fortes acrioribus suppliciis civem perniciosum quam acerbissimum hostem coercerent.

Gone, gone is that valour which was once found in this state, such that brave men would contain a citizen traitor with sharper punishments than the bitterest enemy.

(*Cat.* 1.3)

Yet one might argue that this proverbial Roman severity had merely found a new form. If Romans were traditionally hardest on themselves, Cato with his exemplary act of self-destruction has taken this to its logical conclusion.[91] The latter part of this chapter will consider how, for Seneca at least, Stoic ethics validate and sometimes encourage the would-be philosopher to take his own life.

Final calculations

Seneca's frequent references to and examples of suicide are an aspect of his writing which has disturbed (and fascinated) many readers. They need to be seen as a key part of his project to overcome the fear of death.[92] Seneca also explores in detail examples of individuals who encounter death from disease with equal bravery. Seneca's friend Bassus, for instance, overwhelmed by the infirmities of old age, is praised at length for seeing death coming and welcoming it (*Ep.* 30.9). The wise man never does anything unwillingly; dying well is dying willingly (61.2; 82.17–18). Yet the implication of numerous passages in the letters is that to take one's own life at the moment one chooses may sometimes be a good death. Seneca concludes Letter 69 with further observations on death: *hoc meditare et exerce, ut mortem et excipias et, si ita res suadebit, accersas*, 'consider and practise this – how you may welcome death and, if circumstances recommend, invite it' (69.6). The following letter, Letter 70, offers a lengthy and sustained exploration of the right time to die.

Seneca in Letter 69 invokes Epicurus' advice: *meditare mortem*, 'think on death'. Yet the Epicureans apparently condemned suicide under almost all circumstances – despite their doctrine that 'death is nothing to us' (*Kyria doxa* 2).[93] The philosopher Diodorus when he killed himself was criticised, according to Seneca, for not following the teachings of Epicurus (*De vita beata* 19.1).[94] By contrast Stoicism in imperial Rome, at least in Seneca's rendering of it, seems to endorse even encourage suicide under certain circumstances. A. D. Nock famously referred to 'the Stoic cult of suicide'.[95] Seneca's views on the appropriateness of suicide are to some extent shared by other Stoics (even if his concern with suicide is particularly intense).[96] Epictetus acknowledges Stoic teaching that suicide could be justified under intolerable circumstances, though he seems to insist on a theological endorsement.[97] Closer to Seneca is the view put in the mouth of Cato in Cicero *De finibus* (3.60–2) and that outlined by Diogenes Laertius in his account of Zeno and later Stoics (7.130).[98] According to Diogenes, the Stoics considered self-killing to be an appropriate action, if it would save a friend's life, if it would benefit one's country, or if it would allow one to escape from painful or incurable disease. Seneca invokes this as Stoic tradition. In Letter 104 he comments that Socrates can teach us how to die when it is necessary, Zeno before it is necessary (104.21).[99]

According to Stoic theory as set out by Diogenes Laertius (7.130) one might simply calculate whether the natural advantages of living are outweighed by the corresponding disadvantages.[100] Seneca presents himself as readily resorting to such a process of calculation, in considering whether life continues to be worth living in the face of the physical and mental afflictions of old age (*Ep.* 58.34–5). The term *ratio*, in the sense of calculation, recurs frequently in Seneca's discussions of when is the right time to die.[101] Should one anticipate the executioner or not? Sometimes this may be the appropriate course. But on other occasions to wait is better. An important example here is that of Socrates.

> Socrates potuit abstinentia finire vitam et inedia potius quam veneno mori. Triginta tamen dies in carcere et in expectatione mortis exegit, non hoc animo tamquam omnia fieri possent, tamquam multas spes tam longum tempus reciperet, sed ut praeberet se legibus, ut fruendum amicis extremum Socraten daret.

> Socrates could have brought his life to an end through starvation by abstaining from food rather than dying of the poison. Yet he passed thirty days in prison with death in prospect and not with the thought that anything could happen, that such an extended period brought many hopes but in order that he might show himself obedient to the laws and let his friends benefit from the last days of Socrates.

> (*Ep.* 70.9)

Seneca chooses not to engage with the arguments Socrates is made to advance in the *Phaedo* against suicide, that it is only permissible when one has received a divine sign. Rather he stresses Socrates' wish to demonstrate his own respect for the laws of Athens. At the same time, the desire to benefit others, even though one might experience greater pain oneself, is also shown as a laudable motive for letting the law take its course rather than rushing to embrace death.[102]

The example of Drusus Libo which follows is altogether more ambiguous. Seneca seems at first to be reproaching him for not following his aunt's advice and awaiting execution rather than taking his own life, after his conspiracy against the emperor was discovered. But Seneca then shifts tack: *manus sibi attulit, nec sine causa*, 'He laid violent hands on himself – and not without reason' (70.10). What point is there in living for another few days at one's enemy's pleasure? Significantly this line of debate leads Seneca to the claim:

> Non possis itaque de re in universum pronuntiare, cum mortem vis externa denuntiat, occupanda sit an expectanda. Multa enim sunt quae in utramque partem trahere possunt.

> And so you cannot make a general pronouncement on the matter of whether, when an external force decrees death, you should anticipate it or wait for it. For there are many considerations which may incline a person in one direction or the other.

> (*Ep.* 70.11)

There is no general answer.[103] Thus careful consideration is always needed. Moreover the process of reasoning is itself particularly valuable. This is a key aspect of the contemplation of suicide which could be seen as, for Seneca, the most important philosophical exercise the would-be philosopher undertakes.[104]

Death and freedom

The ability to die bravely could, I suggested earlier, be seen as offering under the principate the prime manifestation of *virtus*, the quality which traditionally distinguished Rome's ruling elite under the republic. Stoic philosophy, at least as Seneca deploys it, provides a crucial medium for the reconfiguration of Roman *virtus*. A more explicitly political characteristic associated with the republic was freedom, *libertas*, understood particularly in the sense of freedom from domination.[105] For Seneca (and for Tacitus as we shall see later), death is also particularly associated with *libertas*. In Letter 24, Cato, on the point of taking his own life, is made to exclaim:

> 'Nihil', inquit, 'egisti, fortuna, omnibus conatibus meis obstando. Non pro mea adhuc sed pro patriae libertate pugnavi, nec agebam tanta pertinacia, ut liber, sed ut inter liberos viverem. Nunc quoniam deploratae sunt res generis humani, Cato deducatur in tutum.'

> 'O fortune,' he said, 'you have achieved nothing by impeding all my enterprises. Until this time, I fought not for my own liberty but for that of my fatherland, nor did I act with such persistence so that I might be free but so that I might live among the free. Now that our state has no future, let Cato be led to safety!'

> (*Ep.* 24.7)

Similarly Seneca has Jupiter in *De providentia* declare that Cato's sword can give him *libertatem, quam patriae non potuit*, 'the freedom it could not give his fatherland' (2.10).[106] Seneca's marked emphasis on the freedom suicide can offer could be read as a counter to the concerns of some Stoics, who concluded that 'if we are supposed to live according to nature, we should wait for nature to release us from life'.[107] Cato's death seems to have prompted an intense debate about the acceptability of suicide. For Brutus – approaching from an Academic perspective – Cato's suicide at first seemed not 'hosion', 'holy', though he seems later to have changed his view on this (Plut. *Brut*. 40.4). Thus Cato's end may ultimately have prompted Seneca's insistence on and elaboration of the relation between death and freedom.

The freedom death can offer is repeatedly stressed in the letters more generally. Death offers *libertas recedendi*, 'the freedom to withdraw' (22.5–6). Thus death is something to be valued rather than feared: *Mihi crede, Lucili, adeo mors timenda non est, ut beneficio eius nihil timendum sit*, 'Believe me, Lucilius, so little is death to be feared that, thanks to death, nothing is to be feared' (24.11). Letter 26 develops this idea at some length: *'meditare mortem'; qui hoc dicit, meditari libertatem iubet*, '"Think on death": one who says this instructs us to think on freedom' (26.10).[108] And Seneca criticises those philosophers who exclude the possibility of committing suicide: *hoc qui dicit, non videt se libertatis viam cludere*, 'One who says this does not see that he is shutting the gate to freedom' (70.14). The slightest of weapons will achieve this end: *scalpello aperitur ad illam magnam libertatem via et puncto securitas constat*, 'A small blade opens the way to great liberty and peace of mind can come through a pin prick' (70.16).

In Stoic philosophy, freedom ('eleutheria' in Greek, *libertas* in Latin) had come to have the sense of 'total independence of the person from all passions and from all wrong desires'.[109] Such an understanding of freedom could reinforce the appeal of death as a means of escape from any situation, no matter how oppressive. A key issue here must be agency.[110] The possibility of death guarantees the perpetual possibility of action, however constrained one's circumstances may be. As Seneca comments:

Qui mori didicit, servire dedidicit; supra omnem potentiam est, certe extra omnem. Quid ad illum carcer, et custodia, et claustra? Liberum ostium habet.

One who has learned to die has unlearned slavery. He is superior to all powers, and certainly beyond their reach. What to him are prison, guards and fetters? He has an open door.

(*Ep.* 26.10)

Here then is at least part of the value in thinking on death, in calculating and recalculating whether and for how long one's life may be worth living. Such exercises serve to keep the possibility of freedom forever before one's eyes.

At the same time there seems to be an ambivalence here, highlighted by Seneca's pervasive use of military imagery. At one point, Seneca comments with regard to the freedom offered by the possibility of suicide: *si pugnare non vultis, licet fugere*, 'if you do not want to fight, you can run away' (*Prov.* 6.7). This reveals a tension in Seneca's use of military metaphor – or perhaps rather in his thinking on suicide.[111] For the Socrates of Plato's *Phaedo*, suicide was no more to be contemplated than deserting one's guard post (62b).[112] Yet that seems to be just what Seneca is advocating in this passage from *De providentia*.

The most extreme – and notorious – formulation of Seneca's celebration of suicide comes in his treatise on anger, *De ira*. Seneca has been describing situations in which anger will inevitably arise and what the consequences might be of concealing or revealing it. Praexaspes has been punished for advising King Cambyses that he should moderate his drinking; the king demonstrates his steadiness of hand by shooting an arrow – through the heart of Praexaspes' son. Praexaspes praises the king's aim – he thus demonstrates that anger can be restrained under the most extreme provocation. Harpagus, the object of another king's cruelty, finds at the king's banquet that he has been served and has eaten the bodies of his own children. He too moderates his anger, flattering the monarch (*De ira* 3.14–15). While these stories purport to show that anger can always be concealed – ostensibly a good thing – they also reveal some profound difficulties for Seneca's position.[113] Ultimately he cannot bring himself to endorse the restraint of either Praexaspes or Harpagus. Praexaspes is a slave in mind, *animo…mancipium* (3.14.3). The gods should curse him. In relation to Harpagus, Seneca comments that he should try *quaerere dignam tam truci portento poenam*, 'to find a punishment worthy of such monstrous ferocity' (3.15.2).[114] For these men, urges Seneca, suicide by any means would surely be the best option. It is to them he offers this advice:

> Quocumque respexeris, ibi malorum finis est. Vides illum praecipitem locum? Illac ad libertatem descenditur. Vides illud mare, illud flumen, illum puteum? Libertas illic in imo sedet. Vides illam arborem brevem, retorridam, infelicem? Pendet inde libertas. Vides iugulum tuum, guttur tuum, cor tuum? Effugia servitutis sunt. Nimis tibi operosos exitus monstro et multum animi ac roboris exigentes? Quaeris quod sit ad libertatem iter? Quaelibet in corpore tuo vena!

Wherever you turn your gaze, there is an end to your troubles. Do you see that cliff? From there you can drop to freedom. Do you see that sea, that river, that well? Freedom lies in its depths. Do you see that stunted, twisted, barren tree? Freedom hangs from it. Do you see your throat, your gullet, your heart? They are the means to escape slavery. Are the ways out I'm showing you too troublesome? Do they require too much bravery, too much strength? Do you ask what may be the way to freedom? Any vein in your body!

(*De ira* 3.15.4)

Detachment, Seneca understands, is and should be impossible. He cannot quite bring himself to advocate any act of resistance to tyranny other than suicide; the individual cheats the tyrant of the pleasure of his murder – the most effective punishment he can devise.[115] Nevertheless the decision to withdraw from the world by deciding on suicide at the same time, motivated as it is by anger, constitutes the Stoic as one deeply implicated in the world and what happens in it. The limitation of suicide, however, is that it can never make the same kind of statement on behalf of social justice that could be conveyed by a more active kind of resistance, such as an attack on the king.[116]

Yet the act of choosing death could convey a specifically political message. To celebrate death as a means of escape is to undermine the power of a regime that seeks to control its subjects through the threat of lethal punishment. This political dimension is explicit in the Stoic Epictetus' discussion of suicide where keen students want to demonstrate by their own deaths that tyrants have power over no-one (1.9.15).[117] Seneca alludes to the general moral weakness which afflicts his contemporaries. Yet even now some show enough spirit to seek security in death:

Respice ad haec nostra tempora, de quorum languore ac deliciis querimur; omnis ordinis homines suggerent, omnis fortunae, omnis aetatis, qui mala sua morte praeciderint.

Think about our own times, whose inertia and fastidiousness we complain about. They will include persons of every rank, of every degree of fortune, of every age who have cut short their own trouble with death.

(*Ep.* 24.11)

It is interesting that Seneca does not, in the letters, refer explicitly to specific *exempla* from times closer to his own.[118] But this more general claim certainly adduces self-inflicted death as a means of displaying qualities opposed to the moral weakness exemplified by *languor* and *delicia*. The political overtones of *libertas* (with which Seneca so closely associates death) are never wholly absent.

In political terms, this is a kind of resistance but one which in some respects carries a heavy price.[119] In Seneca's writing we see what appears to be an increasingly extreme form of the Stoic depreciation of life. At 71.12, for instance, political change is, on one level, to be equated with the change of the seasons, something over which one has no control whatever, something which must simply be accepted. We may well feel uneasy at the implications of a philosophy which effectively discourages its adherents from taking any initiative to change a social order they find repugnant. And yet, once no choice was left, Stoicism, especially as developed in Seneca's writing, could offer a means to make sense of a horrible death, to appropriate it as part of a virtuous life. And even before death was imminent, to think over in advance how one might die was to prepare oneself against the worst, to assume an armour that might prove invincible. In Seneca's writing this acceptance of death could itself bring freedom, even if this *libertas* was very different from that enjoyed by earlier generations of Roman aristocrats.

Seneca is by no means an enthusiastic advocate of suicide under all circumstances. In Letter 24, having first referred to Epicurus' criticism of those *qui mortem concupiscent*, 'who desire death', Seneca himself explicitly criticises those who are obsessed with death. The brave and wise man should avoid that *libido moriendi*, 'longing for death', which has afflicted so many (24.25).[120] At the same time he also concedes that it is sometimes the noblest individuals who are overtaken by the desire for death. There is:

Ad moriendum inconsulta animi inclinatio, quae saepe generosos atque acerrimae indolis viros corripit, saepe ignavos iacentesque; illi contemnunt vitam, hi gravantur.

An unreflecting tendency towards death which often comes upon the noblest and most gifted men, and often upon the idle and abject. The former despise life, while the latter find it tedious.

(24.25)

While apparently condemning those who are simply tired of life, he expresses sympathy with those who despise it.[121] In Letter 30 which, beginning from the particular case of Bassus, discusses death in old age, Seneca praises the inspiration offered both by those who call for death – *qui deposcunt mortem* – and those who meet it in a state of calm and good cheer – *qui hilares eam quietique opperiuntur* (30.12). He goes on to qualify his praise for the former: *illud ex rabie interdum ac repentina indignatione fit*, 'this first attitude is sometimes derived from frenzy and sudden anger'. Yet this is not invariably the case, as *interdum* makes clear. Such statements seem to betray a profound ambivalence on Seneca's part.

This ambivalence needs to be seen in the context of a longstanding philosophical problem, which had been articulated by Plato in the *Phaedo*. Socrates, in this text, is made to depreciate at great length embodied life. The body is a hindrance in the search for wisdom (65a–b). Death by contrast opens up wonderful opportunities for the philosopher.[122] He seems to suggest, in other words, that being dead is always better than being alive.[123] A central concern of the dialogue is the claim that the proper practice of philosophy is preparation for death (63a–64b). 'Those who pursue philosophy properly study nothing but dying and being dead' (64a). Yet, at the same time, Socrates is made to express an explicit condemnation of suicide – unless one has received a divine sign (*Phaedo* 62c).[124] Some at least did read the *Phaedo* as advocating suicide. Cicero refers to Callimachus' epigram concerning Cleombrotos who *cum ei nihil accidisset adversi, e muro se in mare abiecisse lecto Platonis libro*, 'although nothing bad had happened to him, threw himself off a wall into the sea when he had read Plato's book' (*Tusc.* 1.84).[125] Rather Socrates in the *Phaedo* is best taken as arguing that no-one is ready to be released from their bodily concerns, until their soul has been properly prepared through the practice of philosophy. Then and only then will a divine sign sanction the soul's release.[126] To kill oneself before one's soul is ready is to lose the only possibility for self-improvement.[127]

Letter 24 echoes the *Phaedo* in its complaints about the burden imposed by the body (24.17, 25).[128] Seneca's Cato seems to read the *Phaedo* as endorsing suicide.[129] He equips himself with this book, *ut vellet mori* 'so that he might be willing to die', as well as with the sword, *ut posset* 'so that he might have the means' (24.6). The final, apparently inconclusive, paragraph also refers to the impulse toward suicide through *fastidium vitae*, 'distaste for life', an impulse exerted by philosophy itself: *ipsa inpellente philosophia* (24.26).[130] If the arguments of the *Phaedo* present suicide as unjustifiable, the text's heroisation of the dying Socrates, its focus on the physical detail of his death, could work to reinforce the increasing preoccupation of some Romans with dying as a sublime existential process.[131]

Even when circumstances are difficult, however, the option of dying is not always advocated in Seneca's work. In Letter 104 he writes of his wife's love for him, and of his concern for her. For her sake he must go on living:

Interdum, etiam si premunt causae, spiritus in honorem suorum vel cum tormento revocandus et in ipso ore retinendus est, cum bono viro vivendum sit non quamdiu iuvat sed quamdiu oportet. Ille qui non uxorem, non amicum tanti putat, ut diutius in vita commoretur, qui perseverabit mori, delicatus est.

Sometimes, even when good reasons are pressing, life's breath must be recalled and retained at our lips, though our suffering may be great, in honour of those we love, since a good man should live not as long as life is pleasurable, but as long as he ought. The man who does not value his wife or his friend enough to live a little longer but who persists in dying, he is a voluptuary.

(Ep. 104.3)

Here, as in Letter 24, Seneca seems to suggest there can be a kind of self-indulgent pleasure in choosing death which is to be disapproved of. The concern for his wife expressed here is at odds with the stereotype of the Stoic cut off from all human ties. A similar concern is articulated in Letter 78, immediately following Seneca's detailed consideration of brave ways to embrace death in Letter 77. Letter 78 begins with comments on his correspondent Lucilius' ill-health.[132] Seneca goes on to recall similar ailments which he claimed he himself suffered from in his younger days. At first he withstood these attacks:

Deinde succubui et eo perductus sum, ut ipse destillarem ad summam maciem deductus. Saepe impetum cepi abrumpendae vitae; patris me indulgentissimi senectus retinuit. Cogitavi enim non quam fortiter ego mori possem, sed quam ille fortiter desiderare non posset. Itaque imperavi mihi ut viverem. Aliquando enim et vivere fortiter facere est.

Then I succumbed and came to such a state that I was ebbing away, reduced to skin and bone. Often I took it in mind to break off my life. The old age of my most devoted father restrained me. For I considered not how bravely I could die but how he lacked bravery to endure my loss. And so I commanded myself to live. For sometimes it is a brave act to live.

(Ep. 78.1–2)

Seneca's endurance of illness is itself an act of bravery.[133] We might note the reappearance here of the verb *destillare*, used in Letter 24 to describe the hand of Mucius, consumed by the flames. Seneca himself was being consumed by disease. Yet even wrapped in his bed clothes he strove to forge himself into a fit *exemplum*. It is not only in facing death that one may show great heroism. This letter exhorts the ailing reader: in wrestling with disease *insigne prodis exemplum. O quam magna erat gloriae materia, si spectaremur aegri! Ipse te specta! Ipse te lauda!* 'You generate a noble example. O how great would be the scope for glory, if we had an audience for our sick-bed! Be your own audience! Provide your own applause!' (*Ep.* 78.20–1).[134] We may have to play the role of audience for ourselves, yet even when suffering from common ailments we may still aspire to join the glorious ranks of those whose bravery has exemplary power.[135]

But it is above all the prospect of one's own death which can and should be made into a spectacle – at least within the individual's own imagination. Seneca expresses great admiration for Aufidius Bassus who is suffering from a long-drawn-out illness and has death in view: *in conspectus mortem. Eo animo vultuque finem suum spectat, quo alienum spectare nimis securi putares,* 'he looked on his own imminent death with a disposition and expression which you would think too complacent if he were looking on the death of someone else' (*Ep.* 30.3). And if the would-be philosopher should prepare himself by reviewing in his imagination all the misfortunes that might befall him, it is his own death which he must above all contemplate (*Ep.* 70.8).[136]

The end justifies the means

Killing oneself under any circumstances may well have been disapproved of in some contexts in Roman society.[137] My study, which focuses primarily on the literary representation of death, inevitably concentrates on the attitudes of an educated elite, for whom, by and large, killing oneself was perceived as acceptable under certain circumstances. For the Elder Pliny, for instance, the possibility of suicide (*sibi mortem consciscere*) constitutes the greatest gift given to man amid life's sufferings, *optimum in tantis vitae poenis* (*NH* 2.5.27).

Considerable significance, however, is often attached to the particular means chosen. Starvation, *inedia*, appears to have been deemed especially appropriate for the elderly and ill, as in the case of Corellius Rufus (described in Pliny *Ep.* 1.12).[138] By contrast Tacitus tells of the disgraced Papinius, who throws himself from a window – *repentinum et informem exitum* – 'a hasty and unbecoming death' (*Ann.* 6.49.1). References to hanging from a wide range of authors suggest disapproval.[139] Virgil terms the noose *nodum informis leti,* 'the coil of unbecoming death' (*Aen.* 12.603).[140] Much later, the elder emperor Gordian's suicide by hanging is taken as an indication of his base character (SHA *Vita Maximi et Balbini* 4.3).[141] An inscription from Sassina in Umbria records the gift one Horatius Balbus made to the municipality of a public cemetery divided into individual plots. Excluded from burial here are contract gladiators, those who had hanged themselves and those who followed immoral professions for profit.[142] In this case, too, then, death by hanging attracts a particular stigma.

Some scholars have teased out a hierarchy of means by which one might take one's life, hanging, for instance, being associated with lower social status as well as moral weakness.[143] Intermediaries (including doctors) are often presented as playing a role in bringing about someone's death. In some cases, rendering this kind of assistance is seen as a demonstration of a slave's loyalty to his master.[144] By common consent the most prestigious and manly way to meet one's end was by means of a stab wound, preferably with a sword. Martial's use of the phrase *Romana mors*, a Roman death, to describe the suicide of the fatally ill Festus, suggests (as was noted in the Introduction) this was an established way of referring to death inflicted by a sharp weapon.

> Nec tamen obscuro pia polluit ora veneno
>> Aut torsit lenta tristia fata fame,
> Sanctam Romana vitam sed morte peregit
>> Dimisitque animam nobiliore rogo.

> But he did not defile his pure face with some exotic poison, nor did he drag out a miserable end with slow starvation. With a Roman death he made an end to his upright life and dispatched his spirit on a more noble pyre.

> (1.78.5–8)

What might have been a lingering, painful and disfiguring end is pre-empted but not by the slow means of poison or starvation. The superiority of Festus' method serves to align him with the noblest Roman heroes.[145]

Some texts betray a particular fascination with inventive suicides. This is the prime concern of Valerius Maximus in his section 9.12 *de mortibus non vulgaribus*, 'On distinguished deaths', which includes such ingenious approaches as swallowing live coals. Traces of this preoccupation may perhaps be detected in some of the passages of Seneca discussed above.[146] We have seen Seneca marshalling numerous Roman aristocratic heroes of the distant and more recent past. Yet in offering examples of how to find death when you need it, he adduces among his most vivid illustrations a number of conspicuously lowly figures. One important consequence of this approach is to deconstruct the hierarchy of methods:

> Exeat, qua impetum cepit; sive ferrum appetit sive laqueum sive aliquam potionem venas occupantem, pergat et vincula servitutis abrumpat.

Let the soul depart as it feels itself driven to go; whether it seeks the sword or the noose, or some poison that suffuses the veins, let it proceed and burst the bonds of its slavery.

(*Ep.* 70.12)

Here the means one chooses are a matter of personal choice. One should not be concerned about how other people may judge the method one uses. Among the most striking examples described in Letter 70 is that of a German who finds himself bound to fight wild beasts in the Roman arena.

Secessit ad exonerandum corpus; nullum aliud illi dabatur sine custode secretum. Ibi lignum id, quod ad emundanda obscena adhaerente spongia positum est, totum in gulam farsit et interclusis faucibus spiritum elisit.

He withdrew to relieve himself; for he was given no other opportunity to be without a guard. There he took the stick which was placed there with a sponge attached to clean people's private parts. This he stuffed right into his throat and, his windpipe blocked, drove out his life.

(70.20)

This most disgusting means of committing suicide is construed by Seneca as showing proper contempt for death.[147] *Hoc fuit morti contumeliam facere,* 'This was to insult death' (70.20). Death can be despised by the lowest of the low – *hanc rem etiam a contemptissimis posse contemni* (70.22). How much the more should those who have learned the lessons of philosophy be able to face death in the proper spirit. Here, too, the rehearsal in the mind of such scenes enhanced with memorably sordid detail can play an important role in the would-be philosopher's mental preparation for death.

A philosopher's death

The time will come when the would-be philosopher's preparedness is put to the test. In Letter 26 Seneca complains of the physical effects of old age, while expressing relief that his mind is so far unaffected by his advancing years (26.2). Yet death is on the horizon. Seneca reports that he addresses himself in the following terms.

Mors de te pronuntiatura est. Ita dico: disputationes et litterata conloquia et ex praeceptis sapientium verba collecta et eruditus sermo non ostendunt verum robur animi. Est enim oratio etiam timidissimis audax. Quid egeris, tunc apparebit, cum animam ages.

Death will give judgement on you. I say this: debates and erudite conversations and collected sayings from the precepts of philosophers do not reveal true strength of mind. Even the most fearful can make a brave speech. What you have achieved will be revealed at the moment when you send forth your spirit.

(*Ep.* 26.6)

Death is above all the moment at which individuals should be judged.[148] What judgements might be made in relation to the philosopher's own death?

Seneca, as he had anticipated, was offered an opportunity to put into practice the techniques he had been honing for so long, when he received the order to take his own life in 65 CE.[149] Tacitus, in his *Annals*, gives a lengthy description of Seneca's last hours (15.60–4). On the emperor's orders a deputation is sent to instruct Seneca that he is to kill himself, allegedly guilty of involvement in a conspiracy. Nero's centurion forbids Seneca to make changes to his will; Seneca urges his friends to take from him instead the pattern of his life, *imago vitae suae*. Exhorting his companions not to weep, he reminds them of *praecepta sapientiae*, 'the teachings of philosophy' and the *ratio*, 'right reason', *tot per annos meditata ... adversum imminentia*, 'contemplated for so many years in preparation for what lay ahead'. Nero's cruelty was only to be expected. He seeks, also, to console his wife Paulina but she, too, has chosen to kill herself.[150]

Eodem ictu brachia ferro exolvunt. Seneca, quoniam senile corpus et parco victu tenuatum lenta effugia sanguini praebebat, crurum quoque et poplitum venas abrumpit; saevisque cruciatibus defessus, ne dolore suo animum uxoris infringeret atque ipse visendo eius tormenta ad impatientiam delaberetur, suadit in alium cubiculum abscedere. Et novissimo quoque momento suppeditante eloquentia advocatis scriptoribus pleraque tradidit, quae in vulgus edita eius verbis invertere supersedeo ... Seneca interim, durante tractu et lenitudine mortis, Statium Annaeum, diu sibi amicitiae fide et arte medicinae probatum, orat provisum pridem venenum quo damnati publico Atheniensium iudicio extinguerentur promeret; adlatumque hausit frustra, frigidus iam artus et cluso corpore adversum vim veneni. Postremo stagnum calidae aquae introiit, respergens proximos servorum addita voce libare se liquorem illum Iovi liberatori. Exim balneo inlatus et vapore eius exanimatus sine ullo funeris sollemni crematur.

Each with one incision of the blade, the two of them cut their arms. But, his aged body spare from austere living, Seneca's blood flowed too slowly. So he also severed the veins in his ankles and behind his knees. Exhausted by severe pain, he was afraid of weakening his wife's fortitude by betraying his suffering, and that he himself, seeing her agonies, might fail in his endurance, so persuaded her to go to another chamber. Then, in his last moments, he summoned scribes and spoke at length (I see no need to adapt his words which have been published)...

Seneca's death was slow and lingering. He begged Statius Annaeus, a man whom for a long time he had trusted as both friend and doctor, to supply the poison, which had been earlier prepared, of the kind which was formerly used to execute state criminals in Athens. When it came, though, Seneca drank it without effect. For his limbs were already cold and his body numbed against the poison's action. Finally he was placed in a bath of warm water. He sprinkled a little of it on the nearest of the slaves, commenting that it was his libation to Jupiter the liberator. Then he was carried into a vapour bath, where he expired in the steam.

(Ann. 15.63.4–7, 64.3–5)

Tacitus' treatment of Seneca's own death reveals him rising commendably to the occasion for which he had so long prepared himself.[151] Seneca retains control throughout (while his concern for Paulina still shows him a man of feeling). It is he who consoles his friends at his own impending loss. In this Seneca's death echoes that of Socrates – as does his use of hemlock. In contrast to Socrates' easy death, however, Seneca's is long drawn out and acutely painful.[152] Seneca's death is protracted beyond any lesser man's endurance. Like Cato, he takes a long time to die and must make repeated efforts to drive the life from his lean but tough body. Even at the end he is able to formulate last words to communicate with a wider audience (words which Tacitus does not report). Such strength of will-power transforms death into a kind of sublime victory. Seneca's companions have the privilege of drawing inspiration from this most edifying of sights. They serve the crucial role of witnesses to the philosopher's calm as he confronts his end.

Seneca endures a painfully drawn-out end with philosophically inspired courage. He may not have chosen the moment of his death but he finds the resources to embrace it when it comes, to die willingly. Tacitus' account of Seneca's death has inevitably had a significant bearing, not always explicitly acknowledged, on the way readers have responded to Seneca's own voluminous writings on death.[153] Here, at least, he is judged no hypocrite. Seneca's death in a sense rewrites his life.[154] This death provides a final imprimatur on the *imago* Seneca offers his followers (*imaginem vitae suae* 'the image of his life' *Ann.* 15.62.1) – the *imago* already promised in Seneca's letters (*Ep.* 45.3).[155] There could be no more powerful endorsement for the truth and value of Seneca's philosophical writing. At the same time, however, this death scene is to a considerable degree the creation of the historian.[156] In the following chapters we shall consider the role of this and other deaths in Tacitus' own project.

CHAPTER 4

DEFIANCE, COMPLICITY AND THE POLITICS OF SELF-DESTRUCTION

Enforced suicides, such as that of Seneca, and other instances of self-killing have a key role to play in Tacitus' *Annals* and his *Histories*. Such deaths, in Tacitus' writing most strikingly, disclose the conflict between emperors and aristocrats at its most extreme. In this chapter we shall focus on the political significance of these violent aristocratic deaths. Killing oneself on the emperor's orders might seem an act of complicity, an acceptance, even legitimation of his power. Yet, in some cases at least, to take one's own life was construed as a potent criticism of the emperor. Telling details in ancient accounts seem to guide the reader's judgement on individual deaths, presenting us with a defiant hero in one instance or a pathetic victim in another. Yet the same death might be read in quite different ways. Seneca, in his treatise on tranquillity of mind, recounts the behaviour of Julius Canus, when his execution was ordered by Caligula. Canus gave thanks – an act that in some might have been read as a craven move to win clemency but in him, as his calmness in the face of execution later confirmed, was to be differently interpreted. But still there remained an element of ambiguity. These words, suggests Seneca, could be read as a comment on the emperor's cruelty, from which death would offer an escape, or as a reflection on his sanity in supposing genuine the expressions of gratitude he so often received from those whose children had been murdered or property confiscated, or merely as an indication that Canus accepted death as a fortunate escape (*Tranqu. an.* 14.4–6).[1] In this case, we might detect an element of double-speak on Canus' part, an attempt to communicate one message to the emperor and another to his peers.[2]

Roman writers seem to celebrate what is sometimes termed 'political suicide'. Yet they also reveal uneasiness at a form of political protest which might easily appear self-defeating. Those who kill themselves can be criticised for being too concerned with their own self-image. While the motives of those who take their own lives must ultimately remain opaque,

the fascination these deaths held for Roman elite authors and presumably
their readers is evident in much of the literature of the early principate. The
death of the individual can never be fully disentangled from the literary
context in which it is recorded. In Tacitus, above all, as we shall see, there is
an important sense in which this mass of aristocratic deaths must be viewed
as a kind of whole, one deftly manipulated by the historian.

The politics of Cato's death

Even if the motives of dying individuals remain elusive to a degree, earlier
events and their literary reworkings clearly exerted a significant influence.
In particular, it seems evident that from a political (as well as from a
philosophical) point of view, the memory of Cato's death played a role in
determining both how and when individuals chose to die and how others
responded to their deaths. Cato's suicide had offered him an honourable
escape from an impossible situation. A significant consequence of Cato's
death was that it deprived Caesar of the opportunity to exercise his much
vaunted clemency (Plutarch, *Life of the Younger Cato* 66). Indeed this was,
according to Plutarch, Cato's conscious intention in taking his own life;
Caesar was said to have been greatly angered at losing his chance to spare his
enemy: 'I begrudge you your death, as you begrudged me saving your life'
(Plut. *Cat. min.* 72.2).[3] As Paul Plass comments, analysing Roman political
suicide in terms of game theory: 'Cato's death is the paradigmatic case of
suicide as a move to protest repression coupled with a second move anticipating the countermove of *clementia*.'[4] Caesar himself was well aware of
the power of *clementia*. In a letter a few years earlier to Oppius and Balbus,
Caesar explained his clemency toward the defenders of Corfinium, captured
early in the civil war: *haec nova sit ratio vincendi, ut misericordia et liberal-
itate nos muniamus*, 'This is a new procedure of conquest, so we may fortify
ourselves with forgiveness and generosity' (Cic. *Att.* 9.7c.1). This clemency
does not merely replicate force but amplifies its effects.[5] The possibility of
clemency adds a further complexity to the pattern of aristocratic self-killing
as it develops under the descendants of Augustus and their successors.

Seneca, in his treatise on clemency (written under Nero), identifies this
virtue as one particular to rulers: *servavit quidem nemo nisi maior eo, quem
servabat*, 'No-one has saved a life who was not superior to the one he saved'
(*De clementia* 1.21.1).[6] He goes on to underline this point:

> In iis praesertim, quos scit aliquando sibi par fastigium obtinuisse, hoc
> arbitrium adeptus ultionem implevit perfecitque, quantum verae poenae
> satis erat; perdidit enim vitam, qui debet, et quisquis ex alto ad inimici

pedes abiectus alienam de capite regnoque sententiam expectavit, in
servatoris sui gloriam vivit plusque eius nomini confert incolumis, quam
si ex oculis ablatus esset. Adsiduum enim spectaculum alienae virtutis
est; in triumpho cito transisset.

In particular, if he obtains this power over those whose high position he
knows was at one time equal to his own, he has already had his fill of
revenge and completed what is the true punishment. For one who owes
his life to another has lost it. And whoever has been thrown down from
the height of success to the feet of his enemy and waited for a verdict on
his life and his kingdom from another, lives to the glory of the one who
preserves him and, safe, brings greater honour to his name than if he had
been removed from human sight. For he is a lasting spectacle of another
man's virtue; in a triumph he would have passed quickly by.

(*Clem.* 1.21.2)

Seneca urges his dedicatee Nero to aspire to this quality particular to a
princeps, to spare his opponents. But who would want the humiliation of
receiving such clemency?[7] It is hardly surprising Cato chose to deprive
his sometime equal Caesar of this opportunity to turn him into a living
reminder of Caesar's greatness.[8] Cato's suicide was in this respect a highly
effective move. At the end of the civil wars, Julius Caesar celebrated an
actual triumph, ostensibly marking his victory over foreign enemies. Yet in
his triumphal procession, Caesar included not only spoils from Gallic chief-
tains and foreign prisoners of war, but also images of his defeated Roman
opponents. According to Appian (*Bella civilia* 2.101), Caesar chose to parade
an image of Cato in the act of killing himself. In this context, the image of
Cato's suicide was being offered as evidence of his failure. Yet, in Appian's
account, the crowd reacted with grief at this display, unwilling to participate
in Caesar's gloating over his defeated compatriot. Caesar's attempt to appropriate Cato's spectacular countermove to his offer of *clementia* was a failure.
Cato's moral victory was publicly confirmed. Not only this but his suicide
was clearly recognised as – to adapt Seneca's formulation – a *spectaculum
suae virtutis*, 'a spectacle of his own virtue'.

Suicide, then, could function as a dramatically effective political statement,
serving above all to unmask the real distribution of power in Rome. This was
to give it a special potency in a society where the ruler claimed to be merely
the first among equals. Cato himself was to become a metonymy for *libertas*,
both philosophical (discussed above) and political.[9] The political dimension
of Cato's suicide would give it an especial force in relation to those whose
deaths were motivated directly or indirectly by their own political views.

Our main concern in this chapter will be the politics of aristocratic self-destruction after Cato – in the Rome of the early principate. Such is the prominence of self-killing in the literature of and about Rome of the first and second centuries CE that, for one historian: 'it is difficult to avoid thinking of suicide as the characteristic Roman way of death.'[10] The Romans had no word for suicide, as Tim Hill emphasises in his paradoxically entitled *Suicide and the Self*.[11] A variety of terms were employed for acts of self-killing, such as *voluntaria mors* or *mortem consciscere*. However, at least some of the phrases used – *exire* or *migrare e vita*, 'to leave' or 'depart from life', for instance – serve rather to obscure than to highlight the issue of agency. The same terms are used of individuals who are offered a 'free choice of death' as a punishment, following a criminal conviction, and of those who decide of their own volition to take their own lives. As we saw earlier, it is not especially helpful to separate out as a category those who choose to kill themselves.[12] We shall be concerned, then, with a broader notion of self-destruction, which can cover cases where an individual demonstrates some degree of acceptance in meeting a violent death, as well as those where an individual's actions could be construed as provoking a lethal response from the regime. Yet the model offered by Cato – who chose to kill himself – has a bearing on all of these deaths, as I hope to show.

It is, in the end, impossible to separate out events surrounding these deaths themselves from the representation of them – above all in the account of Tacitus. The complex and ambivalent treatment of these deaths in the *Annals* takes centre stage here. Seneca and other Roman writers, such as Valerius Maximus and Suetonius, have important things to say on this topic. The historian and senator Cassius Dio, in his narrative of Rome under the Julio-Claudians (written in the late second and early third century CE), highlights the high casualty rate among aristocrats.[13] 'Virtue was thought to be nothing else than dying nobly,' he comments on the aftermath of Scribonianus' alleged conspiracy against Claudius (Dio 60.16.7). But Dio, a Greek by education and culture, cannot fully comprehend the Roman preference for self-killing; for him forcing a man to kill himself seems worse than executing him (58.15).[14] So, while Dio and other authors will appear, this chapter will concentrate on Tacitus whose vivid, poignant and ironic account of so many deaths has captured the imagination of innumerable readers – and dominated historians' perceptions of this period.

Compulsion, compliance, choice

A number of situations might prompt an individual's self-killing.[15] Of central relevance in the century and a half after Cato's death, particularly from the time of Tiberius, is the Roman tradition of suicide as an alternative to judicial execution. The earliest instance of this apparently dates to 121 BCE; one of the followers of Gaius Gracchus was offered the choice of killing himself instead of being executed (Appian *BC* 1.26). Already at this date suicide could be considered preferable to execution. To be offered the possibility of suicide in place of execution was a recognition of the condemned individual's status. Those involved are almost invariably senators (though there is one recorded instance of a freedman of the emperor Augustus, Suet. *Aug.* 67.2). This offer then was a privilege (though it could also be a challenge which some may have regretted taking up; for Tacitus, the chaotic self-killing of Libo shows him in a poor light, *Ann.* 2.31).[16] Suicide could offer a relatively dignified end. The individual concerned had the opportunity to choose the method of death, to make a display of courage and self-control in the face of death, to die at home in the company of friends and relatives. All these facets of the 'free choice of death' were evidently valued by aristocratic Romans.[17]

A significant proportion of the suicides recorded as taking place in the first century CE are associated with accusations of treason, *maiestas*. Trials generally took place in the senate, in recognition of the status of the defendants. However, the procedures are often unclear and emperors do not seem to have been constrained by them when they considered themselves to be in immediate personal danger.[18] Tacitus and Dio are the main sources for these events (while Suetonius, Valerius Maximus and Seneca also refer to a number of cases). Both historians focus almost exclusively on trials involving members of the elite. They do not, however, always agree on whether an individual was condemned, executed or committed enforced suicide.[19]

A defendant, condemned to death, might take up the offer of *liberum mortis arbitrium*, a free choice of death. This phrase is used twice by Tacitus, at *Annals* 11.3.1 and, as *mortis arbitrium*, at *Annals* 16.33.2, and once by Suetonius in his life of Domitian (*Dom.* 11.3).[20] A large number of the deaths referred to by Tacitus and Dio fall into the category of 'free choice of death'. Such a death would generally be self-inflicted usually with a dagger or sword – thus, on one level at least, still a proper *Romana mors*.

Another category of suicides is often assimilated to this group, yet differs from it in crucial respects. Many individuals, again according to Tacitus and Dio, kill themselves when accused but not yet condemned. Gaius Silius, whose treason trial has been engineered by Sejanus, anticipates imminent conviction *voluntario fine*, 'with a self-inflicted death' (*Ann.* 4.19.4). Similarly, Mamercus Aemilius Scaurus, charged with adultery and magic, 'in a manner worthy of the Aemilii of old, anticipated his condemnation' *ut dignum veteribus Aemiliis, damnationem anteiit* (*Ann.* 6.29.7). Other examples include

Lucius Calpurnius Piso who terminates legal proceedings *ob mortem oppor-tunam*, 'on account of his timely death' (*Ann.* 4.21.4).[21] Women, too, might follow this course of action, for instance Aemilia Lepida, accused of adultery with a slave (*Ann.* 6.40.3).

This practice, also, had precedents in much earlier times; according to Livy, Quintus Fabius was thought to have taken his own life in the course of his trial in 389 BCE: *mors adeo opportuna ut voluntariam magna pars crederet*, 'this death was so timely that most people believed it to have been self-inflicted' (6.1.6–7).[22] These individuals could be seen as exercising a much more significant choice than those in the first category. The decision to die at this point might be read as an acknowledgement of guilt (in this sense it might be seen as parallel to the suicides of defeated generals discussed in Chapter 1). But it might also be read as an acceptance that condemnation was the only possible outcome in a trial which offered a mere charade of justice. The ambiguity of such deaths will be explored further below.

A third category of suicides appears in reaction to accusations which are merely rumoured as forthcoming. The Iunii Blaesi, for instance, on discov-ering the priesthoods they had expected from the emperor had been granted to others, took this as a 'sign of death' *signum mortis* and 'killed themselves' *voluntario exitu*, according to Tacitus (*Ann.* 6.40.3) – their connection with the now disgraced Sejanus no doubt disposing them to a pessimistic reading of the emperor's action.[23] This is one of many instances of aristocrats struggling to interpret signals from the emperor.[24] The ambiguity of such instructions itself constituted part of the apparatus of terror through which the emperors of Roman historiography sought to control members of the elite.[25] Anecdotes of this kind prompt Roland Barthes' reflection 'all these murders have scarcely any causes'.[26] At the same time, we need to be aware that elliptical references in ancient texts are hardly reliable. According to Tacitus, Thrasea Paetus, having fallen out of favour with Nero, was banned from visiting the imperial family at Antium to celebrate the birth of the emperor's daughter. This was *praenuntiam imminentis caedis contumeliam*, 'a snub which portended his looming death' (Tac. *Ann.* 15.23.4). 'Though Thrasea was not forced to kill himself until later, by telescoping the first sign of Nero's displeasure into an "indication of imminent death" ... Tacitus brings out a conjunction that is perfectly real on one political plane by means of another that is factually false,' comments Plass.[27] It is clear that while some of these deaths are institutionally required – the outcome of a legal process – others are not. Yet historians, most particularly Tacitus, often assimilate them. Why might this be?

Rewarding suicide

The reasons so many aristocratic Romans should have chosen to kill themselves are complex. As we have seen in earlier chapters, under many circumstances to take one's own life was an act which could be seen as justifiable, a means to atone for wrong-doing or error, to escape from an impossible situation. For Romans, to kill oneself might paradoxically function as an act of self-constitution. The salvaging of honour is regularly perceived as a significant motive for taking one's own life when on trial. Pliny, for instance, describes his contemporary Classicus, who died, perhaps by his own hand, before the conclusion of his trial, as having 'fled the shame of condemnation through death', *pudorem damnationis morte fugisse* (*Ep.* 3.9.5).

The relative lack of stigma, indeed the positive value, which might be associated with self-killing is also apparent in the provisions of Roman law. Killing oneself, under most circumstances, was treated as acceptable (though traces of disapproval are evident in the comments of some jurists). Legal writings seem to present self-killing as an unexceptionable response to, for instance, indebtedness, *pudore aeris alieni* (*Digest of Justinian* 49.14.45.2). Provided that the act is not evidence or proof of criminal conscience, the law is not concerned with it. Indeed, in the first century CE there were some significant material incentives to suicide for aristocratic defendants. Some allegedly hoped that their convenient suicides would placate the emperor's annoyance and thereby help safeguard surviving family members. The would-be usurper Piso, for example, anxious to protect his wife, is reported to have killed himself for this reason (Tac. *Ann.* 15.59.5).[28]

In later periods, suicide under some circumstances might itself be taken as an admission of guilt, thus leaving the defendant's property forfeit to the imperial treasury (if the alleged crime was one normally punished with the confiscation of property) (*Dig.* 49.14.45.2).[29] At least until the time of Tiberius, however, those who killed themselves before they were actually condemned did not suffer the confiscation of property and denial of burial rights, which would follow execution. Valerius Maximus records an earlier instance of such a death. In the case of C. Licinius Macer, a contemporary of Cicero:

Repetundarum reus, dum sententiae diriberentur, in maenianum conscendit: si quidem, cum M. Ciceronem, qui id iudicium cogebat, prae-textam ponentem vidisset, misit ad eum qui diceret se non damnatum sed reum perisse, nec sua bona hastae posse subici, ac protinus, sudario, quod foret in manu habebat, ore et faucibus suis coartatis, incluso

spiritu poenam morte praecucurrit. Qua cognita re Cicero de eo nihil
pronuntiavit.

On trial for extortion, while the votes were being sorted, he went up to the
balcony. When he saw Marcus Cicero, who was presiding over the court,
remove his magistrate's robe he sent a messenger to report that he had
died not as a condemned man but as a defendant and his property would
not be publicly auctioned. Then he pressed the handkerchief he happened
to have in his hand against his mouth and throat and stopped breathing,
thus dying before sentence had been declared. When Cicero learned this,
he pronounced no verdict.

(Val. Max. 9.12.7)

Thus, comments Valerius, his son the distinguished orator Calvus was saved
from poverty as well as the shame of a conviction in the family. For Valerius,
this is a brave death, *fortis mors* (9.12.8) – if one whose special interest lies
in the bizarre form of self-suffocation deployed by Macer. The anecdote
underlines, also, the devastating financial impact a conviction could have
on the heirs of the defendant.[30]

Tacitus, in his account of events under Tiberius, suggests the reason
many aristocratic defendants killed themselves before sentence had been
passed was at least in part the desire to protect their property.[31]

At Romae caede continua Pomponius Labeo, quem praefuisse Moesiae
rettuli, per abruptas venas sanguinem effudit: aemulataque est coniunx
Paxaea. Nam promptas eius modi mortes metus carnificis faciebat,
et quia damnati publicatis bonis sepultura prohibebantur, eorum qui
de se statuebant humabantur corpora, manebant testamenta, pretium
festinandi.

In Rome the slaughter was continuous. Pomponius Labeo, who, as I
recorded, had been governor of Moesia, slit his veins and bled to death.
His wife Paxaea followed his example. For fear of the executioner made
people quick to choose this way of death, as well as the consideration
that those who were condemned had their property confiscated and were
denied burial, while those who decided for themselves received burial and
had their wills respected – the reward for alacrity.

(Tac. *Ann.* 6.29.1–2)

As often, Tacitus' use of generalisation hints at a widespread phenomenon,
a hint scarcely supported by numerous examples. In this case, Tacitus
has Tiberius insist that Labeo was only to be tried for provincial

maladministration, the punishment for which was exile, and thus the defendant takes responsibility for his own death – and that of his wife. Dio (58.15) comments that, for the accusers and the emperor, such suicides were preferable since blood-guilt was thereby avoided; an element of uncertainty would always remain.[32] Exceptions to the rule, of course, might always be made: a central characteristic of this imperial system is precisely its unpredictability.[33] According to Tacitus, although Gaius Silius anticipated condemnation by suicide *voluntario fine* his property was confiscated nevertheless (*Ann.* 4.20.1). Similarly, when Libo commits suicide partway through his trial, his property is divided among his accusers (*Ann.* 2.32.1).[34]

The degree to which these prescriptions were later subject to alteration remains unclear. References in the *Digest* suggest that the circumstances under which suicide might safeguard a defendant's property were the subject of continuing legal debate. A passage from the *Digest* already referred to comments further that the property of a defendant is not confiscated if an individual commits suicide for the following reasons: *taedium vitae, pudore aeris alieni vel valitudinis alicuius inpatientia*, 'tiredness of life, or from shame over a debt, or from inability to bear some illness' (*Dig.* 49.14.45.2).[35] However, the onus was on the heirs of the defendant to prove such a cause. It is unsurprising, given the financial benefits at stake, that there seems to have been a shift toward seeing suicide as, *prima facie*, an admission of guilt on the part of a defendant (though suicide could still preserve property if the trial had not yet started).[36] However, it remains unclear at what point defendants were effectively deprived of the opportunity to protect their property by taking their own lives, though by the time of Antoninus Pius (at the latest) suicide was taken as equivalent to confession (*Dig.* 48.21.3.1).[37]

The protocol of political suicide

Ancient accounts, particularly that of Tacitus, allow us to distinguish three categories of 'suicide' associated more or less directly with the repeated trials for *maiestas*. There is a sense, I suggested earlier, in which all these deaths are on some level assimilated to the model offered by the death of Cato. But it is helpful here to identify strong and weak versions of the Catonian model. The weak version would stress Cato's calm and dignity as he planned the deed, his bravery and his persistence in attaining death. Numerous invocations of Cato in later texts are especially concerned with his endurance of pain and contempt for death – a preoccupation which could indeed serve to divert attention from the more specifically political dimension of his suicide.[38] As we have seen, Cato might be invoked as an inspiration by anyone facing death. The bravery of Cato's death implicitly informs the death of Tullius

Marcellinus (as described in Seneca's letters), who chooses to kill himself when faced with incurable illness.[39] This aspect of the Catonian model is relevant to all those described as meeting a violent death bravely, whether self-inflicted or not.

There is a measure of redemption in any brave death.[40] Sempronius Gracchus, for instance, a man of noble family but undistinguished life, already in exile for some years (convicted of adultery with Augustus' daughter Julia) is, following Julia's death, to be killed on the orders of Tiberius by a posse of soldiers, Tacitus writes. He asks for a few moments to say goodbye to his wife then offers the soldiers his neck: *constantia mortis haud indignus Sempronio nomine: vita degeneraverat*, 'in the endurance with which he met death not unworthy of his family name, even though in life he had failed to emulate his forebears' (*Ann.* 1.53.8). No matter of principle is at stake here.[41] Yet that word *constantia*, one which repeatedly appears in accounts of Cato's end, lends a Catonian dignity even to the death of this decadent aristocrat.

The strong version of the Catonian model, however, would emphasise an element of choice. A significant number of the individuals whose violent deaths are described or referred to by Tacitus (and other authors) could be seen as having provoked the emperor's action against them. This is notably true of Thrasea Paetus and Barea Soranus, who had offered criticisms of the emperor. It is perhaps also true of Seneca and true too of Helvidius Priscus executed under Vespasian (in the version offered by Epictetus, at any rate).[42] The association of these individuals with Stoic philosophy is certainly relevant; at the very least their philosophical views give them a place from which to speak, help them confront the dangers they run in articulating unwelcome truths to tyrannous rulers.[43] But we could also include in this category others who died in the aftermath of failed conspiracy attempts (such as the company commander Sulpicius Asper, whose bravery in the face of execution offers *constantiae exemplum*, 'an example of endurance', *Ann.* 15.68.1). For Romans the parallel between Cato (who chose to kill himself) and Thrasea (forced to kill himself) and Barea Soranus (executed) was an important one.[44] Agency, in the sense of who did the deed, is of little significance in this context. There is also significant slippage between weak and strong versions of the Catonian model. If all these aristocrats are on some level analogous to Cato, then the emperors under whom they die are, in their turn, cast in the role of Caesar. And all their deaths can be made to carry a political charge.

Many of those who died may well have intended that their ends should be read as commenting on the regime. The idea that an individual's self-inflicted death might be specifically intended to make a point is even to be found enshrined in Roman law. If an accused person chooses to take his own life, his will is still valid, if the act is not an acknowledgement of guilt but motivated rather by weariness of life or the pain of illness, as we have already seen. One passage from the legal commentator Ulpian, writing in the early third century CE, adds to these acceptable motives that of *iactatio*, making a gesture, *ut quidam philosophi*, 'as some philosophers do' (*Dig.* 28.3.6.7).

A number of individual suicides are explicitly described as stirring up *invidia* against the emperor.[45] On one level, suicide might be contrived by the dying individual to look like murder. When Piso, suspected of murdering Tiberius' nephew Germanicus (perhaps as the agent of Tiberius himself), is found dead in prison without a suicide note, rumours circulate that he had actually been executed (*Ann.* 3.16.1). Tacitus has Tiberius complain to the senate that the manner of Piso's death had been calculated to discredit him, *suam invidiam tali morte quaesitam* (3.16.3). Other suicides could also be read as offering a political comment on the emperor. Tiberius is made to express anxiety that the death of his friend Nerva might be so interpreted: *grave conscientiae, grave famae suae, si proximus amicorum nullis moriendi rationibus vitam fugeret*, 'it was a serious blow to his own peace of mind, and to his reputation, if one of his closest friends, having no reason to die, should make an exit from life' (*Ann.* 6.26.1–2).[46] Again Tiberius, with breath-takingly perverse logic, treats Labeo's suicide as malicious, a strategy on the part of the dead man to conceal his real offence – provincial maladminis-tration – by implying he was being persecuted with treason charges (*Ann.* 6.29.2).

Some individuals, resolved on suicide, took full advantage of the freedom of speech offered by imminent death to impugn the emperor. A distin-guished woman, Mallonia, having refused to submit to Tiberius' sexual demands is put on trial but leaves the court room, goes home and stabs herself, *obscaenitate oris hirsute atque olido seni clare exprobrata* 'publicly condemning the hairy stinking old man and his obscenely filthy mouth' (Suet. *Tib.* 45). Instances of emperors seeking to prevent suicides can be read as attempts to forestall such ill-feeling.[47]

At the same time, however, refusing to commit suicide could also work as a strategy to unveil the violence of the regime. When Lucius Silanus, already in exile, is visited by Nero's executioners, he refuses to cooperate.

Illic indignissimum casum sapienter tolerans a centurione ad caedem misso corripitur; saudentique venas abrumpere animum quidem morti destinatum ait, sed non remittere percussori gloriam ministerii. At centurio quamvi inermem praevalidum tamen et irae quam timori propiorem cernens premi a militibus iubet. Nec omisit Silanus obniti

et intendere ictus, quantum manibus nudis valebat, donec a centurione
vulneribus adversis tamquam in pugna caderet.

There, as he endured his entirely undeserved misfortune with philosophical calm, he was seized by a centurion, who had been sent to procure
his death. When the centurion advised him to sever his veins, he replied
that his mind was indeed prepared for death but he would not excuse his
assassin his noble office. However the centurion, perceiving that though
unarmed he was very strong and more inclined to anger than to fear,
gave orders that he be overpowered by the soldiers. Nor did Silanus fail
to resist, laying as many blows as his bare hands allowed until he was laid
low by the centurion, his wounds on his front, as if in battle.

(Tac. *Ann.* 16.9.3–5)

Silanus' resistance reveals no fear of death, as the centurion himself recognises. Rather this is a moment which, if briefly, discloses the raw violence
underlying the regime's authority. A refusal to commit suicide on order
invites execution, thus revealing the true signficance of such a 'suicide'.[48]
Silanus meets a glorious death. He dies as if in battle. His wounds are noble
ones, which serve to align him with Rome's tradition of brave warriors. Only
this time the enemy is Rome's own ruler, the emperor.

One move open to emperors, in the wake of a problematic suicide on
the part of an aristocratic defendant, was to make a retrospective offer of
clementia – invoking the tradition initiated by Julius Caesar. Decimus Junius
Silanus Torquatus, accused of imperial ambitions and foreseeing his own
condemnation, chose to kill himself.

Secutaque Neronis oratio ex more, quamvis sontem et defensioni merito
diffisum victurum tamen fuisse si clementiam iudicis expectasset.

The usual speech from Nero followed: although the man was guilty and
justifiably distrusted he would nevertheless have lived, had he waited for
the judge's mercy.

(*Ann.* 15.35.3)

The emperor laments being deprived of the chance to exercise *clementia* –
and thereby exonerates himself of any guilt for the death. But of course such
a retrospective offer can be never wholly convincing, neatly undermined in
advance as it is by its intended beneficiary/victim.[49]

Paul Plass's analysis of political suicide (he includes 'forced suicides' here
as well as volitional ones), offering penetrating and suggestive accounts
of individual anecdotes, applies game theory to tease out the rules of the

system and the strategies deployed by emperors and their victims.[50] On this model political suicide comes to function as an institution, brought into play from time to time, which works to express the ongoing relations of political power.[51] The practice of suicide is, for Plass, 'shaped by the kind of involuted implicit rules of the kind that governed gift exchange, where meeting obligations could be an insult or clemency where restraint could be aggression'.[52] There is a system here but one which has ambiguity as a central feature – a persuasive and elegant analysis often very much in tune with the grim humour of Tacitus' *Annals*. Nevertheless we might still wonder how far the individuals concerned were aware of themselves as players in this game.

Self-destruction and social ambition

We cannot know how many will have seen their own deaths as an act of political protest. Certainly as an instrument of protest, these deaths could all too easily seem politically futile. Indeed such deaths might even serve to reinforce the emperor's power. Those who conspicuously reject the imperial system can be seen as inviting the emperor's violence, thereby reinforcing the system.[53] Tacitus himself has been read as expressing significant reservations about the value of such deaths. His *Agricola*, a biography of his father-in-law, seems to criticise those who aim for glory through a dramatic end, *ambitiosa mors*. Agricola's career, by contrast, offers a far more satisfactory model for the behaviour of a good senator in bad times, he claims. Agricola's *gloria*, derived from traditional military activities, does put him in danger but his discreet behaviour minimises its impact; he chooses to turn down a prestigious proconsulship (*Agr.* 41). Thus the emperor Domitian:

> moderatione tamen prudentiaque Agricolae leniebatur, quia non contu-macia neque inani iactatione libertatis famam fatumque provocabat. Sciant, quibus moris est inlicita mirari, posse etiam sub malis principibus magnos viros esse, obsequiumque ac modestiam, si industria ac vigor adsint, eo laudis excedere, quo plerique per abrupta sed in nullum rei publicae usum ambitiosa morte inclaruerunt.

> ... was mollified by Agricola's moderation and discretion. Agricola was not in the habit of courting renown and ruin by defiance and a fatuous parade of independence. Those whose habit is to admire what is forbidden should know that men can be great even under bad emperors, and that duty and discretion, if accompanied by energy and an active career, will

bring a man to no less glorious heights than are attained by perilous paths and ostentatious deaths that bring no benefit to the commonwealth.

(*Agr.* 42.3–4)

This passage is unusual in offering a general comment on the phenomenon of conspicuous aristocratic death – and also in expressing disapproval of such ends. Such deaths bring *nullum rei publicae usum*, 'no benefit to the commonwealth' (*Agr.* 42.4). Indeed they may be construed as paradoxically self-serving. They are merely manifestations of *inani iactatione libertatis*, 'the fatuous parade of independence', admired by some, at least, purely because it is forbidden. The adjective *ambitiosa*, connected as it is with the canvassing activities of political candidates, could be read as highlighting the specifically political overtones of such a death, while also suggesting a degree of self-aggrandisement.[54]

A self-inflicted death was often, as we have seen, felt to be more in keeping with aristocratic dignity than an execution. It could serve as a dramatic affirmation of the individual's incontrovertible commitment to traditional senatorial values. Seneca, also, as we saw, and Martial (to be discussed below) suggest dramatic self-destruction may be, on one level, an easy option for those who want to stake a claim to senatorial *virtus*. Such acts could derive from too crude a grasp of ethical behaviour.[55] Certainly they contributed little to preserving the position of the senate itself.[56] Self-destruction should not be seen as the only option for a man of virtue.[57] We must of course remember, however, that Tacitus' assertions here are determined at least in part by the specific agenda of his monograph, the biography of the author's father-in-law, whose career flourished even under a supposedly bad emperor.

And it remains the case that for many ancient writers – Tacitus, Seneca and others too – in at least some circumstances, a brave death might constitute a genuine, legitimate and laudable means to vindicate one's freedom. Dio attributes a comment to Thrasea:

'If it were only me Nero was going to put to death, I could readily forgive the others their excessive flatteries. But even of those who load him with praise he has killed many and will destroy many more. Why should one degrade oneself to no avail then die like a slave, when one could pay nature's debt dying like a free man?'

(62.15.3)

The phrase *liberum mortis arbitrium* – the choice of means to die offered to condemned aristocrats such as Thrasea – can be read simply as the choice

of death worthy of a free man. This was indeed itself a privilege for aristocratic Romans. Yet Tacitus' use of it also exploits the phrase's potential for
rich irony.[58] Part of the power of Tacitus' narrative in the *Annals* above all
lies in its capacity to articulate the contradictions, slippages, paradoxes
– the distortion of language which constitutes the essence of the principate.
Tacitus is painfully alert to the ironies of aristocratic self-destruction. Yet,
as the latter part of this chapter will argue, there is also a sense in which he,
too, is deeply in thrall to the ultimate spectacle of virtue offered by a truly
Roman death.

Senatorial slaughter

A prominent individual may have the power to use his or her death to
criticise the emperor, taking advantage of the freedom of speech only
imminent death can offer, but perhaps the real stimulus to *invidia* against
the emperor is the cumulative power of all these deaths, stacked up by the
historian. Notoriously Tacitus creates the impression that the senatorial
aristocracy is slaughtered, first under Tiberius and then under his successors.
The exact number of deaths he refers to in the *Annals* is not easy to
determine.[59] Tacitus' narrative assimilates executions and suicides. Treason
trials function as the prime symbol of Tiberius' tyranny, even though
Tacitus' own narrative has Tiberius protest at the charges and the accused
are not infrequently acquitted.[60]

In a digression on the nature of his historiographical project, Tacitus
writes:

> Nos saeva iussa, continuas accusationes, fallaces amicitias, perniciem
> innocentium et easdem exitii causas coniungimus, obvia rerum simili-
> tudine et satietate.

> Our subject is a litany of savage orders, ceaseless accusations, false
> friendships, the destruction of innocent people and their deaths, matter
> repugnant for its cloying monotony.

> (Tac. *Ann.* 4.33.3)

There are no gaps between these dreadful events. Tacitus describes the fall of
those associated with Sejanus, presenting the victims as too many to count.

> Inritatusque suppliciis cunctos, qui carcere attinebantur accusati societatis
> cum Seiano, necari iubet. Iacuit immensa strages, omnis sexus, omnis
> aetas, inlustris ignobiles, dispersi aut aggerati.

Provoked by the entreaties he gave orders that all those who were being
held in custody accused of association with Sejanus be put to death. With
no distinction of age or sex, both grand and humble, scattered or piled in
heaps the mass of victims lay.

(*Ann.* 6.19.2–3)

The terms used here are reminiscent of those used in relation to the sack of
cities in war – striking imagery whose significance we shall come back to. A
few chapters later similar terminology reinforces the effect: *At Romae caede
continua*, 'At Rome the massacre was continuous' (*Ann.* 6.29.1).[61]

Yet (after the missing books recounting events under Caligula) under
Claudius things go from bad to worse. Valerius Asiaticus, offered *liberum
mortis arbitrium* by the emperor Claudius, is made to comment that he
would rather have died by the wiles of Tiberius or the violence of Gaius than
by the intrigues of a woman (meaning Messalina) and Vitellius' obscene
tongue (*Ann.* 11.3). Tacitus' narrative returns insistently to the violent deaths
of members of the Roman elite. In particular, in the wake of the conspiracy
to replace Nero with the aristocrat Piso, executions now abounded: *sed
compleri interim urbs funeribus, Capitolium victimis*, 'the city was filled with
funerals, the Capitol with sacrificial victims' (*Ann.* 15.71.1). The remaining
part of the *Annals* is entirely dominated by aristocratic deaths.

A similar preoccupation in relation to aristocratic deaths under Domitian
is manifested in Tacitus' earlier work. One benefit of Agricola's early death
is that:

Evasisse postremum illud tempus, quo Domitianus non iam per intervalla
ac spiramenta temporum, sed continuo et velut uno ictu rem publicam
exhausit.

He had missed that final period, when Domitian, no longer at intervals
and with pauses for breath, but in a continuous and as it were single
attack drained the blood of the commonwealth.

(*Agr.* 44.5)

As scholars have noted, the individuals who died under Domitian do
not seem to have been many.[62] But again things have allegedly gone from
bad to worse. A comment in the *Agricola* compares Nero and Domitian:
*Nero tamen subtraxit oculos suos iussitque scelera, non spectavit: praecipua
sub Domitiano miseriarum pars erat videre et aspici, cum suspiria nostra
subscriberentur*, 'Nero at least withdrew his gaze: he ordered crimes, but
did not observe them. A distinctive part of the suffering under Domitian

was to see him watching us, with even our sighs being noted against us' (*Agr.* 45.2). The *Histories*, too, written before the *Annals* but treating the period afterwards, seem to have had (in the lost portions covering the reign of Domitian) a similar emphasis on the deaths of Domitian's victims.[63]

At *Annals* 4.33 Tacitus contrasted his own material with the traditional subject matter of annalistic history.[64] This contrast reappears in Book 16. Again Tacitus offers an apology for the monotonous nature of his subject matter:

> Etiam si bella externa et obitas pro re publica mortis tanta casuum similitudine memorarem, meque ipsum satias cepisset aliorumque taedium expectarem, quamvis honestos civium exitus, tristis tamen et continuos aspernantium: at nunc patientia servilis tantumque sanguinis domi perditum fatigant animum et maestitia restringunt. Neque aliam defensionem ab iis quibus ista noscentur exegerim quam ne oderim tam segniter pereuntis. Ira illa numinum in res Romanas fuit, quam non, ut in cladibus exercituum aut captivitate urbium, semel edito transire licet. Detur hoc inlustrium virorum posteritati, ut quo modo exequiis a promisca sepultura separantur, ita in traditione supremorum accipiant habeantque propriam memoriam.

> Even if it were foreign wars and deaths encountered for the sake of the republic I was recording with such monotonous detail, I would myself feel surfeited and would anticipate boredom from others, put off by relentlessly tragic material even in the case of the noble deaths of citizens. As it is, slavish passivity and the quantity of blood spilt far from military service exhaust the spirit and weigh it down with grief. Nor can I offer any other defence for those who are remembered thus but that I should not reject those who perished so wretchedly. The cause was heaven's anger against Rome – and not a single outburst to be mentioned once, as when armies are defeated or cities captured. Let this concession be granted to the reputation of distinguished men, that, just as in the manner of their burial they are marked out from the common herd, so too in the recording of their deaths, let each receive separate and enduring record.
>
> (*Ann.* 16.16)

In this passage, Tacitus again uses the term *similitudine*, 'monotonousness', to characterise his own work, as he had done in *Annals* 4.33. The repetitive nature of such subject matter must bore readers. Tacitus claims to separate out deaths, give each his due. Yet outbursts of this kind, we might note, seem to lump together deaths as diverse as the bodged suicide under compulsion

of Libo, the brave suicide under compulsion of the adulterer Sempronius
Gracchus, the apparently unmotivated suicide of Tiberius' friend Nerva,
the execution of Barea Soranus – and the noble, philosophically inspired
suicides of Seneca and Thrasea Paetus. Despite the oppressiveness of the
seemingly endless succession of endings, the infinite varieties of courage
(or its absence) described in the death narratives reveal above all the
unparalleled skill of the historian.[65]

In this passage, as in 4.33, Tacitus appears to draw a sharp distinction
between the foreign wars and noble ends which constitute the proper subject
matter of history and the wretched deaths which he himself must describe.
The contrast Tacitus offers between the traditional content of historiography
and his own project can be seen as a 'technique of claiming to pervert
generic convention in order to do justice to abnormal events'.[66] Tacitus'
history in fact does conform to these generic rules but in a more subtle way.
The narrative of the second half of Tiberius' reign can be read as including
metaphorical equivalents of all those elements which Tacitus claimed were
missing: geographical descriptions, battle scenes and the deaths of famous
men.[67] The *urbs capta* motif which, as we saw, Tacitus invokes in recounting
the deaths of the associates of Sejanus, recurs elsewhere too.[68] The war then
is one between the emperor and the Roman people, but most particularly
the Roman elite. Clearly such a claim serves to indict Rome's emperors. But
what do these deaths say about their victims?

As we have seen in earlier chapters, Roman literature of the republican
period is in many ways less concerned with a virtuous death – particularly as regards death in battle – than is Greek literature. It is under the
principate that a glorious death becomes the only means by which Roman
aristocrats can demonstrate their virtue.[69] At least Romans still know how
to die. Writing of the civil war period following the death of Nero, Tacitus
comments: *supremae clarorum virorum necessitates fortiter toleratae et
laudatis antiquorum mortibus pares exitus*, 'Distinguished men bravely
facing the utmost straits and matching in their ends the famous deaths of
older times' (Tac. *Hist*. 1.3). Tacitus assimilates the struggle between emperor
and senate to warfare. This imagery is to be found in the later Neronian
books as well as Tacitus' account of the second half of Tiberius' reign. Some
of those who are prosecuted in the wake of the Pisonian conspiracy are exiled
velut in agmen et numerum, 'as though to complete the troop and number',
15.71.10 (the terms also serving to emphasise their quantity).[70] The dying
Lucan figures himself as a wounded soldier (*Ann*. 15.70). Nero summons the
senate as if he were going to announce a military victory, *quasi bello gesta
expositurus* (*Ann*. 15.72.1). The execution of Lucius Silanus, discussed above,
figures him as a soldier receiving fatal wounds in battle (*Ann*. 16.9.2).[71]

Tacitus' use of the imagery of civil war in the *Annals* serves to document a collapse of morality, a perversion of law under Rome's emperors very similar to those characterising the episodes of stasis described by Thucydides and Sallust. It is highly likely that such imagery draws on the political invective of the late republic.[72] Issues of morality are never straightforward in Roman accounts of civil war. Yet by elevating the conflict between emperor and senate into a war (even a civil war) a kind of nobility is conferred on those who lose their lives in the struggle. Indeed, as we saw earlier, a noble death takes on a particular value in civil war, when surviving the conflict – and of course prevailing in it – is inevitably compromising.

Tacitus claims his subject matter is *inglorius* (4.32.2). At 16.16 the aristocratic deaths which have come to dominate the narrative are themselves presented as miserable ones – *tam segniter pereuntis*, 'those who die so wretchedly'. The elite is characterised by *patientia servilis*, 'slave-like submission'. Yet *gloria* constitutes a significant outcome of at least some deaths in *Annals*. Silanus, who manages to die a soldier's death in peacetime, is made to refer to the *gloria* of the assassin's task – ironically of course. By implication it is Silanus himself who emerges with true *gloria*. *Gloria* is repeatedly associated with the death of Thrasea Paetus, which occurs just as the manuscript of the *Annals* breaks off. Indeed in the *Histories* he had been termed *exemplar verae gloriae*, 'a model of true glory' (2.91.3).[73] And at *Annals* 4.35 Tacitus describes the trial of Cremutius Cordus (which prompts his suicide) as an act of repression which generates *gloria* for the victim.

Writing death

Intimately connected with the incidence of high-profile deaths is the practice of writing about them, as I have been trying to emphasise. Indeed, the fashion for describing deaths must have reinforced the potency of suicide as a gesture for those who decided to take their own lives, perhaps even tipping the balance in favour of death (in the kind of calculation of benefits Seneca's writing explores at length).[74] The concern with how individuals die was, as we have seen, by no means peculiar to Seneca. Rather Rome in the first and early second centuries CE was characterised by a vogue for death literature. The endless retellings of Cato's death are a symptom of this which also served to fuel the appetite for details of the deaths of other great Romans.

Since the Hellenistic period collections of deaths of philosophers and heroes had appeared, such as the work of Hermippus of Smyrna on the death of the Stoic Chrysippus.[75] However, for Romans the fascination with the details of individual deaths takes on a new urgency in the aftermath of the death of Cato. Earlier works often show a preoccupation with bizarre detail (sometimes with a particular symbolic significance relating for instance to the doctrines taught by a particular philosopher).[76] For Roman writers in the aftermath of the end of the republic, death narratives more often bear a particular political significance.[77] Such writings might take a variety of forms, including poetry and rhetorical *controversiae* (the practice debates around hypothetical court cases which formed a key element in elite education).[78]

It is clear that by the time Tacitus was writing works were in circulation which gathered together details of the deaths of famous men. No specimen of these survives but Pliny mentions Titinius Capito's *exitus inlustrium virorum* 'deaths of famous men' (Pliny *Ep.* 8.12.4).[79] Other known titles include Fannius' account of the victims of Nero (Pliny *Ep.* 5.5.3). Pliny comments that he has died 'leaving his finest work unfinished', *pulcherrimum opus imperfectum reliquit*, and continues: *scribebat ... exitus occisorum aut relegatorum a Nerone et iam tres libros absolverat ... ac tanto magis reliquos perficere cupiebat, quanto frequentius hi lectitabantur*: 'He was bringing out a history of the various people put to death or banished by Nero ... He had already done three volumes and was all the keener to finish the rest, as these were eagerly read by a large public.' Junius Rusticus' biography of Thrasea Paetus and that of Helvidius Priscus by Herennius Senecio, referred to in Tacitus' *Agricola* (2.1), will certainly have included detailed accounts of their deaths. The focus of such literature was partly on those who had died under Domitian but also included, as in the case of Fannius, those who had died in the reign of Nero.

What was at stake in writing about (and reading) such deaths? In celebrating the brave deaths of Domitian's victims, public figures whose careers had prospered under the 'tyrant' Domitian strove to make clear where their own loyalties had really lain.[80] Pliny himself seems keen to emphasise his own intention to attend the recitation of Capito's work: *videor ergo fungi pio munere, quorumque exequias celebrare non licuit, horum quasi funebribus laudationibus seris quidem sed tanto magis veris interesse*: 'It is a pious work, I think, as I could not be present at their funerals to attend this (as I may call it) their funeral oration, late certainly but all the more sincere' (*Ep.* 8.12.5).[81] Pliny makes a number of contributions of his own to the genre, famously recounting the death of Arria – whose daughter, also called Arria, was the wife of Thrasea Paetus.[82] In particular, Pliny presents the death of Corellius Rufus as 'the climactic moment which crystallises the meaning of his entire life'.[83] In presenting Corellius as a Roman Stoic suicide, Pliny implicitly aligns him with such opposition heroes as Cato and Rusticus.[84]

The obsessive, competitive interest of Pliny and his contemporaries in telling and retelling these stories is striking.[85]

Many readers have detected elements of apology in these accounts written under Nerva and Trajan. Pliny's letters are often characterised by moments of defensiveness.[86] This is hardly surprising given the prospering of Pliny's career under Domitian.[87] A similar concern sometimes surfaces in Tacitus' treatment of elite deaths. In the *Agricola*, his earliest surviving work, Tacitus articulates his own survival in terms which suggest a profound alienation from the regime:

> Pauci et, ut sic dixerim, non modo aliorum sed etiam nostri superstites sumus, exemptis e media vita tot annis, quibus iuvenes ad senectutem, senes prope ad ipsos exactae aetatis terminus per silentium venimus?

> The few of us that are left have outlived not only the others but, so to say, our own past selves. With so many years taken from the middle of our lives as we pass from youth to old age, as old men have we not come to the very limit of our lifetimes in silence?

> (*Agr.* 3.2)

As we have seen, in this text Tacitus cannot wholeheartedly embrace the cult of dead victims. He must justify his father-in-law's successful career (and his own). Still Tacitus' account of Agricola's death is also moulded by the fashion for death literature. The account stresses Agricola's *virtus: constans et libens fatum excepisti*, 'with endurance and willingness he accepted his end' (*Agr.* 45.3). Here too, then, an element of Stoic *constantia* may be traced. There are even rumours that Domitian bears some responsibility for Agricola's demise: *constans rumor veneno interceptum*, 'there was a persistent rumour that he had been poisoned' (43.2).[88] The dying man comports himself in such a way as to make no overt reference to this; *tamquam pro virili portione innocentiam principi donares*, 'As though, taking it like a man, he would impute innocence to the emperor' (45.3). His son-in-law chooses to keep it in play however; *nobis nihil compertum adfirmare ausim*, 'I would not dare claim this certain either way' (43.2) – but visits by the emperor's servants to the dying man were, he reports, suspiciously frequent. In spite of all his discretion, Agricola's virtues are still too much for Domitian to stomach. This can easily be read as an attempt on Tacitus' part to have it both ways. Agricola's virtue is guaranteed by Domitian's alleged action against him – though some readers have remained unconvinced.[89] In the *Annals*, by contrast, Tacitus seems generally predisposed to celebrate the distinguished ends of distinguished men. Reservations have sometimes been detected in his account of Seneca's death, for instance,[90] but the concluding section of this chapter will focus on two deaths which, as has already been noted, seem unequivocally positive.

The rest is silence

The final chapters of the surviving text of Tacitus' *Annals* recount Nero's destruction of Barea Soranus and Thrasea Paetus. This is presented as the culmination of the destruction of Roman nobility: 'After the slaughter of so many distinguished men, Nero finally coveted the destruction of virtue itself, with the deaths of Thrasea Paetus and Barea Soranus': *Trucidatis tot insignibus viris ad postremum Nero virtutem ipsam excindere concupivit interfecto Thrasea Paeto et Barea Sorano* (16.21.1).[91] Thrasea in particular had caused Nero persistent annoyance by absenting himself from significant meetings of the senate, such as that following the death of the emperor's mother. Thrasea's enemy Capito, encouraging Nero to act against him, insists Thrasea has never sacrificed for the emperor's welfare and has been absent from the senate for the last three years.[92] Thrasea, suggests Capito, is widely seen as playing Cato to Nero's Caesar (16.22.2) – Thrasea had written a biography of Cato; his admiration for him was notorious.[93] Thrasea is linked with the *secta* of Tubero and Favonius (16.22.7). Such men, Capito argues, may claim to prefer *libertas* to *imperium*, but would attack *libertas* too, if they got their way.[94] Capito finally compares Thrasea to Brutus (notorious as the assassin of Julius Caesar) – by implication, the threat he poses to this Caesar must be forestalled – before suggesting Nero let Thrasea be tried in the senate.

Thrasea, in Tacitus' narrative, is uncertain whether to appear before the senate in his own defence or not and asks his friends for advice.

> Quibus intrari curiam placebat, securos esse de constantia eius disserunt; nihil dicturum nisi qua gloriam augeret. Segnis et pavidos supremis suis secretum circumdare: aspiceret populus virum morti obvium, audiret senatus voces quasi ex aliquo numine supra humanas: posse ipso miraculo etiam Neronem permoveri: sin crudelitati insisteret, distingui certe apud posteros memoriam honesti exitus ab ignavia per silentium pereuntium.

> Some encouraged him to attend. They asserted their own confidence in his ability to stand firm. 'Everything you say will add to your glory. Only the feeble and frightened surround their ends in secrecy. Let the people see a man who goes to meet death, let the senate hear words that seem to come from a superhuman source. Perhaps Nero himself will be moved by

this very miracle. But if he persists in his cruelty, certainly among later generations the memory of a noble death will stand out from the shamefulness of those departing in silence.'

(16.25.1–3)

These friends, we might note, stress their confidence in Thrasea's own *constantia* – his Catonian death is already set up. Others offer different advice; for them, Thrasea's presence in the senate house might tempt some members of that distinguished body to abase themselves still further. *Proinde intemeratus, impollutus, quorum vestigiis et studiis vitam duxerit, eorum gloria peteret finem*: 'Let him then die untarnished, unpolluted, as gloriously as those in whose footsteps and precepts he had lived!' (16.26.5). Yet for both lots of advisers Thrasea's impending death – already characterised in Catonian terms – is a foregone conclusion. And both are concerned it should secure him the greatest possible *gloria*. When the senate meets, Capito and Eprius Marcellus denounce Thrasea, while Barea Soranus is attacked by Ostorius Sabinus. Soranus and his daughter are present and seek in vain to defend themselves. Thrasea, by implication, is absent. All three are condemned, with the concession that they may choose their own deaths, *mortis arbitrium* (16.33.2).[95]

  The first of Thrasea's advisers encouraged him to appear in the senate, lest his absence should make it appear that he went to his death as one of those *ignavia per silentium pereuntium*, 'the shamefulness of those departing in silence' (16.25.3). Yet it is above all Thrasea's *silentium* which his accuser Eprius Marcellus claims to find so galling:

Denique agere senatorem et principis obtrectatores protegere solitus veniret, censeret quid corrigi aut mutari vellet: facilius perlaturos singula increpantem quam nunc silentium perferrent omnia damnantis.

'Let him make an appearance then, this man whose habit is to play the role of senator, to protect the emperor's critics, let him say what it is he wishes to see corrected or changed. They would more easily be able to endure his carping on detail than his present silence by which everything is condemned.'

(16.28.4)

As we have seen, Tacitus elsewhere criticises those who opt for dramatic deaths (*Agr.* 42.4). And he seems to have explicit criticisms to make of Thrasea's earlier behaviour. In the aftermath of Agrippina's death, when other senators congratulated Nero for his narrow escape from his mother's alleged plot, Thrasea who had previously passed over flatteries in silence or else with brief agreement – *silentio vel brevi adsensu priores adulationes transmittere solitus* – this time decides to walk out of the senate, *ac sibi causam periculi fecit, ceteris libertatis initium non præbuit*, 'and thus incurred danger for himself, without bringing others the beginnings of liberty' (*Ann.* 14.12.2).[96] This phrase seems to echo *Agricola* 42.3 (discussed above), where Tacitus explicitly criticised those whose behaviour culminated in *ambitiosa mors*, 'a self-seeking death' of no benefit to the state. Is Tacitus criticising Thrasea here?[97] Or is there perhaps a 'could' implied in *praebuit*, 'did not provide'? For some readers, Thrasea has put himself in mortal danger yet, despite his best efforts, could not bring *libertas* for others.[98] One might also see here a play on *exiit* 'he departed' and *initium* 'beginning'.[99] Indeed, this *exitus*, 'departure', from the senate serves as a prelude to the agonising *exitus* with which the *Annals* reach their premature end.

It is, I think, striking to find Thrasea here linked with *silentium* yet again. Thrasea has made his own silence speak – if ambiguously. It is notable that while Tacitus refers to interventions made by Thrasea in the senate in the past (such as the successful proposal for a more lenient sentence for Antistius, *Ann.* 16.21.2), after the speech he makes at *Annals* 13.49 he does not speak again directly until he has received the order to die, aside from a few words of advice offered to Arulenus Rusticus in which he makes plain he already knows his own end is near, *actam aetatem*, 'my life is done' (*Ann.* 16.26.7). It is evening and Thrasea is in his garden, when the consul's quaestor arrives to deliver the death sentence.[100] The reader here is aligned with the imperial messenger; we are not close enough to hear all of Thrasea's conversation with his friends but may judge from the odd word and from their expressions that they are discussing the nature of the soul and the separation of body and spirit, *de natura animae et dissociatione spiritus corporisque* (*Ann.* 16.34.2) – anyway we could guess what they are discussing, if, that is to say, we have read the *Phaedo*, if we are, as we ought to be, familiar with the death of Cato, the death of Seneca.[101] Thrasea has his veins cut and pours a libation of blood upon the ground. His last recorded words invoke Jupiter the Liberator and offer his death as an example to the young man who brought the death sentence: *in ea tempora natus es quibus firmare animum expediat constantibus exemplis*, 'You have been born into times when it is prudent to strengthen your spirit with examples of endurance' (*Ann.* 16.35.2–3). *Specta*, 'look!' Thrasea exhorts the quaestor – and us, Tacitus' readers. This is the last spectacle of death the *Annals* (or our *Annals*, at any rate) will offer. His lingering death was very painful – and there the manuscript ends.

Death depoliticised?

Such deaths – and their celebration in this kind of protest literature – were perhaps felt to be disingenuous even in antiquity. The political punch of a virtuous death is undercut more than once by Martial, writing under Domitian and his successors. One epigram praises Festus, who, afflicted with painful and disfiguring disease, kills himself with the traditionally favoured Roman blade (in preference to poison or starvation). The poem celebrates a Roman death, *Romana mors*, but disputes the claims of those who seek to appropriate it for a particular political project. It concludes:

> Hanc mortem fatis magni praeferre Catonis
> Fama potest: huius Caesar amicus erat.

> Reputation can prefer this death to the doom of great Cato: this man was Caesar's friend.

> > (1.78.9–10)

Cato's options, Martial implies, were limited. His choice hardly betokens exceptional bravery. Festus' end makes clear that he accepts death, asserts his bravery in anticipating it, demonstrates his respect for Roman tradition – but leaves no unpleasantly political aftertaste.[102]

Conversely another epigram earlier in the same book praises the addressee, Decianus, for following the beliefs of Thrasea and Cato but without finding it necessary to kill himself:

> Quod magni Thraseae consummatique Catonis
> Dogmata sic sequeris salvos ut esse velis,
> Pectore nec nudo strictos incurris in ensis,
> Quod fecisse velim te, Deciane, facis.
> Nolo virum facili redemit qui sanguine famam;
> Hunc volo laudari qui sine morte potest.

> You follow the teachings of great Thrasea and perfect Cato, yet do not wish to harm yourself. In this you do as I would wish, Decianus. The man who buys an easy fame with his blood is not for me. I value him who can win praise without death.

> > (1.8)

In both these poems Martial seems to take issue with those who fetishise – and imitate – Cato's self-aggrandising death as the prime manifestation of virtue. To secure fame with death is an easy option, he suggests – a salvo against his critics Domitian can hardly have been unhappy to read.

Juvenal's satires, written like Tacitus' *Annals* in the time of Trajan, also explore the difficulties of articulating critique under autocracy. Juvenal's first satire laments and celebrates at some length the wealth of vice which flourishes as material for the would-be satirist. He is all set to relaunch satire. Yet the examples sketched out here resemble not figures from Juvenal's own time but monsters of vice from earlier decades, such as the loathsome Crispinus, a prominent figure at the court of Domitian.[103] To tackle the vices of distinguished contemporaries is too dangerous. The satire concludes:

> Experiar quid concedatur in illos
> Quorum Flaminia tegitur cinis atque Latina.

> Let me see what I can get away with against those whose ashes lie along the Flaminian or the Latin way.

> (1.170–1)

Domitian himself was buried beside the Latin way (Suet. *Dom.* 17.3). Many of his predecessors lay in the Mausoleum of Augustus, alongside the via Flaminia. Juvenal has just claimed he is going to revive the traditional freedom of Roman republican satire. He will be a new Lucilius. But what is the point of savaging the dead?[104] Is this 'time-warp' satire to compensate for all the unwritten satires of the previous decades? Seen in these terms, Juvenal's project has much in common with those of Tacitus and Pliny. For at least one modern scholar, Juvenal's handling of his obsession with the past has so much less finesse as to arouse the suspicion that his aim is rather to satirise the 'indignation industry' of his contemporaries.[105]

This suggestion could have important implications for how we read Tacitus. The historian seems to imply that his telling of martyr-tales is a risky undertaking. Can this really have been the case, given the time he was writing?[106] How can he avoid appearing a Roman of compromised integrity, by comparison with, for example, Thrasea? Tacitus, I would suggest, is not unaware of the difficulty of his position. One strategy is precisely to admit his own complicity. Writing of Agricola's early death (in 93 CE), Tacitus comments:

> Non vidit Agricola obsessam curiam et clausum armis senatum et eadem strage tot consularium caedes, tot nobilissimarum feminarum exilia ac fugas ... mox nostrae duxere Helvidium in carcerem manus; nos Maurici Rusticique visus [adflixit], nos innocenti sanguine Senecio perfudit.

Agricola did not see the senate-house besieged, the senate surrounded by armed men, the killing of so many consulars in that same act of butchery, so many most noble women forced into exile or flight ... But soon our own hands led Helvidius to prison, the faces of Mauricus and Rusticus put us to shame, we were drenched with Senecio's innocent blood.

(*Agr.* 45)

Members of the senate – including the author – must take responsibility for the deaths of Helvidius and Senecio.[107] It is possible that Tacitus himself was not actually in Rome at the time these trials took place. This passage may be seen as a strategy to encourage others also to acknowledge their collective guilt. At the same time, in attacking those who admired the 'martyrs' uncritically, Tacitus could also defend his father-in-law (not to mention his own conduct during the reign of Domitian).[108] A salient danger of autocracy is the insidious alienation of members of the Roman elite from their own selves.

History on trial

Tacitus also uses other means to assert his own integrity, I would suggest. One of these is through a surrogate historian. In the year 25 CE, Cremutius Cordus, writes Tacitus, was prosecuted on the novel charge of praising Brutus in his annals and describing Cassius as the last of the Romans. Cremutius knows he will be condemned. Tacitus puts in his mouth an eloquent defence. His speech concludes with some comments on the place of Brutus and Cassius in history. Cremutius is not inciting anyone to civil war, he asserts:

'An illi quidem septuagesimum ante annum perempti, quo modo imaginibus suis noscuntur (quas ne victor quidem abolevit), sic partem memoriae apud scriptores retinent? suum cuique decus posteritas rependit; nec deerunt, si damnatio ingruit, qui non modo Cassii et Bruti sed etiam mei meminerunt.' Egressus dein senatu vitam abstinentia finivit. Libros per aediles cremandos censuere patres; set manserunt, occultati et editi. Quo magis socordiam eorum inridere libet qui praesenti potentia credunt exstingui posse etiam sequentis aevi memoriam. Nam contra punitis ingeniis gliscit auctoritas, neque aliud externi reges aut qui eadem saevitia usi sunt nisi dedecus sibi atque illis gloriam peperere.

'It is seventy years since they died. Is it not right that just as they are made familiar by their statues (even the victor did not deprive them of these) they should be remembered in the works of writers? Posterity gives each his due honour. If I fall victim to condemnation, there will be some who will remember not only Brutus and Cassius but also me.' Then he left the senate and starved himself to death. The senate decreed that the aediles were to burn his books. But they survived, hidden and later circulated. Another reason to mock the stupidity of those who think that present power may serve to eradicate the memory of later generations. On the contrary, the authority of great writers is enhanced by their suppression. All that is achieved by foreign tyrants – and those who use their savage methods – is their own disgrace and the glory of their victims.

(*Ann.* 4.35.2–5)

The destruction of Cordus, described as *perniciabile*, 'ruinous' (34.2), is an instance of the *perniciem innocentium*, 'the ruin of innocents', listed as the materials of Tacitus' history in the previous chapter (33.3). He too, we may infer, should be seen as innocent. Not only this but his death is the only possible outcome of the trial. He is described as *relinquendae vitae certus*, 'certain of his impending death'. His suicide is not premature; the fate of his books, which are to be burned, makes this clear.[109] In presenting the charge against Cordus as a novel one, Tacitus reminds us of how it will be used later; Tacitus had referred in the *Agricola* (2.1) to the burning in 93 CE of the biographies of Thrasea Paetus (whose author was Arulenus Rusticus) and Helvidius Priscus (whose author was Herennius Senecio).[110]

The very act of suppressing the historian serves to confirm the superior and lasting *auctoritas* of history-writing in contrast to the ephemeral *potentia* of governments.[111] Tacitus' use here of the terms *potentia*, 'power', and *auctoritas*, 'authority', is striking. Emperors can only aspire to *potentia* but historians may secure *auctoritas*. Elsewhere the term *auctoritas* – a key word in the emperor Augustus' articulation of his own position – is used only with irony.[112] Here, most unusually, its value is unqualified. Here – as in the case of Thrasea, in my view – the *gloria* of the victim seems unequivocally positive. Here again we find an example which problematises what might look like the dismissal in Tacitus' earlier work of those who take up perilous paths and ostentatious deaths (*Agr.* 42.4).

There are, moreover, compelling reasons for seeing Cordus as standing for Tacitus himself.[113] For he too, like Tacitus, wrote annals recording events in Rome seventy years before his own day. While some aspects of Cordus' speech might seem at variance with comments Tacitus makes in the opening chapters of the *Annals*, the relatively positive assessments of Julius Caesar and of Augustus that Cordus is made to offer can plausibly be read as strategies to make Tiberius appear the more tyrannical. The *egressus* 'departure' of Cordus echoes the terms in which Tacitus described his own historiographical digression a little earlier, *libero egressu*, 'an unconstrained departure' (4.32.2).[114] Most importantly the trial of Cremutius Cordus serves as a manifestation of the dangers run by the historian. Cremutius' work on the civil war has been received as an indirect commentary on the present.[115] At times, writing history could indeed prove suicidal.[116] These dangers are stressed by Tacitus in relation to his own practice in the preceding chapter (at *Ann.* 4.33.4).[117] The danger, he asserts, stems from *figura*, seeing a reference in a text to one person as really a reference to oneself – *ob simili- tudinem morum*, 'on account of similarity of character'.[118] Was Cremutius perhaps protesting too much in his assertion that writing about the past has no implications for the present? Surely there is an invitation here to see a reference to Tacitus in Cremutius. Thus, Tacitus too may be attracted into the category of authors who make the truth known at great personal cost.[119]

It is at this point worth returning to the trademark silence of Thrasea Paetus. Traditionally silence was abhorrent to the Roman aristocrat. Sallust, an author whose influence on Tacitus is widely noted, begins his account of the conspiracy of Catiline as follows: *Omnis homines qui sese student praestare ceteris animalibus summa ope niti decet ne vitam silentio transeant veluti pecora*: 'It is proper for all people who seek to stand out above other creatures to strive with all their might lest they pass through life in silence like cattle' (Sall. *Cat.* 1.1).[120] One may escape silence through deeds worthy of record – and one may also escape silence, as does Sallust himself, by writing.

Silence is the ignominious lot of the honest senator under a tyrannical emperor. Tacitus in the *Agricola*, as we saw, laments the period of silence he and his peers had to endure under Domitian – all we could do, he comments, was be silent, *tacere* (*Agr.* 2.2–3). Indeed, he continues, *prope ad ipsos exactae aetatis terminus per silentium venimus*, 'we came almost to the end point of our lives in silence' (*Agr.* 3.2). It is very tempting to detect in this passage a play on Tacitus' own name. Indeed another programmatic passage from Book 3 of the *Annals* has also been read as offering a play on the author's name: *quod praecipuum munus annalium reor ne virtutes sileantur*, 'this, I consider, is a prime task of history-writing so that virtues are not passed over in silence' (*Ann.* 3.65.1).[121] The historian's duty is to speak, to break the silence. It is Tacitus himself who allows Thrasea's silence to speak, who enables this *spectaculum suae virtutis*, 'the spectacle of his virtue', to become *adsiduum* 'lasting' – if we may revisit the terms in which Seneca discussed the implications of *clementia*. But we might also wonder whether we should not read Thrasea, too, as a surrogate for Tacitus himself.

The end of the historian

It has been a central contention of my work so far that for many Romans the way an individual died could serve to validate – or undermine – the life he or she had lived. As Roland Barthes suggests in his essay on Tacitus and the funerary baroque, in the Tacitean universe of the *Annals* death is construed 'symbolically as the purest moment of life'.[122] Tacitus' work offers death scenes which crucially condition the reader's assessment of the individuals concerned. So finally what about the death of Tacitus himself? Nothing is recorded of how the historian ended his life. Would we read Tacitus differently if he was known to have died gloriously? I suspect we might – just as Tacitus' version of the death of Seneca conditions our reading of Seneca's own work.[123] But in doing so have we perhaps let ourselves be seduced by the distinctively Roman perception that death authenticates life?

Let us conclude with a suggestive example of this way of thinking – and dying – from Tacitus' *Histories*. After the devastating defeat of his forces by the Flavians at Cremona, the emperor Vitellius refuses to acknowledge the weakness of his position. Agrestis, a centurion of *notabili constantia* 'remarkable endurance', strives to make him take action. He seeks to determine the extent of the disaster so that plans may be made to remedy Vitellius' position and goes on a mission to survey the devastation. The Flavians show him the battlefield, the ruined city of Cremona and the captured legions.

> Agrestis ad Vitellium remeavit abnuentique vera esse quae adferret, atque ultro corruptum arguenti 'quando quidem' inquit 'magno documento opus est, nec alius iam tibi aut vitae aut mortis meae usus, dabo cui credas.' Atque ita digressus voluntaria morte dicta firmavit.

> Agrestis returned to Vitellius. Finding that the emperor did not believe his report and even suggested he had been bribed, he said, 'You require some great proof – and my life or death is of no other use to you. Let me give something that you can believe.' Going straight from the emperor's presence, he confirmed his report by committing suicide.

> (Tac. *Hist.* 3.54.3)

The centurion's suicide authenticates his report.[124] Tacitus goes on to offer an alternative version: *Quidem iussu Vitellii interfectum, de fide constantiaque eadem tradidere*, 'Some say he was killed on Vitellius' orders but they agree on his faith and constancy'. The messenger's death bravely faced, whether self-inflicted or not, underwrites the truth of his message.[125]

Tacitus, writing, he alleges, in happier times, when *quae sentias dicere licet*, 'a man can say what he thinks' (*Hist.* 1.1.2),[126] finds himself, I would suggest, in a fix. History-writing is no longer dangerous. He will not – probably – die for what he has written. Yet, if he is to be a credible witness, if we are to believe his message, he too must seem, at the very least, ready to face death. Hence the crucial role in the *Annals* played by the glorious deaths of his surrogates, the historian Cremutius, and Thrasea the constant Stoic, a man whose distinctive and eloquent silence makes him ideally suited to play Tacitus.

CHAPTER 5

DYING IN CHARACTER
STOICISM AND THE ROMAN DEATH SCENE

Dying, for Roman writers, is, as we have seen, not a private act but one which should properly take place in front of an audience. The deaths narrated by Tacitus and others can only be reported, can only have social and political value, because witnesses were present. The bravery of the senator is in a different league from that of the gladiator – but no less spectacular. Indeed, as we saw earlier, the arena might offer an enabling model for an aristocrat embracing a glorious death. The role of both audience and spectacle is figured rather differently in analogies with the theatre. This model too has a significant part in Roman discussions of distinguished deaths. Here again death appears as a performance and – sometimes at least – gains from the piquant contrast between the actor (like the gladiator, a person of lowly status) and the dying aristocrat.[1] The theatre (like the arena) could be invoked in relation to the experience of both the dying subject and those witnessing the death.[2] However, while allusions to the arena focus on the *virtus*, the bravery, of the subject confronting death, invocations of the theatre serve rather to highlight the dying as a process, whose exact details one might plan with an eye to how they would be received. Thus conceived, death can be a complex and subtle act of communication, freighted with allusions historical, literary and philosophical. Sometimes, indeed, death can be an aesthetic act.

The theatre manifests itself in a number of different ways particularly in Roman accounts of suicides. Tacitus, as we have seen, recounts numerous deaths where the subject is committing suicide – or suffering execution (frequently this distinction is blurred, as an individual receives the order to take his or her own life). Some of these have been discussed in detail in earlier chapters. Modern readers, noting the emphasis on the audience and the long-drawn-out nature of these scenes, have commented on their theatricality. In the words of Roland Barthes, they constitute 'an obsessional theatre, a scene even more than a lesson'.[3]

Roman writers often betray significant discomfort in assessing the effect on the viewer of watching gladiatorial deaths. A brave death in combat might be an ennobling, inspiring sight. But it was all too easy to be corrupted by the bloodthirstiness of one's fellow spectators.[4] Such anxieties are not, however, apparent in relation to accounts of aristocratic death scenes. Here the audience is almost always far more select: friends and family, household slaves and ex-slaves. Some among them offer advice. Often the companions exhibit excesses of emotion which throw into still sharper relief the calm of the central subject. However their most crucial function is as witnesses. Witnesses of aristocratic deaths are important, not only because they themselves may be inspired to similar acts of bravery but also because they are the means by which the details of the death are to be transmitted to posterity.[5] Yet the written form of such deaths inevitably raises questions of authorship. How far is the beautifully articulated death the creation of the dying subject – and how far is it the composition of the author who recounts it?

The theatre could offer an apt metaphor for other aspects of human existence besides its conclusion. Stoic philosophers exploit theatrical imagery in relation to more general ideas of personality and character. The theatrical elements which characterise some Roman death narratives take on a significance which relates quite specifically, I shall argue, to the role played by theatrical imagery in some key areas of Stoic philosophy. This is especially evident in Seneca's work (and should perhaps be linked with his own involvement in writing for the theatre, as the author of compelling tragic dramas). We need to be cautious, however, in using the term 'theatrical'. There may be tensions between the different ways in which these texts invoke the 'theatre'. Yet these tensions may themselves enrich our reading of some key death narratives.

Fate

The theatre might be invoked on an imperial death-bed. Augustus, nearing his end, is said to have asked his friends *ecquid iis videretur mimum vitae commode transegisse*, 'whether he had played his role well in the comedy of life' before quoting the final lines from a play of Menander: 'Since the play has been so good, clap your hands / And all of you dismiss us with applause' (Suet. *Aug.* 99.1).[6] Even (or especially?) on his death-bed, the emperor is aware of the scrutiny to which his behaviour is subject. At the same time, the theatrical trope serves to distance the dying man from own death. Augustus' biographer has the elderly emperor invoke comedy as his life nears its natural conclusion.[7] The death of an old man is as natural as the end of a play.

The idea that the end of an individual is fated, predetermined, like that of a play already written, could also convey a more specifically Stoic conception of fate. Cato was well known among his contemporaries for his firm commitment to Stoic philosophy. Cicero terms him *perfectus mea sententia stoicus*, 'in my view the perfect Stoic' (*Paradoxa stoicorum, proem*). The character Cato, who serves as an exponent of Stoic thought in Cicero's treatise on old age, *De senectute* (written after the real Cato's death), is made to observe that nature, as a careful playwright, will not have neglected provision for the end of the play (2.5). The Stoic philosopher Epictetus, writing in the late first century CE, similarly uses the idea of Fortune as playwright who has decided how the drama will conclude:

> Remember that you are an actor in a play, which is as the author wants it to be; short, if he wants it to be short; long if he wants it to be long. If he wants you to act a poor man, a cripple, a public official, or a private person, see that you act it with skill. For it is your job to act well the part that is assigned to you; but to choose it is another's.
>
> (*Ench.* 17)

Such comments generate an alienation effect, establishing a distance between the subject and the part he or she happens to have played in life. This may be seen as one of many Stoic strategies to reconcile oneself to prospect of death (or whatever else awaits). Such matters are merely indifferents. The allusion may serve as a kind of consolation to the dying and those close to them.

A century later another Stoic, the emperor Marcus Aurelius, pursues a similar idea at the close of his *To Himself*:

> Why is it hard, then, if you are dismissed from the city not by a tyrant or an unjust judge, but by Nature who brought you in – just as when the master of the show, who has engaged an actor, dismisses him from the stage? 'But I have not spoken my five acts, only three.' 'You are right, but in life three acts are the whole play.' For it is he, who yesterday caused your composition and today your dissolution, who determines when it is complete; you are the cause of neither. Leave the stage, therefore, with good grace, for he, too, who lets you go, is gracious.
>
> (12.36)[8]

Paradoxically, the artificial structure of drama is used to make sense of the natural process of life and death.[9] A divine playwright/director has complete control; the actor's job is merely to say his lines with conviction.[10] According to this model, too, death is like the end of a play. By implication the individual's life has a shape; fate has determined the end. This consoling analogy is made more complex and problematic, however, by the other ways in which notions of theatricality are invoked.

Performing the Stoic self

In Stoic notions of individual character as they develop in the later republic and under the principate, metaphors and images drawn from the theatre play a significant role. An important instance of this can be seen in the first book of Cicero's *De officiis*, where he sets out the four *personae* theory attributed to the second-century BCE Stoic philosopher Panaetius (1.107–21). Brought up on Rhodes, Panaetius came to Rome in the 140s and seems to have played a vital part in introducing Stoicism to Romans – and in reformulating Stoic philosophy in line with Roman preoccupations. His four *personae* theory offers a helpful model for those seeking to accommodate a commitment to philosophy with involvement in Roman political life, the term *persona* having the sense of 'role' (or, in a theatrical context, 'mask'). The first *persona* is universal (the shared rationality of all human beings), the second individual (the physical, mental and temperamental nature of the individual); the third *persona* is what is imposed by chance (wealth, accidents, opportunities), the fourth that which we assume by deliberate choice (for instance one's profession or career).[11]

Cicero explicitly posits the behaviour of actors as a model in exploring the significance of the second *persona* – the individual's own characteristics:

> Suum quisque igitur noscat ingenium acremque se et bonorum et vitiorum suorum iudicem praebeat, ne scaenici plus quam nos videantur habere prudentiae. ... Ergo histrio hoc videbit in scaena, non videbit sapiens vir in vita? Ad quas igitur res aptissimi erimus, in iis potissimum elaborabimus.

> Everyone therefore should be aware of his own natural ability and show himself an acute judge of his own merits and failings; in this respect we should not let actors show more good sense than we do. ... Shall a player bear this in mind in choosing his role on stage and a wise man fail to do so in selecting his part in life? We shall therefore work most effectively in the role to which we are best adapted.

> (*Off.* 1.114)

The individual should deploy their knowledge of their own strengths and weaknesses – this second *persona* – the better to equip themselves to live up to the demands imposed by first *persona* – universal human nature. One should not attempt to assume a role which, however appropriate it might be for someone else, does not fit with one's own personal character. Cicero's choice of illustration to clarify the nature of the second *persona* serves to flesh out the link with the theatre already evoked by the very notion of the 'persona' (and its Greek equivalent, 'prosopon').

In the course of his exposition of Panaetius' theory, Cicero discusses the death of Cato. Cato's choice of suicide in preference to Caesar's tyranny was a manifestation of his own particular *constantia* and *gravitas*.[12]

> Atque haec differentia naturarum tantam habet vim, ut non numquam mortem sibi ipse consciscere alius debeat, alius non debeat. Num enim alia in causa M. Cato fuit, alia ceteri, qui se in Africa Caesari tradiderunt? Atqui ceteris forsitan vitio datum esset, si se interemissent, propterea quod lenior eorum vita et mores fuerant faciliores, Catoni cum incredibilem tribuisset natura gravitatem eamque ipse perpetua constantia roboravisset semperque in proposito susceptoque consilio permansisset, moriendum potius quam tyranni vultus aspiciendus fuit.

> Indeed, these differences of character have such significance that sometimes one man is under an obligation to take his own life while another is not. For did Marcus Cato find himself in a different situation from the others, the ones who surrendered to Caesar in Africa? Perhaps they would have been criticised, had they killed themselves, given that their lives had been less austere and their characters more adaptable. But Cato had been granted by nature a seriousness too great to credit which he himself reinforced by his unfailing endurance, remaining ever committed to his purpose and fixed resolution. Thus for him it was right to die rather than look on the face of a tyrant.
>
> (*Off.* 1.112)

His earlier life had served to set up certain expectations about how 'Cato' would behave, setting a trajectory – so that one might see Cato's mode of death as implicit in the earlier course of his own life. Cicero's own *persona* did not, it seems, oblige him (in contrast to Cato) to commit suicide, though Cicero, who was also deeply unhappy at the prospect of living under Caesar, is defensive about his own course of action – or rather inaction.[13] He is at some pains then to point out that an act which is appropriate for one person could, because of their different characters, be quite wrong for someone else even under the same circumstances.[14]

Seneca, too, writing a century later and more fully committed than Cicero to Stoicism, invokes the analogy of acting in relation to individual character.

He comments, for instance, that human life generally is characterised by a failure to play one's part well (*Ep.* 80.7). The importance of constancy of character is something he stresses repeatedly:

Sic maxime coarguitur animus imprudens; alius prodit atque alius et, quo turpius nihil iudico, impar sibi est. Magnam rem puta unum hominem agere. Praeter sapientem autem nemo unum agit, ceteri multiformes sumus. ... Mutamus subinde personam et contrariam ei sumimus, quam exuimus.

This is, above all, the sign of a foolish mind: it appears first in one form and then in another, and, which I judge worst of all, it is never like itself. Believe me it is a great thing to play the role of one man. But nobody can act the part of a single person except the wise man: the rest of us slip from one character to another ... We constantly change our mask and put on the very opposite of the one we have discarded.

(*Ep.* 120.22)

Seneca suggests we are called upon to play one single role and that we need to play it constantly and well. The good actor who rises to the challenge of providing a good and consistent performance can be a model for how to live. But consistency is essential.

We can also see a position similar to that set out by Seneca in the writings of Epictetus. Epictetus, too, invokes the 'prosopon', 'mask' or 'character'.[15] For Epictetus, living 'kata prosopon' – in accordance with one's character – signifies living up to the role of one who does not 'sell' himself for matters of indifference but pursues only virtue (*Discourses* 1.2.7). Such a 'role' is exemplified for Epictetus by figures such as Helvidius Priscus, who stand up bravely to political oppression.[16] He recounts a dramatic exchange between Helvidius Priscus and the emperor Vespasian:

Helvidius Priscus ... when Vespasian had sent instructions that he should not attend the senate, answered. 'It is in your power not to let me be a senator; but as long as I am one I must attend.' – 'Well then if you do attend, at least be silent.' – 'Do not ask for my opinion and I will be silent.' – 'But I must ask it.' – 'And I must say what seems to me right.' – 'But if you do I will have you killed.' – 'When did I ever tell you I was immortal? You will do your part and I mine: it is yours to kill and mine to die without trembling; yours to banish me, mine to depart without grieving.'

(*Disc.* 1.2.19–21)

We should note here Helvidius' references to what is expected of one who plays the part of 'senator'. Everyone knows what senators are expected to do in the context of a senatorial meeting. Yet there is also some slippage here. By the end of the conversation, the 'role' is not so much that of the regular senator, respecting the conventions of the curia, but rather that of Helvidius the Stoic, who must say what he really thinks, even if it means death.

Self-consciousness about one's own role is also a preoccupation in plays of the early empire – plays written by the philosopher Seneca. A number of characters, in discussing their own behaviour, repeatedly draw attention to their names. Seneca's Medea wonders if this is this how 'Medea' would behave. '*Medea*,' says the nurse (l. 171), '*fiam*' answers Medea – 'I shall become Medea'. Later – after her ghastly crime (she kills her two children in order to punish her husband) – Medea is made to comment, '*Medea nunc sum*' – 'Now I am Medea' (l. 910).[17] Medea wants to become Medea, to fulfil her role, thus conforming both to her own expectations and to those of her friends and her enemies. The presence of other persons adds substance to the standing of the individual and also renders this claim a kind of existential exercise.[18] Audience and characters always know the end of the story. Indeed Senecan drama displays an almost overwhelming sense of historical and literary self-consciousness. As Wilamowitz famously commented, 'this Medea has read Euripides'.[19]

Such self-consciousness regarding one's name was not confined to the stage. In Roman political life, one could not escape the destiny of one's own name. A particular name might in itself provoke a desire for external fame. Several ancient authors comment on the pressure put on Marcus Brutus to take action against Julius Caesar, stemming, in part at least, from the name he bore. According to Plutarch, messages appeared on the base of a statue of Lucius Brutus, scourge of the Tarquins, 'If only Brutus were alive' and also on the praetor's tribunal in the Forum (when Marcus Brutus occupied that office): 'Brutus, are you sleeping?' and 'You are not really Brutus' (*Brutus* 9.3). His own name obliged Marcus Brutus to follow his famous ancestor and act against tyranny.[20] What did it mean to be called Cato? The moral severity of the Elder Cato was a demanding model to follow. One might read the Younger Cato's choices in life as partially determined by the name he shared with his great-grandfather. The Younger Cato so closely associated himself with the ancient Roman republic that he felt obliged to take his own life when he realised tyranny would prevail. Once Caesar's victory was inevitable, Cato's only course of action was to kill himself.

A key aspect of the acting analogy, particularly as deployed by Seneca, is the role played by the audience. Acting is a success or a failure insofar as it *communicates* the part to those watching. The audience has expectations.

The Stoic conception of the self should be seen as, on one level, intrinsically social. Stoicism itself 'prompts theatrical tropes', comments Thomas Rosenmeyer. Roman Stoic writers, Seneca particularly, encourage the would-be philosopher to put his sufferings on display, just as the hero of a tragedy eagerly conveys his passions to the watching crowd. Seneca's philosophical champions show what Rosenmeyer terms 'a penchant for exhibitionism and truculence'. Their achievements are planned, even contrived, and can only achieve their full meaning when carefully positioned as the central spectacle in a crowded arena.[21]

In Stoicism, the actions of an individual acquire meaning insofar as they are witnessed. In Seneca's Letters, while the Stoic sage may be imagined as totally self-reliant, yet humbler mortals can do no more than aspire to this state. For them, the presence of others, so long as these companions are themselves virtuous, serves as a vital stimulus to act virtuously. When such persons are not actually available, Seneca writes, we must try to imagine them present.[22] In *Ep.* 25.5–6, Seneca advises, imagine all your actions are being scrutinised by some great man such as Scipio, or Cato or Laelius. However, this need seems to have its limits. *Cum iam profeceris tantum ut sit tibi etiam tui reverentia, licebit dimittas paedagogum*, 'When you have made so much progress that you have respect for yourself also, you may send away your tutor', allows Seneca.[23] Is this perhaps the point at which acting ceases to be a relevant analogy?

Helpful here may be possible parallels with the notion of social role as set out by Erving Goffman in his study of self-presentation in the modern western world. Goffman writes of the 'self as a dramatic effect of, rather than a cause of behaviour'.[24] The *cause* of behaviour is rather the desire to project a particular kind of self. The stage analogy here, then, is significantly limited. The emphasis of the analogy is on *techniques* of performance. We might want to say, as Goffman does, that ultimately these techniques, though they are important, are incidental. One does need some of the skills possessed by a good actor – but one needs them for a very different purpose from that of stage performance. The objective is rather the communication of a 'character' whose example will influence the behaviour of others.

However, we should pause before assuming the Stoic conception of the self is strictly parallel to the notion of self explored by Goffman, and concluding, therefore, that the theatrical analogy is strictly limited here also. The challenge of conforming oneself to nature demanded, for the serious Stoic, ceaseless self-scrutiny.[25] This might seem far removed from the world of the stage, so focused on external appearances, on persuasive effect. Yet while the advanced Stoic may not require a numerous audience, even so an audience is still necessary. In Letter 7, Seneca quotes approvingly a comment made by Epicurus, writing to a friend: *satis enim magnum alter alteri theatrum sumus*, 'each of us is sufficient audience for the other' (*Ep.* 7.11). Sometimes the Stoic must even take on this position for himself. Thus the theatre is internalised – the Stoic must himself be simultaneously both actor and audience. In another letter on coping with pain which this time invokes the analogy of the gladiatorial games, Seneca exhorts his reader: *ipse te specta! Ipse te lauda*, 'Be your own spectator; look for your own applause' (78.21).[26] There is a sense, here, in which action can be thought to have meaning only insofar as it is conceived of as spectacle. As Rosenmeyer comments, the self-dramatisation involved in seeing oneself as an actor with an audience 'entails the admission that life has meaning only as a performance, as an aesthetic experience'.[27]

The final curtain

While Seneca and others use the metaphor of the theatre in relation to character generally, it is above all in relation to death that the acting metaphor is invoked. Part of Seneca's Letter 120 exhorting his reader to play one role with constancy was quoted above. He continues:

> Hoc ergo a te exige, ut, qualem institueris praestare te, talem usque ad exitum serves. Effice ut possis laudari, si minus, ut adgnosci.

> This then I ask of you, that you should force yourself to play to the very end of life the character which you assumed at the beginning. See to it that men praise you. If not let them at least identify you.

> (120.22)

The challenge for the would-be Stoic was firstly to establish his own character and then to actualise it, even to the bitter end. Cato above all affirms his own identity in choosing death at a particular point in history. This is to take the Roman Stoic project of self-fashioning to its extreme.[28] Suicide – at least as retrospectively conceptualised – becomes an existential act.[29]

Seneca, in another letter already referred to, writes of individuals being 'assigned' roles in life (*Ep.* 80.7). Just as the actor and the audience know in advance what will happen to the Lord of the Argives as the play unfolds – the part is already written – so in real life, for Stoic thinkers, what will befall the individual is already determined by Fate. The good actor accepts the part he has been given and plays it well; similarly the good Stoic will accept willingly whatever Fate has determined for him. Here the theatre analogy highlights not the particular disposition of one individual as suited to a particular role but rather the role itself as something already determined by Fate.

A further passage from the Letters, while using a similar analogy, offers a significantly different perspective, one which will be our main concern here. Seneca's Letter 77 (developing the theatrical metaphor of the previous letter in Seneca's collection, 76.31) concludes as follows:

> Quomodo fabula, sic vita non quam diu, sed quam bene acta sit, refert. Nihil ad rem pertinet, quo loco desinas. Quocumque voles desine; tantum bonam clausulam inpone.

> Life is like a play – it doesn't matter how long the action is drawn out, but how good the acting is. It makes no difference at what point you stop. Stop whenever you choose; but make sure your conclusion's a good one.

> (77.20)

The letter has been considering how suicide may sometimes be the appropriate course of action.[30] As we see, it ends presenting life as play which needs a good *clausula*, 'conclusion'.[31] Here the Latin *quam bene acta sit* plays both on the sense of 'acting' but also on the sense of 'finishing' – *actum est*.[32] This Stoic is his own playwright. And he takes particular pride in his final lines.[33] Thus might a well-conceived suicide form the equivalent to one of Seneca the playwright's famous *sententiae*. Something memorable, often quoted – witty even. This conception of suicide highlights the sense that it may be an explicitly aesthetic artefact, an artistic creation deserving appreciation from a discerning audience.[34]

There are perhaps problems with Seneca's proliferation of theatrical analogies, which are made to fulfil different purposes in different contexts. There is significant slippage between the focus on the multiplicity of roles played by the individual as compared with roles an actor takes on in different plays; self-actualisation as something to be scrutinised (as in Seneca's exhortation – 'Be your own audience!'); the idea of life as fated – we can no more change what will happen than actors can the ending of the play they are performing. This last notion in particular is effectively deconstructed by Seneca himself. The actor turns playwright and writes his own ending. As often, Seneca pushes metaphors further, so far he perhaps ends up subverting the Stoic position he elsewhere seems to want to endorse. However, while the sophistication of Seneca's engagement with the theatrical may be particular to the writings of this brilliant yet idiosyncratic thinker, it is also a manifestation of a much more widespread tendency among Romans to see the moment of death in theatrical terms. It may be enlightening to explore the theatrical resonances of a number of other descriptions of death in the context of the Stoic emphasis on offering a consistent performance of oneself.

Dying to be Cato?

In Letter 77, as often in Latin literature, we are presented with death as a moment of truth. Death in general was a particular preoccupation of literature produced in Neronian Rome – besides Seneca's own work we might think particularly of his nephew Lucan's epic (discussed in Chapter 1) or Petronius' *Satyricon* (to be explored further in Chapter 6). The high profile of famous deaths in later accounts of the Neronian period is also, as we saw in Chapter 4, due to the mass of death literature produced in the years after Domitian's reign – when Tacitus himself was writing and there seems to have been a particular obsession with death literature.

Cato's death appears to have become the focus of renewed interest in the time of Nero. This may be linked with the publication during this period of Cicero's letters to Atticus, in which Cato's suicide is praised.[35] Cato's death-bed speech was not part of the earliest accounts of his suicide, it appears, and may indeed be the product of Seneca's imagination. However, it seems rapidly to have become an established part of the story of Cato's end. There is good reason to suppose it was included in the biography of Cato by Thrasea Paetus. This work (which has not itself survived) was to become hugely influential.[36] It was apparently the main source used by Plutarch in composing his own biography of Cato early in the next century.[37] The biography was both reflection and reinforcement of Thrasea's own profile as a senator unwilling to moderate his austere principles in deference to Nero.

The life of Cato, from the perspective of later authors, was always already to conclude with his noble suicide. Here is a man who appears to know his part and play it well. Cato must live up to his name. Repeated tellings of the Cato story must have heightened awareness of how a conclusion might condition one's reading of the life which goes before it. Could we see this model as influencing the dying subjects of Nero's time, whose ends were also to be recorded for posterity? Are these, too, instances of spectacular self-actualisation? 'Thus do I become Seneca,' for instance? Tacitus' account might seem to endorse such a reading. A number of the deaths recounted by Tacitus (and other writers, too) have striking features in common. In a number of cases Stoic philosophy is at least implicitly presented as informing both the decision to die and also the details of the death.[38] This Roman suicide is very much a social act, performed in front of an audience. The suicide acts calmly and deliberately. Pain is borne bravely; the term *constantia* (which

Cicero used repeatedly in relation to Cato's suicide) regularly appears. His or her last words play an important part in determining the 'reception' of the death. The deaths of Seneca and Thrasea, particularly, seem self-conscious creations, designed to form fitting conclusions to the narratives of their subjects' lives.

The theatrical analogy here, one might argue, serves a wholly different purpose from the theatrical parallels Stoics sometimes use in articulating ideas of the self. Perhaps we should think of two ways of characterising the idea of performance in relation to dying which are not necessarily linked. Yet we can, I think, make better sense of these theatrical deaths if we look at them in the context both of Stoic exhortations in explicitly theatrical terms to perform one's own personal role well and also in another context, that of the Roman practice of declamation, the role-playing speeches performed by young men as part of their education in preparation for a career in the law-courts and/or the senate.

The starting point for most discussions of the high profile of suicide under the early principate is the death of the Younger Cato, as we have seen. His suicide offered an enabling example to others.[39] This death, which could be read as an enactment of the death of *libertas*, becomes a kind of script for subsequent suicides – though, as often in the Roman theatre, some actors showed a considerable talent for improvisation.[40] Cato too, however, was drawing on a tradition. He seems to have self-consciously presented his own death as an evocation of that of Socrates.[41] The philosopher had been condemned to death in the courts of democratic Athens on charges of corrupting young men. He turned down his friends' offers to help him escape and, according to the accounts of his pupils Plato and Xenophon, accepted and drank the fatal dose of hemlock with great calm, after a lengthy discussion with his companions of the immortality of the soul.[42] The parallel between Cato and Socrates is already implied by Cato's contemporary Cicero, who makes clear that Cato, like Socrates, had received a sign from god sanctioning his departure from life (*Tusc.* 1.74). Seneca in Letter 24 (a letter concerned with the subject of the fear of death) rehearses what he himself terms 'the well-known account' of how Cato *ultima illa nocte Platonis librum legentem posito ad caput gladio*, 'read Plato's book on that last glorious night with a sword laid at his pillow' (*Ep.* 24.6–8).[43] And Plutarch, too, writes that Cato read Plato's *Phaedo* twice in the hours before he died.[44]

Yet there is perhaps a tension here between the idea of being yourself and that of imitating Socrates. And we might see this tension as all the more acute for those who modelled their own deaths on that of Cato.[45] Young Romans were generally encouraged to see Cato as exemplary; it was not only for critics of the emperor that Cato was a role model. Augustus himself (adoptive son of Julius Caesar though he was) is alleged to have praised Cato.[46] The poet Horace, no critic of the autocratic principate, writes of Cato's noble death, *Catonis/nobile letum* (*Odes* 1.12.35–6).[47] And in the schools of rhetoric, too, Cato lived on.[48] Persius, writing under Nero, implies that as one of their exercises Roman schoolboys regularly learned to declaim the speech of the dying Cato. He complains of occasions:

> Grandia si nollem morituri verba Catonis
> Discere non sano multum laudanda magistro.

> when I did not want to recite the noble speech of the dying Cato – a speech which would be much praised by my foolish master.
> (Satires 3.45–6)[49]

Persius' alleged unwillingness to play Cato need not be taken as typical. In Roman declamation schools, the 'Death of Cato' was on one level 'performed' regularly.

Many Romans, then, had rehearsed the role of 'Cato'. While circumstances might not afford the opportunity to emulate Cato in life, a well-chosen end might allow one to aspire to an equally distinguished death.[50] The proliferation of accounts of Cato's end may well have inspired better performances.[51] Did some suppose that impersonating Cato (not to mention other distinguished Romans) might ultimately help the young aristocrat better to perform himself? One might practise Cato's death-bed speech over and over again, experimenting with different variations – even if the Roman aristocrat (like everyone else) would only get one chance to perform his own end.

The Cato 'script' seems to have had an influence on the actual death of Seneca – as Tacitus describes it, at any rate (*Ann.* 15.60–4).[52] Seneca is made to respond to an agent of Nero, sent to interrogate him concerning his alleged involvement in the Pisonian conspiracy, that Nero is more used to experiencing *libertas*, 'the behaviour of a free man', from Seneca than *servitium*, 'slavishness' (15.61.3). *Libertas* was, of course, a term closely associated with the suicide of Cato, particularly in Seneca's own writings.[53] Seneca then receives an order to commit suicide from the emperor – unlike Cato who chooses to die. Like Cato, however, he opts to spend the hours before his death in philosophical conversation with his friends, consoling them at the prospect of his own imminent end. He voices criticisms of Nero which, Tacitus writes, were intended for public hearing. One might compare Cato's presentation of his suicide as itself an indictment of Julius

Caesar. Seneca's final words are taken down for publication (though suicide is essentially a one-off performance, those who did not catch Seneca's speech at the time could at least read the script later). Seneca's death is painful and protracted. The veins are severed, first in his arms and then in his legs also. The blood flows too slowly, however, so Seneca next resorts to poison. This spreads too slowly in his aged limbs and a steam bath is required to hasten his end.[54] Cato, too, had only died with difficulty and persistence; after the wound made in his first attempt had been sewn up by doctors, he famously ripped it open with his own hands.

Like Cato, Seneca evokes the death of Socrates, though not through reading the *Phaedo* (or at least that is not mentioned). Rather we are told, when Seneca's attempt to bleed to death had failed to take effect fast enough, he begged his doctor for *provisum pridem venenum quo damnati publico Atheniensium iudicio extinguerentur promeret; adlatumque hausit,* 'the poison long prepared, such as was earlier used to execute state criminals at Athens' (*Ann.* 15.64.3). Seneca next requests that a libation be offered to Jupiter the Liberator (compare Socrates' request that a cock be offered to Asclepius), then expires in a steam bath.

Tacitus' *Annals* breaks off in the middle of his account of the death of Thrasea Paetus (16.34–5), as we saw earlier. Thrasea, too, expecting to hear his death sentence, discusses philosophical questions concerning the immortality of the soul with a Cynic professor, Demetrius. On receiving news of the senate's decree, Thrasea, like Seneca, slits his veins. He terms the blood which falls on the ground a libation to Jupiter the Liberator – an evocation of the libation requested by Seneca to the same divinity (as well as an allusion to *libertas*).[55] As Cathy Connors comments, he 'seems to construct his last moments as an intertextual re-enactment of Seneca's death scene'.[56] His death can also be read as, specifically, a re-enactment of Cato's re-enactment of Socrates.[57] The parallels with Cato's death (in Plutarch's version) are striking.[58] Among Cato's final companions is a philosopher called Demetrius. Like Cato, Thrasea discusses the nature of the soul and the relations between body and spirit. Thrasea's friends, like Cato's, once his intentions become clear, shed tears and lament his fate. Thrasea dissuades his wife from joining him; similarly Cato dissuades his young friend Statillius.

The issue here, though, is not only whether individuals may have, to some degree, modelled their own deaths on the death-bed scenes of those whom they admired. The narratives resemble each other not only because Thrasea modelled his own death on Cato's but also because Arulenus Rusticus must have modelled his description of Thrasea's death on Thrasea's description of Cato's death.[59] And literary accounts of Cato's death no doubt embellish and reconfigure what they describe. We should remember that Plutarch composed his account of Cato's death *after* the deaths of Seneca, Thrasea and so many others had taken place and been written up. His treatment of Cato's end may well have been influenced by this body of literature recounting later deaths.[60] These *clausulae*, 'conclusions', then may be as much the creations of those who wrote them up as of their original performers.

To what degree, though, can we justify treating these deaths themselves as 'performances'? Perhaps an emphasis on scripts, on replays, is straying too far from properly Stoic notions of performing oneself with constancy, even if, or especially if, that means ending one's own life. Nevertheless self-conscious role-playing seems to have a part in all these accounts. We might remember here Epictetus' presentation of Helvidius Priscus: he has to say these lines – that is his part. There is certainly a strong sense that these deaths would lose a crucial part of their meaning if they had no audience.

Leaving aside, for the moment, Tacitus' role in the creation of Seneca's end, we may think of Seneca as becoming his own playwright, writing his own *clausula*, the last lines of the drama 'Seneca'. But has he played his part well? Has he been consistent? Could he rather be seen as, in Cicero's terms, imitating someone else's nature and abandoning his own? Can he really become 'Seneca' in playing 'Socrates' or 'Cato'? One might well object that Seneca's death is overwritten. Certainly it seems Seneca's mode of death did not find universal favour among his contemporaries. Even Tacitus' account may be read as somewhat critical.[61] Exploring the impact of suicide on the reception of certain authors' work in the twentieth century, Thomas Osborne notes that an author's suicide may well serve to authenticate the seriousness of their work. And yet: 'the irony would be that such a conse-cration cannot come about by the author's will. If the author deliberately intends such effects, then surely the act would be self-defeating.'[62] Was this a view some Romans also held?

It is suggestive to compare here another death, not very Stoic but never-theless rather histrionic: the death of Petronius, again as recounted by Tacitus (*Ann.* 16.18–19). Petronius, arrested by Nero's soldiers and fearing the worst, slits his own wrists – then binds them up again whenever he feels so inclined (in irreverent imitation of Cato, perhaps). Waiting to die, he talks with his friends – in the time-honoured way – but Petronius does not discuss weighty philosophical issues, preferring more trivial topics. He listens to recitations not of discourses on the immortality of the soul but of light lyrics and frivolous poems. His last act is not a sacrifice but the destruction of his own signet ring, after the sealing of a detailed list of Nero's most secret improprieties, to be sent to the emperor. This scene is often read as a parody of a philosophical death. Might this ironic treatment itself betray Tacitean unease at Stoic death theatre?[63] One might also conclude that Petronius, just as much as the others, perhaps more so, is dying a death wholly appropriate to his own role as 'Petronius'.[64]

The metaphor of acting encourages the would-be Stoic to think of his or her own behaviour as intrinsically social. It will always have an audience (even if one must sometimes play that part for oneself). The aim is to *project* a good and consistent character. The theatrical metaphor also fits with Stoic fatalism. The play is already written. The individual's only choice is whether to play the part well or badly. The notion of the theatre can also serve to introduce a kind of metatheatrical distancing which itself complements the Stoic preoccupation with self-scrutiny. What does it mean to be 'Medea', to be 'Cato', to be 'Seneca'? Yet the metaphor of acting also allows scope for moves which could be seen as undermining orthodox Stoicism. The fascination of the stage is hard to resist. The most compelling characters are not always the most virtuous. When the Stoic becomes his own playwright, aesthetics may undermine philosophy.

Not all Stoics felt comfortable with death theatre. Writing some decades after Tacitus, the emperor Marcus Aurelius expressed concern at the theatricalisation of suicides. 'How admirable is the soul which is ready and resolved, if it must this moment be released from the body ... This resolve, too, must arise from a specific decision ... after reflection and with dignity, and so as to convince others, without histrionic display' (11.3).[65] Even this comment however still presents suicide as an act of communication; a serious suicide aims to convey a message to others.

Epilogue: farce

Most of the deaths recounted in the surviving sections of Tacitus' *Annals* take place under the reign of Nero. Theatrical suicides may have seemed especially appropriate under an actor emperor – even if we can never ascertain how far the theatrical elements characterised the original performances and how far they are the creations of later writers.[66] The emperor Nero's own death was probably described by Tacitus in a later part of the *Annals* which has not survived. His end, as presented in Suetonius' account at least (*Nero* 47–9), is highly theatrical.[67] Realising his supporters have finally turned against him, Nero accepts his position is now impossible and looks to make a traditional Roman exit. He repeatedly pronounces *sententiae* which sound as if they might become famous last words. Yet his apparently final exclamation *'qualis artifex pereo!'* 'What an artist dies with me!' is succeeded by another; *'vivo deformiter, turpiter'* 'My life is scandalous, wretched!', he comments in Latin, then continues in Greek. 'This does not befit Nero, it does not befit him. A clear head is what is needed. Come, rouse yourself!'

Like the protagonists of Seneca's tragedies, it seems, Nero must live up to his own well-known character. In their turn, these words too are succeeded by a quotation from the *Iliad*, as horsemen are heard to approach. Even after stabbing himself in the throat, however, Nero is not silent but, in response to a centurion's arrival, croaks out '*sero*', 'Too late' and '*haec est fides!*' 'This is fidelity!'[68]

Nero's actions follow a similar pattern. He rushes from place to place and tries out a vast battery of means to kill himself – poison, a gladiator's sword, drowning in the Tiber and finally a dagger. This last in particular could be read as an echo of the death of Seneca, who also had to use a variety of means to squeeze the life from his aged body. But, in contrast to the death of Seneca, the end of Nero's life is frantic. At first he cannot bring himself to plunge the dagger in but begs his companions to help by setting him an example (those of Cato and Seneca, it seems, are not enough). Finally, as his pursuers draw near, he manages to thrust in the dagger – though even then only with the help of his freedman. Tragedy has descended to farce. In the end, Nero's death – fragmentary, inconsistent but above all theatrical – fully lived up to Nero's life. At last he could become Nero.[69]

CHAPTER 6

TASTING DEATH

The hero of a quintessentially decadent French novel of the 1880s, J. K. Huysmans' *A rebours*, in his quest for ever more recherché pleasures, hosts a funeral dinner party. The invitations, resembling funeral announcements, describe the dinner as marking the decease of the host's virility. The place at table of each guest is marked by a small gravestone, bearing the guest's name. The guests are waited on by naked negresses. Only black foods are served.[1] There is an intriguing eighteenth-century French precedent for Jean Des Esseintes' dinner: in 1783 the great gourmet Grimod de la Reynière, editor of the *Almanach des gourmands*, invited guests (and 300 spectators) to a black dinner which featured a sarcophagus as the centrepiece of the table.[2] But Des Esseintes is also a passionate admirer of the ancient Romans, particularly those of Nero's time and later.[3] It is tempting to see an additional inspiration for his dinner party in a story told about the emperor Domitian, who is said by Dio Cassius to have hosted a similarly funereal dinner party.

This was by no means the only Roman dinner at which death had a conspicuous presence. Our main focus here is a collection of Roman texts associated with the later first century CE, all of which invoke funereal image and metaphor at the dinner table. Nevertheless, the superficial similarity between Huysmans' funereal feast of the French fin-de-siècle and the deathly dinners of the Romans can serve to highlight the rather different, complex (and perhaps unexpected) relationship between dining and death in Roman antiquity.

Convivia or dinner parties are a recurring preoccupation for many Roman writers. These occasions seem to have offered a prime arena for the parading of social status, wealth and cultural sophistication – as well as a context for the furthering of friendships and the pursuit of erotic relations.[4] Dinner parties were also crucially important to the negotiation of relations between Roman emperors and their fellow senators.[5] Indeed, in some contexts, the dinner party functions as a metaphor for imperial rule. 'Observing the emperor's behaviour in the power-laden context of the *convivium* is one way in which Romans of the early empire could render him comprehensible as a locus of concentrated power,' as Matthew Roller comments.[6] Some emperors are celebrated for being generous hosts whose dinner parties respect proper social distinction. Augustus, for instance, in deference to his senatorial and equestrian guests, never invited a freedman to share his table, according to Suetonius (*Aug.* 74). Others are criticised for using dinners to humiliate their guests and parade their own power. Again according to Suetonius, Caligula regularly seduced his female dinner-guests in front of their husbands (*Calig.* 36).[7] Pliny, in his *Panegyric*, praises Trajan at length for his dinner parties, their congenial nature in sharp contrast with those given by his predecessors: *Non tibi semper in medio cibus semperque mensa communis? Non ex convictu nostro mutua voluptas? Non provocas reddisque sermones?* 'Are not your meals always taken in company and the table shared, the dinner and its pleasures partaken of by us all? Do you not encourage our conversation and join in?' (49.5).

Domitian's dinner, as described by Dio (who dates it to approximately 89 CE), unlike those Pliny associates with Trajan, is clearly designed to maximise the discomfiture of his guests:

He prepared a room that was quite black on all sides, ceiling, walls and floor, and had made ready bare couches also black, resting on the bare floor; then he invited his guests to come alone by night and with no attendants. And first he set beside each of them a slab shaped like a grave-stone, with the guest's name on it and also a small lamp of the kind that hangs in tombs. Next beautiful naked boys, also painted black, entered like phantoms, and after circling round the guests in a sinister dance took up their positions at their feet. After this all the things that are usually offered at the sacrifices to the spirits of the dead were in the same manner set before the guests, all of them black and in dishes of a similar colour. As a result of this, each and every one of the guests was filled with fear and trembling – and the constant expectation of having his throat cut the next moment, the more so as on the part of everybody but Domitian there was dead silence, as if they were already in the realms of the dead, while the emperor himself conversed only on topics relating to death and slaughter. Finally he sent them away; but first he removed their slaves, who had been standing in the vestibule, and now gave his guests into the charge of other slaves, whom they did not know, to be transported either in carriages or in litters, and by this procedure he filled them with still greater fear.

(67.9.1–4)

The piquant historicism of Des Esseintes' decadent dinner party could flatter and titillate the erudition of his guests. By contrast Domitian's dinner fills his guests with utter terror by insistently anticipating their deaths – deaths which, as they were well aware, lay within the power of their host. The commonplace rituals of the imperial dinner party are hideously defamiliarised. Guests are given the kinds of food customarily offered to the departed.[8] They are waited on by phantoms. They listen in silence while the emperor talks only of death. They are to think of themselves as dead and immured in a tomb. And such imperial whims were not to be taken lightly. Emperors (allegedly) had been known to signal the wish that a senator should kill himself in the most trivial of asides.[9] In the event, Domitian's guests are not taken off to be executed but are returned to their own homes. Their sense of relief is short-lived, as a messenger immediately arrives from the emperor. The recipient no doubt expects that generous imperial offer *liberum mortis arbitrium*: choose how you die.[10] But their expectations are confounded. The messenger has brought costly gifts, including the funeral slab – which turns out to be made of silver – and the beautiful boy.[11] The ordeal is over – for now. The emperor's malign and ingenious capacity to control the Roman elite has been memorably demonstrated.

The power of the host is an issue regularly explored in Roman dinner-party literature. Hosts humiliate guests whose greed for food and wine – and most of all being seen at the 'right' table – is sufficient to outweigh any sense of their own dignity. Normally guests, too, are culpable, complicit in their own humiliation. In Juvenal's fifth satire, the pitifully scanty meal served by the host to low-ranking guests, such as Trebius, is an index of the degree to which such guests have abased themselves. Interestingly Trebius' portion is itself compared by Juvenal to a funeral offering (5.84–5).[12] But the idea of the host's power has a special resonance when the host is the emperor, and guests have virtually no choice as to whether to attend or not.[13]

Domitian's choice of the *convivium* as a mechanism to terrorise the senatorial elite in Dio's narrative seems in line with what is known of his style of ruling from other sources. Among emperors, Domitian above all seems to have used the role of host to stage his own imperial presence. The poems of Statius celebrate the emperor, presiding over the table, as equal to a god. In *Silvae* 4.2, for instance, the poet expresses incredulity that he is permitted to lie on a couch gazing at the emperor's face.[14] Certainly the *triclinium*, dining room, in Domitian's Palatine palace seems to have been specially constructed to focus all eyes on the host's person in his magnificent setting – a fundamental reorientation of conventional Roman dining space.[15] In Dio's story, the emperor uses the framework of the dinner party to parade and play with his power of life and death over his subjects in an overt and sinister manner. His role as host allows for the unfolding of an exquisitely articulated ritual of torment as guests struggle to interpret the meaning of dishes, drinks, décor and table-talk. What might function as a macabre joke in the home of another host works as a terrifying assertion of the emperor's all-encompassing power – though one which *might* still turn out to be a joke.[16] The guests' fears, as Domitian appreciates, transform into instruments of terror the elaborate conceits of this *convivium*. Their own appetites for food, for wine, for sex (which often played a role in the pleasures a host offered his guests) are transmuted into instruments of torment. To desire the food of the dead, to desire the phantom (however beautiful) is to desire death itself.[17] Even the gifts are transformed into instruments of psychological torture. As David Fredrick comments: 'To accept them and (worse) to want them, the guests must re-enact their powerlessness, terror and humiliation.'[18]

Dining with the dead

Domitian's deathly dinner appears to function as a grotesque, nightmarish parody of proper hospitality. The ideal *convivium*, we might suppose, was far removed from any thought of death. Yet there are nevertheless some distinctive and significant connections between dining and death in Roman society, which should perhaps be brought into consideration here. Reclining banqueters are often shown on funeral monuments of the Greek and Roman worlds. Etruscan sarcophagi in particular feature images of the dead reclining at dinner.[19] What do these images signify? Should they be taken to represent the deceased during life enjoying worldly pleasures, or rather as participating in a banquet of the dead in the life beyond? The appeal of such representations lies partly in their capacity to convey status and privilege but perhaps above all in their ambivalence.[20] Observers could interpret them in accordance with their own beliefs. Dinners were regularly held to mark the occasion of a funeral, with offerings of food made to the deceased themselves (as we have already seen from Dio's narrative). Dinners were also served to commemorate the anniversaries of deaths and for festivals in memory of the dead such as the Parentalia and Feralia. Many individuals left money in their wills, the interest from which was to be used for ceremonial meals, *epulae*, to take place beside the tomb. Indeed tomb complexes sometimes incorporate kitchen areas for the preparation of such meals. This sharing of food was perhaps thought to bring together the living and the dead.[21] Thus Domitian's funereal dinner party can be read as a quite specific anticipation of what constituted a central part of the commemoration of the dead.

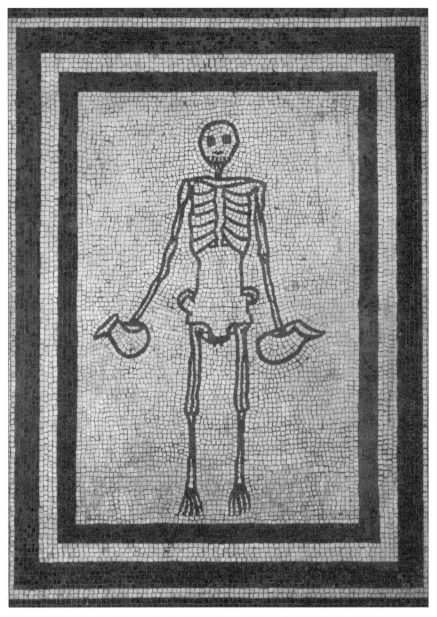

5. Mosaic of skeleton butler from Pompeii, probably first half of first century CE.

6. Silver goblet from Boscoreale.

A number of funerary monuments put words in the mouths of the dead, exhorting the living to enjoy themselves while they can.[22] But such reminders also seem to have had a defined role in the context of Roman dinner parties. Thus the funeral dinner party can also be seen as an extreme version of what appears to have been a regular Roman dinner-party practice in the late republic and early principate – the inclusion of a *memento mori* in the midst of the festivities.[23] A mosaic from a Pompeian house, for instance, depicting a skeleton holding jugs of wine, seems to have been designed for such a purpose (see fig. 5), as do the numerous small silver and bronze skeletons and drinking cups decorated with skeletons which have survived from Roman antiquity.[24] The silver cup found at Boscoreale shown here is decorated with skeletons, identified as celebrated Greek authors and philosophers, Sophocles, Moschion, Zeno and Epicurus (fig. 6). Inscriptions on the cup exhort revellers to seize the moment. Interestingly the theatre is also invoked: 'Life is a stage' reads one inscription.[25] The image of the banquet or symposium here and elsewhere may be seen as functioning to tie together the worlds of the living and the dead. Certainly reminders of death are often invoked as spurs to the enjoyment of the present pleasures of the table in the poems of Horace and Martial.[26] Lucretius, in his *De rerum natura*, treats reasoning of this kind as common, though not conducive to Epicurean tranquillity of mind (3.912–15). As host, then, Domitian is invoking a familiar trope but with a new and vicious twist. For his guests, the imperative *memento mori* takes on a perverse urgency – at any moment liable to telescope into a more peremptory imperative: 'die'.

Playing dead: Trimalchio

Domitian was not the only one to develop the presence of death at the dinner table from a familiar cliché, manifested in a line or two of verse or a model skeleton, into a more elaborate and sustained conceit. A number of other texts associated with the latter part of the first century CE present leading Romans as orchestrating rehearsals not of the deaths of their guests but rather of their own funerals (interestingly, these texts too figure among the reading of the fictional Des Esseintes). Petronius' *Satyricon* (Des Esseintes' favourite work of literature, we are told) notoriously presents the wealthy ex-slave Trimalchio as obsessed with death. This obsession dominates the bizarre dinner party he hosts. An articulated silver skeleton is introduced at an early stage in the dinner party. It is tempting to see this as another example of the kinds of artefact found in Boscoreale and elsewere.[27] The skeleton provokes from Trimalchio a brief poem on death.

> Eheu nos miseros, quam totus homuncio nil est.
> Sic erimus cuncti, postquam nos auferet Orcus.
> Ergo vivamus, dum licet esse bene.

> Alas for us wretched creatures; all humankind is nothing. Thus shall we all be, once Orcus has taken us. Let us live then, while we may live well.
> (*Sat.* 34.10)

While the expression of such sentiments on the part of a Roman host was quite unexceptional, the presence of death at Trimalchio's table turns out to be far more pervasive. One of the seven freedmen guests at the dinner, Gaius Julius Proculus, has been an undertaker, *libitinarius* (38), another, Seleucus, has just come from a funeral feast, a meal which he describes in lurid detail (42),[28] while a third, Habinnas, recounts the funeral from which he has just

come (65).[29] Towards the close of the dinner, Trimalchio reads his will out
to those who are to inherit from him. Then, after the arrival of Habinnas,
who is by trade a monumental mason, Trimalchio orders in great detail an
extremely elaborate (though also absurd) funeral monument (71).[30] Having
described the funeral monument, Trimalchio starts to weep. *Tota denique
familia, tamquam in funus rogata, lamentatione triclinium implevit,* 'Then
all the household, as though summoned to his funeral, filled the dining
room with lamentation' (72). He is haunted by the thought of his own death
– but also seeks to use it as a spur to pleasure. Just as Encolpius, too, starts
to weep, Trimalchio exclaims: *ergo … cum sciamus nos morituros esse, quare
non vivamus?* 'Well, if we know we must die, why don't we do some living?'
and proposes a hot bath.

After the bath (more usually a prelude than a sequel to a dinner),
the guests are escorted into another dining room. The dinner party's
culmination is a fully-fledged rehearsal of Trimalchio's funeral. Trimalchio
instructs his slave:

'Stiche, profer vitalia, in quibus volo me efferri. Profer et unguentem et ex
illa amphora gustum, ex qua iubeo lavari ossa mea.'

Non est moratus Stichus, sed et stragulam albam et praetextam in
triclinium attulit <...> iussitque nos temptare, an bonis lanis essent
confecta. Tum subridens 'Vide tu' inquit 'Stiche, ne ista mures tangant
aut tineae; alioquin te vivum comburam. Ego gloriosus volo efferri, ut
totus mihi populus bene imprecetur.' Statim ampullam nardi aperuit
omnesque nos unxit et 'spero' inquit 'futurum ut aeque me mortuum
iuvet tamquam vivum'. Nam vinum quidem in vinarium iussit infundi
et 'putate vos' ait 'ad parentalia mea invitatos esse'.

Ibat res ad summam nauseam, cum Trimalchio ebrietate turpissima
gravis novum acroama, cornicines, in triclinium iussit adduci, fultusque
cervicalibus multis extendit se super torum extremum et 'fingite me'
inquit 'mortuum esse. Dicite aliquid belli.' Consonuere cornicines funebri
strepitu.

'Stichus, bring me the grave clothes in which I wish to be carried out.
Bring ointment, too, and a sample out of that jar which must be poured
over my bones.'

Stichus did not delay but brought a white winding sheet and robe into
the dining room and … [Trimalchio] instructed us to feel if they were
made of good wool. Then giving a little laugh, he said. 'Take care neither
mouse nor moth spoils them, Stichus, otherwise I will burn you alive.
I want to be carried out in splendour, so that all the people call down

blessings on me.' At once he opened a flask of spikenard, anointed us all and said, 'I hope I shall like this as much in the grave as I do in this life.' Besides this he ordered wine to be poured into a bowl, and said, 'Now you must imagine you have been asked to a festival in my memory.'

It was all getting quite sickening, when Trimalchio, now sodden with drink, had a new set of performers, some trumpeters, brought into the dining room, propped himself up on a heap of cushions, and extended himself on his death-bed, saying, 'Imagine I am dead. Play a lovely tune.' The trumpeters broke into a loud funeral march.

(Sat. 77–8)

Trimalchio stretches himself out on the couch like a corpse (though it may be that some corpses at least were posed as if reclining at a dinner party).[31] This is effectively the end of the dinner party (the trumpeting is interpreted as a summons by the fire brigade, whose arrival disperses the guests).[32] The scene is full of absurdities and confusions. Trimalchio apparently refuses to recognise that he will be in no position to give orders, or to like or dislike anything, after he is dead. In staging a rehearsal of his own funeral he is enabling himself to witness an event normally beyond the human individual's experience.[33] He longs to see how his family, slaves and friends will react. But this desire will clearly be thwarted by the fact that they know him to be alive – and will of course tailor their comments accordingly.

The entire dinner party as orchestrated by its impresario host works to destabilise the relationship between image and reality. The dishes served at dinner are never what they seem – objects presented as raw pea-hen's eggs, for instance, turn out to be made of meal which, on closer inspection, contains a delicious cooked bird, wrapped in spiced egg-yolk (33), while sucking-pigs are revealed to be made of cake (40).[34] Trimalchio the uneducated freedman cannot aspire to the mastery over words boasted by rhetoricians such as his guest Agamemnon. Yet by manipulating the things to which words refer – the endlessly ingenious dishes, the puzzlingly ambiguous events – he can destabilise the power of words to have predictable meaning.[35] The funeral, too, is not a real funeral. Guests are exhorted to use their imagination, with the stimulus offered by a rich array of props. A 'semantic glide' between convivial and funeral couch is explicitly played on here.[36] One striking feature of this pretend funeral is that the process of dying which would normally precede such an event is itself elided. It is almost as if by moving smartly on to the funeral, Trimalchio might avoid altogether the need to die.

On another level, we could read this scene as yet another tactic to humiliate and disconcert his guests. How should they react? As dutiful guests they should go along with whatever their host has prescribed, but does this entail merely admiring his funeral arrangements or engaging in laments for his pretend death? Might not the latter option entangle them still further in absurdities engineered by a knowing and manipulative host who is secretly laughing at their attempts to anticipate what he wants, to humour his apparent ignorance? Certainly as soon as the narrator and his friends have joined in the lamentations which follow Trimalchio's description of his funeral monument, Trimalchio himself at once reverts to cheerfulness and leads his party off to the baths (72.2–4). How far is Trimalchio's stupendous ignorance of the proprieties of dining feigned? Might it not be a strategy to see how far he can push his guests? When Trimalchio leaves the table briefly, the narrator Encolpius is made to observe: 'with the tyrant away we had our freedom and we attempted to draw the conversation of our neighbours', *nos libertatem sine tyranno nacti coepimus invitare convivarum sermones* (41.9). It is tempting to read Trimalchio as figuring for another tyrant, the emperor Nero – a ludicrous host but one whom it might be fatal to offend (and perhaps was to prove so for the author of the *Satyricon*).[37]

An incident related by Tacitus presents Nero himself manipulating guests at a dinner party, though in a way which more obviously anticipates the story of Domitian's funeral discussed above. In the aftermath of the Pisonian conspiracy amid the welter of aristocratic executions/enforced suicides (a number of which have been discussed in earlier chapters) is that of the consul Vestinus Atticus (*Ann.* 15.69). Although no-one has informed against Vestinus, Nero has taken a dislike to him and sends a battalion of the Praetorian Guard to forestall an alleged revolutionary plot. Vestinus is giving a dinner party. When the soldiers enter he at once rises and makes arrangements to take his own life. As for his guests, Tacitus writes:

> Circumdati interim custodia qui simul discubuerant, nec nisi provecta nocte omissi sunt, postquam pavorem eorum, ex mensa exitium opperientium, et imaginatus et inridens Nero satis supplicii luisse ait pro epulis consularibus.

> In the meantime, those who had been at the table with him were surrounded by soldiers and not released until late at night. Nero imagined with amusement their expectation of death after dinner but in the end said they had suffered enough for dining with the consul.

> (*Ann.* 15.69)

Though in this case the emperor is not himself the host, he assumes control of a dinner given by another. Nero takes pleasure imagining the confusion and terror of Atticus' guests as they suppose that they too are condemned. And, like a satirist, he claims to see in the guests' suffering a fit punishment for their social ambition.[38] As in the case of Domitian, the piquancy of the emperor's joke gives a new edge to dinner-party cliché.

The philosopher at table?

This chapter began with an archetypally decadent text, *A rebours*, in which the figure of the Roman funeral dinner is invoked as one of a series of perverse diversions. We might consider further the question of how far Trimalchio's obsessive preoccupation with death at his dinner party could relate to ancient Roman characterisations of decadence. The fragmentary text of the *Satyricon* has been read as offering a moralising, indeed condemnatory picture of Roman morals in decay. Thus the repeated emphasis on impotence and constipation serves as an index of the corrupting effects of *luxuria* on sexual activity and eating, processes essential to life.[39] It is surely not so easy to identify the moral perspective of a work whose central characters are hypocritical chancers, particularly when neither the opening nor the closing sections have survived (and it remains unclear just what proportion of the work as a whole the surviving fragments might represent).[40] Yet the dinner-party episode in particular does seem preoccupied with the relationship between the themes of death and satiation. Trimalchio strives to forget death, to 'seize the day' by eating, satisfying his passionate desire for life, but, in Arrowsmith's words: 'with every mouthful he takes, he tastes death'.[41]

Trimalchio is certainly a man driven by the 'devouring terror of death'. This was a predicament of central concern in Epicurean philosophy generally (though that is not in itself enough to make the *Satyricon* an essentially Epicurean text)[42] – and one to which, as we saw in Chapter 3 above, Lucretius devotes a considerable portion of his *De rerum natura*, composed in the mid first century BCE. Book 3 of *De rerum natura* is concerned almost exclusively with providing reasons why humankind should not fear death, on the grounds that the fear of death is the greatest of evils, responsible for all the worst elements in human behaviour (including gluttony, 3.59–93). Lucretius has a personified Nature pronounce that one should leave life with as little disturbance as a guest leaves a dinner party.

Cur non ut plenus vitae conviva recedis
Aequo animoque capis securam, stulte, quietam?

'Why not withdraw from life as a satisfied man from a dinner party and accept certain quiet with a calm spirit?'

(*DRN* 3.938–9)

Life has a proper shape, just like a well-orchestrated dinner. Well-mannered guests recognise when the time has come to leave.[43] Trimalchio's use of food as a strategy to deny death could be read as a kind of inversion of this philosophical injunction.[44] For Trimalchio, as for the Epicurean philosopher, the banquet functions as a metaphor for life itself. But while for the philosopher this analogy can serve to make easier the departure from life, for Trimalchio it makes the prospect of the actual banquet's conclusion quite unendurable. Trimalchio cannot contemplate satiety. The dinner he gives, composed of an apparently endless succession of grotesque dishes, cannot conclude except with his own death – or at least a rehearsal of it.[45]

Living death

Petronius is not the only author writing under Nero to connect death and eating. Seneca, writing from an explicitly Stoic perspective, articulates this connection in several of his letters.[46] The notion that a life devoted to the satisfaction of bodily cravings, indeed the life of excess more generally, in failing to live up to properly human goals, may be seen as anticipating death, is explored in a number of Seneca's letters:

Non fames nobis ventris nostri magno constat, sed ambitio. Hos itaque, ut ait Sallustius, 'ventri oboedientes' animalium loco numeremus, non hominum, quosdam vero non animalium quidem, sed mortuorum. Vivit is, qui multis usui est, vivit is, qui se utitur; qui vero latitant et torpent, sic in domo sunt, quomodo in conditivo. Horum licet in limine ipso nomen marmori inscribas, mortem suam antecesserunt.

It is not the natural hunger of our bellies that costs us so much but our cravings. Therefore those who, as Sallust puts it, 'listen to their bellies' we should count among animals, and not among humans; and certain people, indeed, should be numbered not even among animals but among the dead. True life is experienced by one who is useful to many; true life is experienced by one who is useful to himself. Those men, however, who creep into a hole and grow torpid are no better off in their homes than if they were in their tombs. Right there on the marble lintel of the house of such a man you may inscribe his name, for he has anticipated his own death.

(*Ep.* 60.3–4)

The man who devotes himself solely to satisfying his animal cravings might as well be dead.⁴⁷ His life is an inversion of life as it ought to be. His home is effectively a tomb – as the vivid detail of the name carved on the door lintel underlines.

In the course of a later letter concerned with charting luxury's drive toward inversion, Seneca attacks the perverse late-night dinner parties of his contemporaries (a glaring instance of devotion to the pleasures of the flesh) by likening them specifically to funeral rituals.

> Sunt qui officia lucis noctisque perverterint nec ante diducant oculos hesterna graves crapula quam adpetere nox coepit ... Hos tu existimas scire quemadmodum vivendum sit, qui nesciunt quando? Et hi mortem timent, in quam se vivi condiderunt? Tam infausti quam nocturnae aves sunt. Licet in vino unguentoque tenebras suas exigant, licet epulis et quidem in multa fericula discoctis totum perversae vigiliae tempus educant, non convivantur, sed iusta sibi faciunt. Mortuis certe interdiu parentatur.

> Some have reversed the functions of light and darkness; they open eyes sodden with yesterday's debauch only at the approach of night ... Do you think that these men know *how* to live who do not know *when* to live? And do these men fear death when they have buried themselves alive? They are as strange as birds of the night. Though they pass the night-time hours with wine and perfume, though they spend every minute of their unnatural waking hours in eating dinners – and those too cooked separately to make up many courses – they are not really banqueting, they are conducting their own funerals. And the dead at least have their banquets by daylight!

> (122.2–3)

Seneca here, as in other letters, is obsessed with time and its misuse – an obsession also shared, if rather differently manifested, by Petronius' Trimalchio.⁴⁸ This kind of 'life' – and Seneca plays on the derivation of *convivium*, banquet, from 'living together' – falls so far short of the proper goals of human life that it comes closer to the denial of life than to its affirmation. Eating, an activity essential to bodily existence, becomes by a characteristically paradoxical move on Seneca's part a marker for life's opposite, death. The dinner of excess is metaphorically transformed into a funeral dinner.

A little further on in the same letter, Seneca develops this image further, offering another vivid comparison to characterise the luxurious:

Aves, quae conviviis conparantur, ut immotae facile pinguescant, in obscuro contineantur; ita sine ulla exercitatione iacentibus tumor pigrum corpus invadit, et superba umbra iners sagina subcrescit. At istorum corpora, qui se tenebris dicaverunt, foeda visuntur. Quippe suspectior illis quam morbo pallentibus color est, languidi et evanidi albent, et in vivis caro morticina est.

Birds that are being prepared for the dinner table, so that they may easily grow fat through lack of exercise, are kept in darkness; and similarly, if men lie around without physical activity, their idle bodies swell up, and in their complacent retirement the fat of indolence grows on them. Moreover, the bodies of those who have devoted themselves to the hours of darkness have a revolting appearance. Their colour is more alarming than that of anaemic invalids; they are indolent and flabby; though still alive they are already carrion.

(122.4)

Here again the luxurious anticipate their own deaths. Now though, instead of consuming a funeral dinner, they have themselves become what is to be consumed. While Seneca repeatedly insists that the body is of no importance to the would-be philosopher (who should instead be perpetually focused on the mind) he nevertheless dwells here as often elsewhere on revealing details of physical appearance: in this instance the pallor and flabby flesh of the luxurious.[49] Their bodies are compared at length to the kinds of luxury foods they themselves consume at their decadent banquets – birds, whose only purpose in life is to be eaten by people who are not hungry. They are bloated, pallid, inert. This self-consciously disgusting comparison brings a suggestion, at the very least, of cannibalism. Their insatiable quest for the pleasures of the flesh causes the luxurious to consume themselves – both metaphorically and literally. Interestingly the Satyricon also explores the idea of eating human flesh.[50] The soi-disant philosopher Eumolpus takes pleasure in mocking the legacy-hunters of Croton by requiring them to eat portions of his dead body in order to qualify for (non-existent) legacies (Sat. 141).[51] In both texts the figure of cannibalism conveys on the moral level a society utterly lacking in civilised values and on the economic (insofar as that may be distinguished) a society concerned only with consumption.

In letters 60 and 122, Seneca treats the life of luxury – and specifically the eating habits of the luxurious – as metaphorically equivalent to death. It is not clear that death is being deliberately invoked by the individuals whose behaviour he attacks. An earlier letter, however, does describe a host who explicitly and repeatedly enacts his own funeral at dinner. Letter 12, which is largely concerned with the issue of old age and the anticipation of death, includes the following anecdote:

Pacuvius, qui Syriam usu suam fecit, cum vino et illis funebribus epulis sibi parentaverat, sic in cubiculum ferebatur a cena, ut inter plausus exoletorum hoc ad symphoniam caneretur: bebiotai, bebiotai! [in Greek] Nullo non se die extulit. Hoc qui ille ex mala conscientia faciebat, nos ex bona faciamus et in somnum ituri laeti hilaresque dicamus:
　　Vixi et quem dederat cursum fortuna peregi.
Crastinum si adiecerit deus, laeti recipiamus.

Pacuvius, who by long occupancy made Syria his own, used to hold a regular burial sacrifice in his own honour, with wine and the usual funeral feasting, and then would have himself carried from the dining room to his chamber, while eunuchs applauded and sang in Greek to a musical accompaniment 'He has lived his life! He has lived his life!' Thus Pacuvius had himself carried out to burial every day. Let us however, do from a good motive what he used to do from a debased one; let us go to our sleep with joy and gladness; let us say:
　　I have lived; the course which fortune set for me is finished.[52]
And if god is pleased to add another day, we should welcome it with glad hearts.

(12.8–9)

Here then we have another instance of the self-conscious rehearsal of death at dinner. The term *parentaverat* refers specifically to rites for the dead.[53] As in the case of Trimalchio's dinner party, the evening culminates with the mock funeral of the host – to great acclaim from his household. This passage in Letter 12 is regularly compared by commentators to the finale to Trimalchio's dinner party, though it is not always clear what significance they attribute to the resemblance. Why exactly should *mala conscientia*, 'bad conscience' provoke Pacuvius to rehearse his own funeral? A comment Seneca makes in Letter 122 is perhaps relevant: *gravis malae conscientiae lux est*, 'light is irksome to a bad conscience' (122.14). Some at least among the luxurious show sufficient awareness of their own plight to appreciate that they may be better off dead. Perhaps in this case, too, like that of Trimalchio the mock funeral serves as a strategy – inevitably unsuccessful – to drive the taste of death from the mouth of the deluded host.

　　For Seneca the anticipation of one's own funeral need not be altogether reprehensible. Seneca criticises Pacuvius in passing but uses this story as a point of departure to develop a rather different line of thought linked to his discussion of old age. The would-be philosopher is encouraged to rehearse his own death. For him it is a strategy to remind himself that death may strike at any moment. This is one means among many to confront and overcome the fear of death.[54] Such a rehearsal, we may imagine, is not to be envisaged as something physically enacted; the crude antics of Pacuvius and others are misguided. Rather the rehearsal is interiorised. Thus Seneca takes a weird fad attributed to the luxurious and transforms it into a philosophically serious *memento mori* exercise. Seneca's friend Bassus, as his own death approaches, behaves as though he is a spectator at his own death-bed (*Ep.* 30.5–6). The would-be philosopher might make the contemplation of his own funeral a similarly edifying exercise.

But if Seneca can be read as appropriating the bizarre habits of the luxurious for his own philosophical project, might we not also see the luxurious themselves – not to mention Domitian or Nero – as self-consciously in dialogue with the tradition of philosophically informed criticism? Might there not be an especially sharp pleasure to be derived from translating hostile philosophical metaphor into dinner table practice? Might drinking from a silver cup decorated with philosophical skeletons perhaps bring special delight to the luxurious? Accused of anticipating his death in a life of excess, might not the more erudite voluptuary deliberately challenge his critics by celebrating his own funeral at the dinner table?

It is relevant at this point to come back to the Platonic tradition. In the *Phaedo* Socrates is made to insist that philosophy is precisely learning how to die: 'Those who really apply themselves in the right way to philosophy are directly and of their own accord preparing themselves for dying and death' (*Phaedo* 63). Real life is life outside the body. Socrates comments a little later: 'The body is a hindrance to the acquisition of knowledge ... The wisdom which we desire ... will be attainable only when we are dead' (65–6).[55] In the Platonic and Stoic traditions, philosophers are to shun the pleasures of the senses since these are seductive reminders of the mortal flesh. But others, we might speculate, could stake their claim to refined hedonism by embracing sensual pleasure precisely as an affirmation of both life *and* mortality – of a life which takes its meaning precisely from its transience.[56]

The death of the author

In Tacitus' account of the aftermath of the unsuccessful Pisonian conspiracy, the senator Petronius (the man commonly identified as the author of the *Satyricon*), condemned to death by Nero, chooses to spend his last hours dining and conversing with his friends about self-consciously trivial subjects. My previous chapter looked at this account in the context of

Roman conceptions of role-playing. Here I would like to press further the philosophical implications of Petronius' death (at least as Tacitus describes it).

Et Cumas usque progressus Petronius illic attinebatur; nec tulit ultra timoris aut spei moras. Neque tamen praeceps vitam expulit, sed incisas venas, ut libitum, obligatas aperire rursum et adloqui amicos, non per seria aut quibus gloriam constantiae peteret. Audiebatque referentis nihil de inmortalitate animae et sapientium placitis, sed levia carmina et facilis versus. Servorum alios largitione, quosdam verberibus adfecit. Iniit epulas, somno indulsit, ut quamquam coacta mors fortuitae similis esset.

Petronius too had reached as far as Cumae and was arrested there. He did not endure delay – with its hopes and fears. Yet his death was not swift. His veins were severed. Then he had them bound and unbound as he chose and conversed with his friends though not on serious matters or such as would secure a glorious reputation for endurance. And he listened to them reciting not on the immortality of the soul or the other topics which please the philosophers but trivial songs and witty poems. He bestowed largesse on some slaves – and beatings on others. He went in to dinner and dozed, so that his death, although enforced, might seem like a natural one.

(*Ann.* 16.19)

This is generally read as an inversion of Roman 'philosophical' deaths, such as that of Seneca himself (at least as described by Tacitus a little earlier in the *Annals*).[57] Certainly the appearance of terms such as *gloria* and *constantia*, which often characterise philosophical death narratives and which Petronius affects to disdain, encourage such a reading.

This death could also, I think, be read as a self-conscious rejection of the model offered by Plato's Socrates in the *Phaedo*. In the *Phaedo* the evening has arrived when Socrates, condemned to death for perverting the youth of Athens, is due to drink the hemlock. A lengthy philosophical discussion explores the fate of the soul after death and stresses the insignificance of embodied life and its pleasures, as we have already seen. Nevertheless Socrates' loyal but dim companion Crito urges him to follow the model of others in his situation who 'have dinner and enjoy their wine ... and only drink the poison quite late at night' (116).[58] Socrates, of course, rejects this suggestion. To act in such a way would be to show himself in thrall to those bodily pleasures he is so soon to leave behind. By contrast Petronius, ordered like Socrates to die, though under somewhat different circumstances, could be said to greet death precisely as the conclusion of a dinner party. He chooses to die at the dinner table. It is all the more tempting to read this death as a deliberate rejection of the Platonic/Stoic tradition, if one accepts firstly that this Petronius was indeed the *Satyricon*'s author and secondly that the dinner-party episode of the *Satyricon*, as a number of scholars have suggestively argued, is a deliberate inversion of another Platonic text, the *Symposium*.[59]

Petronius may have been ordered to die by Nero but he has (as a good Roman should) taken full control of his beautifully orchestrated death scene. This death, unlike that of Trimalchio or Pacuvius, is not mimicry or rehearsal but the real thing. His death, at least as Tacitus describes it, could be said to enact precisely the philosophical death advocated not by Plato but by Lucretius who makes nature advise withdrawal from life as a satisfied man from a dinner party (*De rerum natura* 3.938–9). In this version of the Epicurean tradition, death is not privileged over life (as it sometimes seems to be in Platonic or Stoic writing) – but neither does fear of death spoil even life's final hours.[60]

At the Roman dinner party, the evocation of death is, then, a less 'decadent' practice than it might at first seem – at least sometimes. The *convivium* was a context in which it was quite commonplace to think of death, a practice often perceived as an effective strategy for heightening the pleasure of the moment. But the invocation of mortality, if frequently hackneyed, still had the potential to destabilise the predictable rituals of the dinner table. An obsession with death has taken over – though in quite different ways – the dinner parties of Domitian, Trimalchio and the voluptuaries mocked by Seneca. Petronius himself, by contrast, approaches death lightly and stylishly. His invocation of death at the dinner party could be seen as governed by considerations not so much moral or philosophical as aesthetic. At the same time, though, it makes manifest a recognition that acceptance of mortality alone ensures even the last of life's pleasures will not taste of death.

CHAPTER 7

A FEMININE ENDING?

Dying nobly comes to be represented, in the Rome of the emperors, as the prime site for the display of aristocratic *virtus*, as we have seen – displacing, most notably, achievements on the battlefield. While performance in battle was an area from which Roman women were almost entirely excluded, women too might die a noble death in the contexts increasingly favoured in imperial Rome. Though the vast majority of the deaths we have considered so far have been the deaths of men, dying women are also celebrated in Roman literary texts. A number of issues are raised by these female deaths, however. When women are celebrated for meeting death with courage, are they described in the same terms as their male counterparts? Have these women succeeded in rising above the limitations of their sex? Or how far might such deaths be gendered as distinctively feminine? If women can be seen to provide spectacular displays of *virtus*, might this create problems for constructions of masculinity?

Many of the deaths to be examined here are suicides. For Romans, the act of killing oneself was, as we have seen earlier, not intrinsically shameful but often a strikingly effective means of conveying the dignity and moral status of the individual performing the act. The women who die in the pages of Tacitus, for instance, may seem in many ways closely comparable to the more numerous men who meet their ends in his writing. There is certainly a sense in which female deaths in general and female suicides in particular can command admiration.

The shifting ways in which death has been perceived at different times and in different cultures is fundamentally conditioned by the history of gender.[1] These Roman accounts may be sharply contrasted with, for instance, the representation of female deaths in much nineteenth-century fiction, where as Margaret Higonnet argues, citing most notably *Madame Bovary* and *Anna Karenina*, female suicides generally serve to imply not heroic self-sacrifice but rather disintegration and social victimisation.[2] At the same time, at least some of the Roman death narratives to be examined here reveal an attitude to the dead female body not so very different from that discerned in writing from much later periods.[3] In written texts and visual representations of recent centuries, the female dead body is frequently presented as an object of aesthetic beauty. Such representations serve, in Elisabeth Bronfen's analysis, as a means of simultaneously repressing and articulating culture's unconscious knowledge of death. To the male viewer/ reader these representations of the dead female body may offer a version of death which is reassuringly 'other'.[4] Roman texts seem to share this preoccupation with the dead female body. Romans, as we have seen, insistently envisage death as a spectacle. Where the deaths of women are concerned, the process of dying is important but there is often also a notable focus on the corpse, as a beautiful object on display. At the same time, in some cases at least, the dead female body is made the vehicle of weighty political symbolism.

Suicide's sexual politics

The foundation of the Roman republic, in several versions of the story, is precipitated by the heroic suicide of a woman – Lucretia.[5] In Livy's account (1.57–60), Sextus Tarquinius, son of the Etruscan king of Rome, and Collatinus, away from Rome on campaign against Ardea in 509 BCE, wager bets as to whose wife is the more virtuous. They then hurry back to the city to find Tarquin's wife drinking and entertaining friends, while Collatinus' wife Lucretia is overseeing woolwork with her servants. Collatinus has won the wager, but Tarquin is seized with desire for Lucretia (desire provoked as much by her virtue as by her beauty, *cum forma tum spectata castitas*, according to Livy, 1.57.10). Not long afterwards Tarquin returns to Collatinus' house, accompanied only by a slave. When he finds that the threat of death is not enough to make Lucretia give in to him, he threatens that if she does not accede to his demands, he will kill her and his slave and place their naked bodies in bed together so that her virtue will seem to have been lost in a manner calculated to bring greatest shame on her family. Faced with the threat of losing her good name, Lucretia lets Tarquin have his way. But once he has gone, she summons her father and husband and tells them what has happened. 'Only my body has been violated,' she assures them, 'my mind is blameless. Death shall be my witness.' *Corpus est tantum violatum, animus insons; mors testis erit* (1.58.7). After extracting from her listeners the promise that they will avenge her and dismissing their attempts to assure her that she is guiltless, she continues:

'Vos', inquit, 'videritis, quid illi debeatur: ego me etsi peccato absolvo, supplicio non libero; nec ulla deinde inpudica Lucretiae exemplo vivet.'

'It is for you', she said, 'to decide what he deserves. As for me, though I judge myself innocent, I do not absolve myself of punishment. Thus no unchaste woman shall live by Lucretia's example.'

(1.58.10–11)

She takes out a dagger and kills herself. Among those present is Lucius Junius Brutus; it is he who draws the dripping knife from her wound. He swears an oath by Lucretia's blood – *castissimum ante regiam iniuriam*, 'most chaste until violated by a prince' (1.59.1) – vowing to extract vengeance. He proceeds to drive out the tyrannous Tarquins from Rome, going on to become the first of the city's consuls in the newly founded republic.[6] Livy's Brutus transforms Lucretia's suicide into a sacrifice.[7] Her dead body is put on display in the Forum at Collatia – a spectacle to bring home the nature of the Tarquins' regime to their subjects and thus provoke revolution. Lucretia is, it seems, more powerful as a corpse than as a living woman.[8] In the time Livy was writing, the display of a dead body for political purposes, as a *monumentum* to spur others to action, must have been most obviously familiar from the display of the corpse of Julius Caesar after his assassination in 44 BCE.

The historicity of Lucretia's story is not my concern here. For Livy's readers – and, it seems likely, for earlier generations of Romans, too – the noble female suicide is always already part of Rome's history. This episode is an instrinsic part of the narrative of the republic's inception. A series of formal analogies and correspondences links the account of Lucretia's rape to the political part of the story. The political symbolism is, in many versions, quite evident: 'Lucretia is not simply Lucretia, but the figure of violated Rome; the rape epitomises the wider tyranny of the Tarquins', as Ian Donaldson comments.[9]

Livy's Lucretia would sooner die than suffer rape.[10] Thus the threat of death is not itself sufficient to make Lucretia give in to Tarquin. However, Lucretia would sooner be raped than lose her good name. Livy's Lucretia is preoccupied above all with reputation. Why exactly does Lucretia commit suicide? Her family and friends believe her story and consider her guiltless. Yet her death is to function as 'the ultimate sign of her innocence'.[11] *Mors testis erit*, as Livy makes Lucretia say; 'death shall be my witness'. The violation of her body, though it has happened through no fault of her own, is something she cannot live with. Her honour can only be redeemed through death. But this is not presented as the act of a woman too traumatised to endure the prospect of continued existence. This is the act, rather, of a woman focused on how her life and its end will be read by others.

In thinking of her future reputation, Livy's Lucretia is thinking not only of how she herself will be perceived. She is also thinking of how other women may make use of her example (the Roman preoccupation with exemplarity is, as we have seen, a phenomenon often manifested in accounts of heroic deaths). A Lucretia who survived the rape, no matter how innocent, might always be appropriated as a precedent for Roman women of more dubious chastity. Her suicide – described as a punishment, *supplicium* – functions as a warning for those who might contemplate genuine offences against chastity.[12] Livy's version of the story, we should not forget, was written in the context of a Rome where adultery on the part of a married woman was shortly to become a criminal offence, under the terms of the *lex Iulia de adulteriis coercendis*, the Julian law on controlling adulteries (18 BCE). There is some evidence that the emperor had attempted to pass a measure along such lines earlier in his reign, that is to say before the completion of Livy's first few books.[13] Numerous Augustan writers associate unchecked female sexual misbehaviour with the moral and political chaos of the late republic, a chaos that was finally to be brought under control through the Augustan order.[14] The story of Lucretia resonates with this set of concerns and gives female chastity a distinctively political dimension.

Lucretia is a figure much admired by the Christian writers Jerome and Tertullian.[15] Augustine discusses at length the problems associated with her story in the first book of *The City of God* (1.25–6). The concern with which Augustine addresses Lucretia's suicide is an index of the story's continuing power even in the early fifth century of the Common Era.[16] Augustine wonders whether Lucretia's suicide was motivated by guilt because she had enjoyed sex with Tarquinius. Augustine focuses on difficulties in the narrative. His concern seems in turn to have prompted later writers to engage creatively with the story, speculating further as to how the events might really have occurred or offering variants on Livy's account.[17] The characters in Shakespeare's treatment, *The Rape of Lucrece*, often seem driven by a sense that deeds are superior to words – though both Lucretia and Brutus agonise over how to act.[18]

Livy's Lucretia achieves fame and glory through death – like so many of Rome's exemplary heroes. To kill herself, she uses a dagger, the preferred method for Roman men, as we have seen (Martial's *Romana mors*, 1.78). Nevertheless this suicide which atones for, upstages, rape could be read as a quintessentially feminine suicide. The rape itself is described only in metaphorical terms – *expugnato decori muliebri* 'having taken by storm the woman's honour' – an echo of the campaign against Ardea the men are conducting a few miles away (1.58.5), though the success of the substitute assault on Lucretia contrasts with the failure of the siege of Ardea. However, Livy describes directly the dagger penetrating her body:

> Cultrum, quem sub veste abditum habebat, eum in corde defigit prolapsaque in vulnus moribunda cecidit.

> A knife she had concealed inside her dress she plunged into her heart and collapsing forward onto the wound, died as she fell.

Her movement at once replicates and compensates for Tarquin's violation (1.58.11).[19] For at least some Roman (and indeed later) readers, there is perhaps an element of erotic pleasure to be had from this scene.[20] Lucretia's corpse is further objectified when it is exploited by Brutus as a political symbol.[21]

Violent female deaths also have a distinctive role to play in Virgil's *Aeneid* – like Livy's history, composed in the early years of Augustus' reign. Many men die in the *Aeneid*. Yet their deaths are almost always quick. The only two deaths presented as long drawn out and painful are those of the only two women who die in the poem, the Carthaginian queen Dido and the Italian warrior Camilla, whose deaths round off Books 4 and 11 respectively.[22] Dido welcomes the shipwrecked Aeneas and his companions to Carthage, falls in love with him, then kills herself when her attempts to persuade him to stay are in vain. Camilla dies fighting at the side of her fellow Latins in a vain attempt to drive Aeneas and his supporters from Italy.

The deaths of both Dido and Camilla have a sinisterly erotic dimension.[23] Camilla, whose manly bravery is undone by her feminine weakness for glittering spoils, is pierced through the nipple by a spear.[24] Death is assimilated to defloration. The strategies by which Virgil eroticises the death of Dido have been remarked on by a number of critics.[25]

> At trepida et coeptis immanibus effera Dido
> Sanguineam volvens aciem, maculisque trementis
> Interfusa genas et pallida morte futura,
> Interiora domus inrumpit limina et altos
> Conscendit furibunda rogos ensemque recludit
> Dardanium, non hos quaesitum munus in usus.

> But Dido, trembling and frantic with her terrible plan, burst through the doorway to the inner part of the house. Her eyes were bloodshot and rolling, her cheeks quivered with a flush, and she was pale with the

pallor of imminent death. In a frenzy she climbed the funeral pyre, and unsheathed the Trojan sword, a gift never meant for such a use as this.

(4.642–7)

The contrast between the redness of the blood and the pallor of Dido's face evokes the colour contrasts normally associated with sexual initiation – a reminder of Dido's sexual transgression in having relations with Aeneas. Dido's frantic desire for death is conflated with her sexual passion for Aeneas, as she grasps her lover's sword.[26] It is surely not fanciful to see the imagery here as phallic. At the same time, the metaphorical wound of love Dido sustained earlier (4.65–7) is now succeeded by a real wound.

The parallels between the death of Dido and that of Lucretia are deeply significant. Dido's suicide, like that of Lucretia, is a redemption for sexual *culpa* 'guilt', for so her liaison with Aeneas is termed earlier in Book 4 (*Aen.* 4.170–2).[27] Indeed the death of Dido can be read as the only option left to salvage her honour (as is suggested at 4.534–52). Dido's sufferings are presented as disproportionate to her guilt (as is often the case in tragedy).[28] This is so even if Dido herself argues that she has deserved to die. But though her sufferings are excessive, Dido is nevertheless presented as at fault. This suicide, then, is a recognition of guilt which at the same time serves to compensate for it. In this respect she is unlike Lucretia, whose death serves precisely to demonstrate her innocence. Yet Lucretia, too, kills herself to avenge a sexual transgression.

At the same time, the deaths of both Lucretia and Dido can be read as sacrifices necessary to the foundation and proper development of Rome. The death of Lucretia is, as we have seen, a key moment in the foundation of the Roman republic. Her death is avenged by Brutus – who puts her dead body on display to rouse the feelings of his fellow citizens against the unjust rule of the Tarquins. The death of Dido, on the other hand, can be seen as a necessity for the foundation of the proto-Roman state which is Aeneas' destiny.[29]

Dido, in the *Aeneid*, constitutes a political challenge to the Roman order. As has often been noted, Virgil's handling of Dido's story also resonates with representations of Cleopatra, another foreign queen involved in a liaison with a Roman commander which posed a threat to Rome. Cleopatra, the queen of Egypt, fought alongside her lover Mark Antony in the civil war between Antony and Octavian. Antony and Cleopatra were defeated by Octavian at Actium in 31 BCE. They both committed suicide shortly afterwards in 30 BCE.[30] Both Cleopatra and Dido can be seen as dangerously powerful women, rulers who have usurped the kind of authority which, for Romans, should only be exercised by men. Both are associated with the east (though the Trojan Aeneas is in some respects also associated with the east). And both can be presented as using their feminine charms to ensnare men who should be concentrating on their duty to Rome.

These parallels are stressed within the *Aeneid*, for although the battle of Actium will not take place until centuries after Aeneas' death, his mother Venus persuades Vulcan to make Aeneas a shield on which are depicted important events from Rome's future. The final scene is Augustus' triple triumph of 29 BCE. This is immediately preceded by a representation of his naval victory at Actium (when he was known as Octavian). The description of Octavian's opponents mentions Mark Antony but the focus is on his eastern allies, most particularly his Egyptian wife – an outrage – *nefas Aegyptia coniunx* (8.688). In Roman law, she could scarcely have counted as Antony's legitimate wife, since he was at that time married to Octavian's sister. In this case, as in Dido's, marriage is a delusion.

In the *Aeneid*, as in other Augustan texts, no mention is made of Cleopatra's name:[31]

Regina in mediis patrio vocat agmina sistro,
Necdum etiam geminos a tergo respicit anguis.
Omnigenumque deum monstra et latrator Anubis
Contra Neptunum et Venerem contraque Minervam
Tela tenent.

The queen in the centre called up her columns by sounding the tambourine of her people; nor yet did she think of the pair of asps which fortune held in store for her. Her gods, monstrous forms of every species, even to the barking Anubis, levelled weapons against Neptune, Venus and Minerva herself.

(*Aen.* 8.696–700)

The sinister exoticism of Cleopatra and her minions is stressed. Her death is clearly foreshadowed both with the reference to the asps and also a few lines later, when the routing of the Egyptian fleet is described:

Ipsa videbatur ventis regina vocatis
Vela dare et laxos iam iamque immittere funis.
Illam inter caedes pallentem morte futura
Fecerat ignipotens ...

The queen herself could be seen calling on the winds and setting sail, pictured at the very moment when she shook the sail-sheets loose. The god whose might is fire had fashioned her amid the slaughter, pale with death to come.

(8.707–10)

Virgil describes Cleopatra as *pallentem morte futura*, 'pale with death to come'. This phrase closely echoes his earlier description of Dido at the point of death, *pallida morte futura* (4.644). These queens both display on their bodies portents of their imminent ends.

The poet Propertius, also writing in Augustus' time, develops in one of his elegies a complex parallel between his own 'enslavement' to his mistress and Mark Antony's submission to Cleopatra. Cleopatra was a *meretrix regina*, 'whore-queen' (3.11.39), whose licentiousness knew no bounds. She aspired to take over Rome itself.

> Fugisti tamen in timidi vaga flumina Nili:
> > Accepere tuae Romula vincla manus.
> Bracchia spectavi sacris admorsa colubris,
> > Et trahere occultum membra soporis iter.

Yet you fled to the wandering outlets of the craven Nile: your hands received Roman fetters. I witnessed the sight of your arms bitten by the sacred asps and your limbs channelling the unseen route of the numbing poison.

(Propertius 3.11.51–4)

The imprisoned queen contrived to kill herself. The poet focuses on the sight of her dying body. Cleopatra's suicide aroused Octavian's admiration, according to Plutarch (*Ant.* 86) but thwarted his plan to have her feature as the chief ornament of his triumphal procession (*Ant.* 78).[32] Propertius' use of the term *spectavi*, 'I witnessed', is striking.[33] The poet here puts on display not Cleopatra's death at Alexandria in 30 BCE, but rather the model of the queen's dead body which, in some accounts, was carried in the triple triumph at Rome in 29 BCE. In both Virgil (where Cleopatra is shown figured in silver and gold on Aeneas' shield) and Propertius, the Egyptian queen's dying body is configured as a work of art to elicit triumphal and voyeuristic pleasure from Roman spectators.[34]

These three suicides mark three key moments in Roman – or proto-Roman – history. The death of Dido plays a crucial role in Aeneas' foundation of the community which serves as forerunner to the Rome of Romulus. The death of Lucretia has an essential part to play in the foundation of the Roman republic, while the death of Cleopatra marks the foundation of the Augustan principate. These are political deaths – and yet sex is a central issue in all three cases – at least as Roman writers represent them. Lucretia is in many ways the opposite of Cleopatra: the obedient and virtuous Roman wife could hardly be further removed from the licentious and threatening Egyptian queen. Certainly Cleopatra's suicide is less easily related to sexual *culpa* (though her assimilation to Dido serves to insinuate a connection). Yet in treatments of all three stories, the dead female body is made into a politically resonant object of display for the male Roman viewer.

Gendering virtue

A number of Roman writers, in celebrating Lucretia's action, stress the degree to which she exceeded expectations of female behaviour by assimilating her to a man. Ovid, in the account of Lucretia's rape given in the *Fasti*, his poem on the Roman calendar (2.721–852), praises her as a lady of manly spirit: *animi matrona virilis* (847). More striking, however, is the characterisation offered by Valerius Maximus in his collection of moral anecdotes. Under the rubric of *pudicitia*, which can perhaps be translated as 'sexual honour', he gives a synopsis of Lucretia's story:

> Dux Romanae pudicitiae Lucretia, cuius virilis animus maligno errore fortunae muliebre corpus sortitus est, a Sex. Tarquinio regis Superbi filio per vim stuprum pati coacta, cum gravissimis verbis iniuriam suam in concilio necessariorum deplorasset, ferro se, quod veste tectum attulerat, interemit causamque tam animoso interitu imperium consulare pro regio permutandi populo Romano praebuit.

> The leader of Roman sexual honour is Lucretia, whose manly spirit by a perverse twist of fate was allotted to a woman's body. Through force obliged to suffer rape by Sextus Tarquinius (son of king Tarquinius Superbus), she lamented in the strongest terms the wrong she had suffered before a council of her relatives, then killed herself with a knife which she had brought hidden in her dress and through her courageous death provided the motive for the Roman people to exchange consular rule for that of the kings.
>
> (Val. Max. 6.1.1)

The term *pudicitia* is often translated as 'chastity', a choice which might dispose the modern English reader to associate this quality particularly with women. Indeed, when Livy recounts the circumstances of the foundation of the cult of Pudicitia Plebeia in 295 BCE, Verginia the cult's founder is made to assert that *pudicitia* in women is the characteristic quality which corresponds to *virtus* in men (10.2.7–8).³⁵

Valerius' notion of *pudicitia*, however, is significantly broader. Under this rubric, he has assembled nine stories where the *pudicitia* under threat is that of a woman and six where the potential victim is male.³⁶ While most of the rest of Valerius' virtues are exemplified principally by male characters, this is a virtue expected of both women and men.³⁷ Most of the other stories told by Valerius under this rubric involve the use of violence to defend or avenge *pudicitia*. The story which comes closest to that of Lucretia concerns a Greek woman Hippo, who throws herself into the sea in order to protect her *pudicitia* from male assault (Val. Max. 6.1. Ext. 1).³⁸ We might note, however, that when the victim is male, there is no exploration of the idea of suicide (or pre-emptive killing, on the model of Virginia, stabbed by her father to preserve her from the lusts of a depraved magistrate); violence is used rather against his assailant. It is women who must demonstrate the value they place on their *pudicitia* by surrendering their lives.

Yet Valerius' Lucretia is presented as transcending her sex. He describes her as *dux Romanae pudicitiae*, a term which emphasises not only her temporal priority but also her position as pre-eminent among the defenders of Roman *pudicitia*. The term *dux* is used almost exclusively to refer to males; exceptions to this are themselves anomalous, such as Virgil's Dido (*dux femina facti*, *Aen*. 1.364) and Tacitus' British tribal queen Boudicca (*femina duce*, *Agr*. 16.1; 31.4), the female rulers of foreign peoples.³⁹ For Valerius Maximus, Lucretia exemplifies the specific virtue of *pudicitia*. In doing so she reveals her *virilis animus*, 'manly spirit'.

This usage can be linked to shifting ideas of *virtus* which may be traced in texts associated with the first centuries BCE and CE.⁴⁰ As we have seen, the term *virtus* is generally used in texts of the first century BCE (and earlier) with the sense of 'bravery' and most often in military contexts. However, we do find *virtus* being used in a wider sense (as the opposite of *vitia*) particularly in philosophical writing to approximate to the Greek term 'arete'.⁴¹ Cicero's discussion of *virtus* in the *Tusculans* (*Tusc*. 2.43) may perhaps be read as an attempt to conflate the traditional and the philosophical uses of the term. Cicero, in his parading of etymology, shows himself anxious to tie his definition of virtue to manhood. It is specifically the virtue of a man to display contempt for death and pain. Clearly contempt for death and pain might have a conspicuous part to play on the battlefield. At the same time, however, Cicero's definition leaves scope for others outside the category of *viri* to give evidence of their own *virtus*. Yet when Cicero himself attributes *virtus* to women, he uses the term in a very general sense, and stresses traditionally feminine good behaviour.⁴²

The shift away from an understanding of *virtus* focused on military achievement is further developed in Seneca's writing, a century or so later. In his work, *virtus* can be almost entirely detached from the traditional sphere of warfare. One consequence of this is that physical strength is no longer an issue. In one letter, exhorting the sick to philosophy, Seneca asserts: 'a man can display bravery even when wrapped in his bed clothes' – *et in vestamentis vir fortis apparet* (78.21).[43] Elsewhere Seneca presents us with the brave death-bed scene of an elderly invalid, such as his old school friend Claranus (Letter 66). This letter continues 'virtue is born in any place whatever', *virtutem omni loco nasci* (66.3). If men can exercise *virtus* in their beds, there might also be scope for women, too, to participate in *virtus*. Seneca does occasionally refer to female examples. When he writes of how pain is to be borne, for instance, he comments that even a girl in childbirth can set an example for the endurance of pain (*Ep.* 24.14). Seneca's would-be *sapiens* struggles to transcend *indifferentia* (perceived goods and ills which in reality have no bearing on an individual's *virtus*). One might well suppose that gender difference could count among such *indifferentia*. Is this new philosophical heroism an opportunity, then, for women?

Seneca does sometimes consider women's virtue. Specifically, he addresses consolatory treatises to Marcia and to Helvia (Marcia has lost her son; Helvia, Seneca's own mother, has lost Seneca himself to exile). Strikingly, both are praised for being quite unlike other women. Seneca takes the trouble to address Marcia, he says, because he knows her to be *tam longe ab infirmitate muliebris animi quam a ceteris vitiis recessisse*, 'as far removed from womanish weakness of mind as from all other vices' (*Marc.* 1.1). Similarly, Seneca admonishes his mother: 'You must be as far removed from woman's tears as from her vices', *tantum debes a feminarum lacrimis abesse, quantum vitiis* (16.5).

A passage in the *Ad Marciam* which specifically addresses the question of whether women are capable of *virtus* is of particular interest here. Seneca gives a long list of famous Romans who have borne the deaths of their children bravely. He then writes:

> Scio quid dicas: 'oblitus es feminam te consolari, virorum refers exempla.' Quis autem dixit naturam maligne cum mulierum ingeniis egisse et virtutes illarum in artum retraxisse? Par illis, mihi crede, vigor, par ad honesta, libeat, facultas est; dolorem laboremque ex aequo, si consuevere, patiuntur.

> I know what you are saying: 'You forget that you are comforting a woman; the examples you cite are of men.' But who has claimed that nature has

dealt grudgingly with women's natures and has restricted their virtues to a narrow field? Believe me they have as much force, as much capacity, if they choose, for virtuous action; they are just as capable of enduring pain and trouble when they are used to them.

(Marc. 16.1)

This might seem an unambiguous statement. Seneca's views develop a tradition already to be seen in earlier Stoic writers.[44] And we might compare his comments with similar assertions offered by his near contemporary Musonius Rufus.[45]

We have seen elsewhere Seneca's predilection for citing *exempla* from early Roman history. Here he goes on to mention Lucretia: we are talking, he says, in the city 'where Lucretia and Brutus threw off the authority of the king from Roman subjects; to Brutus we owe liberty, to Lucretia we owe Brutus', *regem Romanis capitibus Lucretia et Brutus deiecerunt: Bruto libertatem debemus, Lucretiae Brutum* (16.2). He also makes a reference to Cloelia, an early Roman heroine who escaped the Etruscans by swimming across the Tiber (Livy 2.13), as well as the reactions of Cornelia, mother of the Scipios, and Cornelia, mother of the Gracchi, to the loss of their children. Cloelia, indeed, has *almost* been included *in viros*, 'among the men' (16.2).

In the *Ad Helviam* (written some time after he was sent into exile to Corsica in 41 CE) Seneca seems even readier to attribute *virtus* or at least the capacity for *virtus* to women. Most of the treatise is devoted to reassuring Helvia as to Seneca's own state of mind – though in exile, he is still happy, he asserts. The final sections, however, address Helvia's own feelings more directly and suggest strategies for subduing her grief: *Sed quanto ista duriora sunt, tanto maior tibi virtus advocanda est et velut cum hoste noto ac saepe iam victo acrius congrediendum*, 'The harder these circumstances are, the more courage must you summon, and you must engage with Fortune the more fiercely, as with an enemy well known and often conquered before' (15.4). Here we have a woman calling on *virtus*, a woman presented as a veteran soldier in life's battles.

Seneca tells his mother she should look for inspiration to women such as Cornelia, mother of the Gracchi, and Rutilia, mother of the exiled Cotta. These positive examples, Seneca describes as 'the women whose conspicuous bravery has placed them in the rank of mighty heroes', *quas conspecta virtus inter magnos viros posuit* (16.5). Here the form of words is very close to that Seneca uses of Cloelia in his address to Marcia. But the difference is significant. While Cloelia is *almost* to be included *in viros* these women, acting precisely in their capacity as mothers, we might note, are to be given this status without qualification.

Earlier instances of 'manly' women in Roman texts may more plausibly be read as transgressive rather than transcendent.[46] Yet the contradictory nature of Seneca's discussions of women's *virtus* in these two texts is striking. In discussing courage in the face of suffering Seneca, like many other Roman writers, chooses to use 'womanly', *muliebriter*, as a pejorative term characterising failure to endure pain (*Ep.* 78.17).[47] Cloelia is to be admired. However, the function of her statue is to fill Roman men with shame that they have been outdone in *virtus* by a mere woman – scarcely a reflection of the 'ethical equality of the sexes'.[48] In both *Ad Helviam* and to a lesser extent in *Ad Marciam* womanliness and manliness are categories which anyone may slip into and out of.[49]

It is notable that when writing of his own family members, Seneca seems more readily able to imagine women as exemplars of *virtus*. But the singular nature of this treatise is evident when one compares it with what Seneca has (or perhaps rather does not have) to say about women in the rest of his philosophical writing. References to women are strikingly rare elsewhere in his prose work, and even in the treatises addressed to Marcia and Helvia almost all the specific examples are of bereaved mothers bearing their loss bravely.[50] The ability to bear physical pain is characterised by Seneca (and Cicero, as we have seen) as an important touchstone of *virtus*. Seneca, particularly in his discussions of illness, develops this idea at considerable length. Yet while Seneca may occasionally refer to anonymous (and low status) female *exempla* like the slave girl giving birth, his named *exempla*, which include Greeks and Romans, figures from myth and figures from history, are almost invariably male; the only significant exceptions here occur, not surprisingly, in the dialogues addressed to Helvia and Marcia, where the focus is predictably on the endurance of suffering rather than more active forms of *virtus*.[51] On the one occasion when Lucretia is mentioned, though her achievement is placed on a level with that of Brutus, there is no specific mention either of rape or of suicide. And strikingly absent are noble deaths (or feats of endurance) of Seneca's own time. Where, we might wonder, is Porcia? Where is Arria?

Lessons in dying

The heroism of some women in the face of death does feature in the work of other writers recounting the history of the late republic and early principate. Porcia, the daughter of Cato and wife of Brutus (the killer of Caesar), is a notable example discussed by Plutarch, Dio and Valerius Maximus.[52] According to Dio, Porcia threatened Brutus that she would kill herself if he did not share with her his political plans – going so far as to stab herself in the thigh with a dagger (44.13). This serves not only to reinforce the threat of suicide but also to make clear that Porcia is capable if necessary of under-going torture without giving anything away.[53] Valerius Maximus includes among the rubric *de amore coniugali*, on conjugal love, Porcia, who, on hearing the news of Brutus' death in 43 BCE, though those with her refused her a dagger, managed to kill herself by swallowing live coals, *muliebri spiritu virilem patris exitum imitata*, 'with her woman's courage imitating the manly death of her father' (Val. Max. 4.6.5).[54] Once again we see Valerius underline the paradox of a woman who performs a manly act. But Valerius' Porcia does more than merely imitate her father in her death; in one respect she outdoes him, for while suicide by the sword was commonplace, she invented a new means of killing oneself, *sed nescio an hoc fortius, quod ille usitato, tu novo genere mortis absumpta es.*

Another notable *exemplum* was that of Arria – like Porcia, part of a family famous for its oppositional stance.[55] Her husband Aulus Caecina Paetus was, under the emperor Claudius, condemned to death for taking part in the conspiracy of Lucius Arruntius Camillus Scribonianus in 42 CE but, it is said, hesitated to take his own life. Arria took the dagger and stabbed herself, encouraging him with the words: '*Paete, non dolet!*', 'It doesn't hurt, Paetus' (Pliny *Letters* 3.16.6). Martial, too, celebrates her in an epigram:

> Casta suo gladium cum traderet Arria Paeto,
>   Quem de visceribus strinxerat ipsa suis,
> 'si qua fides, vulnus quod feci non dolet,' inquit,
>   'sed tu quod facies, hoc mihi, Paete, dolet.'

When chaste Arria handed to her Paetus the sword which she had herself withdrawn from her own entrails, she said, 'If you can believe it, the wound I made does not hurt me, Paetus, but the one you will make, that one will hurt me.'

(1.13)

The word *casta* is highlighted as the first word in this poem. The emphasis is on Arria's loyalty and bravery. Death is not too great a price to pay to ensure her husband's honourable end. Yet there is perhaps a sense in which her specifically sexual fidelity is also demonstrated by her action.

Pliny in his letter commends Arria for offering her husband *et solacium mortis et exemplum*, 'not only consolation but also an example in death' (*Ep.* 3.16).[56] He also emphasises the trouble she had earlier taken to pursue her husband back to Rome after he had been taken prisoner in Illyria. On her return to Rome, she gave further evidence of her loyalty:

Eadem apud Claudium uxori Scriboniani, cum illa profiteretur indicium,
'ego', inquit, 'te audiam, cuius in gremio Scribonianus occisus est, et
vivis?' ex quo manifestum est ei consilium pulcherrimae mortis non
subitum fuisse.

The same Arria, when she encountered at Claudius' palace the wife of
Scribonianus who had just given evidence for the prosecution, said, 'Must
I hear you, when you go on living, though your husband was killed in
your arms?' This remark makes clear that her decision to kill herself so
admirably was not taken on the spur of the moment.

(3.16.9)

Observing that her family members, concerned at her intentions, were
keeping watch over her, she dashed her head violently against a wall and, on
recovering from the blow, asserted: 'I told you, if you would not let me take
an easy path to death, I would find a way no matter how difficult' (3.16.11).
These actions, suggests Pliny, paved the way to her famous suicide.[57]

For Pliny's Arria, it seems, a wife has under some circumstances a duty
to join her husband in death.[58] This might seem an instance of purely
personal integrity.[59] Yet there are in Pliny's treatment of Arria some subtle
qualifications to his admiration. Having repeated *vocem immortalem et
paene divinam: 'Paete, non dolet'*, 'those immortal and almost divine words,
"it doesn't hurt, Paetus"', he goes on to comment: *sed tamen ista facienti
dicentique gloria et aeternitas ante oculos erant*, 'When she spoke and acted
thus, she had before her eyes the prospect of eternal glory' (3.16.6). Her
other deeds, he suggests (including the concealment of her son's death from
her gravely ill husband), are more to be admired than this spectacular and
celebrated display of contempt for death (3.16.13). Pliny labours to express
niceties of moral judgement in his discussion of Arria (as in other letters
recording and commenting on the celebrated deaths of the recent past).
What is it that makes Pliny uneasy here? In part he may be motivated by
deference to Fannia, Arria's granddaughter, whom he cites as his source for
these less well known stories. Fannia herself was celebrated for her loyalty
to her husband, the elder Helvidius Priscus, whom she twice accompanied
into exile. After his execution, she was relegated on her own account for
preserving writings associated with him when they had been banned by the
senate. In another letter, Pliny celebrates Fannia, now gravely ill:

Eritne quam postea uxoribus nostris ostentare possimus? Erit a qua viri
quoque fortitudinis exempla sumamus, quam sic cernentes audientes
miremur, ut illas quae leguntur?

Will there be anyone whom we can afterwards display to our wives. Will there be anyone whom men also can take as an example of courage, a woman at whom we wonder, seeing and hearing her, just as we wonder at others we read about?

(*Ep.* 7.19.7)

Fannia, in her *fortitudo*, is presented as an example for women and also for men. A little earlier, Pliny emphasises Fannia's feminine virtues, her *castitas*, her *sanctitas*, which accompany the unisex virtues of *gravitas* and *constantia* (7.19.4). There is no mention here of the prospect of eternal glory as a spur to her virtuous behaviour.

But there is perhaps a certain defensiveness in Pliny's stress on her continuing physical presence – we can still see and hear her; she is not yet translated to the page. Ought she perhaps to have followed her grandmother's example? Pliny himself, we may suppose, might feel more comfortable with the idea of a wife modelled on Fannia rather than Arria. It is Fannia who is to be paraded as a model for our wives, *uxoribus nostris*. To return to Letter 3.16, we might suspect Pliny of harbouring a sneaking sympathy for Paetus, whose wife's most celebrated action made him seem by comparison cowardly, despite his political daring in conspiring against Claudius and his own suicide. He is to be remembered merely as the addressee of *vocem immortalem et paene divinam*, 'those immortal and almost divine words'.

The remainder of this chapter will focus on one text, Tacitus' *Annals*, which explores at length a number of women's deaths. The section of the *Annals* which might have included Arria's lesson to Paetus has not survived. Nevertheless there are several examples of women whose deaths show some interesting parallels with her case. While some of Tacitus' female characters (such as Aemilia Lepida, *Ann.* 6.40) die, like so many male characters, to avoid prosecution, he also offers instances of aristocratic women who take their own lives apparently out of solidarity with male members of their family. Sextia, for instance, kills herself together with her husband Mamercus Aemilius Scaurus – though it is only he who is threatened with prosecution (6.29). Antistia Pollitta, widow of one of Nero's victims, Rubellius Plautus (assassinated in 62 CE), spends years in a state of conspicuous mourning, then, when her father Lucius Antistius Vetus is about to be tried in connection with the Pisonian conspiracy of 66 CE, goes to remonstrate with Nero. *Modo muliebri eiulatu, aliquando sexum egressa voce infensa clamitabat*: 'She cried like a woman. She also screamed in unwomanly fury' (16.10). When Pollitta's pleas are unsuccessful, she, her father and his mother-in-law Sextia commit suicide together (16.11) – the final stage in an aggressive campaign of protest. In the case of Pollitta, her family's persecution at the hands of Nero has driven her to behaviour which goes beyond what is appropriate for a woman. Tacitus marks this explicitly in relation to her appeal to Nero, where she moves between womanly weeping and unwomanly imprecations. It remains unclear whether in her death too she has transcended her sex.

In his own writings – at least in those addressed to Marcia and particularly to his mother Helvia – Seneca does concede women's capacity for *virtus*. Yet, strikingly, as we have seen, this is never linked with the issue of facing death, even though death constitutes such a dominant theme in Seneca's writing. Tacitus' account in the *Annals* of Seneca's final hours, however, presents him as encouraging and praising his wife Paulina's decision to take her own life, as he is obliged to take his.[60]

Illa contra sibi quoque destinatam mortem adseverat manumque percussoris exposcit. Tum Seneca gloriae eius non adversus, simul amore, ne sibi unice dilectam ad iniurias relinqueret, 'vitae', inquit 'delenimenta monstraveram tibi, tu mortis decus mavis: non invidebo exemplo. Sit huius tam fortis exitus constantia penes utrosque par, claritudinis plus in tuo fine.'

She however insisted that death would be her lot, too, and demanded the knife man's blow. Then Seneca, who was not opposed to her glory and, loving her, did not wish to leave his dearest one vulnerable to injuries later, said: 'I have offered you the comforts of life, you prefer the honour of death. I shall not grudge you your chance to be an example. Though there may be as much endurance shown in both our brave deaths, yours will be the more famous.'

(*Ann.* 15.63.2–4)

Though he is also apparently concerned lest, after his death, she be left vulnerable to Nero's persecution, Seneca makes a point of conceding that Paulina's voluntary end will evoke greater admiration than his own enforced one (a reflection, perhaps, of the more competitive aspects of political gamesmanship).[61] Once again we find future fame linked to a courageous death, here, too, without any explicit suggestion that a desire for fame is a debased motive.

Paulina's bravery is somewhat undercut, however, in Tacitus' account of the aftermath of this attempted double suicide. Nero, in order to protect himself from additional odium, gives orders that Paulina should not be permitted to die. Some people took the view that:

Donec implacabilem Neronem timuerit, famam sociatae cum marito
mortis petivisse, deinde oblata mitiore spe blandimentis vitae evictam;
cui addidit paucos postea annos, laudabili in maritum memoria et ore
ac membris in eum pallorem albentibus ut ostentui esset multum vitalis
spiritus egestum.

As long as she believed Nero's hostility could not be appeased, she sought
the admiration to be gained from joining her husband in death. Then,
when hope was offered of a less harsh fate, she was won over by the attractions of life. She only lived for a few more years, during which she showed
praiseworthy devotion to her husband's memory, while the pallor of her
face and limbs was such as to show she had lost much of her vital spirit.
(15.64)

Paulina is denied the chance of a celebrated end, with or without her own
complicity – as so often, Tacitus leaves this issue unresolved. Nevertheless,
for the rest of her life, her notable pallor serves as a reminder of her
husband's distinguished end and her own attempt to join him.

Certainly it reflects well on a man that he inspires such loyalty, such love.
And it also reflects badly on the emperor; the implication is that these family
members, despite their innocence, had they not chosen to kill themselves
at this point, would later have fallen victim to Nero in their turn.[62] In the
cases described by Tacitus, unlike that of Arria, the companion suicide
does not show the condemned (or soon to be condemned) man how to do
it. Nevertheless, there is perhaps still a sense in which the individual who
volunteers to kill herself may appear significantly braver than the man
who will have to die anyway and is merely taking advantage of *liberum
mortis arbitrium*. This may be read as an act of pure death-defying courage
uncomplicated by calculations of relative advantage.

A fitting end?

In the *Annals*, women of the imperial family rarely have the opportunity
to kill themselves, it seems, though Tacitus leaves ambiguous the question
of who is responsible for the death in exile of Augustus' daughter the Elder
Julia by starvation (*Ann.* 1.53) and the death of her granddaughter, the Elder
Agrippina, by the same means. Neither of these deaths is described at length.
Tacitus comments on that of Agrippina: *voluntate extinctam, nisi si negatis
alimentis adsimulatus est finis qui videretur sponte sumptus*, 'she took her
own life – unless food was denied her so that her death might appear to have
been voluntary' (*Ann.* 6.25). Here, as with some of the ambiguous deaths

discussed in earlier chapters, the element of uncertainty perhaps works to the emperor's advantage, since he need not bear the odium of having killed a relative, while the political force of a recognised act of suicide is muted. Three deaths of imperial women are described at length, however. All three are the victims of assassination ordered by the emperor – Messalina, the Younger Agrippina and Octavia.

The emperor Claudius' wife Messalina is presented by Tacitus (and other authors, too) as a woman consumed with illicit desires.[63] At first she indulges her lusts with low characters such as the actor Mnester (11.36.1–2). But matters become more serious when she sets her sights on a Roman senator, Silius. In Tacitus' account, Silius sees this as an opportunity to make a bid for the empire by marrying Messalina and adopting Britannicus (the son of Claudius and Messalina); the affair culminates in a marriage ceremony, construed by many as an act of treason. Claudius' freedmen succeed in persuading him to condemn his wife to death. To some centurions and a tribune of the guard Narcissus issues the order to kill Messalina:

> Custos et exactor e libertis Euodos datur; isque raptim in hortos praegressus repperit fusam humi, adsidente matre Lepida, quae florenti filiae haud concors supremis eius necessitatibus ad miserationem evicta erat suadebatque ne percussorem opperiretur: transisse vitam neque aliud quam morti decus quaerendum. Sed animo per libidines corrupto nihil honestum inerat; lacrimaeque et questus inriti ducebantur, cum impetu venientium pulsae fores adstititque tribunus per silentium, at libertus increpans multis et servilibus probris. Tunc primum fortunam suam introspexit ferrumque accepit, quod frustra iugulo aut pectori per trepidationem admovens ictu tribuni transigitur.

From the freedmen Euodos was selected to detain her and ensure orders were carried out. He hurried on ahead at once into the gardens where he found her prostrate on the ground. Her mother Lepida was sitting beside her; though distant from her daughter in happier times, now Messalina had been brought so low, she was overcome by pity and was persuading her not to wait for the killer. 'Your life is over; there is nothing more to look for but dignity in death.' But there was no honour in that spirit corrupted by lust. She was pouring forth tears and useless complaints when the doors were broken down by the men rushing in. The tribune stood by in silence; the freedman reviled her with vulgar abuse. Then at last she understood her fate. She took the dagger and drew it tremulously towards her throat and then her breast but in vain. The tribune's blow drove it home.

(*Ann.* 11.37.4–38.1)

Libido, that feminine and effeminising vice, has drained Messalina of
the sense of honour necessary to face death with calm and dignity, despite
her mother's encouragement. Only at the very end does she understand her
situation. She takes the dagger offered to her and moves it uncertainly toward
her throat, her breast. It is a sure sign of moral weakness, in her case, that
she cannot bring herself to take her own life. The tribune's blow drives in
the blade. The penetration of her body by the dagger is foreshadowed by the
executioners' breaking down of the doors. As in the case of Livy's Lucretia, it
is tempting to read Messalina's death, again by means of a blade, as in some
way analogous to a sexual act – a symbolic rape, but one whose victim is as
far removed as conceivable from the supremely innocent Lucretia of Roman
myth; Messalina's illicit liaison with Silius is presented by Tacitus and other
Roman writers as merely the most licentious of her innumerable adulteries.

In the *Annals*, Messalina functions as a figure for feminine desire (and
desire for sex is here, as often, assimilated to desire for wealth).[64] Earlier,
Tacitus asserts that Messalina had acceded to Silius' request for marriage
precisely on account of the magnitude of the *infamia*, 'disgrace', 'bad
reputation', which is the ultimate source of pleasure for the licentious, *cuius
apud prodigos novissima voluptas est* (*Ann.* 11.26.6). If, as so frequently in
Tacitus and elsewhere, one who dies an inspiring and courageous death is
supported by the prospect of glory among future generations, it is surely no
wonder that Tacitus' depraved Messalina is quite unmoved by the possibility
of securing a positive *fama* in years to come.

The death of Messalina's (and Claudius') daughter Octavia is strongly
contrasted with that of her mother. This event, dated to 59 CE, forms the
conclusion to Book XIV of the *Annals*. Octavia, married to the emperor
Nero, is falsely accused, at the instigation of Nero's mistress Poppaea, of
adultery with the freedman Anicetus and sent into exile.

> Ac puella vicesimo aetatis anno inter centuriones et milites, praesagio
> malorum iam vitae exempta, nondum tamen morte adquiescebat.

> So the girl, just nineteen years old, was surrounded by centurions and
> soldiers. The evils that had befallen her made clear her life was over but
> she had not yet resigned herself to death.

> (*Ann.* 14.64.1)

A few days later, however, she receives an explicit order to die. She pleads
with the assassins but to no avail:

> Restringitur vinclis venaeque eius per omnes artus exolvuntur; et quia

pressus pavore sanguis tardius labebatur, praefervidi balnei vapore
enecatur. Additurque atrocior saevitia quod caput amputatum latumque
in urbem Poppaea vidit.

She was bound in chains and veins were opened in each limb. And,
since the girl's terror was such that the blood flowed only slowly, she was
killed by the steam from a very hot bath. On top of this was an act of
appalling savagery: her head was cut off and taken to Rome to be seen
by Poppaea.

(*Ann.* 14.64.3–4)

Her veins are severed according to the pattern that would become commonplace (as Tacitus comments later, *Ann.* 16.17.6). But Octavia does not take her
own life. She is bound and forced. Octavia does not meet death with bravery.
Indeed, she is overcome by fear, *pavor*, to such a degree that the blood flow
is impeded. This is implicitly excusable in such a young girl (though it seems
likely that Tacitus misrepresents her age here in order to heighten the pathos
of the scene).[65] Still, despite the pathos evoked by Octavia's death, the manner
in which she meets it lacks exemplary force. Messalina and Octavia, then,
die deaths neatly balancing their lives. Both these deaths could be described
as distinctively feminine, one exemplifying feminine moral weakness, the
other chaste feminine passivity.

Different again is the account given in the early chapters of Book XIV of
the death of the Younger Agrippina, the mother of Nero (who had succeeded
Messalina as wife of Claudius at the beginning of Book XIII). Book XIV
opens with Nero's reaffirmed decision to have his mother killed. Tacitus'
narrative orchestrates comedy and horror in retailing her escape from a
booby-trapped ship.[66] The murder itself is described briefly. Tacitus rapidly
returns the focus to Nero himself and his reaction to his mother's death. An
elaborate tissue of deception is woven to conceal Nero's matricide. Agrippina
is alleged to have plotted to kill him and, once her lot was discovered, to have
taken her own life in shame (*Ann.* 14.10). The story gains little credence but
many pretend to believe it. Nero is congratulated (14.12).

Agrippina meets death with characteristic fearlessness. Soldiers break
down the doors of her villa. Her servants flee. Agrippina is in her bedroom
with just one companion:

Abeunte dehinc ancilla 'tu quoque me deseris' prolocuta respicit Anicetum
trierarcho Herculeio et Obarito centurione classiario comitatum: ac,
si ad visendum venisset, refotam nuntiaret, sin facinus patraturus,
nihil se de filio credere; non imperatum parricidium. Circumsistunt

lectum percussores et prior trierarchus fusti caput eius adflixit. Iam in mortem centurioni ferrum destringenti protendens uterum 'ventrem feri' exclamavit multisque vulneribus confecta est.

As her maidservant started to leave, she called out 'You, too, are leaving me,' and turned round to see Anicetus, accompanied by a naval commander, Herculeius, and a centurion of the fleet, Obaritus. 'If', she said, 'you have come to visit, you may report back that I am recovered. If you have come to commit a crime, I cannot believe it is my son's work. He has not ordered his mother's death.' The assassins stood on either side of her bed; the naval commander was first. He struck her head with a club. As the centurion bent on killing her extended his dagger, she thrust her womb towards him and called out: 'Strike my stomach'. And after a series of blows she was killed.

(*Ann.* 14.8)

This, too, is an overtly sexual murder. The violation of the woman's body is once again foreshadowed by the breaking down of doors. However, in this case the victim succeeds in appropriating symbolic control of the scene – in marked contrast with the deaths of Messalina and Octavia (the latter's end rounds off the book which begins with Agrippina's death). Agrippina denies the possibility that her son could countenance her murder (a move which can of course be read as another instance of feigning ignorance as a survival strategy).[67] Yet she dies precisely as a mother, for her last words implicitly acknowledge and comment on his guilt. She offers for assault, as if in punishment of it, the part of her body which produced the unfilial Nero. She thus underlines Nero's unspeakable crime in having his mother killed.[68]

I have suggested we might read this matricide as rape. What might be at stake in such a reading? Insofar as Anicetus and his companions are Nero's agents in murdering his mother, they are also, on a symbolic level, his surrogates in her sexual violation. Matricide is compounded by incest. Tacitus claimed earlier that Agrippina, though not chaste, only used sexual relationships for political gain, *nihil domi impudicum, nisi dominationi expediret* (12.7.6). Early in Book XIV, he refers to various reports of incestuous relations between Agrippina and Nero. According to Cluvius Rufus it was Agrippina who had taken the initiative, hoping thereby to retain dominion over her son (*ardore retinendae potentiae*), while Fabius Rusticus presents Nero as making the advances (*Ann.* 14.2).[69] The former version gained greater credence, however, largely because of Agrippina's earlier conduct (culminating in marriage with her own uncle, Claudius, itself judged by some an act of incest): *credibilior novae libidinis meditatio in ea visa est.*[70]

Tacitus does not explicitly endorse either version but moves directly on to Nero's plan for Agrippina's murder: *praegravem ratus interficere constituit* 'finding her intolerable, he decided to kill her' (14.3.2).[71] Ultimately, he suggests, it is incest – whether the threat of incest, the desire for incest or the rumour of incest – that makes Agrippina's continued existence insufferable to Nero. Agrippina's death-bed response can constitute an invitation to read the murder as a lethal re-enactment of incestuous relations between herself and her son (an echo perhaps of the correspondence between Lucretia's rape and her suicide). Thus we might see the sexual dimension even of her murder as turned to Agrippina's own purposes.

The erotically charged corpses of Dido, Lucretia and Cleopatra had been made to serve as political symbols in Augustan Rome. In Tacitus' account of Rome under Nero, the dead body of the emperor's mother is also put on display. Or at least Tacitus reports in the aftermath of Agrippina's end the story, recorded by some, denied by others, that Nero viewed his mother's body after her death and praised her figure: *aspexeritne matrem exanimem Nero et formam corpus eius laudaverit, sunt qui tradiderint, sunt qui abnuant* (14.9.1).[72] Here again we have a female corpse generating voyeuristic pleasure – on the part of a son viewing the mother whom he has had killed and with whom he may or may not have had incestuous relations. Does Agrippina, like Lucretia, figure for Rome? This death, too, marks a new era – of a kind. Rome is now ruled by a man who will stop at nothing.

Though Agrippina explicitly denies the possibility that her son is responsible for her murder, her death-bed behaviour acknowledges his guilt, I have suggested.[73] Tacitus goes on to report the story that Agrippina had known in advance she would meet death at the hands of her son, yet was content to accept this as the price of his attaining supreme power.

> Hunc sui finem multos ante annos crediderat Agrippina contempseratque. Nam consulenti super Nerone responderunt Chaldaei fore ut imperaret matremque occideret; atque illa 'occidat' inquit, 'dum imperet!'

> Agrippina had believed for many years that this would be her end – and had made light of it. For when she sought advice on Nero's future from astrologers, they replied that he would be emperor and would kill his mother. 'Let him kill,' she said, 'provided that he rules!'
>
> (*Ann.* 14.9.5)

Here is a woman who knows how to meet death even at the hands of her own son. Stabbed in the womb, because she is the mother of Nero, Agrippina dies what is on one level precisely a woman's death. Yet we might note here Tacitus' use of the term *contemnere*, 'make light of', 'defy', 'despise', for Agrippina's attitude to her own end. The term recalls Cicero's definition in *Tusculans* of masculine *virtus* – the despising of pain and death.

Indeed Agrippina's masculine traits are repeatedly stressed throughout the *Annals*. Her control over her husband Claudius, indeed over the state itself, is termed *quasi virile servitium*, 'an almost masculine dominion' (*Ann.* 12.7.5). In a number of important respects, her character evokes that of her mother. Like her mother, the Younger Agrippina is termed *atrox*, 'fierce', a term with neutral overtones when applied to men but invariably negative when applied to female characters.[74] In referring to the Elder Agrippina's death, Tacitus comments: *aequi impatiens, dominandi avida, virilibus curis feminarum vitia exuerat*, 'unable to bear a rival and longing for power, with the concerns of a man, she knew no feminine weakness' (6.25.3).[75] Yet the Younger Agrippina outdoes even her mother in her ambition. Arrogating to herself an unprecedentedly public role, she receives homage from the prisoner of war Caratacus and his family:

Atque illi vinclis absoluti Agrippinam quoque, haud procul alio suggestu conspicuam, isdem quibus principem laudibus gratibusque venerati sunt. Novum sane et moribus veterum insolitum, feminam signis Romanis praesidere: ipsa semet parti a maioribus suis imperii sociam ferebat.

They were released from their bonds and paid homage with the same praise and thanks also to Agrippina, conspicuous on another dais close by. This indeed was something new and alien to the customs of former times, that a woman should sit before the Roman standards. She was asserting her partnership in the empire secured by her ancestors.

(*Ann.* 12.37.5–6)

This is the logic of a state where power has come to be inherited; women, too, can point to their noble ancestors and lay claim to legitimate authority. Tacitus' Agrippina presents herself as a co-holder of *imperium*. Nero later claims in justifying his plan for matricide that she demanded *consortium imperii*, 'a share in power' (14.11.1).[76]

Much of Agrippina's behaviour breaches the proprieties of gender distinction. When she seeks to preside with Nero as he receives an embassy from Armenia, scandal is only just averted; Seneca persuades Nero to walk down to meet – and divert – her (*Ann.* 13.5.3). Despite her attempts to lay claim to *imperium*, Agrippina's paradoxical ambition can only ever be contingent on her relational status as great-granddaughter (of Augustus), daughter (of Germanicus), sister (of Caligula), wife (of Claudius), and finally mother.[77] She cannot rule directly. Her goal is to make her son emperor; but when that object is attained she becomes vulnerable.[78] Indeed, once Nero chooses to demote her she at once has no status. Tacitus comments: *nihil rerum mortalium tam instabile ac fluxum est quam fama potentiae non sua vi nixae*, 'nothing in human affairs is so precarious and transient as the fame of a power based on a strength not its own' (*Ann.* 13.19.1).

The institution of the principate, relying as it did (in theory) on the transmission of power within the family, could be seen as legitimating a new role for women of that family within the public sphere, indeed legitimating their appropriation of certain traditionally male forms of behaviour.[79] Tacitus' handling of Agrippina's behaviour sometimes seems to license acknowledgement of her qualifications for rule – those ancestors count for something, and such mastery of the slippery protocols of imperial court politics must command our respect. Tacitus' Agrippina is wily, resourceful, intelligent. Certainly there is a sense in which we are invited to admire her, in spite of her greed and scheming – and perhaps most of all at her moment of death. Yet Agrippina's courage, like the rest of her strengths, is anomalous. Tacitus appropriates the contradictions of the gendered discourse of virtue to make a characteristically pessimistic point. That Agrippina's influence over her son, though inappropriate, restrained him from his worst excesses is merely another indication of Nero's failings.[80] Ultimately her masculine qualities serve precisely as an indictment of the disjointed times in which she is able to flourish. Tacitus' treatment of the death of Nero himself has not survived. We can only speculate that the emperor will have displayed a cowardice appropriately complementing his mother's bravery.[81] Her very virtues betray the terrible truth of the world in which she operates.

Reproach

Nero's persecution of the Roman aristocracy ultimately provokes a plot to assassinate him, with Piso to take his place as emperor. The plot is discovered, however, and many are tortured and executed in its aftermath. One of Nero's victims is a freedwoman called Epicharis.

Atque interim Nero recordatus Volusii Proculi indicio Epicharin attineri ratusque muliebre corpus impar dolori tormentis dilacerari iubet. At illam non verbera, non ignes, non ira eo acrius torquentium ne a femina spernerentur, pervicere quin obiecta denegaret. Sic primus quaestionis dies contemptus. Postero cum ad eosdem cruciatus retraheretur gestamine sellae (nam dissolutis membris insistere nequibat), vinclo fasciae, quam pectori detraxerat, in modum laquei ad arcum sellae restricto indidit cervicem et corporis pondere conisa tenuem iam spiritum expressit, clariore exemplo libertina mulier in tanta necessitate alienos ac prope ignotos protegendo, cum ingenui et viri et equites Romani senatoresque intacti tormentis carissima suorum quisque pignorum proderent. Non enim omittebant Lucanus quoque et Senecio et Quintianus passim conscios edere.

However, in the meantime Nero recalled that, as a result of information from Volusius Proculus, Epicharis was in custody, and thinking that her female body would be unable to endure pain, he gave instructions that she be subjected to the sufferings of torture. But neither the blows, nor the brands, nor the fury of the torturers, which was all the more intense as they strove not to be defeated by a woman, succeeded in breaking down her denial of the charges. Thus was the first day's interrogation disdained. On the following day, when the tortures recommenced with the victim now on a chair (her weakened limbs meant she could no longer stand), she made a loop in the band which had bound her breasts to form a noose, tied it to the back of the chair, inserted her neck and using the weight of her body choked out the feeble breath that remained to her. This example given by a woman who was an ex-slave protecting under such testing circumstances people who were unrelated to her and whom she hardly knew was the more splendid at a time when men who were not merely free-born but equestrians and senators – and who had undergone no torture – betrayed their nearest and dearest. For Lucan, Senecio and Quintianus too had given out the names of all the conspirators.

(*Ann.* 15.57.1–4)

Elsewhere Tacitus comments that the darkest of times are illuminated by distinguished men dying nobly (*Hist.* 1.3.1). But in this passage there is a stark contrast between the brave spirit of a freedwoman and the cowardice of Romans who are male, free-born, equestrians and senators indeed but who cannot endure even the prospect of torture.[82] Tacitus' treatment offers her death as an explicit foil to the inadequate responses of many Roman elite males. The contrast is all the sharper given Tacitus' earlier stress on the unheroic nature of Epicharis' life up until this point (*Ann.* 15.51).[83]

Here the reader is invited to feel admiration for Epicharis, who transcends womanly weakness (as is emphasised by the repetition of *muliebre/mulier*). The mechanism used by Epicharis to choke out her remaining life recalls some of the stories told by Seneca of individuals in extreme circumstances resorting to bizarre or sordid means of killing themselves (as in *Ep.* 77.14).[84]

But the admirable character of her response is overshadowed by the shame associated with the behaviour of Lucan and Senecio. Ultimately even Epicharis' exemplary end should not be read as a celebration of feminine heroism manifested in the contempt for death but rather as yet another insight into the twisted nature of this Rome in which proper distinctions of gender and status are radically confounded.

Conclusion

A significant number of women are acclaimed in Latin texts for meeting death with exemplary bravery. Yet the attribution to them of *virtus* at this most highly charged moment is often deeply problematic. It is striking that, despite the 'ethical equality of the sexes' associated with Stoicism, Seneca's prose, insistently preoccupied though it is with how we should dispose ourselves in the face of death, refuses to engage with the dying female subject. Indeed if a key purpose of the Roman Stoic notion of *virtus* is to offer a new avenue of self-fashioning for male members of the Roman elite, it is perhaps all the more important that this should not be seen as open to women.

Helvia's manliness, by an exquisite Senecan paradox, is especially evident in relation to her *pudicitia*, her sexual virtue. While the *pudicitia* of males is treated by some Roman writers as valuable and vulnerable, they are never called on to demonstrate its value by surrendering their own lives. Rather brave deaths are gendered as distinctively feminine, when they are associated with the defence of *pudicitia* (though even this avenue for female courage is not explored by Seneca). At the same time, bravery in the face of death can function as a demonstration of *castitas* without any suggestion that the sexual virtue of the woman has been compromised. Rather, other admirable and specifically feminine characteristics are in a sense assimilated to this quality. Martial's Arria, for instance, a woman who kills herself to set an example to her husband, is above all *casta* (1.13).

Pliny's admiration for this same Arria is, as we have seen, qualified, and coupled with unease. In Tacitus' *Annals*, the presence of women serves precisely as one of a range of markers of the fundamental impropriety of this history, in which *virtus* is often dissociated from those in whom it should most strikingly inhere.[85] Yet its excrescence elsewhere – even in a female ex-slave – must still command our admiration, if history is not to collapse altogether into undifferentiated badness. Here there is some scope, perhaps, for reading against the grain.

Certainly the celebrated deaths of Roman women often bear a close similarity to those of men remembered for dying bravely. Yet even where the deaths of women resemble male deaths in form, the gender of the dying subject radically affects the meaning of the action. A number of the most symbolically resonant female deaths in Latin literature assimilate the act of killing to rape. The relationship between death and sexuality is highly complex. Sometimes death works to compensate for previous sexual dereliction, most conspicuously in the case of Lucretia. Yet the sexual dimension to a violent death may also seem to aggravate the violation to the woman's body – a body whose outraged beauty is made an object of display.

Another aspect of the link between death and sexuality is made manifest in the story Tacitus reports concerning the execution under Tiberius of the young daughter of the disgraced praetorian prefect, Sejanus.

> Tradunt temporis eius auctores, quia triumvirali supplicio adfici virginem inauditum habebatur, a carnifice laqueum iuxta conpressam.

> The writers of that time record that, since it was unheard of for a virgin to be subjected to capital punishment, she was raped by the executioner with the noose beside her.

> (*Ann.* 5.9)

For this violent death to constitute a 'legitimate' punishment, it should not also serve as a surrogate for defloration.[86] In the twisted logic of Tiberian Rome, this becomes not the reason to spare the girl but the reason to rape her first.

CHAPTER 8

LAUGHING AT DEATH?
CHRISTIAN MARTYRDOM

The Christian writer Tertullian, in his treatise on the games *De spectaculis*, offered, as we saw in Chapter 2, caustic comments on the perverse enthusiasm of pagans for watching spectacles of death. Good Christians should avoid these hideously cruel entertainments. Paradoxically, his bitter attack on the gladiatorial games in particular is one of the texts most often exploited by modern scholars in their attempt to unravel the complexities of the ancient Roman obsession with the sport of watching people kill one another. Yet Tertullian's condemnation of these spectacles takes on a destabilising aspect in the light of the concluding section of *De spectaculis*. Here he describes how Christians who have wisely avoided the games so temptingly on offer in the mortal world may look forward to far superior entertainment in the life beyond, above all on the day of judgement.

Quale autem spectaculum in proximo est adventus domini iam indubitati, iam superbi, iam triumphantis! ... At enim supersunt alia spectacula, ille ultimus et perpetuus iudicii dies, ille nationibus insperatus, ille derisus, cum tanta saeculi vetustas et tot eius nativitates uno igni haurientur. Quae tunc spectaculi latitudo! Quid admirer? Quid rideam? ... Praesides persecutores dominici nominis saevioribus quam ipsi flammis saevierunt insultantes contra Christianos liquescentes? Quos praeterea? Sapientes illos philosophos coram discipulis suis una conflagrantibus erubescentes, quibus nihil ad deum pertinere suadebant, quibus animas aut nullas aut non in pristina corpora redituras adfirmabant?

And yet what a spectacle is imminent in the arrival of our lord now undoubted, now mighty, now in triumph! ... But other spectacles are still to come on that last and eternal day of judgement, that day which the gentiles never thought would come, that day they mocked, when all this old world and all its generations will be consumed in a single fire.

How great then will be the spectacle! What shall I wonder at? What will make me laugh? ... The magistrates who persecuted the name of our Lord melting in flames fiercer than those with which they attacked the Christians. Whom besides these? Those wise philosophers ashamed before their pupils as they blaze together, pupils whom they taught that God concerns himself with nothing and that people either have no souls or else that their souls will never return to their former bodies.

(*Spect.* 30)

This is a spectacle to make the good Christian wonder and laugh, as the erstwhile persecutors of Christ's followers melt in the flames, while even those who offered their students a heretical account of the fate of the soul are to suffer perpetual agony. Similarly edifying torments lie in store, too, for all those athletes, charioteers and actors who presumed during their lives to entertain people with their depraved performances.

Tertullian at least finds the seductive allure of the spectacles traditionally provided by the Roman state impossible to evade altogether. All he can do is offer a Christian substitute, further chilling testimony to the hold the games exercised over spectators of all kinds. This substitute is of course profoundly complicit with just those qualities of cruelty and voyeurism which Tertullian himself so eloquently excoriates earlier in his treatise. Appropriating the model of the arena to convey the edifying spectacle of the suffering of the damned, which the righteous Christian may hope to enjoy in the hereafter, he notoriously discloses the extent to which the attraction exercised by pleasures of watching violence in the arena might ultimately subvert a Christian attempt to condemn those pleasures.[1]

Yet this was not the only spectacle which might give pleasure to the faithful. The accounts of the suffering of Christian martyrs, sufferings which are often alleged to have taken place within the arenas of the Roman empire, can also be seen as offering a Christian alternative to prise the faithful away from the formidably powerful pleasures of witnessing directly the entertainments of the arena (as well as the circus and theatre). The incorporation of such narratives into the Christian liturgy by the late fourth century, if not earlier, constituted an attempt to forge a new and compelling medium for spectacles which would take the place of the profane entertainments of the pagan world.[2] In one of his sermons written in the early fourth century, Augustine, for instance, could comment on the account of the torment and death of the Maccabees: *magnum spectaculum positum est ante oculos fidei nostrae*, 'A great spectacle has been placed before the eyes of our faith' (*Serm.* 301.1).[3]

The uneasy relationship between death and spectacle in the pagan Roman world has been a key preoccupation in my study. Gladiatorial combat, often to the death, was a symbolically central feature of Roman culture. The potent figure of the arena might be deployed to diverse ends. Seneca imagines the gods looking with approval at the death of the Younger Cato, as a spectacular performance of virtue. For his nephew Lucan, by contrast, a parallel with the arena serves to underline the profound futility of civil war in which the purpose of fighting to the death is reduced to a performance without meaning. Yet even texts which describe a death scene involving only a few witnesses, such as the enforced suicides of individual senators condemned under Nero, may present the dying individual as offering a spectacle to be observed for the edification of those watching – and implicitly for later readers also. In the texts of Tertullian and Augustine we are once again confronted by the question of how the reader should relate to descriptions of such spectacles. These concluding pages will consider briefly a few of the continuities and differences between pagan and Christian deployments of spectacular death. One aim is to highlight the longer-term influence of pagan Roman perceptions of a life's conclusion as a privileged moment of truth. But another is to underline some profound differences between pagan and Christian ways of looking at death.

The historical context of Christian martyrdom has been the subject of numerous important studies in recent years. The present discussion can do no more than touch on a few key aspects of this. Certainly a significant change took place between the second and fourth centuries of the common era (though Christian writers often invoke the example of 4 Maccabees, narrating the deaths of Jewish rebels against the tyrant Antiochus in the second century BCE, as a forerunner of Christian martyrdom).[4] How exactly should we understand the term martyr?[5] One approach is to conceive of martyrdom as a discourse, 'a practice of dying for God and of talking about it that changes and develops over time'.[6] From this perspective Christian martyrdom does not constitute a break with Jewish tradition. Indeed both Christian and Jewish texts share a preoccupation with the eroticism and positive appeal of the martyr's death.[7]

At the same time some have stressed continuities with the discourses of the Greco-Roman world. On this view, the development of Christian martyrdom in the second and third centuries could not have happened without the pagan Roman glorification of noble suicide.[8] Certainly Christian writers sometimes express admiration for pagan 'martyrs'. Tertullian, in *Ad martyres* (4) and in his *Apologeticus* (50.7–8), lists brave pagans such as Lucretia or Regulus who have endured death for a noble cause or to preserve their own honour. In part this serves as an argument from the lesser to the greater: if the noblest pagans could achieve a brave death without the support of faith, how much more could the righteous Christian achieve?[9] And Christian martyrs, it is argued, far surpassed even these pagans in their virtue, their piety and their number (Aug. *Civ. dei* 5.14).[10] Such claims can be seen as an attempt to appeal to pagans on their own terms. For both Christians and pagans, the voluntary acceptance of death served as a demonstration of their free agency.[11] The preoccupation with honour, with self-actualisation, is common to both pagan and Christian accounts.[12]

For Roman elite writers of the principate, above all, there was, as we have seen, a privileged kind of truth in an individual's death, a truth which could make retrospective sense of the life that preceded it. A particular value was accorded to an individual's final words, whose veracity was endorsed by their status as final utterance. Similar concerns characterise accounts of Christian martyrdom. Like the senators and soldiers implicated in a conspiracy against the emperor, these individuals too speak freely, liberated from any sense of deference, any fear of retribution by the imminent prospect of death. Similarly, the martyrs address their judges with arresting frankness.[13] In the case of the Christian martyrs, it was precisely the martyr's confession of his or her faith, that 'bearing witness' from which the term martyr derives, which gave sublime value to their suffering.[14] The death of a Christian martyr could be read as bearing witness to a larger truth, the truth of resurrection of the body, the truth of God.

Christian texts (and a handful of pagan ones) present a picture of numerous individuals subjected to torture in an attempt to make them deny their faith. Some Christians, it seems, were condemned to the harshest of punishments envisaged by the Roman legal system: being thrown to the beasts, *damnatio ad bestias*. There was a world of difference between the skill and bravery Romans expected of the trained gladiator or beast fighter on the one hand and the wretched defencelessness of the *noxius* on the other. As witnesses to punishments inflicted in the arena on the miserable *noxii*, audiences expected to see terror, abject suffering, extremes of pain and despair.[15] But when Christians failed to play the role scripted for them, whether in the course of the trial or, once condemned, in the arena, showing themselves not terrified victims but joyous collaborators, the meaning of the ritual was redeployed, appropriated to serve a new purpose.[16] Not all spectators were impressed. Tertullian complains that some pagans mock Christian endurance (*Apol.* 49.4).[17] Others, however, such as the jailer in the account of Perpetua's martyrdom, are said to have been deeply struck by the display of Christian *virtus* (*Perp.* 9).

The spectacular is of key importance here.[18] Already Paul's Letter to the Corinthians figures the role of the apostles in these terms:

For it seems to me God has made us apostles the most abject of mankind. We are like men condemned to die in the arena – a spectacle to the whole universe – angels as well as to men.

(1 Cor. 4.9 trs. New English Bible)

Paul's discussion of voluntary death had a huge influence on the subsequent development of the Christian discourse of martyrdom. In later texts, however, martyrs are encouraged to see themselves as performers, rising to a challenge – and with an audience to impress. It is of crucial importance that they identified themselves not with the misery of the *noxii* but with the bravery of the well-trained athlete or gladiator. The imagery of athleticism is regularly invoked in discussions of Christian martyrdom. The early Christian martyr Ignatius of Antioch exhorts his fellow would-be martyr Polycarp: 'It is like a great athlete to take blows and yet win the fight' (*Ep. ad Poly.* 2.3).[19] Elsewhere, anticipating his own martyrdom, he uses as the model for his oath the oath of the gladiator (*Ep. ad Rom.* 3.3).[20] Other early Christian writers also deploy the figure of the gladiator. Addressing the martyrs, Tertullian in the early years of the third century declares:

Nec tantus sum, ut vos alloquar; verumtamen et gladiatores perfectissimos non tantum magistri et praepositi sui, sed etiam idiotae et supervacui quique adhortantur de longinquo, ut saepe de ipso populo dictata suggesta profuerint.

Not that I have any claim to address you; yet to the most skilled gladiators, not only experts and their trainers give advice, but even non-professionals and any chance onlookers from outside, so that often the comments even of the crowd have been helpful.

(*Ad mart.* 1.2)

The compelling spectacle of Christian martyrdom draws a crowd of curious onlookers, keen to follow every twist and turn of the sublime fight of good against evil.

Female martyrs, too, could figure themselves as fighters in the arena. In the account of her martyrdom, Perpetua (or whoever wrote the account attributed to her) describes a dream on the eve of her execution in which the martyr is herself a wrestler in the arena: *et expoliata sum et facta sum masculus; et coeperunt me favisores mei oleo defricare*, 'My clothes were stripped off, and suddenly I was a man. My seconds began to rub me down with oil.' She defeats her opponent, an Egyptian whom she identifies with the devil (*Perp.* 10).[21] For women in particular the story of Perpetua might function as a narrative of empowerment. Indeed, as such, it posed a challenge to the patriarchal authorities of the early church.[22] Augustine emphasised that her views were not canonical scripture (*De natura et origine animi* 1.10.12). Perpetua's courage, the example she sets, are more than female. This is an instance of a male mind, *virilis animus*, in a female body, he asserts in a sermon delivered on the anniversary of Perpetua's martyrdom (*Serm.* 281). Aspects of this rhetoric are new and specific to Christian discourse. Augustine interprets the snake on which Perpetua ascends to heaven in another of her dreams as a reminder of Eve's fall in the garden of Eden (*Serm.* 280.1).[23] But there are also echoes of the rhetoric found in at least some Roman texts of the early principate. We may remember, for instance, Valerius Maximus' characterisation of Lucretia, who in her exemplary death displayed *virilis animus*, 'a manly spirit', which by an error of fortune had found its way into a female body (6.1.1). Such examples were peculiarly and disconcertingly potent.

The detailed, indeed luxuriant, descriptions of bodily suffering in many of the martyrs' acts have often aroused comment.[24] Christian readers, it seems, can in good conscience enjoy these narratives of suffering, can imagine themselves as witnesses to these most edifying spectacles, absolved of collaboration with the institutionalised cruelty of the arena, through their empathy with and admiration for its victims. There are perhaps echoes here, too, of earlier pagan writers whose identification with the defeated gladiator, as we have seen, could serve to absolve them from challenging the continuing programme of gladiatorial entertainments offered by Rome's emperors. Certainly some non-Christian authors seem fascinated with the detail of physical suffering, Seneca most obviously.[25] But it is particularly the logic of Christian martyrdom which demands an ever increasing amplification of the torments endured by the narrative's victim.[26] For Prudentius, recounting the extraordinarily protracted sufferings of Romanus, God's angel would make an exact record of every detail of the martyr's injuries:

Nec verba solum dissertentis condidit,
Sed ipsa pingens vulnera expressit stilo
Laterum, genarum pectoris et faucium.
    Omnis notata est sanguinis dimensio,
Ut quamque plagam sulcus exaraverit,
Altam, patentem, proximam, longam brevem,
Quae vis doloris, quive segmenti modus;
Guttam cruoris ille nullam perdidit.

He took down not only the words of his discourse but with his pen drew the same wounds he had in his sides, in his cheeks, on his breast, on his throat. The quantity of blood from each was noted and how each wound was gouged out by the gash, whether it was deep or gaping, a graze, long or short, the strength of the pain, the extent of the cut. No drop of blood went unobserved by him.

(Perist. 10.1123–30)

Every wound matters and must be scrupulously recorded. The truth of God is written on the martyr's body, to be transcribed for all eternity in the texts which celebrate him (or her).

The eroticisation of violent death – most particularly a woman's violent death – is a feature of many of the women's death scenes discussed in the previous chapter. The pornography of feminine death manifests itself at greater length and with a somewhat different sensibility in many of the narratives of the deaths of female martyrs written up and celebrated in the early Christian church. The narrative of Perpetua's martyrdom dwells on her exposed flesh (20), which she modestly seeks to cover. Prudentius' eroticised account of deaths of Christian virgins, most strikingly *Peristephanon* 3 on Eulalia and 14 on Agnes, stresses the piquant combination of beautiful flesh and extreme torment. The latter poem gives an account of the martyrdom of Agnes, sent naked to a brothel after refusing the advances of the prefect's son. The martyr takes Christ as her husband; the executioner's sword is to penetrate her flesh.[27]

This combination of female beauty and torture is by no means exclusive to Christian texts. There is a notable parallel, for instance, between the account of the death of a Christian matron falsely accused of adultery given by Jerome (*Ep.* 1) and earlier pagan texts such as Achilles Tatius' *Leucippe*, a Greek romance of the second century CE.[28] Although she is a slave, the heroine Leucippe's endurance of the sufferings inflicted on her as she is raped by her master Thersandros is a testimony to her independence of will, her moral superiority. She invites him to use on her whatever instruments of torture he wishes, he will never conquer her spirit. Both texts offer, in Brent Shaw's words, 'a pornography of power'. Jerome describes how the alleged adulteress, like Leucippe, invites her torturers to do their worst. The executioner tries repeatedly to kill her. The sexual imagery of his attacks on her body with his sword is striking.[29] There is a notable parallel here with the death of the Carthaginian martyr Perpetua, described in the text which frames what are presented as her own words:

Perpetua autem, ut aliquid doloris gustaret, inter ossa conpuncta exulu-
lavit, et errantem dexteram tirunculi gladiatoris ipsa in iugulum suum
transtulit. Fortasse tanta femina aliter non potuisset occidi, quae ab
immundo spiritu timebatur, nisi ipsa voluisset.

Perpetua, however, had yet to taste more pain. She screamed as she
was struck on the bone; then she took the trembling hand of the young
gladiator and guided it to her throat. It was as though so great a woman,
feared as she was by the unclean spirit, could not be dispatched unless
she herself were willing.

(*Perp.* 21.9–10)

As in the case of the matron described by Jerome, the woman's acceptance
of her death serves as a demonstration of her victory over the forces of
oppression, a testimony to the power of her Christian faith. Yet at the same
time we might notice a suggestive similarity between Perpetua's death
and that of the brave gladiator, as described by Seneca and discussed in
Chapter 2. Defeated, he too accepts he must die and, unflinching, *iugulum
adversari praestat et errantem gladium sibi adtemperat*, 'offers his throat to
his opponent and directs the blade to the vital spot' (*Ep.* 30.8). Certainly
the gender of the victim transforms the scene in important respects (not
least in that the modern reader is more readily disposed to detect an erotic
dimension) but this form of death is by no means exclusively feminine. We
have seen earlier how the throat, *iugulum*, was the part of the body most
often referred to as the site of the defeated gladiator's final wound.[30]

Other Christian writers besides Tertullian urge the faithful to avoid
pagan games at all costs. While earlier Christian writers, too, had been
aware that the passions of the martyrs might serve as a substitute for the
entertainments of the amphitheatre, theatre and circus, it is in Augustine's
work above all that the idea of *meliora spectacula* – 'the superior entertainments' – available to the faithful is most fully developed.[31] Augustine,
in one of his *Enarrationes in psalmos*, responds to the question of how
Christians are to manage without traditional entertainments by asserting
that God provides better entertainment in the passions of the martyrs: *haec
munera, haec spectacula edit deus*, 'God is the giver of these spectacles,
of these games' (39.9). Here the Christian God becomes a transcendent
equivalent of the Roman emperor entertaining his people. Augustine uses
the verb *spectare*, 'to watch', with striking frequency in discussion accounts
of martyrdom: *quando leguntur passiones martyrum specto*, 'When the
passions of the martyrs are read, I am spectating' (*Denis* 17.7). For Augustine
the martyr acts have a dual audience, the cruel pagans baying for blood in

the arena, and the Christians who later listen to the narrative of the martyr's suffering (*Denis* 15.1; 4). While the pagans enjoyed the punishment itself, for Christians, claims Augustine, it is rather the cause of the punishment, Christian faith, which is the source of pleasure. Pagans love the torment: *cruciatus*, Christians the bravery: *virtus* (*Caillau* 1, 47.1). For the Christian, appreciation of the martyr act, the distance created by the experience of listening and imagining, as opposed to observing directly, is of crucial importance.[32] *Sed duo genera hominum talia spectacula spectant; unam carnaliam, alteram spiritualiam*, 'But there are two ways in which men watch such spectacles, one fleshly, the other spiritual' (*Serm.* 51.2). As they listen, Christians must labour to visualise these spectacles, inspired by Augustine's skilful deployment of all the traditional armoury of enargeia (the term used by rhetoricians for the creation of a vivid verbal picture, whether true or false).[33] It is notable how few visual representations of martyrdom survive by comparison with written accounts. The consumption of such images was perhaps less susceptible to control by the church authorities, whose accompanying commentaries glossed the recitations of martyr acts to the faithful.[34]

Unlike the performers of the pagan games, Christian martyr-performers are examples to be imitated. Discussing the Maccabees, Augustine comments: *laudabilis est spectator, si fuerit imitator*, 'The spectator is praiseworthy if he becomes an imitator.' At the theatre, by contrast, *et spectator turpis est, et imitator infamis*: 'the spectator is shameful and the imitator infamous' (*Denis* 17.7). Augustine's criticisms of the moral value of acting draw on a long pagan tradition.[35] But we might also be reminded of the ambivalence some pagan Roman writers express toward performances in the arena. Here the skill of the performer does not lie in imitation: the blows, the wounds, the deaths are real enough. And yet the performance is both real and not real, both an *exemplum* – showing the audience how to fight and how to die – and a *spectaculum* – a source of entertainment.[36] Gladiators die but for no larger cause. Hence, as we have seen, the appeal and the appositeness of the figure of the arena to convey the futility of civil war.

At the same time we might also map Augustine's two responses to the spectacle of martyrdom – pagan cruelty on the one hand, Christian admiration on the other – back onto the responses set out in pagan texts to different kinds of death scene. Gladiators die before a great crowd, whose responses are disturbingly volatile. Aristocratic commentators express some admiration for the gladiators themselves but hesitate to identify completely with the emotions of the onlookers more generally. In the narratives of senatorial death in Seneca and Tacitus – chamber performances, as it were – the select group of onlookers draw only inspiration; these deaths are clearly marked as *exempla* not *spectacula*. Thrasea Paetus, for instance, as we saw, is made by Tacitus to offer his own end as an example of endurance in the face of death, advising the emperor's messenger: *in ea tempora natus es quibus firmare animum expediat constantibus exemplis*, 'You have been born into times when it is prudent to strengthen your spirit with examples of endurance' (*Ann.* 16.35.2). The exemplary value of these acts might also be available through the narrating text to those not present at the time – just as Augustine's congregation could derive benefit from hearing accounts of the passions of the martyrs. And yet for Augustine's pagan predecessors, too, there is significant slippage between the exemplary and the spectacular. Repeatedly using the verb *spectare*, Seneca imagines the dying Cato as a fighter in the arena, the gods his delighted audience. Perhaps it is helpful to see this strategy as a deliberately risky one, an act of spiritual daring for Stoic as for Christian, to imagine the scene of suffering without succumbing to the temptation to dwell luxuriantly on the tortured flesh.

In the case of both pagan and Christian death-texts, we may wonder how far the experience of reading or listening to another's painful death did indeed serve as a spur to imitation. I suggested in Chapter 4 that the deaths of both Thrasea and Cremutius Cordus in Tacitus' *Annals* instead of being taken as models could be read as surrogates for the death of the author. Like Trimalchio in Petronius' *Satyricon*, we may find ourselves overwhelmingly curious as to the nature and aftermath of our own ends.[37] And yet, as Freud observes, it is impossible for us to conceive of our own deaths. Whenever we try to do so, we find ourselves in the position of spectator – and consequently survivor, of the very death we are seeking to imagine.[38] Keith Hopkins comments in relation to Christian martyr acts that 'They enable readers (or listeners) vicariously to act out the effrontery of opposition with impunity ... the reader survives, and can read the story again and again ... Each time the story of faithful death was retold, the event recurred, at least in each believer's mind.'[39] Martyr acts have their particular place in the self-definition of the Christian church, but it is not implausible that for pagan aristocrats, preoccupied with their own embattled honour a few decades earlier, in the context of a culture so intensely focused on death as a moment of truth, the death-texts we have been considering could be both uplifting and reassuring. For some, the act of reading was itself courageous enough.

The elevation of the virtue of endurance – 'hypomone' is frequently the Greek term used, *patientia* in Latin – is certainly a striking feature of the literature of martyrdom. This might seem a dramatic shift in values away from more active virtues such as 'andreia', the active bravery closely associated both with masculinity and with the elite in earlier centuries.

These texts of the second century CE show us passivity as a legitimately male quality; Augustine advises his congregation that while in time of persecution the Christian needs the qualities of the soldier, in peacetime it is constancy that wins the crown (*Serm.* 303.2).[40] How far the new importance of 'endurance' is a specifically Christian phenomenon is less clear. We might see a significant continuity with the stress on *patientia* in Seneca's work in particular.[41] Seneca too paradoxically dismisses the value of the body, yet privileges its sufferings and ultimately its extinction as opportunities for communicating the virtuous disposition of the sufferer.[42]

The passivity of Christian martyrs was paradoxical – to win, they had to lose.[43] Yet this kind of paradox has many close counterparts in pagan texts. Several distinctive characteristics of at least some Christian thinking on martyrdom might seem to be anticipated in pagan authors, Seneca above all, whose works have been a central preoccupation of earlier chapters. Carlin Barton contends persuasively that if we insist on too radical a distinction between Roman and Christian values 'we fail to see the degree to which the proud Roman *animus* was already turned against itself, nor how deeply in love with victory and glory was the humble Christian'.[44] In Seneca's treatise on providence, the Stoic sage experiences *summa felicitas*, 'highest happiness', even as he meets death. His ability to rise above any injury renders him *continuo gaudio elatus*, 'elated with unceasing joy' (*Const. sap.* 9.3). To what degree does this transcendent felicity foreshadow the fierce joy of the Christian martyr?[45] In a number of texts, as we have seen, Seneca urges his reader to be the spectator of his own acts of virtue. To be the spectator of one's own death is impossible. In the passage from *De providentia* which describes the death of Cato, Seneca invokes god to play the part of the spectator. Like the Christian god, the Stoic gods function as omniscient witnesses, whose judgement may always be relied on. Yet ultimately the Stoic gods are insubstantial figures whose enjoyment of the spectacle of virtue will never translate into heavenly rewards for the virtuous individual.

Just as Seneca had advised his readers to make use of the examples of Mucius and Cato to transcend their own more mundane sufferings as they lay sick in bed, Augustine several times advises the faithful to imitate the martyrs when faced with the challenge of illness.[46] Similarly, the *Acts of the Martyrs* offered readers and listeners an understanding of themselves as sufferers, whose experience of suffering gave them a kind of power.[47] In later centuries, too, the examples of the Christian martyrs were regularly invoked to underpin the endurance of more commonplace sufferings. Yet while the conceit appears similar, the Christian texts hold out possibilities entirely absent from the work of Seneca and his contemporaries. The martyrs have beaten a path to heaven. To follow the example of Cato is its own reward.

This is a stark doctrine. The Stoic sage, unlike the Christian martyr, is often no more than an ideal, never actualised, impossible to attain.

The greatest contrast with pagan discourses is offered by the notion of death as a happy ending. According to Tertullian, Arrius Antoninus, a proconsul of Asia in the second century, was completely thrown by Christians clamouring to undergo judicial execution (*Ad Scap.* 5).[48] Ignatius proclaims his desire for death (*Ep. ad Rom.*). Christians longed to make a sacrifice of themselves in imitation of Christ. Ignatius urges: 'Allow me to follow the example of the passion of my Lord!' (6.3). His contemporary Polycarp advised the Philippians: 'Let us then be imitators of [Christ's] endurance and if we suffer for his name's sake let us glorify him. For this is the example which he gave us in himself' (*To the Philippians* 8.2).[49] It was precisely in suffering that Christians could come closest to God.

This is death as rebirth. Ignatius urges his fellow Christians in Rome not to prevent his martyr's death: 'Do not obstruct my coming to life – do not wish me to die' (6.1.2). No pagan writer embraces death quite so warmly. Death is the avenue to eternal life. Minucius Felix has the Christian apologist Octavius declare:

'Quam pulchrum spectaculum deo, cum Christianus cum dolore congreditur, cum adversum minas et supplicia et tormenta componitur, cum strepitum mortis et horrorem carnificis inridens inculcat, cum libertatem suam adversus reges et principes erigit, soli deo, cuius est, cedit, cum triumphator et victor ipsi, qui adversum se sententiam dixit, insultat! ...'

'How beautiful a spectacle for God, when a Christian confronts pain, when he is matched against threats, and punishments and torture, when laughing he tramples the noise of death and the horror of the executioner, when he asserts his liberty against kings and princes, ceding only to God, to whom he belongs, when triumphant and victorious he defies the man who pronounced judgement on him ...'

(*Octavius* 37.1)

If there are parallels with the spectacle of Mucius burning off his right hand, if there are parallels with the gladiator in the arena, if there are parallels with the aristocratic suicide, yet there must remain a great gulf between the *libido moriendi* which stems from a kind of desperation with this life and that which takes its spur from eager anticipation of the life to come. Only Christians laugh in the face of death.

The characteristics of 'the conceptual system of posthumous recognition and anticipated reward' are already associated with an older Jewish tradition of martyrdom evident in 2 and 4 Maccabees.[50] The doctrine of resurrection, an idea which had already had some currency in earlier Jewish discourses, came to be asserted with notable force around 200 CE, just at the time when the discourse of martyrdom was itself becoming a particularly prominent strand in Christian self-definition.[51] By the end of the second century, Christian writers were devoting whole treatises to this topic, with a new stress on the material continuity of the specific individual. It was above all the martyr's mutilated corpse which was thought of as the body redeemed and raised by Christ. Literal physical resurrection would be the ultimate demonstration of the martyr's victory over his or her excruciating death.[52] The prospect of martyrdom and its intense agonies was made more bearable by the idea that the flesh might assume a foretaste of incorruption.[53] For Christians more generally the promise of resurrection might numb death's sting, reassuring them of the survival of each individual in the face of the pain of death and the horror of putrefaction. As Caroline Bynum comments: 'Resurrection is victory over partition and putrefaction; it is both the anaesthesia of glory and the reunion of particles of the self. Resurrection guarantees not only the justice denied to the living; it guarantees the rest and reassemblage – the burial – denied to the dead.'[54] This hope above all could give courage – indeed bring joy – to the martyr: Perpetua is described entering heaven: *Deo gratias, ut quomodo in carne hilaris fui, hilarior sim et hic modo*, 'Thanks be to God that I am happier here now than I was in the flesh.'[55] It is above all this anticipation of the life to come which serves to differentiate Christian approaches to death from pagan ones.

Christian martyrs often seem to be protected from experiencing bodily pain.[56] Romanus, for instance, in Prudentius' *Peristephanon*, as his torturers intensify their efforts assures the judge *non dolet*, 'it does not hurt' (10.460). Other Christians refute docetic beliefs, according to which the physical sufferings of Christ were not real, stressing rather that it is precisely the physical suffering of the martyr which gives value to his or her act.[57] Yet even where their physical suffering is not muted by divine intervention, nevertheless the prospect of heaven, so tantalisingly imminent, is presented as offering them the means to transcend the torments of the flesh. The martyrs' ability to laugh in the face of even the most painful end is the most telling testament to the power of their god to redeem them from the extremes of human misery with the promise of an eternal life of bliss.

By contrast accounts of the deaths of pagan Romans could convey only the bleakest of consolations. In the works of pagan authors an awareness of death, quickened by a joke, image or poem, could sharpen the intensity of the moment and its transient pleasures. The hope of an afterlife, beyond that offered by reputation, makes only rare appearances, and even some of those can be seen as fantasies, on some level acknowledged as such. The frequent sight of violent death made death no less fearful. The fascination with death – often in its most gruesomely physical aspect – betrayed by Roman elite writers may sometimes grate against modern sensibilities. Their inclination to identify death with a kind of freedom can seem a counsel of despair. And yet, in embracing death as an intrinsic and supremely important part of life, perhaps they can still offer a model of courage to confront death with a steady gaze, to know death as the end, a strategy to transcend death which does not seek to deny its finality – an acceptance of mortality.

NOTES

Notes to Introduction

1. Martial 1.78. This poem is discussed further in Chapter 4 below. Translations are my own except where otherwise indicated.
2. Other versions of Cato's death may be found in Appian *BC* 2.98–9; Dio 43.11.4–5; Florus 2.13; Livy *Per.* 114; *B.Afr.* 88.3–4. Appian's in particular (composed in the second century CE) focuses on the gory nature of Cato's death. See Geiger (1979) for the relationships between these texts and their possible sources. Cf. Trapp (1999) on Plutarch, whose treatment will be discussed further in Chapter 5 below.
3. Scipio, too, had committed suicide and is celebrated for this by later writers such as Seneca (*Ep.* 24.9–10). At the time of writing, however, Cicero may not have been fully aware of the circumstances of his death (Griffin 1986: 200–1).
4. See van Hooff (1990: 10–11).
5. The circumstances of Cassius' suicide were disputed (Plut. *Brut.* 43). Some attempted suicide but survived to be thought less than committed, for example, Nero's ancestor Domitius Ahenobarbus whose vacillations, as described by Suetonius (*Nero* 2; cf. Pliny *NH* 7.186), foreshadow those of his descendant the emperor at the biography's conclusion.
6. See most recently Griffin (1989); Sedley (1997).
7. Cic. *Att.* 12.21.1 [S B 260]; 13.46.2 [S B 338]. According to Plutarch, Brutus initially disapproved of Cato's suicide but later changed his mind (Plut. *Brut.* 40.4). On the death of Brutus, see also Dio 47.49.1–2. Dio has Brutus declaim some lines spoken by Hercules in a tragic drama before asking a companion to kill him.
8. Debate focused on his conduct in Cyprus and his marriage to Marcia as well as the circumstances of his death. Geiger (1979: 54–5).
9. Cf. Tac. *Ann.* 4.34. In Plutarch's own time, he claims, 'Both treatises have many keen readers, on account of Caesar and of Cato' (*Caes.* 54.6).
10. Geiger (1979); Griffin (1986: 198). There were biographies of Cato by Munatius Rufus and by Thrasea Paetus.
11. See, for instance, 1.128, 2.390: Cato as poem's moral centre; 2.301–5: Cato's commitment to *libertas*; 9.208–14: Cato would rather die than be complicit in the tyranny of Caesar. On Lucan's treatment of Cato, see Hill (2004: 222–9).
12. Cf. Schunk (1964: 57); Griffin (1986: 197).
13. On the later reception of Cato's death, see particularly Goar (1987) and Donaldson (1982: 143–68). Cato's mode of death of course made him an especially problematic figure for Christian writers opposed to suicide. Augustine, for instance, offers lowlier motives for his death, *Civ. dei* 1.22–4. In this respect there are strong

parallels between Cato and Lucretia, whose death will be discussed in Chapter 7. On the reception of Cato's death in early eighteenth-century Britain, see Edwards (2005b).

14. On Montaigne's relationship with classical authors, see Quint (1998) and O'Brien (2005). In the earlier essays (in a more strictly Stoic vein) Montaigne appears to express greatest admiration for the death of Cato. In the later work, 'On cruelty', he argues rather that the death of Socrates is the more beautiful.

15. See Dollimore (1998: 87).

16. Montaigne (1991: 687).

17. Nepos writes: *subito febris decessit leviorque morbus esse coepit. Tamen propositum nihilo setius peregit*, 'suddenly the fever abated and the illness became more bearable. Nevertheless he carried out his plan all the same' (*Att.* 22.3).

18. Montaigne (1991: 689).

19. Cf. Quint (1998: 47).

20. Montaigne's most extended comparison of Stoicism and Christianity comes in his 'Apology for Raimond Sebond'.

21. Montaigne (1991: 687). Another earlier essay 'On Cato the Younger' focuses specifically on the figure of Cato (1991: 257–61).

22. See Chapter 2 below.

23. Cf. Quint (1998: 45–6); Edwards (2005b).

24. There are also works on the subject of Cato's death by Lethière, Boucher, Le Brun and others. On the fashion for history painting, see Rosenblum (1967: Ch. 2).

25. This is the main focus of Toynbee (1971); Reece (1977); Scheid (1984); Walker (1985); von Hesberg and Zanker (1987); Morris (1992); Bassett (1992); Hinard (1995); Hope and Marshall (2000).

26. Cf., for example, Hopkins (1983: 221–6) and, on attitudes to the death of children in a culture with a high level of infant mortality, Golden (1988); Shaw (1991).

27. Van Hooff (1990), Grisé (1982), Griffin (1986) and most recently Hill (2004).

28. Hopkins (1984), Barton (1993), Plass (1995).

29. Derrida (1993: 55). Indeed a significant number of twentieth-century French thinkers have been especially drawn to Roman Stoic views on death. Foucault's exploration of suicide as a work of art, for instance, seems significantly influenced by Roman models (Foucault 1994 vol. IV: 251–60).

30. On the role of metaphor in structuring thought see Lakoff and Johnson (2003).

31. Though Augustus too apparently desired an easy end, *exitus facilis*, according to Suetonius *Aug.* 99.1.

32. See Lounsbury (1987: Ch. 4).

33. Champlin (1991).

34. Important modern discussions of Roman funerary ritual include: Scheid (1984); Flower (1996); Bodel (1999); Sumi (2002). Feldherr (2000) suggestively explores the detail of Roman funerary ritual in relation to Catullus' poem on the death of his brother.

35. There was a significant tradition of consolation literature in Roman antiquity. On this see further, for example, Scourfield (1993: 15–33); White (1995); Erskine (1997); Wilson (1997).

36. See Houghton (2005) on Propertius. On the propensity of the Roman lover to suicide, see Hill (2004: 87–120).

37. See Dollimore (1998) for a thought-provoking exploration of this issue in relation to later periods.

38. Seale (1998: 8); Walter (1994: 109–16, 131–2). Cf. Flemming (2005) on the relevance of Roman practice to modern debates about euthanasia. For Dollimore the preoccupation of many recent studies with the need for a 'healthier' attitude to death overlooks the inevitably traumatic nature of death (1998).

39. See, for instance, Prof. Rosi Braidotti's Leverhulme-funded research project at Birkbeck College on 'Ways of dying'.
40. (1962: 281–5, §47). Suggestively discussed by Derrida (1993: 35–7).
41. Cited by Goodwin and Bronfen (1993: 3).
42. Cf. Metcalf and Huntingdon (1991). Among anthropologists and others debate continues concerning the degree to which we can isolate aspects of the experience of death and particularly bereavement which are universal rather than culturally specific. Do emotions themselves vary between cultures or are they merely expressed in significantly different ways? Cf. Bloch and Parry (1982).
43. Other important studies include Vovelle (1983), McManners (1981).
44. The most sustained use of Ariès' model in relation to the ancient world is to be found in Sourvinou-Inwood's 1995 study of ancient Greek attitudes to death. This is an ambitious and thought-provoking if not always ultimately convincing project. See Morris (1989) on her earlier work.
45. Whaley (1981), for instance, articulates some important criticisms of Ariès' work.
46. First published 1897. On Durkheim's study of suicide, see Gane (2005).
47. For attempts to articulate a more nuanced approach to self-killing in different cultures see the collection of essays in *Economy and Society* 34.2 (2005).
48. This point, also made by earlier scholars (Alvarez (2002: 74–85); Grisé (1982: 21–8); van Hooff (1990: 80–1)), is articulated with particular clarity by Hill (2004: 4–7; 15–21). Cf. Flemming (2005).
49. This issue will be revisited in Chapter 4.
50. Hill (2004: 11). Hill draws attention to the difficulties in applying a Durkheimian model of suicide – one predicated on a post-enlightenment Cartesian notion of the self – to a society in which the identity of the individual can only be understood in social terms; the aristocratic social audience is paramount (2004: 15–21).
51. Hill (2004: 202).
52. Maurice Pinguet's compelling study (1993) of attitudes to voluntary death in Japanese culture opens with a discussion of the death of Cato. There are clear affinities between the honour and value associated with certain acts of self-destruction in ancient Roman and in traditional Japanese culture. It is tempting to trace in Pinguet's study the influence of the Roman historian Paul Veyne (a colleague of Pinguet's in the Collège de France).
53. Elements of this argument were foreshadowed in his 1955 article, 'The pornography of death'. Others too, most notably Freud and Walter Benjamin, identified a tendency to deny death in modern culture but differed as to its origins (cf. Dollimore 1998: 119–27).
54. Kübler-Ross (1970).
55. See, for example, Seale (1998); Walter (1994).
56. Thus the cancer patient serves as model for the self-aware death (Seale 1998).
57. See, for example, Bloch and Parry (1982); Metcalf and Huntingdon (1991). There are some exceptions to this. See for instance Laidlaw's discussion (2005) of deliberate deaths of Jain ascetics.
58. Specifically, Dollimore (influenced particularly by the work of Georges Bataille) traces the ways in which a link between death and desire, vividly articulated in Renaissance literature, comes in the late twentieth century to be redeployed in relation to male homosexual desire, under the shadow of the spread of Aids.
59. Goodwin and Bronfen (1993).
60. Canetti (1962: 227).
61. Tertullian is referring specifically to the alleged origins of gladiatorial combat as an entertainment associated with aristocratic funerals. Cf. Hopkins (1983: 30). Discussed further in Chapter 2 below.

62. As Goodwin and Bronfen suggest (1993: 22).
63. Goodwin and Bronfen (1993: 13).
64. Bronfen (1992). Bronfen examines a series of case studies drawn from western literature and art of the eighteenth to the twentieth centuries.
65. Nevertheless, there are also, as we shall see particularly in Chapter 7, revealing differences between the ways women's deaths are figured in Roman texts, and the nineteenth-century material discussed by Bronfen.
66. This model is of course heavily indebted to that articulated in Laura Mulvey's classic article 'Visual pleasure and narrative cinema' of 1975 (Screen 16 (1975) 6–18, reprinted in Mulvey (1989)). For the term 'sadistic voyeurism', see Mulvey (1989: 22). Mulvey's work has been refined by many subsequent studies which have explored the role of the female viewer and the importance of masochism as a source of pleasure. See, for example, E. Ann Kaplan (1983); Studlar (1988).
67. Later critics, refining Mulvey's 1975 model, particularly stressed the importance of masochism in analysing responses to film. See esp. Studlar (1988).
68. This is well emphasised by Eldred (2002: 66–7).
69. Freud (1985: 77).
70. On attitudes to the afterlife, see Bremmer (2002).
71. Toynbee (1971: 61–4); Scheid (1984); Dunbabin (2003: 103–32).
72. Examples are conveniently collected by Lattimore (1942: esp. Chs 2 and 3); see too Rohde (1925).
73. Lattimore (1942: 78–86). The Christian Tertullian criticised pagans for their inconsistent beliefs in this respect (Resurr. 1.2).
74. For a discussion of some of the inconsistencies in the Odyssey's picture of the underworld and the issues these may raise, see Sourvinou-Inwood (1995: 17–107); Bremmer (2002: 4–6). On the Greek tradition of underworld accounts, see Edmonds (2004).
75. Clinton (1989). Cf. Burkert (1987).
76. Plutarch fr. 178 Sandbach (from the De anima) is the clearest indication of this. Cf. Lucian Downward Journey 22. See Graf (1999); Reinhardt (2004: 36).
77. See Bremmer (2002: Ch. 2) and, on Pythagoreanism, Kahn (2001: Ch. 7); on Orphism, Edmonds (2004: 29–109).
78. Bernstein (1993: Ch. 2) offers a helpful account of the variations. Cf. Edmonds (2004: 159–220) on Phaedo.
79. It is striking that Cicero, unlike Plato and (later) Virgil, is not concerned to explore any corresponding punishment for the souls of the wicked.
80. The story of Er is, it seems, referred to in the comments introducing the Somnium Scipionis, Rep. 6.3.
81. On the problems inherent in Cicero's definition of virtus, a definition which conflates aristocratic status and ethical merit, see Long (1995: 228). See now also Zetzel (forthcoming).
82. This is a theme pursued in earlier philosophical literature which can be plausibly connected with the idea associated with mystery cults that the soul might travel beyond the evidence of the senses to a true vision of the cosmos. Cf. Jones (1926). On Seneca's moves to identify with the cosmos, see Inwood (2005: 319).
83. It is tempting to see a resonance here with Virgil's treatment of the soul after death in Aeneid 6.
84. On possible Orphic and Pythagorean as well as Platonic influences here, see Luck (1973); Feeney (1986); Bernstein (1993: Ch. 2).
85. Feeney (1986).
86. West (1990).
87. In an epigram in his 'Garland' composed around 100 BCE. Cf. West (1990: 237).

88. For a subtle and rich account of the relationship between Roman literature and religion more generally, see Feeney (1998).

89. Even while attacking the stories of Sisyphus and Tantalus as fantasies, Lucretius aligns his own hexameter poem with Homer's *Odyssey*, making a bid for epic stature. Cf. Segal (1989).

90. See Feeney (1986).

91. See Spentzou and Fowler (2002).

92. Chthonic forces are associated with poetic inspiration in many other texts, too. Seneca's tragedy *Thyestes*, for instance, is launched by the appearance of Tantalus from the underworld, a figure whose passionate rage, *furor*, provides the creative, dramaturgical impetus for the play (Schiesaro 2003: 26–36). Cf. Medea's invocation of the Furies in the opening speech of Seneca's *Medea* (2003: 45–6).

Notes to Chapter 1: Dying for Rome? The glorious death of a commander

1. Important modern discussions of Roman funerary ritual include: Scheid (1984); Flower (1996); Bodel (1999); Sumi (2002). Feldherr (2000) suggestively explores the detail of Roman funerary ritual in relation to Catullus' poem on the death of his brother.

2. Cf. *Tusc.* 1.32 and *Rhet. Her.* 4.57, citing the example of Decius, discussed below.

3. Cf. Tac. *Hist.* 1.3.1. Moles (1998) reads Tac. *Ann.* 4.32–3 as a nuanced critique of Cic. *Fam.* 5.12.

4. On the militarised nature of Roman society, see Hopkins (1978: Ch. 1); Harris (1985); Rich and Shipley (1993).

5. 'Das Gedicht vom Tod', Marg (1973: 10).

6. Vernant (1991: 51).

7. Fr. 10.1–2, trs. D. Gerber (Loeb edition). Cf. Vernant (1991: 64–5; 88–9). Tyrtaeus elsewhere celebrates those who have fought bravely and survived, as Loraux emphasises in her discussion of the ideology of the beautiful death among the Spartans (1995: Ch. 3).

8. On the origins of this practice see Bradeen (1969: appendix 1). Many other Greek cities, too, had rituals to honour the war dead and acknowledged their obligation to them (Loraux 1986: 18).

9. As Loraux has so tellingly emphasised (1986: 99).

10. On this see Bradeen (1969).

11. Cf. Loraux (1986: 42).

12. On the civil war context, see Sordi (1990b).

13. A passage from Appian (*BC* 1.43), recounting events during the Social War in 90 BCE, describes an ambush in which many Romans were killed. Their numerous corpses, brought back to Rome for burial, provoked grief and despondency. In consequence of this the senate decreed that in future those killed in battle should be buried where they fell, lest the sight of their bodies discourage others from joining the army. On this see Valvo (1990). Pliny claims that the practice of cremation gained currency among Romans after it became known that the bodies of those fallen in battle were later exhumed (*NH* 7.187).

14. Plutarch (*Publ.* 9.6) similarly emphasises that this Roman custom predates the Athenian funeral oration.

15. For an example of the topics such a speech might cover, see the summary of the panegyric of Lucius Metellus, offered by Pliny (*NH* 7.139–40).

16. On the erotic nature of the imagery used here see Fowler (1987) and Oliensis (1997).

17. On the number and gruesomeness of the war deaths described in the *Aeneid*, see

Heuzé (1985). As he emphasises, in some ways the killing in the *Aeneid* is significantly more relentless than that in the *Iliad* (1985: 116).

18. This is distinguished from *devotio hostium* by Versnel (1976) (and termed *devotio ducis*). In his view only *devotio hostium* constitutes a true *devotio*; the enemy will only become the property of the gods if the gods bring about the requested defeat. The so-called *devotio* of the Decii constitutes rather a form of *consecratio*, since the general is transferred at once to the infernal gods. However, Roman authors commonly use the term *devotio* to refer to Decius Mus. This broader sense of *devotio* is explored by Hardie (1993: Ch.2), Barton (1993: 40–4); and Leigh (1993) and (1997: 132–4). For Leigh invocations of *devotio* in Latin literature are 'the ultimate expression of a military code which expected courage from a general and heroism in defeat' (1993: 105).

19. Here the Romans are fighting Gauls and Samnites.

20. P. Decius Mus, cos. 340. Cicero refers to the *devotio* of a third Decius (son of the second), *Fin.* 2.60–1; *Tusc.* 1.89.

21. Cf. Leigh (1997: 131).

22. Cf. Versnel (1981: 153). The term *devovisse* also occurs in Livy's account of the still more mythical prototype of the Decii, Marcus Curtius (7.6.4). Livy continues: *equo ... exornato insidentem, armatum se in specum immisisse*, 'armed and mounted on a horse, splendidly adorned, he plunged into the chasm' (7.6.5).

23. Feldherr (1998: 84).

24. Feldherr (1998: 103).

25. See Barton (1993: 41–2) on this passage.

26. Cf. *Rhet. Her.* 4.57; Val. Max. 5.6.5; Sen. *Ep.* 67.9. For a full list of references to the Decii, see Litchfield (1914).

27. See Feldherr (1998: 92).

28. Rosenstein comments: 'Whatever else they may have thought about him, the historians knew how their audiences expected a man of his rank to die' (1990: 117).

29. Examples listed by Rosenstein (1990: 118 n.7). Harris (1985: 40) comments that, except during the most intense years of the Hannibalic war, consular deaths in war are rare. However, it seems to have been quite common for tribunes to lose their lives in more severe campaigns.

30. Rosenstein (1990: 121). Minor defeats, however, seem to have been tolerated and indeed to have had little impact on a general's subsequent political career (though it should be noted that the size of Rosenstein's sample is small).

31. According to Livy, the senate had no sympathy for the soldiers taken prisoner after Cannae and refused to ransom them, on the grounds that they should have fought their way out – or else died in the attempt (22.59.60). Valerius Maximus presents as admirable the centurion Publius Crassus Mulianus who, captured by a barbarian, thrusts his staff into the man's eye to provoke a soldier's death (3.2.12). On Roman military discipline see Barzanò (1990), Goldsworthy (1996), Harris (2006).

32. On the qualities expected of a Roman commander more generally, see Harris (1985: Ch.1); Goldsworthy (1996: Ch.4).

33. Cf., for example, Front. *Strat.* 2.8.11; Dion. Hal. 6.9.4 (writing about the fifth century BCE).

34. Cf. Barzanò (1990). On Roman military discipline more generally, see Goldsworthy (1996), Harris (2006).

35. See Harris (2006) on this.

36. As Schunk stresses (1964: 57, n.2).

37. See, too, Claudius' boast after his British campaign (*ILS* 216) and Velleius Paterculus' favourable comments on Tiberius' campaign in Germany (2.97.4).

38. (1998: 1).

39. For a wide-ranging exploration of this theme see Jal (1963). Roman texts of the first century CE preoccupied with civil war include Seneca *Thyestes*, Statius *Thebaid*. On this theme in the latter part of the century see McGuire (1997).

40. Jal (1963: 48).

41. The poem is sometimes known by the title *Pharsalia*. Ahl (1976) argues this was the original title but most other scholars favour *Bellum civile*.

42. On this passage see Henderson (1998: esp. 177–81).

43. A detailed discussion is offered by Wilkins (1994), esp. Ch. 2.

44. See Vretska (1976) *ad loc.* and Skard (1956).

45. Also to be located in this tradition, as Barton (1993: 32) suggests, is the later account by Florus of the death of the rebel gladiator Spartacus – like Catiline a morally ambiguous figure. *Tandem eruptione facta digna viris obiere morte et, quod sub gladiatore duce oportuit, sine missione pugnatum est. Spartacus ipse in primo agmine fortissime dimicans quasi imperator occisus est*: 'At last they made a sally and met an end worthy of men. The battle was fought to the death, as befitted those fighting under the leadership of a gladiator. Spartacus himself fought most valiantly in the front rank and fell as became a general' (Florus 2.8.14).

46. It is striking, as Wilkins comments (1994: 54), that *audacia* seems to be valued negatively earlier in the monograph but is apparently treated as a positive quality in the concluding paragraphs.

47. As McGushin notes (*ad loc.*), the alliterative combination of *luctus* and *laetitia* is later used by Livy to characterise the Roman army's emotions on recovering the body of their commander Aulus, killed in conflict with the Samnites (9.22.10).

48. On the open-endedness of the *Cat.* as mirroring the open-endedness of the civil war, see Peta Fowler (1997: 134). Ash stresses the influence of Sallust's *Catiline* on Virgil's depiction of quasi-civil conflict between Trojans and Italians in the latter part of the *Aeneid* (2002).

49. On this question see Batstone (1988), Feeney (1994), Gunderson (2000), Levene (2000).

50. Elsewhere too Lucan comments that victory in war is worse than defeat. Cf. 7.123; 4.258–9. Similarly Seneca suggests a virtuous man might in civil war prefer to be conquered rather than to conquer (*Ben.* 4.32.2; *Ep.* 14.13; Tac. *Hist.* 1.50). On this as a topos of civil war narratives, see Ahl (1976: 145, 245 n. 16).

51. The story also appears in Livy *Per.* 79; Val. Max. 5.5.4 (in both cases associated with the civil conflict of 87 BCE); Aug. *Civ. dei* 2.25. Tacitus also uses a version of this story associated with the fighting between Strabo and Cinna in the civil war of 87 BCE (Sisenna is cited as his source). Tacitus contrasts this with the civil wars of 68–9 CE in which, he asserts, a trooper who had killed his own brother then demanded a reward from his leaders (*Hist.* 3.51). On this see Woodman (1998: 13–16).

52. This aspect of the poem is usefully discussed by Roller (1996), who relates it to the conflict between *virtus* and *pietas* in Lucan's representation of Pompey.

53. Cf. Hill (2004: 198–201).

54. Though some disasters might be so extensive that the commander's suicide offered little compensation, for example, that of Varus, after losing three legions to the Germans (Tac. *Ann.* 1.61).

55. Of course this can be read as a reprise of the wars between Trojans and Latins in the second half of the *Aeneid*. Aeneas and Latinus were also to become father-in-law and son-in-law. On the theme of wars worse than civil more generally, see Jal (1963: 36).

56. Cf., for example, 2.150–1; 7.180; 7.320–5; 7.624–30.

57. (1998: 166). On the increasingly problematic value of *virtus* in Lucan, see also Fantham (1995).

58. See Hill (2004: 215–18).
59. Domitius had earlier been pardoned by Caesar. See 2.478–525.
60. On this see Masters (1994: esp. 163–8).
61. See Bartsch (1997: 16); Most (1992).
62. Contrast Book 2 where the gruesome deaths described are those of named individuals but are located in the time of Sulla in the 80s BCE. See esp. 2.118–93.
63. See Hardie (1993: 30). On *devotio* as a motive in Lucan see also Barton (1993: 44–5); Eldred (2002).
64. See Fantham (1995).
65. Cf. 7.117–20: 'The first missile hurled in this fatal war is welcome to find its lodging in my head, if that head could fall without influence on the issue and without the destruction of our cause; for to me victory is no more welcome than defeat ...'
66. Discussed by Bartsch (1997: 79–80). Cf. Leigh, who disposes effectively of the case for Pompey made by Rambaud and others (1993: 128–43).
67. See for instance *Hist.* 1.50.2. The relationship between Tacitus' *Histories* and Lucan is discussed by O'Gorman (1995). She suggestively argues that this passage echoes elements in the speech Lucan places in the mouth of a civil war veteran in Book 2 of his epic (68–232).
68. On this motif, see Jal (1963: 401); Woodman (1998: 13–16).
69. Cf. particularly the description of Antonius leading his troops (3.17) and Sall. *Cat.* 60.
70. The parallels are also marked in Plutarch's treatments of the two deaths. Schunk sees Otho's death as very much in the Stoic-philosophical tradition (1964: 49).
71. Ash (1999: 88). As Ash points out, there is also a nice contrast here with the suicide of Nero who in Suetonius' account (*Nero* 49.2) tries the points of two *pugiones* before throwing them away in fear. For further discussion of Suetonius' account of Nero's death, see Chapter 5 below.
72. Shochat (1981) argues that Tacitus does not make a convincing case against Otho. For Ash, Tacitus' representation of Otho serves as a foil to Galba and Piso but the complexity of his characterisation derives ultimately from the conflicting propaganda circulating during and after the civil war. Vespasian and his supporters appear to have emphasised the heroism of Otho's death to denigrate Vitellius and also to win over Otho's own supporters. As she notes, the most negative remarks on Otho are attributed to other characters rather than presented as authorial comment (Ash 1999: 83–93).
73. Haynes' recent study more plausibly presents the Tacitean Otho as successful in his attempt to retain imperial power precisely insofar as he eludes categorisation as an exemplar either of Neronian vice or of Galban virtue: 'Tacitus depicts Otho ... as playing upon the desire of the *volgus* by staying just out of reach' (2003: 63, cf. 56–7).
74. On the details of Tacitus' description of Otho's death see Hutchinson (1993: 257–61). Keitel suggests numerous parallels between Tacitus' Otho and Sallust's Catiline, particularly in terms of their speeches. As she notes, both foreshadow in their first speeches the ways they will eventually meet their ends (1987).
75. See Plass (1995: 82). He comments: 'What is strange is that suicide may well be the right, perhaps the only, thing to do' (1995: 83).
76. According to Plutarch (*Otho* 18), Otho's tomb was a focus of veneration – a further indication of the respect inspired by his suicide. His account has a soldier commit suicide as a demonstration of loyalty *prior* to Otho's death (*Otho* 15.3).
77. Note also Martial 1.78 which again disparages the death of Cato. This is discussed further below in Chapter 4.

78. It is perhaps also relevant that Otho, opposed to Vitellius, was seen positively under Vespasian and his successors, who had defeated Vitellius (cf. Ash 1999: 87). He was also related to the future Nerva, who succeeded Domitian in 96 CE (Otho's brother, Otho Titianus, was married to Nerva's sister Cocceia).

79. Grisé (1982), Griffin (1986), Hill (2004). This will be discussed further in Chapters 3 and 4.

80. Contrast Augustine's argument (Civ. dei 1.17–21), where suicide is assimilated to murder.

81. Martindale (1993: 48). Cf. Bartsch (1997: 24–5); Hill (2004: Ch. 9).

82. A link also made by others, e.g. Virg. Aen. 6.833; Calp. Sic. 1.46–50. However it is elaborated with much greater insistence in Lucan.

83. Cf. Hill: 'Lucan's writing contains an implicit but powerful critique of the practice of aristocratic suicide' (2004: 215). Lucan's own enforced suicide, in the wake of the Pisonian conspiracy, he chose (if we believe Tac. Ann. 15.70) to conflate with a non-suicidal death in the Bellum civile. The passage Lucan allegedly recited is following Suetonius De viris illustribus and the grammarian Vacca's fifth-century Life, sometimes identified with 3.635–46 (see Hill 2004: 233–6). Tucker (1987) argues that his was an execution rather than a forced suicide.

84. The Vulteius incident is also recorded in Livy Per. 110; by Florus 2.13.33–4. On the theme of mutual suicide see Bayet (1971).

85. Seneca has Cato invoke the examples of Petreius and Juba as a spur to his own suicide (Prov. 2.10). One motive for this practice must have been that those captured were usually killed rather than kept as prisoners (cf. e.g. Dio 47.48 on the situation in 42 BCE).

86. The parallels with Scaeva are noted by Ahl (1976: 117–20), Marti (1966) and Hill (2004: 215–21). Vulteius with his blind dedication to Caesar cannot constitute a paradigm of virtus except in a parodic sense.

87. On this see Inwood (2005: Ch. 11). This issue will be discussed further in Chapter 3 below.

88. See, for example, Ep. 58.34–5 and also 70.10, discussed below (pp. 99–100).

89. See, for example, Sen. Ep. 24, discussed in Chapter Three below.

90. Martindale (1984: 69).

91. Elsewhere, as Leigh points out, deaths at sea (in these cases as a result of storms) are lamented precisely because, unlike deaths in battle, they are not associated with loss to the enemy (Leigh 1997: 262–4).

92. See Eldred (2002: 72–3).

93. Eldred (2002: 61).

94. Eldred (2002: 66–7). Eldred draws here on Laura Mulvey's classic 1976 analysis of the dynamics of spectatorial pleasure in relation to Hollywood film (Mulvey 1989), as well as the work of Mulvey's later critics. For Eldred the Vulteius episode offers a disturbing reworking of the death of Palinurus (Aen. 5) in particular but also the notion of the sacrifice of the one for the many more generally in Virgil's epic.

95. Eldred (2002: 73).

96. As Hill emphasises, the inadequacy of witnesses is a key issue for Lucan (2004: 215).

97. Cf. Eldred (2002: 76).

98. Cf. Ahl (1976: Ch. 3), Leigh (1997: 260–1). Other episodes in the poem where gladiatorial metaphors are significant include 6.60–3, 6.191–2. Tacitus also exploits the parallel (cf. e.g. Hist. 3.83), where those looking on as the emperor Galba is killed in the Roman Forum derive pleasure from the spectacle). This is discussed by Levene (1997: 146–7). On gladiatorial combat as a metaphor for civil war, see also Jal (1963: 341–5); Barton (1993: 36–9).

99. As Leigh suggests (1997: 235) – though the spectacles of the arena could also be seen as exemplary on some level, as we shall see in Chapter 2.

100. Cf. Eldred (2002: 57–8).

101. This cycle of myths was popular in late first-century Rome, forming the basis most notably of Statius' *Thebaid*. Cf. McGuire who sees the Vulteius episode in Lucan as foreshadowing the concerns of later epicists, writing in the aftermath of the civil wars of 68–70 CE (1997: 89–90). On this see also Fantham (1995); Henderson (1998: Ch. 6) on Statius.

102. Cf. Ahl (1976: 120).

103. Pompey's death is problematic. He attempts to flee, fearfully entrusting himself to a boat to reach Lesbos (8.39). Then on by another boat, together with his wife Cornelia, heading east. Pompey even thinks about enlisting help from the Parthians. Eventually he and supporters head for Egypt, despite doubts about Pharaoh's loyalty. Lucan protests that in the logic of civil war, Pompey should die at the hands of Romans not foreigners (8.547–9). Invited into the Egyptian boat, Pompey, despite his fears, prefers death to appearing fearful and accepts the invitation. (8.576). In the boat it is, however, a Roman, Septimius who had once served under Pompey, who kills him (606–8). Pompey endures death bravely watched by his wife and son. Septimius cuts off and parades Pompey's head, which is preserved and kept as a trophy by the Egyptians (8.667–91). His body is thrown in the sea.

104. On the evidence for the intended end of the poem see Masters (1992: Ch. 7). On this topic see also Hill (2004: 225) who argues that the poem was intended to include Cato's death.

105. Hardie suggests however that the manner of Cato's death served to rule out the possibility of a resolution to what he terms the 'sacrificial crisis': 'Turning his hand on himself, acting out the roles of both sacrificer and sacrificed in one person, he confounded utterly the distinction between killer and killed on which the logic of Girardian victimisation rests' (1993: 31).

Notes to Chapter 2: Death as spectacle: looking at death in the arena

1. Mark Twain in his *The Innocents Abroad* (1869) satirically congratulated himself that he had written at length about the Colosseum, 'yet have never once used the phrase "butcher'd to make a Roman holiday". I am the only free white man of mature age to have accomplished this since Byron originated the expression' (1969: 259). On Byron and Twain's treatments and the issue of modern responses to the Colosseum more generally see Hopkins and Beard (2005: esp. Ch. 1).

2. Modern evocations of the Roman arena almost invariably legitimate their own graphic display of gladiatorial combat with expressions of (more or less explicitly Christian) moral superiority. Among toga movies, for instance, as Fitzgerald comments, only *Spartacus* offers a moment when 'the audience is actually *accused* of complicity with the Roman spectators who command the spectacle of men killing each other', as the gladiator Draba hurls his trident at the camera (2001: 28).

3. A complexity well emphasised in recent years by Barton, to whose discussion in particular I am much indebted. Also important is the work of Ville (1981), Hopkins (1983), Wiedemann (1992), Gunderson (1996; 2003), Plass (1995), Hopkins and Beard (2005).

4. Earlier scholars, principally Hopkins (1983) and Wiedemann (1992), have also considered aspects of this.

5. The arena is invoked as a model for combat, particularly single combat, in warfare by Virgil (see Hardie 1986: 151–4) and Livy (see Feldherr (1998: Ch. 3), though he stresses the spectacles in general rather than the arena more specifically). The

arena offers an especially potent metaphor for civil war as we saw in Chapter 1.

6. See, for example, the essays in *The Roman Gaze: Vision, Power and the Body*, ed. D. Fredrick (2002), most particularly Eldred's essay on Lucan. The arena itself is briefly discussed in Fredrick's own essay.

7. The deceased will sometimes have specified the sum to be spent and the nature of the spectacle to be provided. Cf. Veyne (1976: 42).

8. Val. Max. 2.4.7. For debates about the origins of the games, see Ville (1981: Ch. 1).

9. For details of known *munera* see Ville (1981: Ch. 2).

10. Cf. Hopkins (1983: 6–7).

11. On aristocratic funerals, see Chapter 1. Wealthy Romans sometimes provided gladiatorial fights as entertainment for dinner-party guests, according to Athenaeus *Deipn.* 153e–154d.

12. Wiedemann (1992: 5–7) argues against the view that *munera* were sometimes given by republican magistrates in their public capacity. On this see too Baltrusch (1988); Futtrell (1997: Ch. 1).

13. Further changes in organisation are listed by Hopkins (1983: 6).

14. Though as Edmondson points out (1996: 76) this argument is based only on the lack of evidence for the provision of games by those outside the imperial family. Ville provides a catalogue of known *munera* down to the death of Domitian and discusses changes in the pattern of provision. By the time of Tiberius, *munera* no longer seem to be associated with funerals (Ville 1981: 99–106, 116–21, 129–55). Certainly the most spectacular *munera* were given by the imperial family.

15. Cf. Hopkins (1983: 7, 20). For detailed discussion of visual representations of gladiatorial combat, see Brown (1992).

16. Their simultaneous exaltation and degradation is most vividly conveyed by Barton's provocative study *The Sorrows of the Ancient Romans* (1993). See also Ville (1981: 329–44); Wiedemann (1992: Ch. 3); Edwards (1997b).

17. Barton (1993: 47).

18. On *noxii*, see Kyle (1998: 91–5). Capital punishment in the arena was sometimes carried out in the context of quasi-theatrical shows. On these, see Coleman (1990); Fitzgerald (2007).

19. Some imperial shows, however, do seem to have subverted these categories. See Ville (1960: 283); Kyle (1998: 78).

20. The different grades of gladiator are clearly analysed by Kyle (1998: 84).

21. This is well emphasised by Kyle (1998: Ch. 3).

22. On the ethnic origins of gladiators, see Ville (1981: 264–7); Wiedemann (1992: 113–15).

23. This was seen as an appropriate punishment for a slave who had committed a serious offence, such as murder (Wiedemann 1992: 105). A master could, it seems, condemn his own slave to be a gladiator. Such individuals might – if they survived – retire from the arena after three years and achieve freedom after five years (*Collatio Mosaicorum et Romanorum legum* 11.7.4). Under Augustus they were banned from becoming Roman citizens (*lex Aelia Sentia*, Gaius *Inst.* 1.13).

24. Cf. Hopkins (1983: 25). On the proportion of slave to free gladiators, see Ville (1981: 227, 255); Kyle (1998: 89).

25. Kyle (1998: 79). Advertisements also distinguish between gladiators and *noxii*.

26. See Ville (1981: 47). On the mechanisms by which free men became gladiators, see Kyle (1998: 87 and 114, n. 86).

27. Referred to by Seneca, *Ep.* 37.1, 71.2–3; Petronius *Sat.* 117. Ville (1981: 246–55) discusses the gladiator's oath in detail. Cf. Barton (1993: 2, 14–17). Barton assumes all gladiators, including slaves, swore the oath. The evidence for this is discussed by Guarino (1983) who takes the view that the gladiator's oath was sacral rather

than juridical in status and that slave gladiators could not have been induced to fight without the threat of divine sanction. The argument seems to me inconclusive. Slaves, after all, may well have been inspired by the prospect of financial gain and, ultimately, the possibility of securing their freedom.

28. Hopkins (1983: 24). Pompeian graffiti, for instance, attest to gladiators with the names of free Roman citizens (Wiedemann 1992: 107).

29. See Tert. *Spect.* 22, specifying their exclusion from all public honours and a good many distinctions. Tertullian's comments also apply to actors and charioteers. On the parallels between these professions see Edwards (1997b). It is, however, difficult to reconstruct exactly what disabilities applied to gladiators, since most surviving legal material is to be found in compilations assembled after gladiatorial shows had been banned in the fourth century CE (Wiedemann 1992: 156-8). Under the *lex Aelia Sentia* of 4 CE, freed slave gladiators took the same status as subject foreigners who had fought against Rome and surrendered. They could never become Roman citizens or Latins. They could not make a valid will or receive anything under the will of another (Gaius *Inst.* 1.13).

30. As Ville comments: 'Ce qui est infamant dans la gladiature n'est pas l'activité meutrière elle-même, mais le caractère public de l'exhibition' (1981: 270).

31. For example, *Phil.* 6.5.13; *Rosc. Am.* 3.8; 6.17.

32. For example, Manilius 4.220-6. Cf. Ville on the motivation of volunteers (1983: 227).

33. See, for example, Dio 59.10.4; Suet. *Calig.* 35.2. It is sometimes specified that this was without loss of life. See Suet. *Nero* 12.

34. Cf. Levick (1983); Lebek (1990); Bartsch (1994: Ch. 1); Edwards (1997b).

35. See Greenidge (1894: 69-70).

36. Cf. Barton (1993: Ch. 1); Edwards (1997b).

37. Calculations are offered by Ville (1981: 318-23); Clavel-Lévêque (1984: 203); Wiedemann (1992: 119-22). These are analysed by Kyle (1998: 86-7).

38. See Kyle (1998: Ch. 5).

39. Hopkins and Beard (2005: 86-94). Recent research by Karl Grosschmidt and Fabian Kanz at the University of Vienna, analysing the remains of 67 bodies from Ephesus identified as gladiators, reinforces the view that deaths in the arena were regular occurrences (*New Scientist* 22 Jan. 2005: 14).

40. For discussion of the different arms and armour and the different fighting styles associated with different types of gladiator, see Daremberg and Saglio (1896: 2.1563-1600); Robert (1940: 64-73) and more recently Junkelmann (2000). Gladiatorial typology is, however, problematised by Hopkins and Beard (2005: 63-4).

41. Edmondson (1996: 72).

42. As Wiedemann points out (1992: Ch. 1, esp. 38).

43. Athenaeus compares gladiatorial combat with the single combat of earlier days (*Deipn.* 4.155a). See Oakley (1985: esp. 405-7) on single combat. As Plass points out, 'though true single combat is exceptional in real war, combat is experienced individually' (1995: 20).

44. For Barton, the arena offered Romans a 'simplified and purified soldiery' (1993: 33).

45. See Le Roux (1990); Wiedemann (1992: 45-6); Welch (1994); Kyle (1998: Ch. 2).

46. For example, Val. Max. 2.3.2 on 105 BCE. At the same time, there was a strong sense that gladiators should not fight as soldiers in the Roman army, from which numerous legislative enactments excluded them.

47. Hopkins (1983: 2), though he plays down the popularity of gladiatorial games under the republic when military experience was less of a rarity for Romans. This need not, as Wiedemann argues (1992: 39-40), entail a hydraulic theory of violence.

48. Wiedemann (1992: 35–40. Cf. 165). On *virtus* more generally see Chapter 3.
49. See, for example, Tac. *Ann*. 15.32. Cf. Cébeillac-Gervasoni and Zevi (1976). For other references, see Kyle (1998: 115, n.94). On women and *virtus* see further Chapter 7 below.
50. For Hopkins (1983: 23) and Wiedemann (1992: 37) this suggests that on occasion, martial ability might be separated out from masculinity. For a more pessimistic reading of this see Gunderson (1996: 143). Similarly marginal seems to be the role assigned to female bull-fighters in modern Spain. Cf. Mitchell (1991: 157–8). This is one among many suggestive parallels between the Roman arena and the Spanish bull-fight.
51. Bergmann (1999: 22).
52. Cf. Fitzgerald (2007).
53. Gunderson (2003: 644).
54. On the role of the gladiatorial games in affirming the emperor's authority – while also allowing limited scope for it to be contested – see Hopkins (1983: esp. 18–19), Clavel-Lévêque (1984), Wiedemann (1992: Ch. 5), Plass (1995).
55. On the arena as a space where moral and political order was reaffirmed, see Hopkins (1983: 11–12); Plass (1995: 3–77); Gunderson (1996: 133–6). Wiedemann (1992: 46) comments on the 'liminality' of what went on in the arena.
56. Cf. Tert. *Spect*. 25. Cf. Parker (1999) on the theatre.
57. See Edmondson (1996: 82, 100–1); Edwards and Woolf (2003: 1); Fitzgerald (2007).
58. Well emphasised in recent years by Clavel-Lévêque (1984), Edmondson (1996) and Gunderson (1996), esp. 142–3 on undifferentiated seating for women as a means of asserting their political marginality.
59. Edmondson points out that rules about seating were not rigidly enforced (1996: 100). Cf. Hopkins and Beard who emphasise that others besides senators themselves must often have occupied the 2000 or so seats in the front rows of the Colosseum (2005: 111–12).
60. Indeed, as Gunderson comments, the arena was productive of the emperor's subjectivity, to the extent that even a refusal to participate (Tiberius, for instance, chose to stay away) became 'a display of non-participation' (1996: 127). This material is discussed by Yavetz (1969: 18–24); Veyne (1976: 685–9); Millar (1977: 368–75); Wallace-Hadrill (1982); Wiedemann (1995: Ch. 5); Gunderson (1996: 126–33).
61. Cf. Bartsch (1994: 2).
62. On this aspect of the arena, see Hopkins (1983: 14–15).
63. On the power of the people as a potent fantasy, see Hopkins and Beard (2005: 41).
64. Debord contrasts this with the diffuse spectacle of consumerism characteristic of the modern western world which is the primary focus of his own study (1967: 41–2).
65. Barton suggestively explores in particular the parallel between the gladiator's oath, the *auctoramentum*, and the ritual of *devotio* (1993: 15, 40–6). There are however some crucial differences. For a discussion of *devotio*, see Chapter 1 above.
66. On elite performers in the arena, see particularly Wiedemann (1992: 130–3), Barton (1993: 25–31), Edwards (1997b).
67. Expressively explored by Barton (1993: 27–34).
68. For a detailed discussion of this see Edmondson (1996: 70–1).
69. Discussed by Hopkins and Beard (2005: 49–50).
70. Ville (1981: 17).
71. On occasion a fight might be announced as *munus sine missione*, that is to say with no *missio* permitted (such fights were banned by Augustus according to Suet. *Aug*. 45.3).

72. Ville (1981: 410–15).
73. Interestingly, Martial also has animals pausing, *Spect.* 30. Cf. Gunderson (2003: 656).
74. Some texts give grounds for thinking that on occasion, the *editor* would allow the defeated gladiator to recommence the fight rather than being killed (or let off). Ville (1981: 416).
75. For the latest contribution to the continuing debate as to the gestures used to indicate the gladiator's fate, see Corbeill (2004: Ch. 2).
76. For example, Cic. *Tusc.* 2.41 (quoted below). Cf. Ville (1981: 417).
77. On the different ways of killing the defeated gladiator see Ville (1981: 424–5).
78. Libitina was a divinity associated with funerals. By contrast the corpses of condemned criminals were dragged off with hooks. See Kyle (1998: Ch. 5).
79. Kyle's detailed study (1998) makes clear that gladiators often received proper burial (and sometimes epitaphs also) paid for by relatives or by burial societies. It is less clear what happened to the bodies of slave and condemned gladiators. Gladiators were sometimes excluded from normal burial. Cf. *CIL* 11.6528 (= *ILS* 7846). Discussed by Hopkins (1983: 23); Kyle (1998: 161); Bodel (1986).
80. Ville (1981: 423).
81. 'Le combat gladiatorien n'était pas de l'escrime un peu trop poussée, un combat qui finissait mal, selon la décision objective du sort des armes; c'était une tragédie tendue vers son épilogue, une mise à mort physique et, en tout cas, une mise à mort morale: contraindre un homme à consentir à la sentence de son éventuel égorgement' (1981: 424).
82. As Barton suggests (1993: 35, n. 87).
83. Cf. Horace *Epist.* 1.1.6; Pet. *Sat.* 45.11. This issue is discussed by Ville (1981: 419–20).
84. For the Greek Christian Athenagoras, Christians had renounced the arena spectacles 'since we regard seeing a man killed as much like killing him' (*Embassy* 35.5).
85. The idea that the dead need human blood is, however, also to be found in Varro who comments (according to Servius *Ad. Aen.* 3.67): *mulieres in exequiis et luctu solitas ora lacerare ut sanguine ostenso inferis satisfaciant* (10.519). This is discussed by Ville with editorial additions by Veyne (1981: 9–10). They explain this as a Hellenistic *aition* for gladiatorial games.
86. Cf. Prudentius *Contr. Symm.* 1.379–80; 2.1125–6.
87. Cf. Wiedemann (1992: 151–5).
88. Most recently by Futtrell (1997: esp. Ch. 5).
89. As Ville and Veyne emphasise (Ville 1981: 13). Cf. Potter (2001).
90. As Plass suggests (1995: 19–22). Cf. Barton (1993: 24).
91. Cf. Barton (1993: 34).
92. Cf. Ville 'le public scrute avidement le visage du malheureux' (1981: 424).
93. See Wistrand (1990).
94. On the importance of the gladiator's death for judging his worth, see Seneca *Tranqu. an.* 11.5–6, discussed below.
95. Cf. Brown (1995: 384).
96. (1992: 35). Cf. Vogt (1983).
97. Plass (1995: 23). Cf. Wiedemann (1992: 35): 'Instead of seeing a gladiatorial combat as a public display of killing it might be useful to see it as a demonstration of the power to overcome death.'
98. Visual representations of gladiators about to die, dying or just dead regularly show them both with and without helmets. Those without are normally identified as *retiarii*. Juvenal (8.199–210) asserts that for an aristocrat to enter the arena as a *retiarius* was especially shameful since the lack of helmet meant he was readily recognised.

99. The gladiators falling to the ground by accident were treated as if they had submitted. Cf. Dio who disapproves of Claudius' intense interest in the spectacle of gladiatorial slaughter (60.13.1–5). Suetonius' account of the pleasure Vitellius took in witnessing executions (*Vit.* 14) is similarly critical. Note also the comment Tacitus makes concerning Drusus' excessive pleasure in the sight of blood spilt in the arena – *quamquam vili sanguine nimis gaudens*, 'as though taking excessive pleasure in cheap bloodshed' (*Ann.* 1.76).

100. See Mitchell (1991: Ch. 5) on sexualised responses of the part of spectators to bull-fights in contemporary Spain (in this context he makes deft use of material relating to the Roman arena as an analogy). For a psychological approach to the relationship between sexual pleasure and death, see Bataille (1962) who argues that we experience the pull of annihilation most intensely through sexual desire.

101. The link between violence and eroticism in Roman culture is briefly explored by Ville (1981: 343) and Hopkins (1983: 21–3). The erotic pleasure some Romans seem to feel at spectacles of cruelty is also discussed by Barton (1993: 47–50) and Gunderson (1996: 144–5).

102. See Hopkins (1983: 21–3). We might note, however, that the *retiarius* can be characterised as effeminate. Seneca in *Naturales quaestiones* 7.31 in an attack on his contemporaries' abandonment of masculinity comments on the man who 'runs off to the indecent section of the gladiators' school, and, hired for death, selects a disgraceful form of armament in which to practise his sickness', *in obscaenam ludi partem fugit et, locatus ad mortem, infame armaturae genus in quo morbum suum exerceat legit*. Cf. Gunderson (1996: 145–6).

103. Cf. Fowler (1987: 186–7).

104. This play of looks is effectively conveyed in some visual images of the arena games. See S. Brown (1992).

105. This term is derived from Mulvey's highly influential analysis of spectatorial pleasure in relation to Hollywood film. Gladiatorial combat normally culminates in the death or release of the defeated gladiator – this might be seen as parallel to 'punishment' and 'forgiveness' in Mulvey's classic formulation (1989: 21–2). On 'sadistic voyeurism', see further Introduction above.

106. See, for example, Suet. *Titus* 8 on that emperor's keenness for gladiators in Thracian arms (also Suet. *Calig.* 55).

107. On the sociology of spectator-sports generally see Elias (1986). The role played by betting may be significant here. On the evidence for this in connection with gladiatorial games, see Toner (1995: Ch. 8).

108. Bergamín, cited by Mitchell (1991: 172).

109. Eldred (2002), discussed in Chapter 1 above.

110. We might note that critics of Mulvey's characterisation of cinematic pleasure take issue with her assumption that the viewer can sustain a stable identification with the male lead character. More recent work has focused rather on the viewer's passive pleasure, emphasising masochism in theories of looking. Cf. Kaplan (1983); Studlar (1988).

111. The figure of the lover as victim is often read as taking on a feminine role. Studlar (following Deleuze) problematises the Freudian assumption that masochism should be seen as the pathological exaggeration of natural feminine traits (1988: 10).

112. See Wiedemann (1992: 38–9).

113. 'The writers of the Neronian period were both victims and spectators', as Barton emphasises (1993: 25).

114. Though in the context of current affairs reporting it is becoming increasingly common to show images of , for example, war casualties – provided they are not British or American. On this phenomenon, see Sontag (2003).

115. See the now classic discussion of the phenomenon of public execution in Foucault (1977).
116. Boswell (1928: 280–1) cited by Plass (1995: 21n).
117. Cf. Bronfen (1992: x).
118. Seale (1998: 3). Compare Elias Canetti's comment, quoted in the Introduction (p. 11).
119. Cf. Wiedemann (1992: 37); Gunderson (1996: 137–8).
120. Cf. Gunderson (1996: 137). On the paradoxical combination of slavery and freedom in the gladiator, see Barton (1993: 15), though the unilateral nature of the *auctoramentum* would seem to make it crucially different from the *devotio* to which she compares it.
121. Cf. Chapter 1 above.
122. This account is suggestively discussed by Richlin (1999). Other versions are also included in later chapters of Sen. *Suas.* 6 (cf. Roller 1997). Furse (forthcoming) promises to bring out some important characteristic of the tensions between them.
123. Barton (1993: 39).
124. Wistrand (1990) provides a complete list of instances.
125. *Vetus proverbium est gladiatorem in harena capere consilium: aliquid adversarii vultus, aliquid manus mota, aliquid ipsa inclinatio corporis intuentem monet* (*Ep.* 22.1).
126. For a similar treatment, see Letter 66 on the failing health of Claranus. On these letters see Edwards (1999) and Chapter 3 below.
127. As Gunderson notes: 'This volition, especially if a good gladiator did confess to it, must be seen as an ideological effect: both parties, audience and fighter, have an interest in this. The fights are thereby rendered cultural and ordered as opposed to the spectacles expressly enacting punishments' (1996: 137 n. 85).
128. Cf. Barton (1993: 18–19).
129. See Barton (1989: esp. 9–12); (1993: 34). This issue is in many ways the chief preoccupation of Barton's work on the arena (1993: esp. 1–46). For her it is the gladiator's combination of reckless courage and despair which is so compelling for dispossessed aristocrats.
130. Barton (1993: 39).
131. Gunderson invokes Florence Dupont's notion of the society of spectacle in this context (1996: 136). For him, the gladiator functions as 'an excluded and abject space which acts as the defining limit for the aristocratic norm. For Cicero and Seneca, the gladiator plays Remus to the normative aristocrat's Romulus: he is the brother who must be slain that an empire may be founded' (1996: 139).
132. See Wistrand (1990). Similarly, *Ep.* 95.33 discusses those fighting unarmed, *nudus inermisque*.
133. (1996: 135–6).
134. According to Dio, he insisted on blunt weapons to mitigate the cruelty of gladiatorial combats (Dio 71.29.3–4).
135. Cf. 4.4 (a true gladiator complains when there are fewer shows put on). Note too the discussion in Chapter 3 (p. 92) of Seneca's stress on the role of adversity more generally in stimulating *virtus*.
136. Cf., for example, *Ep.* 24.6–8, Tandoi (1965–6). We shall return later to this preoccupation in more detail.
137. Montaigne's reworking of this passage is discussed in the Introduction (pp. 3–5).
138. One might compare *Ep.* 37.2 and *Tranqu. an.* 11.5 where Fortune appears as a cosmic *editor*. Cf. Cic. *Nat. deor.* 3.15 on *devotio* as entertainment for the gods, a passage discussed by Barton (1993: 41–2). Seneca returns to the example of Cato at *Prov.* 3.14.

139. Compare the comment made by the Elder Pliny, who observes that a mortal is more fortunate than a god *namque nec sibi potest mortem consciscere, si velit, quod homini dedit optimum in tantis vitae poenis*: 'because the god cannot, if he wishes, take his own life, something he has granted as a supreme benefit to humankind amid the great trials of life' (*NH* 2.27).

140. Seneca is elsewhere careful to draw between *voluptas*, pleasure (as properly understood), which Stoics find reprehensible, and *gaudium*, joy, the elation of a spirit which trusts in the goodness and truth of its own possession and may only be attained by the wise (*Ep.* 59.1).

Notes to Chapter 3: Fighting the fear of death

1. Epicurus himself had established a philosophical community in Athens at the end of the fourth century BCE over which he presided until his death in 276.

2. As Warren stresses (2004: 6), other Epicurean texts also seem to have been concerned with this topic, e.g. Xenocrates' work *On Death* (Diog. Laert. 4.12) and Antisthenes' *On Dying, On Life and Death, On Things in Hades* (Diog. Laert. 6.15–18).

3. This is effectively analysed by Nussbaum (1994: 195–201).

4. Nussbaum (1994: 226, 231–2).

5. Cf. Diog. Laert. 10.125–6.

6. Helpfully set out in Warren's study of Epicurean approaches to the fear of death (2004: 4).

7. Cf., for example, 3.845–69. There is extensive philosophical debate about the validity of this complex of arguments (the key issues being whether all harms need to be perceived and how to identify the subject of the harm of death). On this in relation to ancient philosophy see esp. Furley (1986); Nussbaum (1994: 204–12); Warren (2004: esp. 215). For the modern philosophical debate which explicitly draws on Epicurean ideas see also Feldman (1992).

8. This is often termed the Symmetry argument. Discussed by Nussbaum (1994: 203, 206–7); Warren (2004: Ch. 3).

9. This argument on its own clearly does nothing to counter concerns about premature death (Nussbaum 1994: 211, 214). It also seems to rely on a notion of pleasure rather at odds with a strictly Epicurean hedonism (Warren 2004: 217). Nevertheless, as Nussbaum movingly argues, this argument suggests another, that it is precisely the temporally unfolding nature of human life, determined by its finitude, which ultimately confers meaning on human activity (1994: 225–38). Reinhardt offers an alternative interpretation of this argument (2002). For a different aspect of this argument, see Chapter 6 below.

10. On the persuasiveness of this argument, see Nussbaum (1994: 222–5).

11. Much of this picture is drawn from the description of the underworld in *Odyssey* 11. These myths are also attacked by Diogenes of Oenanda fr. 14 Chilton, col. 1. On the structure of this passage in relation to the rest of Book 3, see Reinhardt (2004).

12. Lucretius' account of Sisyphus closely follows that of Homer (*Odyssey* 11.593–600). As West points out, the final line of this passage can also suggest the candidate (*petitor*) rushing back to the Campus Martius in pursuit of re-election (1969: 102). Cf. Jocelyn (1986).

13. Cf. Nussbaum (1994: 218–19). Nussbaum goes on to highlight some problems with this argument, stressing political activities such as the attempt to make just laws which do not appear to be self-negating (1994: 220).

14. Though physical suffering more generally is a recurrent preoccupation; Book 3 dwells often on aspects of bodily decomposition, as part of the argument to prove

the mortality of the soul. Cf. Segal (1990: 13). For Segal, Lucretius' focus on bodily disintegration and the violation of corporeal boundaries more generally works as an indirect expression of anxieties over the process of dying (Segal 1990: Chs 6 and 7).

15. Though this model is not a particularly powerful one in Roman culture. See Chapter 1 above.

16. On the relationship between Thucydides' plague narrative and the funeral oration he attributes to Pericles, see Woodman (1988: 32–40, 35 cited here). For the debate concerning Thucydides' use of and response to medical writings here, see Hornblower (1991: 316–18).

17. For an illuminating account of Lucretius' reworking of Thucydides, see Commager (1957). Commager perhaps underestimates the symbolic significance of the plague narrative within Thucydides' history, however. People became indifferent to written law and to fear of the gods (2.53.1, 4). They disregarded honour (2.53.3). Funerary ritual is abandoned (2.52.4). Death is stripped of its social significance. It ceases to be an event around which social meaning crystallises, reduced instead to a bald medical fact.

18. Cf. 3.48–58.

19. At Thucydides *Histories* 2.49.7–8 it is the disease itself which is responsible for the loss of people's extremities.

20. The plague narrative also serves to underline Lucretius' stature as an epic poet. For important echoes of the plague which opens the *Iliad* and the funeral which concludes it, see Gale (1994: 112–13) and P. Fowler (1997). Segal compares the role of the plague in Lucretius' poem with that of Plato's myths, fulfilling several symbolic functions and having a number of layers of meaning (1990: 191–2).

21. It is fear of death, he claims, which makes people abase themselves to religion, whose evils are exemplified by Agamemnon's sacrifice of his daughter Iphigeneia, vividly described in Book 1, 1.80–101. As Nussbaum emphasises, for Lucretius, rather than the fear of death being a creation of religion, it is religion which is a symptom of the fear of death (1994: 200).

22. Though it seems likely that some lines have been transposed and that lines 1247–51 should be the concluding lines, as they are a close translation of the concluding section of Thucydides' account. On this see P. Fowler (1997). Many readers have found the poem's bleak ending deeply pessimistic.

23. Cf. Segal (1990: 35).

24. For example, Diog. Laert. 10.22; Cic. *Fin.* 2.96; Sen. *Ep.* 22.5–6.

25. Cf. Segal (1990: 34).

26. On the central role of *Tusc.* see Schofield (2002: 102).

27. As Douglas emphasises in the introduction to his commentary, Cicero chooses not to engage with a significant number of issues and arguments which had preoccupied Plato in his treatment of these topics, such as what happens to the souls of the wicked and whether the souls of the virtuous undergo purification (1985: 17).

28. Cf. *Tusc.* 1.48. For a similar depreciation of the power of tales of the afterlife, cf. *Nat. deor.* 2.5 where Lucilius Balbus is made to set out a Stoic position (to be criticised by Cotta in Book 3).

29. Warren (2004: 44).

30. *Tusc.* 1.97–9 = *Apol.* 40.c–42a; *Tusc.* 1.53–4 = *Phaedr.* 245c–246a. On the role of these passages, see Hill (2004: 54–7). See too the comments in Juv. 2.149–52; Pliny *NH* 2.158, as well as Sen. *Ep.* 24.18, which is discussed below.

31. Lucretius presents dying as a fleeting process (3.208–30). Warren (2004: 13–15) notes that Epicureans in general 'have surprisingly little to say about the ethical significance of the process of dying'.

32. Though Cicero does praise the death of Cato, as we saw in the Introduction above, he is not especially concerned with its details.

33. Death is also an important concern in the tragedies, which there is not space to consider here. On suicide in the *Phaedra* see now Hill (2004: esp. 159–75).

34. His phrase is echoed at 24.4, where the thought is attributed to Seneca's correspondent Lucilius. Cf. 120.18, which offers a more extended development of this theme. The relationship between death and time in Seneca's letters will be explored further in James Ker's forthcoming book.

35. There is perhaps an echo of Plato *Phaedo* (64a).

36. Though Seneca does several times refer to the Epicurean maxim that intense pain lasts only a short time, while lasting pain is bearable (e.g. 24.14; 30.14; 78.7; 94.7).

37. On the fear of death as the greatest fear, see also, for example, *Helv.* 13.3; *Naturales quaestiones* 2.2.

38. A commonplace, too, in the Epicurean tradition, cf. Epicurus *Sent. Vat.* 31 and Philodemus *De morte* 37.27–9.

39. As Mayer notes (1991: 159), Letters 24 – and also 71 – make more extensive use of *exempla* than most others. It is in his other prose works that Seneca tends to use *exempla* more frequently. Rutilius, Mucius, Socrates and Cato occur together at *Prov.* 4.3; Rutilius, Socrates and Cato at *Marc.* 22.3; *Tranqu. an.* 16.1.

40. Seneca also invokes the death of Socrates at *Ep.* 13.14; 67.7; 70.9; 71.17; 98.12; 104.27–8.

41. 2.12–13. Ogilvie (1970) argues that Livy's version of the story is probably an early third-century fabrication. It is likely that a version of the story also featured in Ennius *Annales*. On the Livy passage see Fitzgerald (2007). For a suggestive discussion of Seneca's deployment of other passages from Livy, see Henderson (2004: esp. 93–9).

42. Notably at 66.51; 76.20; 98.12. See, too, *Ben.* 4.27.2; 7.15.2. On later treatments of Mucius, see Fitzgerald (2007) who discusses particularly Martial 1.21; 8.30; 10.25.

43. For Seneca's use of Cato, see also Chapter 2 above. Cato appears with great frequency in the letters, e.g. 67.7, 67.12; 71.15–19. Mayer highlights the skill with which Seneca structures these examples (1991: 153–5).

44. Cf. Quintilian *Inst.* 12.4.1.

45. *Decantatae in omnibus scholis istae fabulae sunt*, 'those stories have been played through in all the schools', as he imagines a critic's comment (24.6).

46. On the relationship between memory and living presence, see also *Ep.* 102.30; 104.21.

47. Seneca regularly privileges action over words. Cf. *Ep.* 52.8.

48. In Letter 95 Seneca comments once again on the value of attending to *exempla*. We should *narrare et exponere*, 'relate and set forth' *Catonis illud ultimum ac fortissimum vulnus per quod libertas emisit animam*, 'that last and bravest wound of Cato, through which liberty sent forth his soul' (95.72).

49. Seneca's fascination with Mucius' hand in some ways anticipates that of Martial. There is however a significant contrast between the spectacle as played out in the would-be philosopher's mind and the scene Martial evokes in which the role of Mucius is replayed in the amphitheatre by a condemned criminal. In this treatment, as Fitzgerald (2007) comments, the story is diminished 'from exemplary drama to fascinating spectacle (and spectacle of fascination)'.

50. Cf. Val. Max. 3.3.1 where Mucius also figures as an *exemplum* of *patientia*.

51. We might compare the terms in which Seneca invokes the death of Cato in *De providentia*, discussed in Chapter 2 (pp. 75–7), and the death scenes to be described in Chapter 4.

52. Relevant here is the comment made by Armisen-Marchetti (1986: 185) on the related practice of *praemeditatio* (the contemplation of possible misfortunes) which, she suggests, 'offre l'occasion d'user l'imagination au service de la raison'.
53. Cf. Inwood (2005: 295).
54. Seneca comments that his admirable friend Claranus facing death is *in exemplar editus* (*Ep.* 66.4).
55. Discussed by Flower (1996: 171–5); Roller (2001: 22–3).
56. See Harris (1985: 10–41) on the link between aristocratic values and the military ethos of the mid–late republic.
57. Cf. McDonnell (2003: 236). His emphasis on the 'courageous' aspect of *virtus* leads him to offer compelling criticisms of the account of *virtus* put forward by Eisenhut (1973). On Livy's use of *virtus*, see Moore (1989).
58. On this see McDonnell (2003). See also McDonnell (2006), which I did not have the opportunity to consult.
59. I am grateful to David Wray for allowing me to consult his unpublished discussion of this passage. The implications of Cicero's definition in terms of conceptions of gender will be discussed in Chapter 7 below. The Greek term 'arête' is also linked etymologically with 'aner' (man) but the abstract noun 'andreia' (also linked with 'aner') is the term usually used for bravery. On this see Rosen and Sluiter (2003: Introduction).
60. On the problems inherent in Cicero's conception of *virtus* see Long (1995).
61. See Schofield (forthcoming) on Brutus, and Zetzel (forthcoming).
62. Cf. 66.48 on the last day of Epicurus' life, characterised but not compromised by extreme pain – *beatae vitae clausulam*.
63. Letter 67 also provides some striking examples of this. Here, Cato (again) and Regulus, as Roller has recently emphasised, 'directly contradict the traditional understanding of *virtus* as brilliant valour displayed in battle' (2001: 104). Cato is described as worshipping virtue with offerings of sweat and blood (67.12).
64. Strikingly, Seneca uses death as an analogy for virtue at 66.43 – virtue has no degree just as death has no degree.
65. Cf., for example, the formulation put in the mouth of Cato by Cicero (*Fin.* 3.21–2).
66. This claim serves to undercut the assertion made in the following letter that Seneca does not desire hardships (67.4). For a positive valuation of hardship see also 68; 71.5, 18–19, 28.
67. Cf. Lavery (1980: 149). Note also the analogy Seneca draws with the training of athletes (78.16).
68. On the relationship between Seneca's writing and his career, see Griffin (1976).
69. For the classic formulation of this shift see Hopkins and Burton in Hopkins (1983: esp. 171–5).
70. Cf. Roller (2001: 101–2).
71. Roller (2001: 104).
72. Cicero also adduces Mucius as an instance of Roman patriotism, *Sest.* 48.
73. Wright (1974: 60) on *Const. sap.*; Lavery (1980); Wilson (1997: 62–5); Veyne (2003: 135); Inwood (2005: 50–1).
74. For Inwood, Seneca's vivid imagery, in externalising and reifying the passions, has a distorting effect (2005: 50 on *De ira* 1.8.2).
75. Cf. *Ep.* 98.12.
76. Compare Seneca's comment about the Scipios at *Ep.* 24.10, discussed above. Inwood (2005: 184) sees Seneca's discussion of the fear of death at *Naturales quaestiones* 6.32 as a response to Lucretius.
77. Cf. Hill who sees important parallels between Lucretius and Seneca in this respect (2004: 148).

78. Wilson offers a nice analysis of this letter, stressing its interconnectedness with the rest of the collection (1987: esp. 110–19).
79. For example, 48.6; 49.8.
80. Though he returns, at paragraph 19, to the uselessness of such reasoning.
81. On the fate of the soul after death see also, for example, *Ep.* 71.14 and 16; 102 (to be discussed below).
82. Contrast Lucretius 3.978–1023. Seneca suggests it is unnecessary to bother, as the Epicureans do, with such poetical fancies which no-one really believes (24.18).
83. This could be read as an implicit criticism of the Epicurean position, discussed above, which seems to assume that the only significant requirement for overcoming the fear of death is to offer a convincing argument against the possibility of post-mortem survival. (cf. Epicurus *L. Men.* 124).
84. Cf. the comments made by Reinhardt (2004) with regard to Lucretius' deployment of the figure of *katabasis* in Book 3 of *De rerum natura*.
85. Though it may be helpful here to distinguish what Seneca terms the involuntary manifestations of fear which even the bravest soldier may experience (*De ira* 2.3.2). Cf. Inwood (2005: 60).
86. Cf. *Ep.* 53.11, quoted in Chapter 2 above (p. 77).
87. Cf. Wilson (1997: 61).
88. On the Stoic idea of virtue more generally, Nussbaum comments, 'virtue ... is not an inert inner condition: it is imagined as a striving or straining' (1994: 363).
89. Similar examples, including that of the Spartans at Thermopylae, are offered to counter the fear of death by Cicero, *Tusc.* 1.100–2. On the problematic identity of the anonymous Roman general Seneca also refers to here, see Mayer (1991: 151–2).
90. This picks up on the military imagery introduced earlier in the letter where philosophy is described as *inexpugnabilis murus, quem fortuna multis machinis lacessitum non transit*, 'an impregnable wall which, though often hit by siege engines, gives no opening to fortune' (82.5). This could be read as an implicit response to Epicurus' claim 'when it comes to death we humans all live in an unwalled city' (*Sent. Vat.* 31).
91. With Mucius Scaevola as his rugged forerunner. Indeed Livy's Mucius is described by the Etruscan Porsenna as making war on himself: *in te magis quam in me hostilia agis* (2.12.14).
92. Cf. Griffin (1976: 384).
93. Cf. Warren (2001: 92).
94. Though note *Ep.* 12.10–11. On Epicurean attitudes to suicide, see also Hill (2004: Ch. 3) who stresses that some texts offer a rather different picture, most notably Cic. *Fin.* 1.49, where the Epicurean Torquatus asserts that the individual may leave life whenever he or she chooses, as though leaving the theatre.
95. Nock (1933: 197).
96. According to Griffin (1976: Ch. 11). However, for John Rist, Seneca's interest in suicide far exceeds that of other Stoics. 'Seneca's wise man is in love with death', comments Rist (1969: 249). For a comprehensive account of Seneca's comments on suicide see Tadic-Gilloteaux (1963). Hill (2004: Ch. 7) also discusses these texts in detail, arguing that Seneca 'produces very little that is philosophically innovative' with regard to suicide (2004: 147).
97. Cf. 3.24.101–2. Long comments: 'Epictetus shows none of Seneca's fascination with suicide, nor does he treat it, like Seneca, as the supreme test of Stoic freedom' (2002: 203–4). Cf. Droge and Tabor (1992: 34–7).
98. Though Rist (1969: 239–41) argues that according to the position set out by Cicero's Cato, only the *sapiens* is ever in a position to know when it is right to kill himself. On the vagueness of this Ciceronian account, see Hill (2004: 36–41).

99. As Griffin suggests (1976: 373), it makes most sense to interpret Seneca's Zeno not as making an arbitrary decision but as perceiving the increasing weakness of his body (cf. *Ep.* 58.34).

100. Cf. Cic. *Fin.* 3.60–1. On the notion of the balance sheet, see van Hooff (1990: 122); Griffin (1986: 200).

101. For example, *Ep.* 14.2; 24.24; 98.16. Griffin (1976: 376–80) discusses some specific examples of such calculations in the letters. On the discourse of *rationes* in relation to planning one's death see also Pliny *Ep.* 1.12.3–5 on the death of Corellius Rufus. On this see Hoffer (1999: 148), who stresses Pliny's use of financial imagery.

102. Compare the example Seneca offers in Letter 98 of an elderly friend who, despite suffering pain, continues to live while he may be of service to his companions (98.15–18).

103. Cf. Inwood (2005: 106, 113) on the discussion of situational factors in *Ep.* 71.

104. Cf. Hill (2004: 151–7).

105. Wirszubski (1950); Brunt (1988); see Arena (2008).

106. Cf. too *Ep.* 95.72 quoted above.

107. As Griffin suggests (1976: 375).

108. Seneca here claims to be quoting Epicurus. Further examples in the letters include: 66.13, 16; 70.14, 24–5. *De providentia* also returns to this theme: *adtendite modo et videbitis quam brevis ad libertatem et quam expedita ducat via*, 'only observe and you will see what a short and easy path leads to liberty' (*Prov.* 6.7). See too *Marc.* 20.2–3.

109. Bobzien (1998: 339). As Inwood comments, this constitutes an 'internalisation of social and political reality'. On this issue, see particularly Inwood (2005: Ch. 11 'Seneca on freedom and autonomy').

110. Inwood (2005: 306). Contrast the view of Hill, who argues that in Roman discussions of suicide the central issue is not agency but rather honour (2004: 11). His approach rightly emphasises the Roman tendency to categorise together voluntary and enforced suicides. Yet even in the case of the latter there might be considered some scope for agency which though limited is nevertheless highly valued. This issue will be considered further below in Chapter 4.

111. Lavery comments: 'the suicide would appear to be a deserter in battle and a soldier who surrenders to fortune' (1980: 150). Another aspect of this problem is discussed by Griffin: 'If the virtue of the wise man's actions lies in its intentions, not its result, what danger of disgraceful action can he be said to avoid through suicide?' (1976: 380–1).

112. The term 'phrouria' can also have the sense of 'prison' as well as 'guard-post'.

113. As Nussbaum emphasises: 'The twistings and turnings of the text contain a far more complex message' (1994: 437, cf. 435).

114. Nussbaum stresses the vehemence of Seneca's language here and comments: 'Seneca never seriously doubts that a parent will *feel* anger inside himself at these incidents, nor does he even try to suggest that it would be a good thing if he didn't' (1994: 434).

115. Cf. Nussbaum (1994: 436–7).

116. Cf. Nussbaum (1994: 436) and Barton (1994: 59).

117. This is discussed further in Chapter 4.

118. Though the death of Cremutius Cordus, Marcia's father, is discussed briefly in *Marc.* 1.2, while that of Julius Canus receives extended treatment in *Tranqu. an.* 14.4–10.

119. Cf. Nussbaum (1994: 468).

120. For Stoic criticism of the desire for death, see also Epictetus *Disc.* 1.9.12 and 2.15.4–12.

121. Disapproval of those who kill themselves for frivolous reasons, out of boredom or

under the influence of extreme emotion: *Helv.* 10.9–10; *Tranqu. an.* 2.14–15; *De ira* 2.36.5–6; *Ep.* 4.4. Hill (2004: 175–8) offers a suggestive discussion of Seneca's *fastidiosi*, stressing the influence of as well as the contrast with Lucretius. This picture is linked with the idea of the debauched life as a living death which Seneca explores elsewhere (to be discussed in Chapter 6 below).

122. The afterlife is considered at several points, particularly 63c.

123. Cf. Warren (2001: 92).

124. The response Socrates is made to give to Cebes – worried that the philosopher promotes the benefits of death, yet disapproves of self-killing – is, as Warren comments, 'famously difficult to interpret' (2001: 95).

125. Augustine specifies *Phaedo* in his version (*Civ. dei* 1.22). In Plato's *Laws*, composed some years later, a somewhat different position is articulated: suicide is prohibited but it is made clear that this does not cover the case of those, such as Socrates, condemned to drink poison, and exceptions are also made for those whose suicide is provoked by shame or unavoidable misfortune (*Laws* 873c–d). Cooper (1999) argues that Socrates in the *Phaedo* does not endorse very firmly the prohibition of suicide, though he also notes the more general tendency of Plato's work to defend existing practice (or at least an idealised version of it) in Greek city states. In Athens, suicides were punished by being buried with their right hands amputated (Aeschines 3.244). For Cooper there is a very strong contrast between the Platonic and Stoic positions.

126. As Warren suggests (2001: 104). While this reading is a persuasive one, he does concede that the argument would have been clearer if it had been made explicit that suicide is in fact prohibited only for those for whom it is not beneficial (2001: 105).

127. A similarly negative view of suicide is to be found in the closing section of Cic. *Rep.* 6.15. At *Tusc.* 1.74, Cicero explicitly discusses the role of divine signs in legitimating suicide. These passages are discussed by Hill who suggests they are not to be taken literally in view of their role in relation to mythical accounts of the afterlife (2004: 48–54).

128. Cf. Sen. *Ep.* 66 and the comments of Inwood (2005: 268–9).

129. Perhaps choosing to take Caesar's offer of clemency as a divine sign.

130. This is perhaps qualified by a variant formulation in *Ep.* 74.21: *species quodam atque umbra virtutis in mortem voluntariam trudit*, though Seneca's argument here is rather how much the more will people despise death when armed with real virtue.

131. On the *Phaedo*'s preoccupation with the corporeality of Socrates see Loraux (1995: Ch. 8 'Therefore Socrates is immortal').

132. One of many strategies to reinforce the carefully constructed impression that this is a series of actual letters. On the importance of the letters' status as letters, see Edwards (1997a) and Wilson (2001).

133. Parallel to the reservations expressed in Letter 78 is the articulation of concern for Seneca's wife in letter 104.3–4. Compare the concerns which the preface to Book 4 of *Naturales quaestiones*, also addressed to Lucilius, puts in Lucilius' mouth (*NQ* 4. pr. 17).

134. Cf. too *Ep.* 54 in which Seneca explores the value of using what appear to be the symptoms of asthma as an opportunity to rehearse preparation for death. See Edwards (1999: esp. 261–2).

135. This issue is explored further in Edwards (1999). Cf. Bartsch (2001).

136. Cf. Armisen-Marchetti (1986).

137. See for instance the rules of the burial club in Lanuvium (136 CE) which stipulate that if a member committed suicide he or she would forfeit the right to a funeral: *quisquis ex quacumque causa mortem sibi adsciveri[t] eius ratio funeris non*

habebitur (*CIL* 14.2112 = *ILS* 7846). This is discussed by J.-L.Voisin (1987); see too Veyne (1981). For a different perspective on the disapproval of suicide, see Grisé (1982). On the phenomenon of burial clubs, see Hopkins (1983: 211–17).

138. Cf. the death of Atticus, as described by Cornelius Nepos (*Atticus* 21–2), though it is also presented as the method chosen by some defendants killing themselves before or as a consequence of condemnation, e.g. Cremutius Cordus (Tac. *Ann.* 4.35.5). This method is also recommended to Valerius Asiaticus, condemned by Claudius (*Ann.* 11.3).

139. See Veyne (1981: 243).

140. On the suicide of Amata, see M.Voisin (1979). On the feminine associations of death by hanging in the Greek world, see King (1983); Loraux (1995: 101–15).

141. Cf. Hill (2004: 190).

142. *Extra au[c]torateis et quei sibi [la]queo manu attulissent et quei quaestum spurcum professi essent* (*CIL* 11.6528). Discussed by J.-L.Voisin (1987); Kyle (1998: 161). On the treatment of the bodies of suicides more generally, see Grisé (1982: Ch.4).

143. Grisé (1982: 94–123); van Hooff (1990: Ch.2, esp. 69–70 on hanging and social status).

144. On the implications of this in relation to questions of agency, see Flemming (2005).

145. On the politics of this poem, see Chapter 4 below.

146. Most obviously *Prov.* 6.9; *De ira* 3.15.4.

147. As Bartsch notes (2005: 80–1) 'a shameful form of bodily humiliation here becomes a badge of pride', an index of the degree to which the Stoic devalorisation of the body evident in Seneca's writing might be in conflict with traditional Roman elite attitudes to bodily integrity.

148. Cf. Seneca's comment in another letter: *dubitas ergo, an optimum sit memorabilem mori et in aliquo opere virtutis?* 'Do you doubt then that the very best thing is to die a memorable death, performing an act of virtue?' (*Ep.* 67.9).

149. The political context for this will be discussed in detail in Chapter 4.

150. Paulina, however, survives. Tacitus' treatment of her suicide attempt is discussed in Chapter 7 below.

151. On Tacitus' description, see particularly Griffin (1976: 369–88); Hutchinson (1993: 263–8); Veyne (2003: 170–2); Hill (2004: 178–82). On the death scene in relation to Seneca's own discussion of how the philosopher should take care of his body in life, see Edwards (2005a).

152. Though as Gill argues, given the usual effects of hemlock poisoning, the ease of Socrates' death in the *Phaedo* is likely to be very much a Platonic construct (1973).

153. See, for example, Nussbaum (1994: 437).

154. As Beat Schönegg comments (1999: 243): 'Mit seinem Selbstmord hat Seneca sein ganzes Werk neu geschrieben, er hat ihm, sterbend, in dem kurzen Augenblick eines Leidschlags diejenige Rechtschaffenheit geschenkt, die es brauchte, um als unvergänglicher Besitz in die Nachwelt einzugehen.'

155. This is a phenomenon not without parallels in the modern world; take, for example, the impact of Sylvia Plath's suicide on subsequent responses to her work discussed by Alvarez (2002: 5–34), with the comments of Osborne (2005: 287–8). As Osborne goes on to observe: 'an author's suicide inevitably affects the functioning of the name' (2005: 289). This is of course especially the case for an author whose work shows such a marked preoccupation with suicide. Further implications of this will be discussed in Chapter 5.

156. Dio's account is rather less favourable, suggesting that Seneca forced Paulina to commit suicide as a demonstration of the efficacy of his own teachings against the fear of death, and that Seneca himself was finished off by Nero's soldiers (62.25).

Notes to Chapter 4: Defiance, complicity and the politics of self-destruction

1. This passage is suggestively discussed by Roller (2001: 120–4).
2. Cf. Bartsch (1994: Ch. 3).
3. Similar comments are recorded by Plutarch in *Sayings of the Romans* Caesar 13; Dio 43.12.1. Cf. Val. Max. *Catonis quoque morte Caesar audita et se illius gloriae invidere et illum suae invidisse dixit... et hercule divinorum Caesaris opera non parva pars Catonis salus fuisset:* 'Also when he heard of the death of Cato, Caesar said that he grudged him his glory, just as Cato had grudged Caesar his ... And indeed, saving Cato would have been no minor part of Caesar's achievements' (5.1.10).
4. These dynamics also emerge clearly from Cassius Dio's account (43.10–13). Cf. Plass (1995: 108–9).
5. Cf. Roller (2001: 183). On *clementia* see also Hill (2004: 226).
6. On Seneca's *De clementia* see S. M. Braund, forthcoming edition.
7. Cf. Tacitus' criticism of the German prince Marobduus who chooses to live on in Italy after his defeat rather than killing himself (*Ann.* 2.63).
8. Augustine concludes that Cato *ne ab illo etiam sibi parceretur... erubuit*, 'Cato would have been embarrassed at receiving Caear's pardon' (*Civ. dei.* 1.23). On the dilemma posed by clemency – lack of it is despotic, while its exercise is also despotic – see Dyer (1990) on Cicero *Pro Marcello*. See also Roller (2001: 183–93) on *clementia* as gift-exchange.
9. Discussed by Roller (2001: 278–9). Cf. Val. Max. 6.2.5; Lucan *BC* 9.28–30; Sen. *Const. sap.* 2.2; *Ep.* 95.72. On philosophical *libertas* offered by death see Chapter 3 above.
10. Griffin (1986: 64). Other recent studies of this topic include: Grisé (1982); van Hooff (1990); Plass (1995); Hill (2004).
11. Hill (2004: 6–7). Indeed Hill finds himself offering a rather strained re-definition of suicide as 'any death possessing implications for the social standing of the deceased' (2004: 11). On terminology, see also Griffin (1986: 68–70).
12. On this see the Introduction above.
13. See for instance in relation to the reign of Claudius, Dio 60.11.8; 60.14–15.
14. Cf. Hill (2004: 188).
15. 'So thoroughly does the act of suicide come to permeate aristocratic culture during this time that ... it is committed virtually automatically under certain generally recognised conditions', comments Hill (2004: 183).
16. Though Seneca endorses Drusus Libo's decision to kill himself. Cf. *Ep.* 70.10, discussed in Chapter 3 above.
17. Cf. Plass (1995: Ch. 7). Very occasionally the offer of 'free choice of death' allowed the victim to evade execution: Marsus pretends to be starving himself to death, anticipating the imminent end of the emperor Tiberius (*Ann.* 6.48).
18. As Plass comments (1995: 93). On the procedure with regard to *maiestas* trials, see Garnsey (1970: 18–29, 43–9). Certainly by the time of Domitian, emperors claimed independent capital jurisdiction over senators, although a number of them undertook not to receive charges of treason (Garnsey 1970: 44–5). Cf. Dio 67.2.4.
19. For some significant divergences, see Hill (2004: 185).
20. See Hill (2004: 7–8, 197). Curiously this practice is referred to only once in the *Digest of Justinian*, a compilation of Roman legislation assembled in the sixth century CE; governors are here forbidden to authorise a choice of death, although this had been permitted in an earlier ruling: *Nec liberam mortis facultatem concedendi ius praesides habent ... Divi tamen fratres rescripserunt permittentes liberam mortis facultatem*: 'They do not have the right to allow a free choice of

death. However the deified brothers wrote in a rescript allowing the free choice of death' (48.19.8.1, A.Watson trs.).

21. As well as: Publius Vitellius *Ann.* 5.8.3; Sextius Vistilius *Ann.* 6.9; Taurus *Ann.* 12.59; Clodius Quirinalis *Ann.* 13.30.

22. Other early examples include Appius 449 BCE (Livy 3.58.6) (cf. Dion. Hal. *Ant. rom.* 11.46.3); Spurius Oppius 449 BCE (Livy 3.58.9); Brutulus Papius (truce-breaker) 322 BCE (Livy 8.39.14); M. Laetorius Mergus, third century BCE (Valerius Max. 6.1.11). See van Hooff (1990: 112–13).

23. On undermotivation, see Hill (2004: 188).

24. Similarly, Pompeius Macer and his son kill themselves when they learn that Tiberius is angered at the elder Macer's association with Pompey and at the divine honours he received from the Greeks (*Ann.* 6.18.2). See Plass (1995: 92; 100–1). On the uninterpretability of imperial signs more generally, see O'Gorman (2000).

25. A similar effect is generated by the apparent shift towards increasingly trivial grounds for treason accusations. One equestrian was allegedly condemned to death because of a dream he had had which was interpreted as portending the death of the emperor Claudius (*Ann.* 11.4).

26. Barthes (1982: 163).

27. Plass (1995: 92). Rogers (1952) examines this issue in detail, arguing that Tacitus habitually omits the principal charges brought against defendants, misleadingly placing emphasis instead on more trivial matters which formed a subsidiary part of the prosecutor's case.

28. Plass (1995: 102).

29. *Eius bona, qui sibi ob aliquod admissum flagitium mortem conscivit et manus intulit, fisco vindicantur*: 'The property of a person who has committed suicide and laid hands on himself because of some crime committed is forfeit to the imperial treasury' (A.Watson trs.).

30. Cf. Hill (2004: 190–1). Grisé terms this 'suicide salvateur' (1982: 249–58). She identifies 56 separate instances in the period from the beginning of the republic to the death of Nero.

31. Correspondingly, a pre-emptive suicide might be made to look like execution in order to avoid conceding property. Cf. Tac. *Ann.* 6.40.1. on the case of Vibulenus Agrippa.

32. Cf. 67.3.4; Tac. *Ann.* 6.25.1.

33. On exceptions Hill (2004: 191). Rogers, with a rather touching faith in the law-abiding nature of all emperors, contends that trial proceedings were not quashed by the defendant's suicide if the indictment was either a charge of *repetundae* or the more serious form of *maiestas* (1952: 281–2).

34. Perhaps also relevant here is Tacitus' report that a proposal was made that accusers should forfeit their rewards, if a defendant on a treason charge killed himself before the trial was finished (*Ann.* 4.30.3–5).

35. Cf. *Dig.* 29.5.1.23: *si quis non metu criminis imminentis, sed taedio vitae vel inpatientia doloris sibi manus intulit, eius testamentum aperiri et recitari mortis casus non impedit*: 'If a person has committed suicide not through fear of imminent exposure of a crime but because weary of life or unable to bear pain the way in which his death happened does not hinder the opening or reading of his will' (A.Watson trs.).

36. *Dig.* 48.21.3.pr. On the tendency to stigmatise suicide in later legal prescriptions, see Veyne (1981: esp. 228–34). He argues that one can see traces of a tradition more hostile to suicide associated with non-elite sections of Roman society seeping into these later comments.

37. Crook (1967: 276).

38. Hill (2004: 179–80). Cf. Griffin (1986: 74); Hutchinson (1993: 274).

39. *Ep.* 77.5–9. Cf. Griffin (1986: 67) on the death of Atticus.

40. And there are many brave deaths even among those who are killed simply because they are very rich or happen to have a particularly aristocratic ancestry, e.g. Valerius Asiaticus *Ann.* 11.3.

41. Though there was inevitably a political dimension to the charge of adultery with a member of the imperial family. Cf. Edwards (1993: Ch. 1).

42. *Arrian's Discourses of Epictetus* 1.2.19–21. This passage is discussed further in Chapter 5 below.

43. Cf. Sen. *Tranqu. an.* 14 and the discussion by Roller (2001: 119–24) and, more generally, Griffin (1986). Wilson (2003) argues that the role of Stoicism was effectively politicised by the trial of Thrasea. Thereafter it became closely associated with opposition to the emperor.

44. Cf. Griffin (1986: 69–70, 195). Marcus Aurelius, for instance, refers to Cato in the same terms as Thrasea Paetus (forced to commit suicide) and Helvidius Priscus (executed) (*To Himself* 1.14).

45. Plass (1995: 97); Hill (2004: 192).

46. Lucius Junius Silanus' choice of the day of Claudius' marriage to Agrippina to commit suicide was perhaps motivated by a desire to increase ill-feeling – *ad invidiam*, comments Tacitus (*Ann.* 12.8.1).

47. Plass (1995: 101).

48. Cf. Plass (1995: 131). He also comments on this same incident 'the execution (murder) implicit in suicide is made explicit' (1995: 103).

49. Compare Tiberius' reported complaint (*Ann.* 3.50.2) about those who forestall his clemency by killing themselves. On this see Plass (1995: 113); Hill (2004: 209). Other examples include Tiberius' comment on Libo (*Ann.* 2.31.4). On one occasion Nero is said to have supported a capital charge in order that he might win favour later by intervening to mitigate the penalty (*Ann.* 14.48–9).

50. As he comments: 'Every group has rules for governing behaviour; game theory tries to identify and assess the various strategies possible within their limits' (1995: 87).

51. Cf. Plass (1995: 84).

52. (1995: 91).

53. As Plass observes: 'the danger of aggressive rejection of collaboration was that inviting a demonstration of the emperor's power might very well also confirm it' (1995: 130).

54. Hill (2004: 9–10). On this passage see also Syme (1958: 24–6) and Freudenberg (2001: 224).

55. Hill suggests rather that on Tacitus' interpretation the political suicides of Domitian's reign 'were attempting to acquire a superior social standing simply by acting as though they already possessed it' (2004: 10). But it is difficult to think of any specific example which exactly fits this description.

56. Tacitus' disapproval of some of these deaths, Hill suggests, is to be seen as a comment on the lack of fit between a particular individual and the social status their act of self-destruction attempts to lay claim to. He comments 'at the same time that suicide was becoming a crucial means of senatorial self-reflection and definition, it was equally coming to prove less and less capable of furnishing this reflection and definition with any positive content' (2004: 211).

57. Note also *Ann.* 4.20.3 in praise of Marcus Lepidus, who mitigates the severity of the *maiestas* laws while retaining the favour of Tiberius.

58. Hill takes earlier scholars to task for wanting to find irony in Tacitus' use of the phrase with reference to the privilege granted to some condemned members of the senatorial class to choose their own mode of death (2004: 193–7, taking issue most notably with Plass 1995: 96).

59. On frequency: Grisé (1982: 53–7). It is impossible to separate incidence from Roman authors' concern to write about them, as van Hooff comments in relation to self-killings (1990: 10–11), though he devotes much space to consideration of what the actual figures may have been. Cf. Hill (2004: 185).
60. See Walker (1952: 20–2).
61. As Griffin notes, the 'massacre' does not seem to have been as indiscriminate as Tacitus here suggests. 'Every one courted Sejanus when he was in favour, but it was the little men – knights and *novi homines* – who perished when he fell' (1976: 49). Cf. Syme (1958: 384–5, 406).
62. See Jones (1992: 119–25).
63. Cf. *Hist.* 1.3; 4.50 on the informer Baebius Massa. Freudenberg (2001: 218) comments 'we can be sure that the noble deaths of Massa's victims in the blood-letting of autumn 93CE down to the last days of Domitian's reign were a prominent feature of his *Histories*' last book'.
64. This passage is suggestively discussed in Woodman (1988: 180–90).
65. Hutchinson (1993: 264).
66. In Woodman's helpful formulation (1988: 186).
67. 'Providing, through the further alternative of "metahistory", precisely the elements which he earlier professed to exclude', observes Woodman (1988: 190). Cf. Keitel's comment: 'Through graphic descriptions and similes, the historian implied that the princeps was waging a kind of war in peacetime against his own people' (1984: 306).
68. As Keitel notes (1984), the use of this imagery in describing the conflict between emperor and senate is far more evident in Tacitus than in the accounts of Suetonius and Dio.
69. Griffin (1986: 197–8) in explaining the fashion for suicide stresses 'the restriction of traditional opportunities for acquiring glory that was imposed by the autocratic system of government'. Cf. Hopkins and Burton in Hopkins (1983: 120–3); Barton (1993: 28); Hill (2004: 191–2).
70. Cf. *eodem agmine* (16.17.1).
71. Cf. the death of Ostorius Scapula, *Ann.* 16.15.2.
72. Cf. Keitel (1984: 306).
73. Though we might also note that Tacitus comments critically in relation to Thrasea's son-in-law Helvidius, *etiam sapientibus cupido gloriae novissima exuitur* 'even with philosophers the passion for fame is the last weakness to be discarded' (*Hist.* 4.6.1).
74. As discussed in Chapter 3 above.
75. Quoted by Diogenes Laertius (7.184–5).
76. Chitwood (2004). Valerius Maximus' section 9.12, *De mortibus non vulgaribus*, also reflects this tradition. The entertainment value of curious deaths sits somewhat uneasily with edifying displays of courage.
77. Geiger (1979: 61–6).
78. Cf., for example, the poem composed by the poet Persius (*Vita* 44–7).
79. On genre of deaths of famous men Marx (1937); Bardon (1956: 207–9); Griffin (1986: 197–8); Hill (2004: 187).
80. Cf. *Ep.* 9.13 making clear that Pliny has recently published a collection of speeches in defence of Helvidius Priscus (the Younger) executed by Domitian in 93 CE. The speeches were only published after Domitian's death. As Freudenberg comments (2001: 232): 'Pliny, when it really mattered, three years before when he could have "defended" the man, said nothing. But now that Domitian has died, when it really matters to him, he has plenty to say.' Pliny's attack on his fellow senator Certus did not lead to any formal motion against him. Still according to Pliny (*Ep.* 9.13.24–5), when Certus fell fatally ill shortly afterwards, he was

hounded by an *imago* of Pliny himself wielding a sword. Cf. Freudenberg (2001: 233–4).

81. On Pliny's preoccupation with such deaths, see Freudenberg (2001: 215–19, 225–9). Capito himself, like Pliny, had prospered under Domitian, as Syme emphasises (1958: 92); cf. Freudenberg (2001: 227–8). An earlier letter praised Capito for obtaining permission from the emperor to set up a statue in the Forum to Lucius Silanus, one of Nero's victims (*Ep.* 1.17). Matthew McNamara's forthcoming work promises to explore further Pliny's obituary letters, exposing the role that the dead could play in the ongoing negotiations for power and status between senatorial elites and princeps which characterised the early imperial period.

82. See Chapter 7 below for a discussion of Pliny *Ep.* 3.16 on the death of Arria, grand-mother of Fannia. Fannia's defiance of Domitian is recounted in *Ep.* 7.19, a letter which parades Pliny's friendship with her.

83. In Stanley Hoffer's words (1999: 141). This letter is also discussion by Hutchinson (1993: 270).

84. Though Corellius is a martyr in reverse. He chose to stay alive heroically for the republic, in order to use his authority to help establish the 'new republican' emperors Nerva and Trajan. Pliny stresses the severe pain (apparently due to gout) which he endured so long before finally taking his own life. Cf. Hoffer (1999: 147).

85. Cf. Freudenberg (2001: 217).

86. Hoffer provides a thorough and subtle account (1999). Cf. Hutchinson (1993: 268–71).

87. Cf. Syme (1958: 77, 83). As Syme notes, these successes are glossed over in the letters. 'Just where was Pliny when Domitian went down?' asks Freudenberg (2001: 229).

88. The repetition of *constans* here balances – and perhaps undercuts – its earlier use to describe Agricola's disposition in the face of death.

89. Note Freudenberg on the implausibility of this (2001: 222–4).

90. For example, by Griffin (1976: 368). This issue will be explored in more detail in Chapter 5.

91. Syme (1958: 557) sees this as an evocation of Cato, who was termed *homo Virtuti simillimus*, 'the man most like Virtue herself' (Vell. Pat. 2.35.2). Cf. Sen. *Tranqu. an.* 16.1: *Cato ille, virtutium viva imago*, 'that Cato, the living image of Virtue'.

92. According to Tacitus, Capito was responsible for reviving the treason law in 62 CE by bringing a charge against Antistius Sosianus for reciting some verses satirising the emperor at a dinner party. It was believed, alleges Tacitus, that the intention was for the emperor to win popularity by intervening to veto the senate's condem-nation. However Thrasea pre-empts this by proposing exile rather than death, a penalty endorsed by the senate and grudgingly accepted by the emperor (*Ann.* 14.48–9).

93. Cf. Plut. *Cat. min.* 25; 37. On the biography see further Chapter 5 below. On Thrasea's ideological position more generally, see Wirszubski (1950: 138–43). Rogers (1952) argues that Thrasea may well have been involved in an actual conspiracy against Nero.

94. Q. Aelius Tubero was an opponent of the Gracchi in the second century BCE. His strict Stoicism is emphasised by Cicero, *Brut.* 117. Cf. Sen. *Ep.* 95.72. Favonius was an opponent of Julius Caesar, killed after Philippi in 42 BCE; he is mentioned in Cicero's letters as an imitator of Cato's Stoic austerity (e.g. *Att.* 7.15.2).

95. Rogers argues that Tacitus suppresses the actual charges made against Thrasea and Barea (1952: 290, 296).

96. Though note Tacitus' comment on Thrasea's intervention in the trial of Antistius: *libertas Thraseae servitium aliorum rupit*, 'Thrasea's outspokenness punctured the

servility of others' (14.49.1). On Thrasea's conduct after the death of Agrippina, see also Dio 61.15.2 quoted above (p. 126).

97. For Beryl Walker, Thrasea is 'the subject of some of Tacitus' most taunting criticisms' (1952: 229–30).

98. Henderson (1998: 296–7); Syme (1958: 556).

99. Cf. Henderson (1998: 296–7).

100. Tacitus' account of the death of Thrasea probably derives from the biography written by Arulenus Rusticus, a work fatal to its author according to Tacitus (*Agr.* 2.1). Cf. Syme (1958: 298).

101. As Henderson comments (1998: 298): 'This is another repeat, degraded by late-comer repetition, but the best available.' For a list of the parallels between Plutarch's account of the death of Cato and Tacitus' account of the death of Thrasea, see Geiger (1979: 62–3). On this see further Chapter 5 below.

102. The implications of this poem as an index of the huge influence of Cato's suicide are underlined by Griffin (1986: 197). The poem does however sit curiously with Martial's criticism elsewhere of Fannius, who committed suicide to avoid dying at the hands of the enemy: *hic, rogo, non furor est, ne moriare mori*, 'Is this not madness, I ask, to kill yourself to avoid dying?' (2.80). See Chapter 1 above for a discussion of Martial 6.32, which compares the suicides of Cato and Otho to the detriment of the former.

103. See Townend (1973: 149); Bartsch (1994: 92); Freudenberg (2001: 213–14).

104. On different approaches on the part of modern scholars to this apparent contradiction, see Anderson (1982: 207–8).

105. Freudenberg (2001: 214–15, 239).

106. Cf. Freudenberg (2001: 220).

107. The former, son of the Helvidius Priscus executed under Vespasian, was executed for an apparent allusion to Domitian in a play he had written. As regards Senecio, Pliny (*Ep.* 7.19.6) notes that Senecio's books were burned by order of the senate. On these events, see also Suet. *Dom.* 10.3. There is some inconsistency. See Jones (1992: 123). On the corporate guilt of the senate see also Dio 59.16.2 (Caligula comments on the reign of Tiberius) and Tac. *Hist.* 4.8. Cf. Garnsey (1970: 47).

108. Syme (1958: 25).

109. His histories did survive, it seems, to reappear as permitted reading in the time of Caligula (Suet. *Calig.* 16), while Quintilian is later able to admire the *libertas* of his writing (10.1.104). See Griffin (1976: 33). For an earlier instance of book-burning cf. the destruction of the works of Labienus at the end of Augustus' reign (Dio 56.27.1).

110. Though as Moles (1998) notes, Tacitus elsewhere makes clear that while it was generally true that only *facta* rather than *dicta* were punished under Augustus, he was the first to apply the treason law to libellous writings when he prosecuted Cassius Severus for his attacks on members of the elite, *Ann.* 1.72.

111. Effectively emphasised by Moles (1998). For O'Gorman (2000: 102) Tacitus' claim that tyrannical suppression of literature only secures glory for the artist 'is ironically undercut by his claim in the digression that glory, perpetuated in historical memory, is subject to hostile reinterpretation by future readers'.

112. Syme (1958: 412–13). Cf. Augustus' account of his own achievements, *Res gestae* (esp. 34.3).

113. The defence of *libertas* in Cordus' speech echoes that of the speech to the plebeian assembly in 73 BCE of Licinius Macer in Sallust's *Histories* 3.84. Marincola suggests (1997: 251) that the echo is particularly significant as Licinius is the only other figure known to be a historian to make a speech in Roman history-writing. The identification is by no means secure, however, as Tim Cornell points out (personal correspondence).

114. As Moles notes (1998).
115. On the problems of construing Cremutius' speech, see Martin and Woodman (1989) *ad loc.*
116. Cf. Henderson (1998: 13).
117. Cf. Marincola (1997: 252); Freudenberg (2001: 236).
118. See Pliny *Paneg.* 3.4 with the discussions by Ahl (1984a) and (1984b); Sinclair (1991); Bartsch (1994: 65–71, 93–7). On this passage see Martin and Woodman (1989), Moles (1998).
119. Cf. Moles (1998).
120. At *Ann.* 3.30.2, for instance, Sallust is referred to as *rerum Romanarum florentissimus auctor*, 'the most outstanding author of Roman history'. On Sallustian echoes in the *Annals* see esp. Woodman (1988: 180); Syme (1958: 196–9, 353–6).
121. The problems with construing this passage – and its implications – are usefully discussed by Moles (1998).
122. Barthes (1982: 166).
123. On this see Chapter 3 above.
124. Cf. Dio 46.51.3.
125. A parallel story is to be found in relation to Otho (Suet. *Otho* 10; Dio 64.11). These are discussed by Plass (1995: 107–8). For van Hooff (1990: 18–19) these are instances of suicide as proof of loyalty.
126. Cf. *Agr.* 3.1. Ahl comments: 'We should beware of taking Tacitus at his word' (1984a: 207).

Notes to Chapter 5: Dying in character: Stoicism and the Roman death scene

1. Roman writers often express hostility to the stage. Cf. Dupont (1985); Edwards (1993: Ch. 3).
2. Though interestingly, in tragedy at any rate, deaths were rarely portrayed on stage. Cf. Shelton (2000).
3. (1982: 163). Cf. Griffin (1986: 65). Malissard (1990) and Woodman (1993) discuss other manifestations of the theatrical in Tacitus.
4. See Chapter 2 above.
5. We might note the uncertainty surrounding the circumstances under which Cassius died – the only witness, his freedman, has disappeared (Plut. *Brut.* 43).
6. *PCG* VIII.925 (p. 275). I am grateful to Eric Handley for drawing the significance of this quotation to my attention. On imperial deaths, see van Hooff (2003).
7. Though some took the view that Livia had hastened his end, anxious that a planned reconciliation with his grandson Agrippa Postumus might imperil her own son Tiberius' succession (Dio 66.30.1–2).
8. Compare the comment made by the philosopher Demonax, as reported in Lucian's biography, who at an advanced age chose to starve himself to death, quoting the words of the heralds at the games: 'Here ends a contest awarded the fairest of prizes; the time calls us and forbids delay' (*Demonax* 65–7).
9. There is a parallel here with the model of life as a feast which is adumbrated in Lucretius 3.938–9 and in a Stoic discussion of acceptable motives for suicide, *Stoicorum veterorum fragmenta* 3.768. This will be discussed further in the next chapter.
10. The notion of performance is also relevant for Stoic thought, Nussbaum suggests, in the sense that 'though *pietas* and reverence for duty may produce much loyal and quasi-committed action, the Stoic goes through the motions like one playing a role' (1994: 501).
11. Cf. Gill (1988).
12. Terms Cicero had also used of Cato in *Att.* 12.4, discussed above (p. 2). For a

careful discussion of Cicero's treatment of the ethics of suicide more generally, see Hill (2004: Ch. 2).

13. *Fam.* 9.18.2 [SB191]; 7.3.4 [SB183]; 4.13.2 [SB225]. Cf. Plut. *Cat. Min.* 59, 66; *Cicero* 38.1; also Brunt (1975: 15). The Elder Seneca cites several of the rhetoricians known for their performance speeches offering advice to Cicero as to whether or not he should concede to Mark Antony. Some comments compare Cicero unfavourably with others, such as Cato, who had taken their own lives (e.g. Cestius *ap. Suas.* 6.10). The Elder Seneca comments on Cicero's own death: *omnium adversorum nihil ut viro dignum erat tulit praeter mortem*, 'of all these disasters he faced none but his death as becomes a man' (6.22). The circumstances of Cicero's death are discussed briefly in Chapter 2 above (pp. 71–2).

14. Compare here Epictetus' comment (1.2.25–9) that as a philosopher, he would rather die than shave off his beard, though such a sacrifice might seem insignificant to someone else. This reasoning should not however be thought of as validating the actions of those who, in actualising their own evil characters, go against the require- ments of common human rationality (Panaetius' first *persona*). Cf. Gill (1994).

15. Brunt argues persuasively that Epictetus' notion of the prosopon largely overlapped with the *persona* of Panaetius (1975: Appendix 5).

16. Gill (1994: 4620).

17. Discussing another Senecan tragedy, the *Thyestes*, Braden remarks on 'Atreus' confrontation with a self-image to live up to'. He continues: 'Indeed part of what he sets before himself – like Nero [in *Octavia*] and Medea – is his own name' (1985: 42–6).

18. Rosenmeyer (1989: 52) – also with reference to Seneca's Hercules.

19. Wilamowitz (1919: vol. III, 162). Cf. Boyle (1997: 129).

20. On the extent to which Brutus may have been motivated by Stoic views, see Griffin (1989: 10–11); Sedley (1997). On individuals referring to themselves by name in the third person, see Segal (1982) and Hutchinson (1993: 275 n. 32).

21. Rosenmeyer (1989: 47–8). Cf. Boyle (1997: 116).

22. For a longer discussion of this particularly in relation to Seneca's advice on how to bear physical pain, see Edwards (1999). Cf. too Rosenmeyer (1989: 52); Boyle (1997: 115–16).

23. Cf. *Ep.* 11.8–10.

24. Goffman (1959: 243, 245).

25. See, for example, Sen. *Ep.* 16.2.

26. On this see further Chapter 3 above.

27. Rosenmeyer (1989: 48).

28. On Stoic self-fashioning, see Edwards (1997a).

29. Cf. Hill (2004); Leeman (1971).

30. On this issue, see further Chapter 3 above.

31. Cf. Connors (1994: 228).

32. Cf. *Oxford Latin Dictionary, s.v. agere* 21c.

33. Cf. Boyle on last lines of Seneca's tragedies (1997: 83–4).

34. Foucault (intimately familiar with Seneca's work) offers a suggestively similar comment: 'Il n'y pas une conduite qui ne soit plus belle, qui, par conséquent, mérite d'être réfléchie avec d'autant d'attention, que le suicide'; 'There is no behaviour which is more beautiful – and which in consequence merits contemplation with greater atttention – than suicide' (1994: 256).

35. Cf. Geiger (1979: 71). Some of Cicero's comments are quoted in the Introduction (p. 2). On Cato's reception see also Goar (1987).

36. Cf. Tandoi (1965: esp. 329–36). Seneca discusses Cato's death at length in *Prov.* 2.9–12 (on which see above, pp. 75–7), as well as *Ep.* 24.6–8 and 71.8–16 (on which see above, Chapter 3).

37. On Plutarch's treatment, see Trapp (1999).
38. On the association of Stoicism and suicide, see Chapter 3 above.
39. Griffin observes: 'Stoicism, not alone but via the powerful example of Cato, made suicide not tolerated or acceptable – for it was that already – but fashionable and esteemed' (1986: 197, cf. 200).
40. Connors comments generally on accounts of a Roman suicides: 'a text is produced or reenacted in the final moments of life' (1994: 228).
41. Geiger comments: 'Cato's own death was the first of Roman to be modelled consciously on Socrates'' (1979: 63). In relation to Plutarch's account of Cato's end, Trapp argues that, in important respects, a contrast is drawn between Socrates, condemned to death, and Cato who chooses to kill himself. The *Life of Phocion*, which Plutarch chose to be counterpart to that of Cato, offers an account of Phocion's death which is far closer to that of Socrates. For Trapp (1999) this is a riposte to earlier Roman heroisations of Cato. On Plutarch's treatment of deaths more generally, see Pelling (1997).
42. See in particular Plato *Phaedo* and Xenophon *The Last Days of Socrates*.
43. Cf. *Ep.* 71.11. Letter 24 is discussed in more detail in Chapter 3 above.
44. While the *Phaedo* is usually read as arguing against suicide, its focus on the unimportance of bodily existence for the philosopher has sometimes been seen as an encouragement to take one's own life (Warren 2001). Callimachus seems to associate reading the *Phaedo* with suicide (epigr. 23 Pf. = Page and Gow *Hell. Epigr.* Call. 53). See further above (pp. 104–5).
45. Shelton comments suggestively in relation to the arena spectacles in which condemned criminals were made to act out mythical stories (such as that of Orpheus) which culminated in their own actual deaths: 'In each of these charades, the victims were degraded by having their own identities obliterated and being forced to die as someone else' (1990: 98). On these 'fatal charades' see also Coleman (1990); Barton (1993); Fitzgerald (2007).
46. Macrob. *Sat.* 2.4.18.
47. In Virgil's *Aeneid* Cato is not segregated in the underworld with the sad souls who have taken their own lives but appears as a commanding figure, dispensing laws (*Aen.* 8.666–70).
48. Cf. Goar (1987: 30–1). On the afterlife of Cato more generally see Donaldson (1973), (1982); Edwards (2005b).
49. On the textual problems associated with these lines, see Tandoi (1965–6).
50. Sometimes by means of the kind of short-cut to *gloria* about which Seneca and Tacitus express reservations (see Chapters 3 and 4 above).
51. As Griffin emphasises (1986: 198).
52. On Tacitus' treatment, see also Chapter 3 above.
53. See Chapter 3 above.
54. For a more detailed discussion of Seneca's death in relation to his own discussions of how the would-be philosopher should look after his body in life, see Edwards (2005a). On Seneca's death scene see also Griffin (1976: 369–88); Hill (2004: 178–82).
55. Cf. Geiger (1979: 64).
56. Connors (1994: 228). Cf. Griffin (1976: 369–72).
57. Geiger (1979: 62–7).
58. Geiger (1979: 62–3), though cf. Trapp's view, in note 41 above.
59. As Geiger stresses (1979: 64). On Thrasea's sources see (1979: 65–7).
60. Geiger (1979: 64).
61. A more hostile tradition is preserved by Dio 62.25. Elements of criticism have also been detected in Tacitus' account. Cf., for example, Griffin (1976: 368).
62. Osborne (2005: 290).

63. Griffin comments: 'For Tacitus … Seneca's end was admirable but a shade histrionic; he clearly preferred the panache of Petronius' (1976: 368).
64. We shall return to this death from a different perspective in Chapter 6.
65. Cited by Griffin (1986: 197).
66. On Nero as actor-emperor, see Edwards (1994).
67. Though the mise-en-scène is very different from the calmly domestic settings of the noble suicides Tacitus describes. As Malissard notes, it is only in the case of Otho that Tacitus presents an imperial death thus (1990: 119). On emperors' deaths more generally, see van Hooff (2003) and on the deaths of bad emperors Arand (2002).
68. On Nero's last words see Connors (1994: 230).
69. Nero is alleged to have exclaimed on the completion of his monstrous new palace, the Golden House, *se … quasi hominem tandem habitare coepisse*, 'At last I have begun to live like a human being' (Suet. *Nero* 31.2).

Notes to Chapter 6: Tasting death

1. *Against Nature* (R. Baldick trs. (1959: 27).
2. See Lucan and Gray (1995: 69–70).
3. As a child he has a great facility for Latin but no aptitude for Greek (1959: 18). His favourite Roman authors are precisely those whom 'minds drilled in conformity by repetitious university lectures lump together under the generic name of "the Decadence"' (1959: 40). He hates Virgil, Ovid, Horace, Cicero, Caesar and virtually all the other authors recommended by his schoolmasters. He admires Lucan but his real passion is for Petronius, though he also enjoys Apuleius.
4. Cf. D'Arms (1984), (1990), (1999); Gowers (1993).
5. On this see Goddard (1994).
6. Cf. Roller (2001: 135).
7. For discussion of critiques of divisive dinner parties, see D'Arms (1984), (1990); Gowers (1993: 211–19); Roller (2001: 135–46).
8. Snakes and eggs are often referred to in such contexts. On the food offered to the dead, see Scheid (1984).
9. See Plass (1995: 92–3). The difficulty of reading potentially lethal signals from the emperor is discussed further in Chapter 4 above.
10. On this offer, which can be read both as a recognition of aristocratic privilege and as a parade of imperial whim, see Chapter 4 above.
11. This episode is suggestively discussed by Fredrick (2003) in relation to Domitian's building programme.
12. The resonance of this with the Dio passage is pointed out by Gowers (1993: 214–15).
13. For manipulative hosts see, for example, Juv. 5. Cf. Gowers (1993: 212–19); D'Arms (1999).
14. On this poem see Bek (1983: 90–1); Coleman (1988).
15. See Bek (1983: 90–1); Gibson, De Laine and Claridge (1994). Another banqueting hall built by Domitian seems to have been constructed with a view of the Mausoleum of Augustus. Cf. Martial 2.54 and Grottanelli's discussion (1995: 68). The preoccupation of accounts of lavish dinner parties more generally with their visual dimension is nicely highlighted by D'Arms (1999).
16. A number of individuals are alleged to have met their ends at the imperial table, most strikingly Tiberius' son Drusus (Tac. *Ann.* 4.7–8) and Claudius' son Britannicus (*Ann.* 13.16). While the latter was deliberately poisoned by Nero (according to Tacitus), Drusus' death allegedly resulted from a plot by Sejanus. It is notable that both are members of the imperial family.

17. Cf. Fredrick (2003: 213).
18. Fredrick (2003: 214).
19. On the Etruscan material see Toynbee (1971: 12); Murray (1988); Dunbabin (2003: Ch. 1). For the representation of banqueters more generally, see Dunbabin (2003: 104–40).
20. Cf. Dunbabin (2003: 109).
21. For Toynbee the many representations of funerary banquets carved on tombstones or painted on the walls of mausolea 'bear witness to the special importance of the ceremonial meal eaten at the tomb' (1971: 62, cf. 51, and 136 on the existence of kitchens adjacent to tombs for the preparation of commemorative meals). Cf. Scheid (1984); Dunbabin (2003: 125–32). One of the characters in Petronius' *Satyricon* describes a funeral meal he has just attended (42). On funeral food see Gowers (1993: 215). Cf. Augustine *Confessions* 6.2; Plut. *Crassus* 19; *Quaestiones Romanae* 95. Note too Tertullian, who criticises the inconsistency of pagans: *sed vulgus inridet, existimans nihil superesse post mortem, et tamen defunctis parentat et quidem inpensissimo officio pro moribus eorum, pro temporibus esculentorum, ut, quos negant sentire quidquam, etiam desiderare praesumant,* 'But the common people mock, thinking that nothing survives death, and yet they make offerings to the dead with most costly ceremony in accordance with their individual preferences of things to eat, so that they claim they can feel nothing yet assume them to have wants' (*Resurr.* 1.2).
22. Cf. Dunbabin (2003: 126).
23. Some Greek and Roman texts attribute a similar practice to Egyptians. Cf., for example, Silius Italicus *Punica* 12.474–6); Plutarch *On Isis* 17; *The Dinner of the Seven Sages* 2. Both Dunbabin (1986) and, more strongly, Grottanelli (1995) suggest the Roman practice was perhaps adopted from the east.
24. Dunbabin's article offers a full and nuanced account of these artefacts in relation to the themes of *memento mori* and *carpe diem* in Latin literature (1986). These topics are discussed further in Dunbabin (2003: 132–40).
25. On the use of theatrical similes in relation to the transience of human life, see Chapter 5 above. On the Boscoreale cups, see Dunbabin (1986: 224–30).
26. Horace *Odes* 1.4.11; 2.3.14; Martial 2.59; 5.64. Cf. too the pseudo-Virgilian *Copa*, discussed by Dunbabin (1986) and Grottanelli (1995).
27. See Dunbabin (1986: esp. 196).
28. For an analysis of this in Bakhtinian terms, see Gowers (1993: 30–1).
29. Arrowsmith comments: 'If Trimalchio turns a feast into a funeral, Habinnas turns a funeral into a feast' (1966: 312).
30. On the detail of this account, which like many other passages in the *Satyricon* plays on a confusion between representation and reality, see Slater (1990: 76–7; 217–18). There is some evidence to suggest that by the Neronian period elaborate funeral monuments were no longer in fashion among the Roman aristocracy (Mouritsen 2005).
31. So Grottanelli surmises on the basis of the relief showing a funeral cortège from Amiternum (1995: 75).
32. Thus the guests do find themselves with precisely the poor end to a dinner party – lamenting someone else's death – which they had feared earlier when it seemed as if the death of one of the entertainers might bring a halt to the party; *malum exitum cenae, ne necesse haberent alienum mortuum plorare,* Encolpius is made to comment (54).
33. Cf. Bartsch (2001: 1).
34. On the interpretative challenge posed by the dishes served at Trimalchio's dinner, see Slater (1990: 59–64).
35. As Dupont comments (1977: 96–9).

36. Dunbabin (2003: 112–13).
37. On Trimalchio as a figure for Nero, see Walsh (1970: 137–9). In my view, the parallel is not so much a matter of specific details in the text echoing known details of court life but rather an exploration of the relationship between an all-powerful host and his guests.
38. Cf. Henderson (1998: 261).
39. See the highly influential article of Arrowsmith (1966).
40. For criticism of Arrowsmith, see, for example, Sullivan (1968: 256); Slater (1987).
41. Arrowsmith (1966: 308).
42. On the Epicureanism of Petronius, see Raith (1963); Arrowsmith (1966).
43. Cf. Epicurus *L. Men.* 126. The idea of life as a banquet is also explored in some Stoic texts, see, for example, *Stoicorum veterorum fragmenta* 3.768; Sen. *Ep.* 77.8. Reinhardt (2002) argues that we need not see Lucretius' simile as necessarily implying life itself has a structure like a banquet. Rather the dying individual should emulate the contented manner characteristic of the departing dinner-guest.
44. Perhaps relevant here is the ironic comment Petronius puts in the mouth of the rhetorician Agamemnon, that Trimalchio looks set to put all the philosophers out of work (*Sat.* 56).
45. The comments put in the mouth of Encolpius underline repeatedly that this dinner fails to follow the usual conventions for the succession of courses. The guests have no idea what to expect next and no sense of where the meal might conclude.
46. We might also compare Persius *Satires* 3.88–106, in which a young man devoted to a life of excess ends up expiring at the dinner table. Cf. Grottanelli (1995).
47. Compare, too, *Puto, aeque qui in odoribus iacet, mortuus est quam qui rapitus unco. Otium sine litteris mors est et homini vivi sepultura.* 'I think the man who reclines in perfumed luxury is just as dead as the corpse being dragged away with a hook. Retirement without literary study is a living death, being buried alive' (*Ep.* 82.3). A related theme is explored in *Ep.* 55.4 where leisure is compared to death (on which see Henderson (2004: 75–7)). This analogy is also made elsewhere, e.g. Lucretius 3.1046 on life as living death.
48. For a perceptive discussion of time in Seneca's letters in the context of inversions of night and day in Roman literature more generally see Ker (2004). On Petronius, see Arrowsmith (1966: 307–8) as well as Rimell (2002: 184–8). This preoccupation is also to be found in the criticisms made of Nero's own dinner parties. Cf. Goddard (1994: 72–3).
49. On Seneca's ambivalent treatment of bodies more generally, see Edwards (1999) and (2005a).
50. Cf. Connors (1994: 230); Gowers (1993: 30–1). Arrowsmith, linking the cena and the episode at Croton, terms cannibalism the 'master metaphor of *Satyricon*' (1966: 316).
51. *'Omnes qui in testamento meo legata habent, praeter libertos meos hac condicione percipient, quae dedi, si corpus meum in partes conciderint et astante populo comederint',* 'All those who are given legacies in my will, with the exception of my freedmen, take possession of them only on the condition I have stipulated, namely that they divide up my corpse into pieces and consume them, in the presence of the populace'. On this passage see Conte (1987). Sullivan (1985: 1684) reads Sen. *Ep.* 122 as a critique of Petronius.
52. Virg. *Aen.* 4.653. The line is taken from the speech of Dido about to take her own life.
53. Cf. Scarpat *ad loc.* on *parentaverat*. Henderson has some suggestive comments on Pacuvius' funeral (2004: 6–7, 26). The letter is also helpfully discussed by Habinek (1982). Grottanelli takes Seneca to suggest that the ritual is a Syrian practice and explores an interesting parallel with Lucian *On Grief* 21 (1995: 66–7).

54. A particular preoccupation of Seneca's Letters, as we saw in Chapter 3 above.

55. Cf. the notion of the body itself as a tomb, discussed by Warren (2001: 97–8).

56. Cf. the words Seneca puts in the mouth of an imagined voluptuary: '*virtus et philosophia et iustitia verborum inanium crepitus est. una felicitas est bene vitae facere. Esse, bibere, frui patrimonio, hoc est vivere, hoc est se mortalem esse meminisse*', 'Virtue and philosophy and justice is a buzz of empty words. The only true happiness is to live a nice life. Eating, drinking, enjoying your estate – that is living, that is the reminder that you are mortal' (*Ep.* 123.10).

57. See, for example, Griffin (1986); Hill (2004: 247–51). On this episode see further Chapter 5 above.

58. Examples of this pattern of behaviour are also to be found in Roman texts. See, for example, Libo who, according to Tacitus, having been condemned by Tiberius, arranges a dinner as his last pleasure on earth (*Ann.* 2.31.1). Plutarch's account of the last days of Antony and Cleopatra is also relevant here (*Ant.* 71.3).

59. The Greek symposium or drinking party seems to have been regarded as the social counterpart to the Roman *convivium*. Petronius' harnessing of the *Symposium* is persuasively argued for by Dupont (1977); Conte (1996: 120–1). Cf. Cameron (1969). For Petronius' death as an Epicurean act, see Highet (1941: 187, 194).

60. Cf. Epicurus *L. Men.* 124: 'A correct understanding that death is nothing to us makes the mortality of life enjoyable, not by adding infinite time, but by ridding us of the desire for immortality' (trs. Long and Sedley). See Nussbaum (1994: 226). This issue is discussed briefly in Chapter 3 above.

Notes to Chapter 7: A feminine ending?

1. Cf. Goodwin and Bronfen (1993: 5).

2. Higonnet (1985: 71).

3. Goodwin and Bronfen (1993: 13).

4. As Bronfen comments (1992: xi): 'Because the feminine body is culturally constructed as the superlative site of alterity, culture uses art to dream the deaths of beautiful women'. Her book examines a series of case studies drawn from western literature and art of the eighteenth to the twentieth centuries.

5. On Livy's version see Ogilvie (1970) *ad loc.* Extended versions are also to be found in Dion. of Hal. *Ant. rom.* 4.64–82; Ovid *Fasti* 2.721–852; Plutarch *Mulierum virtutes* 14. As Beard comments, 'in Roman myth rape repeatedly marks moments of political change' (1999: 2). A perceptive reading of Livy's version is offered in Langlands (2006: esp. Ch. 2). On the origins of the Lucretia story, see Wiseman (1998).

6. The nature of the connection between Brutus (a cousin of both Tarquinius and Collatinus) and Lucretia has seemed tenuous to at least some readers, prompting versions of the story in more recent centuries in which the two are lovers. Cf. Donaldson (1982: 128–33).

7. Feldherr (1997: 148–52).

8. Cf. Joplin (1990: 64).

9. (1982: 9). Cf. Joplin (1990: 64).

10. Though it is striking that Tarquin does not choose to use his physical strength to force himself on her but rather obtains her compliance through the threat to her good name. 'His goal is to persuade Lucretia, not to brutalise her', as Langlands emphasises (2006: 89–90).

11. Cf. Donaldson (1982: 22); Langlands (2006: 94–5).

12. 'Her suicide leaves no anomaly for the patriarchal future', as Joshel comments (1992: 125) – an example nicely reinforced by the story of Appius and Virginia,

associated with the plebeian uprising that ended the domination of the decemvirate. Virginia was allegedly stabbed to death by her father Virginius, so that she could not fall victim to the lusts of the decemvir Appius Claudius (see e.g. Livy 3.44–8).

13. See Badian (1985).
14. Edwards (1993: Ch. 1). 'Lucretia becomes a mouthpiece for the ideology that demonises her', in Joplin's words (1990: 63).
15. Jerome *Against Jovinianus* Bk. 1; Tert. *Ad mart.*; *De monogamia*.
16. On this see further Chapter 8 below.
17. Cf. Donaldson (1982: 83). See also Jed (1989) on Coluccio Salutati's fourteenth-century reworking of this story.
18. Cf. Donaldson (1982: 42–4).
19. Cf. Donaldson (1982: 22). Joplin (1990: 67) comments on the parallel between wound and vagina.
20. This aspect of the story is especially highlighted in some of the later visual images discussed by Donaldson (1982: Ch. 1).
21. On display and spectacle in relation to Livy's treatment of Lucretia, see Feldherr (1998: 194–202).
22. Heuzé (1985: esp. 116–33).
23. In Roman epic female death is pervasively sexualised, as Keith has recently argued (2000: 104). Erotic terminology is also sometimes used to describe the deaths of beautiful young men, as Fowler emphasises in his study of defloration imagery (1987). Cf. Oliensis (1997).
24. This scene, as Oliensis writes, 'figures a grotesquely accelerated sexual maturation, from virgin to bride to nursing mother' (1997: 308–9). On Camilla's death see also Fowler (1987).
25. Heuzé (1985). Gillis comments 'In this scene of thanatos, there are many quiet yet obvious memories of eros' (1983: 44, cf. 37–48).
26. As Keith argues (2000: 115).
27. The exact nature of Dido's *culpa* has been the subject of extensive scholarly debate. Moles (1984) persuasively argues that the issue is not her betrayal of her husband Sychaeus but the intrinsically illicit nature of her love-making with Aeneas.
28. Wlosok sees this disproportion as essential to tragedy (1999: 60).
29. Cf. Keith (2000: 115–16).
30. The only detailed account of Cleopatra's death to survive is that of Plutarch, written more than a hundred years later (*Ant.* 84–6). Though a captive, she succeeds in having poison smuggled in to her and kills herself. On representations of Cleopatra's death, see Gurval (forthcoming).
31. Wyke (2002: Ch. 6) and others have persuasively argued that the motifs deployed by Virgil here, as well as by Horace (*Epode* 9; *Ode* 1.37) and Propertius (3.11; 4.6), should be traced back to Octavian's own propaganda, as he agitated for support in the run-up to Actium and its immediate aftermath.
32. Interestingly, Horace's treatment of the dying Cleopatra presents her as transcending her sex: *nec muliebriter/expavit ensem*, 'nor did she, like a woman, take fear at the sword' (1.37.22–3).
33. This is sometimes amended, following Markland, to *spectasti*, 'You witnessed'.
34. Wyke (2002: 207–8, 240–1); Fedeli (1985: 384–5). For the triumph, Plut. *Ant.* 86; Dio 51.21.7–8.
35. See Moore (1989: 123).
36. On Valerius Maximus' treatment of *pudicitia* and on the significance of the term more generally in Roman culture see Langlands (2006).
37. See too Wray (forthcoming).

38. Cf. Langlands (2006: 170–3).
39. On the use of *dux* with *femina* see Santoro L'hoir (1994).
40. As Wray (forthcoming) notes, Valerius appears to be offering a pointed revision of Livy who refers to Lucretia's *muliebrem animum* (1.58).
41. Cf. Roller (2001: 26); McDonnell (2006); Zetzel (forthcoming). On this, see further pp. 91–2 above.
42. Cf. Wray (forthcoming). For attributions of *virtus* to women in some inscriptions, see Eisenhut (1973: 210–11); Roller (2001: 24).
43. On this passage and Seneca's use of *virtus* more generally see further Chapter 3 above.
44. See Wray (forthcoming).
45. On Musonius Rufus, see Nussbaum (2002).
46. As Wray argues (forthcoming).
47. Cicero uses the term *muliebriter* similarly. See, for example, *Tusc.* 2.48.
48. Wray (forthcoming) comments: 'Given his stoically informed positing of an ethical equality of the sexes, and given that Roman vernacular morality of the late republic and early empire appears ... to have had no trouble accepting that a woman could attain and exhibit exemplary virtue as a woman, what philosophical or rhetorical gain does Seneca seek in equating the virtue of a virtuous woman with literal manhood?'
49. Cf. Wray (forthcoming).
50. Cf. Nussbaum (2002) on Musonius Rufus, whose treatment of women stresses their capacity for *virtus* in general terms but adduces only the tamest of examples of, for instance, women's bravery.
51. Female figures appear rarely in the letters. Only a handful are named – Socrates' insufferable wife Xanthippe, Maecenas' wife Terentia and Seneca's own wife Paulina, whom Seneca ignores when she tells him not to go to Nomentum (104.2), though cf. 104.3–4. The only female exemplary figures are Harpaste, a slave in Seneca's household who won't acknowledge that she has lost her sight (50.2ff), and the mythological characters Hecuba (47.12), Niobe (63.2) and Penelope (88.8), all of whom are referred to only fleetingly.
52. On Porcia and Brutus see Moles (1997: esp. 159–61).
53. The versions told by Val. Max. 3.2.15 and Plut. *Brut.* 13.3–6 do not mention suicide but emphasise Porcia's ability to endure pain as a test of her character.
54. Plutarch (*Brut.* 53.4) argues that Valerius Maximus and Nicolaus are wrong in reporting her to have died after Brutus.
55. On Arria and other members of her family in relation to a tradition of 'dissident history', see O'Gorman (2000: 124–6). The Elder Arria was also celebrated in a lost poem by Persius (Suet. *Vita Persii*).
56. Cf. Pliny's discussion of the double suicide of the elderly couple from Como (*Ep.* 6.24.2–5). On the issue of wives dying to help their husbands more generally, see Treggiari (1991: 485–9).
57. In Dio's account, though Arria apparently survives the famous stabbing, she succeeds in killing herself not long after her husband's death (60.15).
58. Though Pliny is careful to emphasise that this is not always appropriate. Arria's daughter (also called Arria) was wife of P. Clodius Thrasea Paetus. She is said to have wanted to kill herself after her husband's suicide in 66 CE but was persuaded by him to live on to look after their daughter Fannia (Pliny *Ep.* 7.19).
59. Cf. Plass (1995: 86).
60. In Dio's version, by contrast, Seneca is criticised for persuading his wife to die with him (65.25.1).
61. Plass (1995: 110).
62. Cf. Plass (1995: 109).

63. Tacitus' account of Messalina is suggestively analysed by Joshel (1995). See also Levick (1990).
64. This is well emphasised by Joshel (1995).
65. Gallivan (1974) argues persuasively that she was older.
66. Cf. Scott (1974). On this passage see also Ginsburg (2006: 46–53).
67. Cf. 14.6.1, *solum insidiarum remedium esse, si non intellegerentur,* 'the only defence against an attack was not to recognise it as such'.
68. The art with which this scene is composed is suggestively discussed by Quinn (1963: 110–29). Dio's account of Agrippina's death is briefer. He gives her last words as: 'Strike here, Anicetus, strike here for this bore Nero' (62.13.5).
69. This is foreshadowed at 13.3. Cf. Henderson (1998: 288). More graphic versions of the incest story appear in Suet. *Nero* 28 and Dio 61.11.4.
70. See O'Gorman (2000: 139–40). On the rumours of incest as a manifestation of hostility to the endogamous nature of the Julio-Claudians, see Ginsburg (2006: 130).
71. On the tensions in Tacitus' account of Nero's motivation, see Ginsburg (2006: 47).
72. This incident is also referred to by Suetonius (*Nero* 34).
73. O'Gorman sees these as different versions of Agrippina's end which are in tension with one another (2000: 138–43). She suggestively links Agrippina's reported last words with the later death of the pregnant Poppaea, kicked in the stomach by Nero, but also sees this as a reminder of Agrippina's own route to power (her fecundity had recommended her to Claudius, *Ann.* 12.2.3).
74. On this see Michael Kaplan (1979). The mother is described as 'semper atrox' (*Ann.* 4.52.2); the term *atrox* is also applied to the daughter (12.22.1; 13.13.3).
75. Tacitus also suggests parallels with Livia her paternal great-grandmother (whom Agrippina is expressly said to imitate 12.69). On these see Henderson (1998: 278–85) and O'Gorman (2000: 126–38). As Santoro L'hoir (1994) observes, there are numerous thematic links also with particularly Livia but also other female characters in the *Annals*. Ginsburg also notes parallels with Augustus (Agrippina's great-grandfather) and with Sejanus (2006: 54).
76. Through her young son Nero she exercises *dominatio* over Rome (*Ann.* 13.2).
77. On her unprecedented number of imperial connections see *Ann.* 12.42.
78. Cf. O'Gorman (2000: 133).
79. For this view, see, for example, Hallett (1989: 67).
80. The drastic deterioration in Nero's rule after her death suggests not only the degree to which she controlled her son but also the positive nature of her influence (14.13.2).
81. Certainly the description of Nero's suicide in Suetonius' biography insistently emphasises his inability to act decisively. See pp. 159–60 above.
82. A somewhat similar instance of bravery is offered in the story of the peasant assassin of Piso (governor of Spain), who kills himself to pre-empt interrogation, thus protecting his associates (*Ann.* 4.45). For the defiance of other women under torture, see *Ann.* 14.60.
83. We might compare this with Tacitus' treatment of Otho's paradoxically virtuous death, discussed above in Chapter 1.
84. These are discussed on pp. 107–9 above.
85. Cf. Henderson (1998: 262).
86. Cf. Suet. *Tib.* 61. Dio (47.6) relates what could be read as a parallel instance in which a youth is made to assume the *toga virilis* before being executed.

Notes to Chapter 8: Laughing at death? Christian martyrdom

1. As Edward Gibbon noted in Ch. 15 of *The Decline and Fall of the Roman Empire*. Cf., for example, Goldhill (2002: 391–3); Wiedemann (1992: 150). A similarly vengeful account of the deaths to be suffered by those who persecute the Christians is to be found in Lactantius *De mortibus persecutorum* (On the Deaths of the Persecutors).
2. Cf. Grig (2004: 34).
3. For a suggestive exploration of Augustine's language here and elsewhere, see Grig (2004: 42–53).
4. On this, see Shaw (1996: 276–84). Boyarin (1999: 115–17) sees strong similarities between this text and Ignatius *Letter to the Romans* and dates it to the first or even second century CE. For Augustine's sermons given on the feast of the Maccabees, see *Serm.* 300, 301; *Denis* 17.
5. Debate continues over how the term martyrdom may most helpfully be defined. See, for example, Frend (1965); Droge and Tabor (1992: 75); Bowersock (1995: esp. 5–8); Boyarin (1999); Grig (2004: 8–11). Van Hooff (1990) also considers briefly some points of comparison in the concluding section of his study.
6. As Boyarin suggests (1999: 94).
7. Boyarin (1999: 127).
8. Bowersock (1995: 72). Continuities are also emphasised by Droge and Tabor (1992) (particularly in relation to the death of Socrates) and by Barton (1994).
9. Carlson (1948). Cf. Bowersock (1995: 63–4); Straw (2001).
10. Cf. Minucius Felix *Octavia* 37.4–5; John Chrysostom *Homilies on I Corinthians* 4.7.
11. Cf. Straw (2001).
12. Straw comments: 'Both Romans and Christians shared the model of the failed hero, who redeems his honour through bold acts of the will' (2001: 50). P. Brown too stresses that the courage of the martyr can be seen as parallel to that of the philosopher (1992: Ch. 2). Ammianus Marcellinus, for instance, expresses admiration at the fortitude of martyrs who achieve a *gloriosam mortem* (22.11.10).
13. Cf. Grig (2004: 22). There are parallels with the so-called pagan martyr acts which also frequently appear in the form of a judicial prosecution (see Musurillo 1954).
14. For some Christians, the martyr's death had the effect of effacing any previous sins and rendered the martyr as if newly baptised. Cf. Droge and Tabor (1992: 132). Tertullian comments: 'The sole key to unlock paradise is your own life's blood' (*De anima* 55.5).
15. Potter writes of 'a picture of society's power painted upon the canvas provided by the bodies of the condemned to the agents of the central government' (1993: 53). It is the spectacle of the death of the *noxius* which is the concern of Seneca's Letter 7. Kyle documents in impressive detail what is known of the fate of the *noxii* (1998). Cf. Coleman on the details of punishments of Christians (1990: 47).
16. The focus on judicial execution – a process which necessarily brought guilt on the officials involved and sometimes at least was thought to inspire an excessive keenness to die on the part of would-be martyrs – was felt to be increasingly problematic by some church fathers (Cyprian *Epistulae* 81.1, 4; Clement of Alexandria *Stromateis* 4.4; 4.15). The polemic context of comments such as those made by Clement also needs to be taken account of (cf. Grig. 2004: 19). The condemnation of suicide on the part of some Christians, most particularly Augustine in *Civ. dei.* 1.19, was in part a response to and had significant implications for voluntary martyrs (cf. Bowersock 1995: 62–74, stressing the importance of the Platonic tradition as an influence).
17. Christians were similarly criticised for worshipping Christ, whose condemnation

and death made him a source of mockery, *ludibrium* (Minucius Felix *Octavius* 93.7).

18. On developing visual protocols particularly associated with the second century CE see Goldhill (2002). Potter (1993) explores the role of judicial process as itself a form of spectacle, through the example of some martyr acts. He suggests state authorities became increasingly unwilling to make a spectacle of the deaths of upper-class Christians, however.

19. See, for example, Grig (2004: 17). Other instances of the imagery of athleticism include Blandina, one of the martyrs of Lyons (Eusebius *HE* 5.1). See too the concluding section of 4 Maccabees.

20. Cf. Straw (2001) and Barton who, discussing at length the significance of the *sacramentum*, suggests the model of the gladiator also underlies Christian invocations of the soldier (1994: esp. 56).

21. Musurillo trs. Shaw comments: 'As with many Christian texts, elements of both gladiatorial and athletic contests are merged into a single, mixed literary type' (1993: 28). Wiedemann observes: 'For a Christian lady, playing the ambivalent figure of a gladiator might be as subconsciously attractive as for the pagan women of high status satirised by Juvenal' (Wiedemann 1992: 151).

22. Whose strategies to contain it are brilliantly analysed by Shaw (1993: 28–30). See too Cameron (1989).

23. See Shaw (1993: 37–41).

24. Important recent studies include Shaw (1993), (1996); Grig (2002), (2004: esp. Ch. 4). As they stress, late antique pagan texts also show an increased preoccupation with the detail of pain and suffering.

25. See Edwards (1999).

26. As Grig comments: 'The greater the violence, the greater the possibility for victory: the more endurance, fortitude, immunity can be shown' (2004: 66). Cf. Barton (1994); Delehaye (1921: 284).

27. Cf. Grig (2004: 82), also Fowler (1987: 186–7). This focus on the sufferings of the flesh is also to be linked with the Christian preoccupation with abstinence, a preoccupation whose diverse forms are suggestively explored by Brown (1989). For Brown it is Tertullian who first articulates the role that continence might have as a means by which those unable to secure martyrdom may find a path to the holy spirit (1989: 76–80).

28. As Shaw emphasises (1996: 269–74). Cf. Goldhill (1995: Ch. 3).

29. Cf. Shaw, who comments: 'she offers a quintessential female part, her throat, to the executioner's sword' (1996: 273).

30. On parallels between the gladiator and the martyr, see Barton (1994).

31. Grig (2004: 42–3).

32. Cf. Grig (2004: 45).

33. Cf. Grig (2004: 44).

34. As Conybeare (2005) suggests in her review of Grig (2004).

35. Grig (2004: 45). Cf. Edwards (1993: Ch. 3).

36. As Gunderson argues (2003: 644). Here we perhaps come closer to the more edifying sense of *spectaculum* explored by Feldherr in relation to some episodes in Livy. See above pp. 25–6.

37. Cf. Bartsch (2001: 1).

38. Freud 'Reflections on war and death' (1963: 122).

39. Hopkins (1999: 114–15).

40. Cf. Shaw (1996: 280).

41. Rather underemphasised by Shaw. For a somewhat different evaluation of the significance of *patientia* in Seneca's Stoicism, see Bartsch (2005: esp. 81–3); Edwards (2005c).

42. (1995: esp. 142–99). The degree to which Christian explorations of the suffering body may be seen as drawing on contemporary pagan discourses is stressed by Perkins. Christian writings occasionally acknowledge continuities. See, for example, Tert. *Apol.* 50.14 who approves the sentiments of Cicero and Seneca exhorting their readers to the endurance of pain and death but goes on to comment: *nec tamen tantos inveniunt verba discipulos quantos Christiani factis docendo*, 'Their words never find so many pupils as the Christians do through their deeds'.
43. Cf. Shaw (1996: 312).
44. Barton (1994: 60).
45. As Barton contends (1994: 55, n.101).
46. *Serm.* 286.7; 328.8. Cf. Grig (2004: 50–1).
47. Cf. Perkins (1995: 142).
48. On the phenomenon of Christians volunteering for martyrdom see de Ste Croix (1974); Lane Fox (1986: 419–92); Droge and Tabor (1992: esp. Ch.6); Hopkins (1999: 111–37).
49. See Lane Fox (1986: 441); Droge and Tabor (1992: 130–2).
50. Bowersock (1995: 5). As Boyarin stresses, these features do not, in themselves, serve to differentiate Christian martyrdom sharply from earlier Jewish tradition (1999: 95).
51. See Bynum (1995: esp. 21–58).
52. Cf. Bynum (1995: 43–4).
53. Bynum (1995: 45).
54. Bynum (1995: 58).
55. Musurillo (1972: 121).
56. Cf. Bynum (1995: 45–6). This is a point also made by some critics of Perkins' work. See, for example, Trout (1998: 562–4).
57. For example, Ignatius *Ep. ad Trall.* 10.1.

ABBREVIATIONS OF
ANCIENT AUTHORS, TEXTS
AND COLLECTIONS

In the case of most works cited, parallel Latin (or Greek) and English texts are conveniently available in the Loeb Classical Library editions.

Appian	*BC*	*Bella civilia* (Civil Wars)
Athenaeus	*Deipn.*	*Deipnosophistae* (Philosophers at Table)
Aug.	*Civ. dei*	Augustine *De civitate dei* (The City of God)
	Serm.	*Sermo* (Sermon) in *Corpus Christianorum series latina* Vol. 51
	Caillau Denis	These additional sermons are included in *Miscellanea Agostiniana: testi e studi* 2 vols (Roma 1930–1)
	Enarr. in psalmos	*Enarrationes in psalmos* (Commentaries on the Psalms) in *Corpus Christianorum series latina* Vol. 38
Aulus Gellius		*Noctes Atticae* (Attic Nights)
B. Afr. (anonymous)		*Bellum Africum* (Africa War)
Caesar	*BC*	*Bellum civile* (Civil War)
	BG	*Bellum Gallicum* (Gallic War)
Calp. Sic.		Calpurnius Siculus
Cic.	*Att.*	Cicero *Ad Atticum* (Letters to Atticus)
	Brut.	*Ad Brutum* (To Brutus)
	Cat.	*In Catilinam* (Against Catiline)
	Fam.	*Ad familiares* (Letters to his Friends)
	Fin.	*De finibus* (On Ends)
	Leg.	*De legibus* (On the Laws)
	Mil.	*Pro Milone* (On Behalf of Milo)
	Off.	*De officiis* (On Duties)
	Nat. deor.	*De natura deorum* (On the Nature of the Gods)
	Phil.	*Orationes philippicae* (Speeches against Mark Antony)
	Rep.	*De re publica* (On the State)
	Rosc. Am.	*Pro Roscio Amerino* (On Behalf of Roscius from Ameria)

	SB	D. R. Shackleton-Bailey (whose now standard editions of Cicero's letters use his own numbering)
	Sest.	*Pro Sestio* (On Behalf of Sestius)
	Tusc.	*Tusculanae disputationes* (Tusculan Disputations)
	Verr.	*In Verrem* (Against Verres)
CIL		*Corpus Inscriptionum Latinarum* (Collection of Latin Inscriptions)
Dig.		*Digesta* (Digest of Justinian) trs. and ed. T. Mommsen, P. Krüger, A. Watson, 4 vols (Philadelphia 1985)
Dio		Dio Cassius
Diog. Laert.		Diogenes Laertius
Dion. Hal.	*Ant. rom.*	Dionysius of Halicarnassus *Antiquitates romanae* (Roman antiquities)
Epictetus	*Disc.*	*Discourses*
	Ench.	*Encheiridion* (Handbook)
Epicurus	*L. Men.*	*Letter to Menoeceus*
	Kyria doxa	*Key Doctrines*
	Sent. Vat.	*Vatican Sayings* (Epicurus texts in A. A. Long and D. N. Sedley *The Hellenistic Philosophers*, 2 vols (Cambridge 1987)
Eusebius	*HE*	*Historia ecclesiastica* (Church History)
Florus		*Epitome de Tito Livio bellorum* (Epitome of Livy's Roman Wars)
Front.	*Strat.*	Frontinus *Strategemata* (On Stratagems)
Gaius	*Inst.*	*Institutes* (Teaching course) ed. and trs. W. M. Gordon and O. F. Robinson (1988)
Ignatius	*Ep. ad Poly.*	*Epistula ad Polycarpum* (Letters to Polycarp)
	Ep. ad Rom.	*Epistulae ad Romanos* (Letters to the Romans)
	Ep. ad Trall.	*Epistulae ad Tralleanos* (Letters to the Tralleans)
ILS		*Inscriptiones Latinae selectae* ed. H. Dessau (1892–1916)
Jerome	*Ep.*	*Epistulae* (Letters)
Juv.		Juvenal *Saturae* (Satires)
Lact.	*Div. inst.*	Lactantius *Divinae institutiones* (Divine Institutes)
	Mort. pers.	*De mortibus persecutorum* (On the Deaths of the Persecutors)
Livy		*Ab urbe condita* (From the Foundation of the City)
	Per.	*Periochae* (Summaries of lost books)
Luc.	*DRN*	Lucretius *De rerum natura* (On the Nature of the Universe)
Lucan	*BC*	*Bellum civile* (Civil War)
Macrob.	*Sat.*	Macrobius *Saturnalia*
Mart.	*Spect.*	Martial *Spectacula* (Spectacles)
Nep.	*Att.*	Cornelius Nepos *Atticus*

PCG		*Poetae comici graeci* (Greek Comic Poets) ed. R. Kassel and C. Austin (Berlin 1983)
Perp.		Martyrdom of Perpetua (in *Acts of the Christian Martyrs* ed. F. Musurillo Oxford 1972)
Pet.	*Sat.*	Petronius *Satyricon*
Plato	*Apol.*	*Apology*
	Phaedr.	*Phaedrus*
Pliny	*Ep.*	Pliny (Younger) *Epistulae* (Letters)
	Paneg.	*Panegyricus* (Panegyric)
Pliny	*NH*	Pliny (Elder) *Naturales historiae* (Natural Histories)
Plut.	*Ant.*	Plutarch *Life of Antony*
	Brut.	*Life of Brutus*
	Caes.	*Life of Julius Caesar*
	Cat. min.	*Life of the Younger Cato*
	Crassus	*Life of Crassus*
	Otho	*Life of Otho*
	Publ.	*Life of Publicola*
Polyb.		Polybius
Prudentius	*Contra Symm.*	*Contra Symmachum* (Against Symmachus)
	Perist.	*Peristephanon* (On the Crowns of the Martyrs)
Quint.	*Inst.*	Quintilian *Institutio oratoria* (The Education of an Orator)
Rhet. Her.		*Rhetorica ad Herennium* (To Herennius On the Art of Oratory)
Sall.	*Cat.*	Sallust *Bellum Catilinae* (The War against Catiline)
Sen.	*Ben.*	Seneca (Younger) *De beneficiis* (On benefits)
	Clem.	*De clementia* (On Mercy)
	Const. sap.	*De constantia sapientis* (On the Endurance of the Wise Man)
	Ep.	*Epistulae morales* (Letters)
	Helv.	*Ad Helviam* (To Helvia)
	Marc.	*Ad Marciam* (To Marcia)
	Prov.	*De providentia* (On Providence)
	Tranqu. an.	*De tranquillitate animi* (On Tranquillity of Mind)
[Sen.]	*Anth. Lat.*	fragments attributed to Seneca in *Anthologia Latina* ed. D. R. Shackleton-Bailey (Stuttgart 1982)
Sen.	*Suas.*	Seneca (Elder) *Suasoriae* (Persuasive Speeches)
SHA		Scriptores Historiae Augustae (Authors of the Augustan History)
Serv.	*Ad Aen.*	Servius *Ad Aeneida* (Commentary on Virgil's *Aeneid*)
Suet.	*Aug.*	Suetonius *Life of Augustus*
	Calig.	*Life of Caligula*

	Claud.	*Life of Claudius*
	Dom.	*Life of Domitian*
	Iul.	*Life of Julius Caesar*
	Nero	*Life of Nero*
	Tib.	*Life of Tiberius*
	Vit.	*Life of Vitellius*
Tac.	*Agr.*	Tacitus *Agricola*
	Ann.	*Annales* (Annals)
	Hist.	*Historiae* (Histories)
Tert.	*Ad Scap.*	Tertullian *Ad Scapulam* (To Scapula)
	Ad mart.	*Ad martyres* (To the Martyrs)
	Apol.	*Apologeticus* (Apology)
	Resurr.	*De resurrectione* (On the Resurrection)
	Spect.	*De spectaculis* (On the Spectacles)
Val. Max.		Valerius Maximus
Vell. Pat.		Velleius Paterculus
Virg.	*Geo.*	Virgil *Georgics*
	Aen.	*Aeneid*

BIBLIOGRAPHY

Ahl, F. *Lucan: An Introduction* (Ithaca 1976)
—— 'The art of safe criticism in Greece and Rome', *American Journal of Philology* 105 (1984a) 174–208
—— 'Politics and power in Roman poetry', *Aufstieg und Niedergang der römischen Welt* 2.32.1 (1984b) 40–110
Alvarez, A. *The Savage God: A Study of Suicide* (London 2002; first edn 1971)
Anderson, W. S. *Essays in Roman Satire* (Princeton, 1982)
Arand, Tobias *Das schmäliche Ende. Der Tod des schlechten Kaisers und seine literarische Gestaltung in der römischen Historiographie* (Frankfurt am Main 2002)
Arena, Valentina *'Libertas' and the Practice of Politics in the Late Roman Republic* (2008)
Ariès, Philippe, *The Hour of Our Death* (London 1981), trs. by Helen Weaver of *L'Homme devant la mort* (Paris 1976)
Armisen-Marchetti, M. 'Imagination et méditation chez Sénèque: l'exemple de la *praemeditatio*', *Revue des Etudes Latines* 64 (1986) 185–95
Arrowsmith, William 'Luxury and death in the Satyricon' *Arion* 5 (1966) 304–31
Ash, Rhiannon *Ordering Anarchy: Armies and Leaders in Tacitus' Histories* (London 1999)
—— 'Epic encounters? Ancient historial battle narratives and the epic tradition' 253–73 in D. Levene and D. Nelis (eds) *Clio and the Poets* (Leiden 2002)
Auguet, R. *Cruelty and Civilisation: The Roman Games*, trs. from French (London 1972)
Aune, D. C. 'Mastery of the passions: Philo, 4 Maccabees and earliest Christianity' 125–58 in W. E. Helleman (ed.) *Hellenization Revisited: Shaping a Christian Response within the Greco-Roman World* (Lanham, Maryland 1994)
Badian, Edward 'A phantom marriage law' *Philologus* 129 (1985) 82–98
Baltrusch, E. 'Die Verstaatlichung der Gladiatorenspiele' *Hermes* 116.2 (1988) 324–37
Bardon, H. *La Littérature latine inconnue*, vol. II (Paris, 1956) 207–9
Barnes, T. D. *Tertullian: A Historical and Literary Study* (rev. edn Oxford 1985)
Barthes, Roland 'Tacitus and the funerary baroque' 162–6 in Susan Sontag (ed.) *Barthes: Selected Writings* (London 1982)
Barton, Carlin 'The scandal of the arena' *Representations* 27 (1989) 1–36
—— *The Sorrows of the Ancient Romans* (Princeton 1993)
—— 'Savage miracles: the redemption of lost honour in Roman society and the sacrament of the gladiator and the martyr' *Representations* 45 (1994) 41–71
—— *Roman Honour: The Fire in the Bones* (Berkeley 2001)
Bartsch, Shadi, *Actors in the Audience* (Cambridge, Mass. 1994)
—— *Ideology in Cold Blood: A Reading of Lucan's 'Civil War'* (Cambridge, Mass. 1997)

—— 'The self as audience: paradoxes of identity in imperial Rome' *Pegasus* 44 (2001) 1–12

—— 'Eros and the Roman philosopher' 59–83 in Bartsch and Bartscherer (2005)

—— and T. Bartscherer (eds) *Erotikon: Essays on Eros, Ancient and Modern* (Chicago 2005)

Barzanò, Alberto 'Libenter cupit commori qui sine dubio scit se esse moriturum: la morte per la patria in Roma repubblicana' 157–70 in Sordi (1990)

Bassett, S. *Death in Towns: Urban Responses to the Dying and the Dead 100–1600* (Leicester 1992)

Bataille, Georges *Erotism: Death and Sensuality* trs. M. Dalwood (San Francisco 1962)

Batstone, W.W. 'The antithesis of virtue: Sallust's synkrisis and the crisis of the late republic' *Classical Antiquity* 7 (1988) 1–29

Bayet, J. 'Le suicide mutuel dans la mentalité des Romains' 130–76 in *Croyances et rites dans la Rome antique* (Paris 1971)

Beard, Mary 'The erotics of rape: Livy, Ovid and the Sabine women', 1–10 in P. Setälä and L. Savunen (eds) *Female Networks and the Public Sphere* (Rome 1999)

Bek, Lise '*Quaestiones conviviales*: the idea of the triclinium and the staging of convivial ceremony from Rome to Byzantium' *Analecta Romana Instituti Danici* Suppl. 12 (1983) 81–109

Bergmann, Bettina 'Introduction: the art of ancient spectacle' 9–35 in Bergmann and Kondoleon (1999)

Bergmann, B. and C. Kondoleon (eds) *The Art of Ancient Spectacle* (Yale, New Haven 1999)

Bernstein, Alan E. *The Formation of Hell: Death and Retribution in the Ancient and Early Christian Worlds* (Ithaca 1993)

Bloch, Maurice and Jonathan Parry *Death and the Regeneration of Life* (Cambridge 1982)

Bobzien, Susanne *Determinism and Freedom in Stoic Philosophy* (Oxford 1998)

Bodel, John 'Graveyards and groves: a study of the *lex Lucerina*', *American Journal of Ancient History* 11 (1986) 1–133

—— 'Death on display: looking at Roman funerals' 258–81 in Bergmann and Kondoleon (1999)

Boswell, James *The Hypochondriack* Vol. II, ed. M. Bailey (Stanford 1928)

Bowersock, Glen *Martyrdom and Rome* (Cambridge 1995)

Bowlby, John *Loss: Sadness and Depression* (London 1980)

Boyarin, Daniel *Dying for God: Martyrdom and the Making of Christianity and Judaism* (Stanford 1999)

Boyle, A. J. *Tragic Seneca: An Essay in the Theatrical Tradition* (London 1997)

—— and W. J. Dominik (eds) *Flavian Rome: Culture, Image, Text* (Leiden 2003)

Bradeen, D. 'The Athenian casualty lists' *Classical Quarterly* 19 (1969) 145–59

Braden, Gordon *Renaissance Tragedy and the Senecan Tradition: Anger's Privilege* (New Haven 1985)

Braund, S. M. and C. Gill (eds) *The Passions in Roman Thought and Literature* (Cambridge 1997)

Bremmer, Jan *The Rise and Fall of the Afterlife* (London 2002)

Bronfen, Elisabeth *Over her Dead Body: Death, Femininity and the Aesthetic* (Manchester 1992)

Brown, Peter *The Body and Society: Men, Women and Sexual Renunciation in Early Christianity* (London 1989)

—— *Power and Persuasion in Late Antiquity: Towards a Christian Empire* (Madison 1992)

—— *Authority and the Sacred: Aspects of the Christianisation of the Roman World* (Cambridge 1995)

Brown, Shelby 'Death as decoration: scenes from the arena on Roman domestic mosaics' 180–211 in A. Richlin (ed.) *Pornography and Representation in Greece and Rome* (New York 1992)

—— 'Explaining the arena: did the Romans "need" gladiators?' *Journal of Roman Archaeology* 8 (1995) 376–84

Brunt, P. A. 'Stoicism and the principate' *Papers of the British School at Rome* 43 (1975) 7–35

—— 'Libertas in the republic' ch. 6 in *idem The Fall of the Roman Republic* (Oxford 1988)

Burkert, Walter *Ancient Mystery Cults* (Cambridge, Mass. 1987)

Bynum, C. W. *The Resurrection of the Body in Western Christianity, 200–1336* (New York 1995)

Cameron, Averil 'Petronius and Plato' *Classical Quarterly* 19 (1969) 367–70

—— 'Virginity as metaphor: women and the rhetoric of early Christianity' 184–205 in A. Cameron (ed.) *History as Text* (London 1989)

Canetti, Elias *Crowds and Power* (London 1962), trs. by Carol Stewart of original German edn (1960)

Carlson, Mary Louise 'Pagan examples of fortitude in the Latin Christian apologists' *Classical Philology* 43 (1948) 93–104

Cébeillac-Gervasoni, M. and F. Zevi 'Révisions et nouveautés pour trois inscriptions d'Ostie: des femmes gladiateurs dans une inscription d'Ostie' *Mélanges de l'Ecole Française de Rome: Antiquité* 88 (1976) 602–20

Champlin, E. *Final Judgements: Duty and Emotion in Roman Wills 200 BC–AD 250* (Berkeley 1991)

Chitwood, Ava *Death by Philosophy: The Biographical Tradition in the Life and Death of the Archaic Philosophers Empedocles, Heraclitus, and Democritus* (Ann Arbor 2004)

Clark, Kate *The Virgin and the Bride: Idealised Womanhood in Late Antiquity* (Cambridge, Mass. 1996)

Clavel-Lévêque, M. *L'Empire en jeux* (Paris 1984)

—— 'L'espace des jeux dans le monde romaine' *Aufstieg und Niedergang der römischen Welt* 2.16.3 (1986) 2405–563

Clinton, K., 'The Eleusinian mysteries: Roman initiates and benefactors, second century BC to AD 267' *Aufstieg und Niedergang der römischen Welt* 2.18.2 (1989) 1499–539

Coarelli, F. 'L'armamento e le classi dei gladiatori' 153–73 in A. La Regina (ed.) *Sangue e arena* (Rome 2001)

Coleman, Kathleen (ed.) *Statius Silvae IV* (Oxford 1988)

—— 'Fatal charades: Roman executions staged as mythological enactments' *Journal of Roman Studies* 80 (1990) 44–73

Commager, H. S., Jr 'Lucretius' interpretation of the plague' *Harvard Studies in Classical Philology* 62 (1957) 105–18

Connors, C. 'Famous last words: authorship and death in the *Satyricon* and Neronian Rome' 225–35 in Elsner and Masters (1994)

Conte, Gian Biagio 'Petronius *Sat.* 141.4' *Classical Quarterly* 37 (1987) 529–32

—— *The Hidden Author: An Interpretation of Petronius' Satyricon* (Berkeley 1996)

Conybeare, Catherine 'Suffering bodies' *Times Literary Supplement* (15 April 2005) 9

Cooper, J. 'Greek philosophers on euthanasia and suicide' 515–41 in *idem Reason and Emotion: Essays in Ancient Moral Philosophy and Ethical Theory* (Princeton 1999)

Corbeill, Anthony *Nature Embodied: Gesture in Ancient Rome* (Princeton 2004)

Cormack, M. (ed.) *Sacrificing the Self: Perspectives on Martyrdom and Religion* (Oxford 2001)

Crook, John *The Law and Life of Rome* (London 1967)

Daremberg, C. and S. Saglio (eds) *Dictionnaire des antiquitiés grecques et romains* (Paris 1877–1919)

D'Arms, J.H. 'Control, companionship and clientela: some social functions of the Roman communal meal' *Echos du monde classique* 28 (1984) 327–48

—— 'The Roman *convivium* and the idea of equality' 308–20 in O.Murray (ed.) *Sympotica* (Oxford 1990)

—— 'Performing culture: Roman spectacle and the banquets of the powerful' 301–19 in Bergmann and Kondoleon (1999)

Debord, Guy *The Society of the Spectacle* (New York 1994) trs. by D.Nicholson-Smith of original French edn (1967)

Delehaye, H. *Les Passions des martyrs et les genres littéraires* (Brussels 1921)

Derrida, Jacques, *Aporias: Dying – Awaiting (one another at) the 'Limits of Truth'* trs. T.Dutoit (Stanford 1993)

Diels, H. and W.Kranz (eds) *Die Fragmente der Vorsokratiker* 5th edn 3 vols (Berlin 1950–2)

Dollimore, Jonathan *Death, Desire and Loss in Western Culture* (London 1998)

Donaldson, Ian 'Cato in tears' in R.F.Brissenden (ed.) *Studies in the Eighteenth Century* 2 (Canberra 1973)

—— *The Rapes of Lucretia: A Myth and its Transformations* (Oxford 1982)

Douglas, A.E. (ed. and trs.) *Cicero Tusculan Disputations* I (Warminster 1985)

Droge, A.J. and J.D.Tabor *A Noble Death: Suicide and Martyrdom among Christians and Jews in Antiquity* (New York 1992)

Dunbabin, K.M. '*Sic erimus cuncti*... the skeleton in Greco-Roman art' *Jahrbuch des Deutschen Archäologischen Instituts* 101 (1986) 185–225

—— *The Roman Banquet: Images of Conviviality* (Cambridge 2003)

Dupont, Florence *Le Plaisir et la Loi: du Banquet de Platon au Satiricon* (Paris 1977)

—— *L'Acteur-roi* (Paris 1985)

Durkheim, Emile *Suicide: A Study in Sociology* (London 1952) trs. by J.A.Spaulding and G.Simpson of original French edn (1897)

Dyer, J. 'Rhetoric and intention in Cicero's *Pro Marcello*' *Journal of Roman Studies* 80 (1990) 17–30

Earl, D. *The Moral and Political Tradition of Rome* (London 1967)

Edmondson, J.C. 'Dynamic arenas: gladiatorial presentations in the city of Rome and the construction of Roman society in the early empire' 69–112 in W.J.Slater (ed.) *Roman Theater and Society* (Ann Arbor 1996)

Edmunds, Radcliffe G. III *Myths of the Underworld Journey: Plato, Aristophanes and the Orphic Gold Tablets* (Cambridge 2004)

Edwards, Catharine *The Politics of Immorality in Ancient Rome* (Cambridge 1993)

—— 'Beware of imitations: theatre and the subversion of imperial identity' 83–97 in Elsner and Masters (1994)

—— 'Self-scrutiny and self-transformation in Seneca's Letters' *Greece & Rome* 44.1 (1997a) 23–38

—— 'Unspeakable professions: public performance and prostitution in ancient Rome' 66–95 in J.Hallett and M.Skinner (eds) *Roman Sexualities* (Princeton 1997b)

—— 'The suffering body: philosophy and pain in Seneca's Letters' 252–68 in J.Porter (ed.) *Constructions of the Classical Body* (Ann Arbor 1999)

—— 'Archetypally Roman? Representing Seneca's ageing body' 13–22 in A.Hopkins and M.Wyke (eds) *Roman Bodies* (London 2005a)

—— 'Modelling Roman suicide? The afterlife of Cato' *Economy and Society* 34.2 (2005b) 200–22

—— 'Response to Bartsch' 84–90 in Bartsch and Bartscherer (2005c)

Edwards, Catharine and Greg Woolf (eds) *Rome the Cosmopolis* (Cambridge 2003)

Eisenhut, W. *Virtus romana* (Munich 1973)

Eldred, Katherine 'The ship of fools: epic vision in Lucan's Vulteius episode' 57–85 in Fredrick (2002)

Elias, Norbert 'An essay on sport and violence' 150–74 in N. Elias and E. Dunning (eds) *Quest for Excitement: Sport and Leisure in the Civilising Process* (Oxford 1986)

Elsner, J. and J. Masters (eds) *Reflections of Nero* (London 1994)

Erskine, Andrew 'Cicero and the expression of grief' 36–47 in Braund and Gill (1997)

Fantham, Elaine 'The ambiguity of *virtus* in Lucan's *Civil War* and Statius' *Thebaid*' *Arachnion - A Journal of Ancient Literature and History on the Web* (8 Dec. 1995) (http://www.cisi.unito.it/arachne/num3/fantham.html)

Fedeli, P. *Properzio. Il libro terzo delle Elegie* (Bari 1985)

Feeney, Denis 'History and revelation in Vergil's underworld' *Proceedings of the Cambridge Philological Society* 212 (1986) 1–24

—— 'Beginning Sallust's *Catiline*' *Prudentia* 26 (1994) 139–46

—— *Literature and Religion at Rome: Cultures, Contexts and Beliefs* (Cambridge 1998)

Feldherr, A. 'Livy's revolution: civic identity and the creation of the *res publica*' 136–57 in T. Habinek and A. Schiesaro (eds) *The Roman Cultural Revolution* (Cambridge 1997)

—— *Spectacle and Society in Livy's History* (Berkeley 1998)

—— '*Non inter nota sepulchra*: Catullus 101 and Roman funerary ritual' *Classical Antiquity* 19.2 (2000) 209–31

Feldman, Fred *Confrontations with the Reaper: A Philosophical Study of the Nature and Value of Death* (Oxford 1992)

Fitzgerald, William 'Oppositions, anxieties and ambiguities in the toga movie' 23–49 in S. Joshel, M. Malamud and D. McGuire (eds) *Imperial Projections: Ancient Rome in Modern Popular Culture* (Baltimore 2001)

—— *Martial: The World of the Epigram* (Chicago 2007)

Flemming, Rebecca 'Suicide, euthanasia and medicine' *Economy and Society* 34.2 (2005) 295–321

Flower, Harriet *Ancestor Masks and Aristocratic Power in Roman Culture* (Oxford 1996)

Foucault, Michel *Discipline and Punish: The Birth of the Prison* trs. A. Sheridan (London 1977)

—— 'Conversation avec Werner Schroeter' 251–60 in D. Defert and F. Ewald (eds) *Dits et écrits 1954–88* Vol. IV (Paris 1994)

Fowler, Don 'Vergil on killing virgins' 185–98 in M. Whitby *et al.* (eds) *Homo viator: Classical Essays for John Bramble* (Bristol 1987)

Fowler, Peta 'Lucretian conclusions' 112–38 in Roberts, Dunn and Fowler (1997)

Fredrick, David 'Introduction: invisible Rome' 1–30 in *idem* (ed.) *The Roman Gaze: Vision, Power and the Body* (Baltimore 2002)

—— 'Architecture and surveillance in Flavian Rome' 199–227 in Boyle and Dominik (2003)

Frend, W. H. C. *Martyrdom and Persecution in the Early Church: A Study of Conflict from the Maccabees to Donatus* (Oxford 1965)

Freud, Sigmund 'Reflections on war and death', trs. E. Colburn Mayne in P. Rieff (ed.) *Sigmund Freud: Character and Culture* (New York 1963)

—— 'Our attitude towards death', trs. J. Strachey in A. Dixon (ed.) *Civilisation, Society and Religion*, Penguin Freud Library Vol. 12 (London 1985)

Freudenberg, Kirk *Satires of Rome: Threatening Poses from Lucilius to Juvenal* (Cambridge 2001)

Furley, D. J. 'Nothing to us?' 75–91 in M. Schofield and G. Striker (eds) *The Norms of Nature* (Cambridge 1986)

Futrell, Alison *Blood in the Arena: The Spectacle of Roman Power* (Austin, Texas 1997)

Gale, Monica *Myth and Poetry in Lucretius* (Cambridge 1994)

Gallivan, P. A. 'Confusion concerning the age of Octavia' *Latomus* 33.1 (1974) 116–17

Gane, Mike 'Durkheim's scenography of suicide' *Economy & Society* 34 (2005) 223–40

Garnsey, P. D. A. *Social Status and Legal Privilege in the Roman Empire* (Oxford 1970)

Geiger, J. 'Munatius Rufus and Thrasea Paetus on Cato the younger' *Athenaeum* 57 (1979) 48–72

Gelzer, M. *Caesar: Politician and Statesman* (Oxford 1968)

Gibbon, Edward *The Decline and Fall of the Roman Empire* ed. D.Womersley, 3 vols (London 1994)

Gibson, Sheila, Janet De Laine and Amanda Claridge 'The triclinium of the Domus Flavia: a new reconstruction' *Papers of the British School at Rome* 49 (1994) 66–97

Gill, Christopher 'The death of Socrates' *Classical Quarterly* 23 (1973) 25–8

—— 'Personhood and personality: the four-*personae* theory in Cicero's *De officiis* I' *Oxford Studies in Ancient Philosophy* 6 (1988) 169–99

—— 'Peace of mind and being yourself: Panaetius to Plutarch' *Aufstieg und Niedergang der römischen Welt* 2.36.7 (1994) 4599–640

Gillis, D. *Eros and Death in the 'Aeneid'* (Rome 1983)

Ginsburg, Judith *Representing Agrippina* (Oxford 2006)

Goar, R.J. *The Legend of Cato Uticensis from the First Century BC to the Fifth Century AD* (Brussels 1987)

Goddard, Justin 'The tyrant at table' 67–82 in Elsner and Masters (1994)

Goffman, Erving *The Presentation of Self in Everyday Life* (London 1959)

Golden, Mark 'Did the ancients care when their children died?' *Greece & Rome* 35 (1988) 152–63

Goldhill, Simon *Foucault's Virginity: Ancient Erotic Fiction and the History of Sexuality* (Cambridge 1995)

—— 'The erotic eye: visual stimulation and cultural conflict' 154–94 in *idem* (ed.) *Being Greek under Rome* (Cambridge 2001)

—— 'The erotic experience of looking: cultural conflict and the gaze in empire culture' 374–99 in M.C.Nussbaum and J.Sihvola (eds) *The Sleep of Reason: Erotic Experience and Sexual Ethics in Ancient Greece and Rome* (Chicago 2002)

Goldsworthy, A. *The Roman Army at War 100 BC–AD 200* (Oxford 1996)

Goodwin, S.W. and E.Bronfen (eds) *Death and Representation* (Baltimore and London 1993)

Gorer, Geoffrey *Death, Grief and Mourning in Contemporary Britain* (London 1965)

Gowers, Emily *The Loaded Table: Representations of Food in Roman Literature* (Oxford 1993)

Graf, F. 'Katabasis' 327–30 in *Der Neue Pauly* 6 (Stuttgart 1999)

Green, C.M. 'The necessary murder: myth, ritual and civil war in Lucan, Book 3' *Classical Antiquity* 13.2 (1994) 203–33

Greenidge, A.J.H. *Infamia* (Oxford 1894)

Griffin, Miriam *Seneca: A Philosopher in Politics* (Oxford 1976)

—— 'Philosophy, Cato and Roman suicide' *Greece & Rome* 33 (1986) 64–77 and 192–202

—— 'Philosophy, politics and politicians at Rome' 1–37 in J.Barnes and M.Griffin (eds) *Philosophia togata* (Oxford 1989)

Grig, Lucy 'Torture and truth in late antique martyrology' *Early Medieval Europe* 11.4 (2002) 321–36

—— *Making Martyrs in Late Antiquity* (London 2004)

Grisé, Y. *Le Suicide dans la Rome antique* (Montreal and Paris 1982)

Grottanelli, C. 'Wine and death – east and west' 62–89 in O.Murray and M.Tecușan (eds) *In vino veritas* (London 1995)

Guarino, A. 'I *gladiatores* e l'*auctoramentum*' *Labeo* 29 (1983) 7–24

Gunderson, Eric 'The ideology of the arena' *Classical Antiquity* 15.1 (1996) 113–51

—— 'The history of mind and the philosophy of history in Sallust's *Bellum Catilinae*' *Ramus* 29.2 (2000) 85–126

—— 'The Flavian amphitheatre: all the world as stage' 637–58 in Boyle and Dominik (2003)

Gurval, R. A. 'Dying like a queen: the story of Cleopatra and the asp(s) in antiquity' in
    M. Miles (ed.) *Cleopatra and Egyptomania* (Berkeley forthcoming)
Habinek, Thomas 'Seneca's circles: *Ep.* 12.6–9' *Classical Antiquity* 1 (1982) 66–9
Hallett, Judith 'Woman as same and other in the classical Roman elite' *Helios* 16.1 (1989)
    59–78
Hardie, A. 'The *Georgics*, the mysteries and the muses at Rome' *Proceedings of the
    Cambridge Philological Society* 48 (2002) 175–208
Hardie, Philip *Virgil's Aeneid: Cosmos and Imperium* (Oxford 1986)
—— *The Epic Successors of Virgil* (Cambridge 1993)
Harris, W. V. *War and Imperialism in Republican Rome 327–70 BC* (Oxford 1985; first
    edn 1979)
—— 'Readings in the narrative literature of Roman courage' 300–20 in Sheila Dillon
    and Katherine Welch (eds) *Representations of War in Ancient Rome* (Cambridge
    2006)
Haynes, Holly *The History of Make-believe: Tacitus on Imperial Rome* (Berkeley 2003)
Heidegger, Martin *Being and Time* trs. J. Macquarrie and E. Robinson (Oxford 1962)
Henderson, John *Fighting for Rome: Poets and Caesar, History and Civil War* (Cambridge
    1998)
Henten, Jan Willem van and Friedrich Avemarie *Martyrdom and Noble Death: Selected
    Texts from Greco-Roman, Jewish and Christian Antiquity* (London 2002)
Hesberg, H. von and P. Zanker *Römische Gräberstraße. Selbstdarstellung – Standard*
    (Munich 1987)
Heuzé, P. *L'Image du corps dans l'oeuvre de Virgile* (Rome 1985)
Highet, Gilbert 'Petronius the moralist' *Transactions of the American Philological
    Association* 72 (1941) 176–94
Higonnet, Margaret 'Speaking silences: women's suicide' 68–83 in S. R. Suleiman (ed.)
    The Female Body in Western Culture: Contemporary Perspectives (Cambridge, Mass.
    1985)
Hill, T. D. *Ambitiosa mors: Suicide and the Self in Roman Thought and Literature*
    (London 2004)
Hinard, F. (ed.) *La Mort, les morts et l'au-delà dans le monde romain* (Caen 1987)
—— *La Mort au quotidien dans le monde romain* (Paris 1995)
Hoffer, Stanley *The Anxieties of the Younger Pliny* (Atlanta 1999)
Hooff, A. J. L. van *From Autothanasia to Suicide: Self-killing in Classical Antiquity*
    (London 1990)
—— 'The imperial art of dying' 99–116 in L. de Blois *et al.* (eds) *The Representation and
    Perception of Roman Imperial Power* (Amsterdam 2003)
Hope, V. and E. Marshall (eds) *Death and Disease in the Ancient City* (London 2000)
Hopkins, Keith *Conquerors and Slaves* (Cambridge 1978)
—— *Death and Renewal* (Cambridge 1983)
—— *A World Full of Gods: Pagans, Jews and Christians in the Roman Empire* (London
    1999)
—— and Mary Beard *The Colosseum* (London 2005)
Hornblower, Simon *A Commentary on Thucydides* Vol. 1: *Books I–III* (Oxford 1991)
Horsfall, Nicholas 'Dido in the light of history' *Proceedings of the Virgil Society* (1973–4)
    13.1–13, repr. in S. J. Harrison *Oxford Readings in Virgil's Aeneid* (Oxford 1990)
Houghton, Luke *Death and the Elegists: Latin Love Poetry and the Culture of the Grave*
    (unpublished PhD diss., Cambridge 2005)
Hutchinson, G. O. *Latin Literature from Seneca to Juvenal* (Oxford 1993)
Huysmans, J. K. *Against Nature* (Harmondsworth 1959), trs. by Robert Baldick of *A
    rebours* (Paris 1888)
Inwood, Brad *Reading Seneca* (Oxford 2005)
Jal, P. *La Guerre civile à Rome* (Paris 1963)

Janssen, L. F. 'Some unexplored aspects of the *devotio Deciana*' *Mnemosyne* 4 [34] (1981) 357–81

Jed, S. H. *Chaste Thinking: The Rape of Lucretia and the Birth of Humanism* (Bloomington, Indiana 1989)

Jocelyn, H. (1986) 'Lucretius, his copyists and the horror of the underworld' *Acta Classica* 29 (1986) 43–56

Jones, B. W. *The Emperor Domitian* (London 1992)

Jones, R. M. 'Posidonius and the flight of the mind through the universe' *Classical Philology* 21 (1926) 97–113

Joplin, P. K. 'Ritual work on human flesh: Livy's Lucretia and the rape of the body politic' *Helios* 17.1 (1990) 51–70

Joshel, S. 'The body female and the body politic: Livy's Lucretia and Verginia' 112–30 in A. Richlin (ed.) *Pornography and Representation in Ancient Greece and Rome* (Oxford 1992)

—— 'Female desire and the discourse of empire: Tacitus' Messalina' *Signs* 21.1 (1995) 50–82

Junkelmann, M. 'Familia gladiatorial: the heroes of the amphitheatre' 31–74 in E. Köhne and C. Ewigleben (eds) *Gladiators and Caesars: The Power of Spectacle in Ancient Rome* (English edn R. Jackson) (Berkeley 2000)

Kahn, C. H., *Pythagoras and the Pythagoreans: A Brief History* (Indianapolis 2001)

Kaplan, E. Ann 'Is the gaze male?' 309–27 in Ann Barr Snitow, C. Stansell and S. Thompson (eds) *Powers of Desire: The Politics of Sexuality* (New York 1983)

Kaplan, Michael '*Agrippina semper atrox*: a study in Tacitus' characterisation of women' 410–17 in C. Deroux (ed.) *Studies in Latin Literature and Roman History* Vol. I, Collection Latomus Vol. 164 (Brussels 1979)

Keegan, John *The Face of Battle* (London 1976)

Keitel, E. 'Principate and civil war in the *Annals* of Tacitus' *American Journal of Philology* 105 (1984) 306–25

—— 'Otho's exhortations in Tacitus' *Histories*' *Greece & Rome* 34 (1987) 73–82

Keith, Alison *Engendering Rome: Woman in Latin Epic* (Cambridge 2000)

Kennedy, D. F. *Rethinking Reality: Lucretius and the Textualisation of Nature* (Ann Arbor 2002)

Ker, J. 'Nocturnal writers in imperial Rome' *Classical Philology* 99 (2004) 209–42

King, Helen '"Bound to bleed": Artemis and Greek women' 109–27 in A. Cameron and A. Kuhrt (eds) *Images of Women in Antiquity* (London 1983)

Kraus, C. S. and A. J. Woodman *Latin Historians* (Oxford 1997)

Kübler-Ross, Elisabeth *On Death and Dying* (London 1970)

Kyle, Donald *Spectacles of Death in Ancient Rome* (London 1998)

Laidlaw, James 'A life worth leaving: fasting to death as telos of a Jain religious life' *Economy & Society* 34 (2005) 178–99

Lakoff, George and Mark Johnson *Metaphors We Live By* (Chicago 2003; first edn 1980)

Lane Fox, Robin *Pagans and Christians in the Mediterranean World from the Second Century AD to the Conversion of Constantine* (London 1986)

Langlands, Rebecca *Sexual Morality in Ancient Rome* (Cambridge 2006)

Lattimore, R. *Themes in Greek and Latin Epitaphs* (Urbana 1942)

Lavery, G. B. 'Metaphors of war and travel in Seneca's prose works' *Greece & Rome* 27 (1980) 147–57

Lebek, W. D. 'Standeswürde und Berufsverbot unter Tiberius: das SC der Tabula Larinas' *Zeitschrift für Papyrologie und Epigrafik* 81 (1990) 37–96

Leeman, A. D. 'Das Todeserlebnis im Denken Senecas' *Gymnasium* 78 (1971) 322–33

Leigh, Matthew 'Hopelessly devoted to you: traces of the Decii in Virgil's *Aeneid*' *Proceedings of the Virgil Society* 21 (1993) 89–110

—— *Lucan: Spectacle and Engagement* (Oxford 1997)

Le Roux, P. 'L'amphithéâtre et le soldat sous l'empire romain' 203–16 in C. Domergue, C. Landes and J.-M. Paillier (eds) *Spectacula I: gladiateurs et amphithéâtres* (Lattes 1990)

Levene, D. S. 'Pity, fear and the historical audience' 128–49 in Braund and Gill (1997)

—— 'Sallust's *Catiline* and Cato the censor' *Classical Quarterly* 50.1 (2000) 170–91

Levick, B. 'The *senatus consultum* from Larinum' *Journal of Roman Studies* 73 (1983) 97–115

—— *Claudius* (London 1990)

Lim, R. 'In the "temple of laughter": visual and literary representations of spectators at Roman games' 343–65 in Bergmann and Kondoleon (1999)

Litchfield, H. W. 'National *exempla virtutis* in Roman literature' *Harvard Studies in Classical Philology* 25 (1914) 1–74

Long, A. A. 'Cicero's politics in *De officiis*' 213–40 in A. Laks and M. Schofield (eds) *Justice and Generosity* (Cambridge 1995)

—— *Epictetus: A Stoic and Socratic Guide to Life* (Oxford 2002)

Loraux, Nicole *The Invention of Athens: The Funeral Oration in the Classical City* trs. A. Sheridan (Cambridge, Mass. 1986)

—— *The Experiences of Tiresias: The Feminine and the Greek Man* trs. P. Wissing (Princeton 1995)

Lounsbury, R. *The Arts of Suetonius: An Introduction* (New York 1987)

Lucan, M. and D. Gray *The Decadent Cookbook* (Sawtry, Cambs. 1995)

Luck, G. 'Virgil and the mystery religions' *American Journal of Philology* 94 (1973) 147–66

McDonnell, Myles 'Roman men and Greek virtue' 235–61 in Rosen and Sluiter (2003)

—— *Roman Manliness: Virtus and the Roman Republic* (Cambridge 2006)

McGuire, D. T. *Acts of Silence: Civil War, Tyranny and Suicide in the Flavian Epics* (New York 1997)

McGushin, P. *Bellum Catilinae: A Commentary* (Leiden 1977)

McManners, John *Death and the Enlightenment* (Oxford 1981)

Malissard, A. 'Tacite et le théâtre ou la mort en scène' 213–22 in J. Blänsdorf *Theater und Gesellschaft* (Tübingen 1990)

Marg, Walter 'Zur Eigenart der Odyssee' *Antike & Abendland* 18 (1973) 1–14

Marincola, John *Authority and Tradition in Ancient Historiography* (Cambridge 1997)

Marti, Berthe 'Cassius Scaeva and Lucan's inventio' 239–57 in L. Wallach (ed.) The Classical Tradition: Literary and Historical Studies in Honor of H. Caplan (Ithaca 1966)

Martin, R. H. and A. J. Woodman (eds) *Tacitus Annals 4* (Cambridge 1989)

Martindale, C. A. 'The politician Lucan' *Greece & Rome* n.s. 31 (1984) 64–79

—— *Redeeming the Text* (Cambridge 1993)

Marx, F. A. 'Tacitus und die Literatur der exitus illustrium virorum' *Philologus* 92 (1937) 83–103

Masters, Jamie *Poetry and Civil War in Lucan's Bellum Civile* (Cambridge 1992)

—— 'Deceiving the reader: the political mission of Lucan *Bellum civile* 7' 151–77 in Elsner and Masters (1994)

Mayer, Roland 'Roman historical exempla in Seneca' 141–69 in *Sénèque et la prose latine*, Entretiens sur l'antiquité classique Vol. 36 (Geneva 1991)

Metcalf, P. and R. Huntingdon *Celebrations of Death: The Anthropology of Mortuary Ritual* (2nd edn, Cambridge 1991)

Millar, F. G. B. *The Emperor in the Roman World (31BC to AD337)* (London 1977)

Miller, F. D. 'Epicurus on the art of dying' *Southern Journal of Philosophy* 14 (1976) 169–77

Mitchell, T. *Blood Sport: A Social History of Spanish Bull-fighting* (Philadelphia 1991)

Moles, John 'Aristotle and Dido's hamartia' in I. McAuslan and P. Walcot (eds) *Virgil* (Oxford 1990; first edn 1984)

—— 'Plutarch's *Brutus* and Brutus' Greek and Latin letters' in J. Mossman (ed.) *Plutarch in his Intellectual World* (London 1997)

—— 'Cry Freedom: Tacitus Annals 4.32–35' *Histos* 2 (1998)

Montaigne, M. de *Essays* trs. and ed. M. A. Screech (Harmondsworth 1991)

Moore, Timothy *Artistry and Ideology: Livy's Vocabulary of Virtue* (Frankfurt 1989)

Morris, Ian 'Attitudes towards death in archaic Greece' *Classical Antiquity* 8 (1989) 296–320

—— *Death Ritual and Social Structure in Classical Antiquity* (Cambridge 1992)

Most, G. '*Disiecti membra poetae*: the rhetoric of dismemberment in Neronian poetry' 391–419 in R. Hexter and D. Selden (eds) *Innovations of Antiquity* (New Haven 1992)

Mouritsen, Henrik 'Freedmen and decurions: epitaphs and social history in imperial Italy' *Journal of Roman Studies* 95 (2005) 38–63

Mulvey, Laura 'Visual pleasure and narrative cinema' *Screen* (1975), repr. in *eadem Visual and Other Pleasures* (London 1989)

Murray, Oswyn 'Death and the symposium' *Annali del Istituto Universitario Orientale di Napoli* [Archeologia e storia antica] 10 (1988) 239–57

Musurillo, H. *The Acts of the Pagan Martyrs* (Oxford 1954)

—— *The Acts of the Christian Martyrs* (Oxford 1972)

Nock, A. D. *Conversion: The Old and the New in Religion from Alexander the Great to Augustine of Hippo* (Oxford 1933)

Nussbaum, Martha *The Therapy of Desire: Theory and Practice in Hellenistic Ethics* (Princeton 1994)

—— 'The incomplete feminism of Musonius Rufus, Platonist, Stoic and Roman' 283–326 in M. C. Nussbaum and J. Sihvola (eds) *The Sleep of Reason: Erotic Experience and Sexual Ethics in Ancient Greece and Rome* (Chicago 2002)

Oakley, S. 'Single combat in the Roman republic' *Classical Quarterly* 79 (1985) 392–410

O'Brien, John 'Montaigne and antiquity: fancies and grotesques' 53–73 in U. Langer *The Cambridge Companion to Montaigne* (Cambridge 2005)

Ogilvie, R. M. *A Commentary of Livy Books 1–5* (2nd edn Oxford 1970)

O'Gorman, E. 'Shifting ground: Lucan, Tacitus and the landscape of civil war' *Hermathena* 158 (1995) 117–31

—— *Irony and Misreading in the Annals of Tacitus* (Cambridge 2000)

Oliensis, E. 'Sons and lovers: sexuality and gender in Virgil's poetry' 294–311 in C. Martindale (ed.) *The Cambridge Companion to Virgil* (Cambridge 1997)

Osborne, Thomas '"Fascinated dispossession": suicide and the aesthetics of freedom' *Economy and Society* 34.2 (2005) 280–94

Parker, Holt 'The observed of all observers: spectacle, applause, and cultural poetics in the Roman theatre audience' 163–79 in Bergmann and Kondoleon (1999)

Pelling, Christopher 'Is death the end? Closure in Plutarch's *Lives*' 228–50 in Roberts, Dunn and Fowler (1997)

Perkins, Judith *The Suffering Self: Pain and Narrative Representation in the Early Christian Era* (London 1995)

Pinguet, Maurice *Voluntary Death in Japan* (Oxford 1993), trs. by Rosemary Morris of original French edn (Paris 1984)

Plass, Paul *The Game of Death in Ancient Rome: Arena Sport and Political Suicide* (Madison 1995)

Potter, D. 'Martyrdom as spectacle' 53–88 in Ruth Scodel (ed.) *Theatre and Society in the Classical World* (Ann Arbor 1993)

—— review of Wiedemann (London 1992)

—— 'Death as spectacle and subsequent disposal' *Journal of Roman Archaeology* 14 (2001) 478–84

Quinn, Kenneth *Latin Explorations* (London 1963)

Quint, David *Montaigne and the Quality of Mercy* (Princeton 1998)

Raith, Oskar *Petronius ein Epikureer* (Nuremberg 1963)

Rawson, E. 'Discrimina ordinum: the *lex Iulia theatralis*' *Papers of the British School at Rome* 53 (1987) 97–113

Reece, R. (ed.) *Burial in the Roman World* (London 1977)

Reinhardt, Tobias 'The speech of nature in Lucretius *DRN* 3.931–71' *Classical Quarterly* 52 (2002) 291–304

—— 'Readers in the Underworld: Lucretius, *De rerum natura* 3.912–1075' *Journal of Roman Studies* 94 (2004) 27–46

Rich, J. and G. Shipley (eds) *War and Society in the Roman World* (London 1993)

Richlin, Amy 'Cicero's head' 190–211 in J. Porter (ed.) *Constructions of the Classical Body* (Ann Arbor 1999)

Rimell, Victoria *Petronius and the Anatomy of Fiction* (Cambridge 2002)

Rist, John *Stoic Philosophy* (Cambridge 1969)

Robert, Louis *Les Gladiateurs dans l'orient grec* (Paris 1940)

Roberts, Deborah, Francis Dunn and Don Fowler *Classical Closure: Reading the End in Greek and Latin Literature* (Princeton 1997)

Rogers, R. S. 'A Tacitean pattern in narrating treason trials' *Transactions of the American Philological Association* 83 (1952) 279–311

Rohde, E. *Psyche* (London 1925), trs. by W. B. Hillis of 8th German edn

Roller, Matthew 'Ethical contradiction and the fractured community in Lucan's *Bellum civile*' *Classical Antiquity* 15 (1996) 319–47

—— 'Color-blindness: Cicero's death, declamation and the production of oratory' *Classical Philology* 92 (1997) 109–30

—— *Constructing Autocracy: Aristocrats and Emperors in Julio-Claudian Rome* (Princeton 2001)

Rosen, R. M. and I. Sluiter (eds) *Andreia: Studies in Manliness and Courage in Classical Antiquity* (Leiden 2003)

Rosenblum, R. *Transformations in Late Eighteenth-century Art* (Princeton 1967)

Rosenmeyer, T. G. *Senecan Drama and Stoic Cosmology* (Berkeley 1989)

Rosenstein, N. *Imperatores victi: Military Defeat and Aristocratic Competition in the Middle and Late Republic* (Berkeley 1990)

Rutz, W. 'Amor mortis bei Lucan' *Hermes* 88 (1960) 462–75

Ste Croix, G. E. M. de 'Why were the early Christians persecuted?' 210–49 in M. I. Finley (ed.) *Studies in Ancient Society* (London 1974)

Salisbury, Joyce E. *Perpetua's Passion: The Death and Memory of a Young Roman Woman* (New York 1997)

Sandbach, F. H. *The Stoics* (London 1975)

Santoro L'hoir, F. 'Tacitus and women's usurpation of power' *Classical World* 88.1 (1994) 5–25

Saylor, W. 'Lux extrema: Lucan *Pharsalia* 4.402–581' *Transactions of the American Philological Association* 120 (1990) 291–300

Scarpat, G. *Lettere a Lucilio: libro primo (Epp. I–XII)* (Brescia 1975)

Scheid, John 'Contraria facere: renversements et déplacements dans les rites funeraires' *Annali del Istituto Universitario Orientale di Napoli* [Archeologia e storia antica] 6 (1984) 117–39

Schiesaro, A. *The Passions in Play: Thyestes and the Dynamics of Senecan Drama* (Cambridge 2003)

Schofield, Malcolm 'Academic therapy: Philo of Larissa and Cicero's project in the *Tusculans*' 91–107 in G. Clark and T. Rajak (eds) *Philosophy and Power in the Greco-Roman World: Essays in Honour of Miriam Griffin* (Oxford 2002)

—— 'Cicero, Brutus, virtue, happiness: Tusculan Disputations 5' (forthcoming)

Schönegg, Beat *Senecas epistulae morales als philosophisches Kunstwerk* (Bern 1999)

Schunk, P. 'Studien zur Darstellung des Endes von Galba, Otho und Vitellius in den

Historien des Tacitus' *Symbolae Osloenses* 39 (1964) 38–82

Scott, R. D. 'The death of Nero's mother' *Latomus* 33.1 (1974) 105–15

Scourfield, D. *Consoling Heliodorus: A Commentary on Jerome, letter 60* (Oxford 1993)

Seale, Clive *Constructing Death: The Sociology of Dying and Bereavement* (Cambridge 1998)

Sedley, David 'The ethics of Brutus and Cassius' *Journal of Roman Studies* 87 (1997) 41–53

Segal, Charles '*Nomen sacrum*: Medea and other names in Senecan tragedy' *Maia* 34 (1982) 241–6

—— 'Poetic immortality and the fear of death: the second proem of the *De rerum natura*' *Harvard Studies in Classical Philology* 92 (1989) 193–202

—— *Lucretius on Death and Anxiety* (Princeton 1990)

Shaw, Brent 'The cultural meaning of death: age and gender in the Roman family' 66–90 in D. Kertzer and R. Saller (eds) *The Family in Italy from Antiquity to the Present* (New Haven 1991)

—— 'The passion of Perpetua' *Past and Present* 139 (1993) 1–45

—— 'Body/Power/Identity: Passions of the Martyrs' *Journal of Early Christian Studies* 4.3 (1996) 269–312

—— 'Judicial Nightmares and Christian Memory' *Journal of Early Christian Studies* 11.4 (2003) 533–63

Shelton, Jo-Ann 'The spectacle of death in Seneca *Troades*' 87–118 in G. Harrison (ed.) *Seneca in Performance* (London 2000)

Shochat, Y. 'Tacitus' attitude to Otho' *Latomus* 40.1 (1981) 365–77

Sinclair, Patrick 'Rhetorical generalizations in Annales 1–6. A review of the problem of innuendo and Tacitus' integrity' *Aufstieg und Niedergang der römischen Welt* 2.33.4 (1991) 2795–829

Skard, E. *Sallust und seine Vorgänger. Eine sprachliche Untersuchung*, Symbolae Osloenses Suppl. 15 (Oslo 1956)

Slater, Niall 'Against interpretation: Petronius and art criticism' *Ramus* 16 (1987) 165–76

—— *Reading Petronius* (Baltimore 1990)

Sontag, S. *Regarding the Pain of Others* (New York 2003)

Sordi, M. (ed.) *Dulce et decorum est pro patria mori: la morte in combattimento nell' antichità* (Milan 1990)

Sordi, M. 'Cicerone e il primo epitafio romano' 171–9 in Sordi (1990)

Sourvinou-Inwood, C. *'Reading' Greek Death* (Oxford 1995)

Späth, Thomas *Männlichkeit und Weiblichkeit bei Tacitus: zur Konstruktion der Geschlechter in der römischen Kaiserzeit* (Frankfurt 1994)

Spentzou, E. and D. Fowler (eds) *Cultivating the Muse: Struggles for Power and Inspiration in Classical Literature* (Oxford 2002)

Stableford, Brian (ed.) *The Second Dedalus Book of Decadence: The Black Feast* (Sawtry, Cambs. 1992)

Straw, C. '"A very special death": Christian martyrdom in its classical context' 39–57 in Cormack (2001)

Studlar, G. *In the Realm of Pleasure: Von Sternberg, Dietrich and the Masochistic Aesthetic* (Urbana 1988)

Sullivan, J. P. *The Satyricon of Petronius: A Literary Study* (London 1968)

—— 'Petronius' *Satyricon* in its Neronian context' *Aufstieg und Niedergang der römischen Welt* 2.32.3 (1985) 1666–86

Sumi, G. 'Impersonating the dead: mimes at Roman funerals' *American Journal of Philology* 123 (2002) 559–86

Syme, R. *Tacitus* (Oxford 1958)

—— *Sallust* (Cambridge 1964)

Tadic-Gilloteaux, N. 'Sénèque face au suicide' *L'Antiquité classique* 32 (1963) 541–51

Tandoi, V. '*Moritura verba Catonis*' *Maia* 17 (1965) 315–39, 18 (1966) 20–41

Tanner, R.G. 'Martyrdom in Saint Ignatius of Antioch and the Stoic view of suicide' 201–5 in E.A.Livingstone (ed.) *Studia patristica* Vol.16.2 (Berlin 1985)

Thompson, L. and R.T. Bruère 'The Virgilian background of Lucan's fourth book' *Classical Philology* 65 (1970) 152–72

Toner, J.P. *Leisure and Ancient Rome* (Oxford 1995)

Townend, G.B. 'The literary substratum to Juvenal's satires' *Journal of Roman Studies* 63 (1973) 148–60

Toynbee, J.M.C. *Death and Burial in the Roman World* (London 1971)

Trapp, M.B. 'Socrates, the *Phaedo* and the lives of Phocion and Cato' 487–99 in A.Pérez Jimenez (ed.) *Plutarco, Platon y Aristoteles* (Madrid 1999)

—— 'Beyond Plato and Xenophon: some other ancient Socrateses' in *idem* (ed.) *Socrates from Antiquity to the Enlightenment* (Aldershot 2007)

Treggiari, Susan *Roman Marriage: iusti coniuges from the Time of Cicero to the Time of Ulpian* (Oxford 1991)

Trout, D.E. review of Perkins 1995 in *Church History* 67.3 (1998) 562–4

Tucker, R. 'Tacitus and the death of Lucan' *Latomus* 46 (1987) 330–7

Twain, Mark *The Innocents Abroad* (New York 1969)

Valvo, A. '"Legibus soluti virtutis causa" nelle disposizioni della X Tabula' 145–55 in Sordi (1990)

Vernant, Jean-Pierre *Mortals and Immortals: Collected Essays*, trs. and ed. F. Zeitlin (Princeton 1991)

Versnel, H.S. 'Two types of Roman *devotio*' *Mnemosyne* 29 (1976) 365–400

—— 'Self-sacrifice, compensation and the anonymous gods' 135–94 in *Le Sacrifice dans l'antiquité*, Entretiens sur l'antiquité classique Vol. 27 (Geneva 1981)

Veyne, Paul *Le Pain et le Cirque: sociologie historique d'un pluralisme politique* (Paris 1976)

—— 'Suicide, fisc, esclavage, capital et droit romain' *Latomus* 40.1 (1981) 217–68

—— *Seneca: The Life of a Stoic* trs. D.Sullivan (New York and London 2003)

Ville, Georges *La Gladiature en occident des origines jusqu'à la mort de Domitien* ed. P.Veyne (Rome 1981)

Vogt, Joseph 'Der sterbende Sklave. Vorbild menschlicher Vollendung' 6–16 in *idem Sklaverei und Humanität. Ergänzungsheft* (Wiesbaden 1983)

Voisin, J.-L. 'Apicata, Antinous et quelques autres. Notes d'épigraphie sur la mort volontaire à Rome' *Mélanges de l'Ecole française de Rome: Antiquité* 99 (1987) 257–80

Voisin, M. 'Le suicide d'Amata' *Revue des Etudes Latines* 57 (1979) 254–66

Vovelle, Michel *La mort et l'Occident, de 1300 à nos jours* (Paris 1983)

Vretska, K. (ed.) *C.Sallustius Crispus, de Catilinae coniuratione* 2 vols (Heidelberg 1976)

Walker, Beryl *The Annals of Tacitus: A Study in the Writing of History* (Manchester 1952)

Walker, S. *Memorials to the Roman Dead* (London 1985)

Wallace-Hadrill, Andrew '*Civilis princeps*: between citizen and king' *Journal of Roman Studies* 72 (1982) 32–48

Walsh, P. *The Roman Novel: The 'Satyricon' of Petronius and the 'Metamorphoses' of Apuleius* (Cambridge 1970)

Walter, T. *The Revival of Death* (London 1994)

Warren, James 'Socratic suicide' *Journal of Hellenic Studies* 121 (2001) 91–106

—— *Facing Death: Epicurus and his Critics* (Oxford 2004)

Welch, K. 'The Roman arena in late republican Italy: a new interpretation' *Journal of Roman Archaeology* 4 (1994) 59–80

West, D.A. *The Imagery and Poetry of Lucretius* (Edinburgh 1969)

—— 'The bough and the gate' 224–38 in S. Harrison (ed.) *Oxford Readings in Vergil's Aeneid* (Oxford 1990)

Whaley, Joachim *Mirrors of Mortality: Studies in the Social History of Death* (London 1981)

White, S. 'Cicero and the therapists' in J. Powell (ed.) *Cicero the Philosopher* (Oxford 1995)

Wiedemann, Thomas *Emperors and Gladiators* (London 1992)

Wilamowitz von Möllendorf, U. *Griechische Tragödien* (Berlin 1919)

Wilkins, A. T. *Villain or Hero? Sallust's Portrayal of Catiline* (New York 1994)

Williams, G. D. 'Cleombrotos of Ambracia: interpretations of a suicide from Callimachus to Augustine' *Classical Quarterly* 45 (1995) 154–69

Wilson, Marcus 'Seneca's Epistles to Lucilius: a revaluation' *Ramus* 16 (1987) 102–21

—— 'Subjugation of grief in Seneca's "Epistles"' 48–67 in Braund and Gill (1997)

—— 'Seneca's Epistles reclassified' 164–88 in S. J. Harrison (ed.) *Texts, Ideas and Classical Literature* (Oxford 2001)

—— 'After the silence: Tacitus, Suetonius, Juvenal' 523–42 in Boyle and Dominik (2003)

Wirszubski, C. *Libertas as a Political Idea at Rome during the Late Republic and Early Principate* (Cambridge 1950)

Wiseman, T. P. 'Roman republic year 1' *Greece & Rome* 45 (1998) 19–25

Wistrand, M. 'Violence and entertainment in Seneca the Younger' *Eranos* 88 (1990) 31–46

—— *Entertainment and Violence in Ancient Rome: The Attitudes of Roman Writers of the First Century AD* (Göteborg 1992)

Wlosok, A. 'The Dido tragedy in Virgil: a contribution to the question of the tragic in the *Aeneid*' 158–81 in P. Hardie (ed.) *Virgil: Critical Assessments* Vol. IV (London 1999; first edn 1976)

Woodman, A. J. *Rhetoric in Classical Historiography* (London 1988)

—— 'Amateur dramatics at the court of Nero: Tacitus *Annals* 15.48–74' 104–28 in A. J. Woodman and T. J. Luce (eds) *Tacitus and the Tacitean Tradition* (Princeton 1993)

—— *Tacitus Reviewed* (Oxford 1998)

Wray, David 'Manly matrons and Stoic virtue in Seneca and Valerius Maximus' (forthcoming)

Wright, J. R. G. 'Form and content in the moral essays' 39–69 in C. D. N. Costa (ed.) *Seneca* (London 1974)

Wyke, Maria *The Roman Mistress* (Oxford 2002)

Yavetz, Zwi *Plebs and Princeps* (London 1969)

Zetzel, J. E. G. 'Strength and wisdom are not opposing values' (forthcoming)

INDEX

Where relevant, individuals are listed under the more familiar English forms of their names

Achilles Tatius 213
Aemilia Lepida 118, 194
Aemilius Scaurus, Mamercus 117, 194
Aeneas 16–17, 23–4, 96, 183–5
Aestheticisation 4–6, 12, 144, 153, 178, 180–1, 186, 206, 213
Afterlife 6, 13–20, 79–82, 85–6, 96, 164, 207–8, 217–20
Agency 10, 101–2, 122, 210
Agnes 213
Agrestis 142
Agricola, Gnaeus Julius 28, 125–6, 128, 133, 138–9
Agrippina (Elder) 196–7, 202
Agrippina (Younger) 135, 197, 199–203
Antistia Pollitta 194–5
Antony, Mark 22, 70–1, 184–5
Appian 115, 117
Arena (see also Gladiators) 11, 13, 44, Ch. 2 passim, 109, 144, 207–9, 212, 214–15
Ariès, Philippe 9–10
Arria (Elder) 132, 191–4, 196, 205
Arria (Younger) 132
Arrowsmith, William 171
Arulenus Rusticus, Q. Junius 132, 140, 157
Asper, Sulpicius 122
Athens 21–2, 82–3, 155, 157, 177
Atticus 154; death of 2–4
Audience, self as 4, 106–7, 151–3, 159, 217

Aufidius Bassus 73, 104, 176
Augustine 64–6, 182, 208–10, 212, 214–17
Augustus 2, 21–3, 48–9, 54, 140, 156, 182–3, 185, 196, 201–2; death of 145
Aurelius, Marcus 75, 146, 159

Barbarians 26, 46, 51–2
Barea Soranus, Q. Marcius 122, 130, 134–6
Barthes, Roland 118, 142, 144
Barton, Carlin 5, 49, 71, 74, 217
Bereavement 8, 10, 189–91
Bergamín, José 67
Bergmann, Bettina 53
Blaesi, Iunii 118
Boswell, James 68–9
Boudicca 188
Bronfen, Elisabeth 10–12, 180
Brutus, Lucius Junius 22, 150, 181, 183–4, 190–1
Brutus, Marcus Junius 2–3, 21, 40, 101, 134, 139–40, 150, 191
Bull-fighting 67
Bynum, Caroline 219
Byron, Lord 46

Caesar, Gaius Julius 1–3, 28, 33–4, 40–1, 43–5, 48, 91, 114–15, 122, 124, 134, 140, 148, 150, 156–7, 181; death of 7
Caligula 54, 61, 113–14, 128, 162, 203
Camilla 183

Canetti, Elias 11, 13
Cannibalism 174–5
Canus, Julius 113–14
Capito 134–5
Cassius Longinus, Gaius 2, 139–40
Catiline, Lucius Sergius 29–31, 36, 97
Cato, Marcus Porcius (Younger) 1–5,
    9–10, 12, 33–5, 37–8, 45, 75–6, 78, 87,
    89–90, 100–1, 111, 114–16, 121–2, 131–2,
    134–7, 146, 148, 150–2, 154–9, 192, 209,
    216–17
Christianity 4, 6–7, 9, 11, 46, 49, 58–60,
    63–6, 207–20
Cicero, Marcus Tullius 2–3, 14–17, 20–2,
    24, 27–9, 50, 52, 52, 60–2, 65–7, 69–73,
    85–8, 90–2, 97, 114, 119–20, 146–8,
    154–5, 188; death of 71
Civil war 1–3, 12–13, 24, 28–45, 70, 80,
    88, 92, 115, 130–1, 184, 209
Claranus 189
Classicus 119
Claudius 62, 128, 192–4, 197–8, 200, 203
Clemency 114–15, 124
Cleopatra 184–7, 201
Cloelia 190
Colosseum 46, 55
Commemoration 5, 8, 13–14
Connors, Cathy 157
Consolation 8, 69, 85, 189–91, 219
Constantia 122, 133, 136, 142, 148, 154–5,
    177, 194–5
Corellius Rufus 132
Cornelia 190
Cowardice 27, 34, 37, 54, 60–1, 75, 80,
    194, 198, 203–4
Crassus, Publius Licinius 32
Cremutius Cordus, Aulus 131, 139–41,
    143, 216

Death, beautiful 21, 23–4
Death, desire for 4, 43, 104–6, 184, 218
Death, good 24, 73
Death in battle 6, 7, 12, Ch. 1 passim, 61,
    124, 129–30, 183, 188
Death-literature 131–4, 154, 157–8
Death, rehearsals for 175–6, 178
Death, Roman 1, 6, 108, 117, 127, 137, 182
Death, sudden 7

Debord, Guy 54
Decadence 161, 171–6, 178
Decius Mus (father and son) 25–7, 30, 32,
    34, 44–5
Declamation 155–6
Democritus 84–5
Demography 5, 11
Derrida, Jacques 6
Des Esseintes, Jean 161, 163, 167
Devotio 25–7, 30, 34–5, 38, 41, 44
Dido 12, 17, 183–8, 201
Dining 6, 81, 161–78
Dio, Cassius 49, 55, 116, 126–7, 161–4,
    191–2
Diogenes Laertius 98–9
Dionysius of Halicarnassus 22–4, 27
Dollimore, Jonathan 10
Domitian 52, 117, 125–6, 128, 132–3,
    137–9, 141, 154, 161–7, 176
Domitius 33–4
Donaldson, Ian 181
Drusus Libo 99–100, 117, 121, 130
Durkheim, Emile 9–10

Eldred, Katherine 43
Emperors 49, 50–5, 67, 74, 113–43, 161–4,
    214
Endurance see Constantia
Ennius 25
Epicharis 203–5
Epictetus 146, 149–50, 158
Epicurus 79, 83, 98, 152, 166; death
    of 84–5
Eroticism 8, 10, 12, 53, 63–8, 76–7, 164,
    183–4, 209, 213
Eulalia 213
Euryalus 23

Family 8, 13, 19, 117, 119, 145
Fannia 193–4
Fannius 132
Fear 63, 73, 78–112, 118, 162–4, 171, 176,
    199
Feldherr, Andrew 26
Flaminius, Gaius 27
Fredrick, David 164
Freedom 3, 31, 34, 42, 100–4, 115, 123,
    125–7, 134, 136, 155–7, 170, 210, 220

Freud, Sigmund 12–13, 216
Funerals 8, 19–23, 47–9, 59–60, 132, 164,
 167–70, 173, 175

Gaius (emperor) *see* Caligula
Game-theory 114, 124–5
Gender 7, 10–12, 20, 43, 49, 53, 63, 66–7,
 90–1, Ch. 7 *passim*, 212, 214
Gladiators (*see also* Arena) Ch. 2 *passim*;
 elite as 50–1, 55, 58, 74; faces of,
 exposed 62–3; as metaphor 69–78,
 211–12, 214; oath of 49–50, 70, 72
Glory 20–1, 27, 61, 74, 124–5, 130–1, 134,
 139–40, 144, 177, 193
Goffman, Erving 151–2
Goodwin, Sarah 11
Gorer, Geoffrey 10
Gracchus, Gaius 117
Guilt 32–3, 39–40, 118–19, 121, 139, 182,
 184, 187, 198, 201
Gunderson, Eric 53, 75

Heidegger, Martin 9
Helvia 189–91, 195, 205
Helvidius Priscus 122, 132, 138–40, 149–
 50, 158, 193
Henderson, John 28, 33
Herennius Senecio 132, 138–40
Higonnet, Margaret 179
Hill, Tim 10, 116
History-painting 4–5
History-writing 20–1, 78, 118, 127–31,
 138–41
Homer 14, 17, 21, 23–4, 34, 51
Honour (*see also* Pudicitia) 10, 13, 27, 54,
 71–2, 75, 119, 180, 184, 198, 210
Hopkins, Keith 5, 216
Horace 156, 167
Huysmans, J.K. 161, 171

Ignatius of Antioch 211, 218
Illness 1, 3–4, 73, 82–4, 106–7, 189, 217
Infamia 49–51, 61
Initiation 7, 14–15

Jerome 182, 213–14
Judaism 209, 219
Julia (Elder) 196

Juvenal 58, 63–4, 138, 163

Lactantius 58–9, 163
Law 119–21, 123, 210
Licinius Macer, Gaius 119–20
Livy 12, 25–7, 30, 47, 52, 56, 63, 71–2, 88,
 94, 118, 180–3, 187–8
Lucan 3, 6, 12–13, 24, 33–6, 39–45, 47, 67,
 154, 209; death of 130, 204–5
Lucretia 12, 180–3, 187–8, 190–1, 201, 206,
 209, 212
Lucretius 17, 78–86, 95, 167, 171–2, 178

Maiestas 120–1, 123, 127, 131, 134–6,
 139–41
Mallonia 123
Marcellus, Eprius 135
Marcia 189–91, 195
Martial 1, 3, 38–9, 55, 108, 126, 137–8, 167,
 182, 192, 205
Martindale, Charles 39, 42
Martyrs (Christian) 50, 207–20
Masochism 12–13, 43, 67–8
Medea 150, 159
Messalina 128, 197–9
Milo, Titus Annius 60, 69–70
Minucius Felix 218
Montaigne, Michel de 3–5
Mortuary ritual (*see also* Funerals) 5, 10,
 58, 107, 162–4, 168–9
Mysteries (*see* Initiation)

Nature 14–15, 80–1, 146
Nepos, Cornelius 4
Nero 7, 13, 28, 34–6, 52, 68, 86, 110, 114–
 15, 118, 124, 126, 128, 130, 134–6, 154,
 156, 158–60, 161, 170–1, 176, 178, 194–5,
 198–204; death of 159–60
Nerva (emperor) 133
Nerva (friend of Tiberius) 123, 130
Nisus 23
Nock, A. D. 98
Noxii 50, 61, 210–11

Octavia 197–9
Octavian *see* Augustus
Orpheus 17
Osborne, Thomas 158

Otho 36–9
Ovid 53, 67–8, 187

Pacuvius 175–6, 178
Pain 65, 67, 77, 87–90, 111, 121, 136, 154–5, 183, 188–91, 212–13, 219
Pallas 23
Panaetius 147–8
Parentalia 13, 164
Paul 210–11
Paulina 105–6, 110, 195–6
Perpetua 210–14, 219
Persius 156
Persona ('role') 146–59
Petronius 154, 167–72, 174, 216; death of 158–9, 176–8
Philosophy 15–18, 47, 69–77, 123, 131–2, 156–8, 166–7, 176–7; Epicurean 17, 79–85, 166–7, 171–2, 178; Stoic 2–4, 16, 42, 45, 74, 122, 145–54, 159, 172, 176, 189–90, 205, 216–18
Piso, Gaius Calpurnius 119, 128, 130, 156, 170, 176, 194, 203–4
Piso, Gnaeus Calpurnius 118, 123
Plass, Paul 5, 61, 114, 118, 124–5
Plato 2–3, 15–16, 86, 90, 176–8; Phaedo 2, 99, 102, 105, 136, 155, 157, 176–7
Pleasure 4, 12, 20–1, 26, 43, 46, 58–9, 61–8, 76–7, 80, 161, 171–4, 176–8, 183, 186, 198, 208, 219
Pliny (Elder) 7, 13–14, 48, 61, 107
Pliny (Younger) 8, 17, 52–3, 107, 119, 132–3, 138, 162, 192–4, 205
Plutarch 1–3, 14, 38, 91, 101, 150, 154, 157–8, 186, 191–2
Polybius 8, 19–22, 24, 27–8
Polycarp 211, 218
Pompey 31, 33, 35
Pomponius Labeo 120–1, 123
Porcia 191–2
Propertius 8, 186
Prudentius 64, 66, 212–13, 219
Psychoanalysis 10, 12–13, 216
Pudicitia ('sexual honour') Ch. 7 passim
Punishment 10, 40–1, 62–3, 68–9, Ch. 4 passim, 182, 206–8, 210, 215

Quintus Fabius 118

Rape 180–3, 198, 200–1, 206
Religion (see also Christianity, Judaism) 7, 13–18, 59–60, 64, 83, 207–20
Republic 3, 47, 68, 74, 100, 138, 150, 181, 184
Roller, Matthew 94, 162
Romanus 212–13, 219
Romulus 28–9
Rosenmeyer, Thomas 151–2
Rubellius Plautus 194
Rutilia 190

Sacrifice, human 59–60; self (see also Devotio) 9–10, 24–7, 179
Sallust 24, 29–31, 36, 91, 131, 141, 172
Satire 138
Scaevola, Gaius Mucius 32, 87–8, 94, 106, 217–18
Schopenhauer, Arthur 9
Scipio Aemilianus, dream of 15–16, 88, 92
Scipio, Q.Caecilius Metellus Pius 2, 88
Seale, Clive 69
Sejanus 117–18, 127, 130, 206
Sempronius Gracchus 122, 130
Seneca 3–4, 6, 16–18, 31–2, 42, 47, 49–50, 61, 66–7, 72–9, 86–90, 92–107, 113–17, 126, 131, 145, 148–59, 172–8, 189–91, 195–6, 202, 204–5, 209, 212, 214–15, 217; death of 110–13, 130, 136, 143, 159–60
Sextia 194
Shaw, Brent 213
Silanus, Decimus Junius Torquatus 124
Silanus, Lucius 123–4, 130–1
Silence 134–6, 141, 143
Silius, Gaius 117, 121, 197–8
Slavery 50–1, 61, 70, 101–2, 131, 156
Socrates, death of 3, 15, 84, 87, 89, 99, 102, 105, 111, 155, 157–8, 176–8
Spartans 97
Spectacle, death as 11–12, 26, 43–5, Ch. 2 passim, 106–7, 115, 127, 136, 141, 144, 180–1, 186–7, 205–20
Statius 163
Suetonius 7, 38, 54, 62, 67, 116–17, 145, 159–60, 162
Suicide 7, 9–10, 12–13, 31–3, 36–9,

45, 75–9, 87, 112–16, 121, 179–206;
definitions of 9–10, 116; as alternative
to execution 117–21, 126–8, 135, 163,
196; as metaphor 39–45; methods
of 1, 3–4, 37–8, 102–3, 108–9, 111, 117,
137, 159–60, 182–3, 192, 196–7, 204–5; of
terminally ill 1, 3–4, 104–5, 121

Tacitus, Cornelius 13, 17, 20–1, 24, 28,
35–8, 49, 93, 100, 107, 110–14, 116–36,
138–44, 154, 156–9, 177–9, 194–206,
215–16; death of 142–3
Tarquin 180–3
Tertullian 11, 49, 59–60, 62–3, 69, 182,
207–11, 214
Theatre 6, 50, 84, Ch. 5 *passim*, 166–7,
215
Thrasea Paetus, P. Clodius 118, 122,
126–7, 130–2, 134–7, 140–1, 143, 154–5,
157–8, 216
Thucydides 21, 82–3, 131
Tiberius 122, 120, 118, 123, 127–8, 130,
140, 206
Titinius Capito, Gnaeus Octavius 132
Titus 55, 67
Tombs 13–14, 59, 168–9, 172–3
Trajan 52–3, 55, 133, 162
Treason (*see Maiestas*)
Trimalchio 167–72, 175, 178, 216
Triumph 114–15, 186
Truth, death as a moment of 5, 7–8, 87,
109–12, 142–3, 209–10, 216
Tullius Marcellinus 121–2

Turnus 24
Tyrtaeus 21

Valerius Asiaticus 128
Valerius Maximus 108, 116, 119–20, 187–8,
191–2, 212
Vernant, Jean-Pierre 21
Vespasian 122, 149–50
Vestinus Atticus 170–1
Ville, Georges 58
Virgil 6, 12, 16–17, 23–4, 96, 107, 183–8
Virginia 188
Virtus ('Virtue', 'Manliness') 7–8, 15, 28,
31–6, 41–5, 51–3, 66–7, 71, 77–9, 90–8,
116, 126, 130, 144, 179, 188–91, 195,
202–3, 205–6, 209–10, 215
Vitellius 142
Voyeurism 69, 186, 201, 208; sadistic 12,
66–7
Vulteius 12–13, 40–5, 67

Warfare 19–45, 51–2, 125, 188; as
metaphor 6, 90–7, 189, 217
Wiedemann, Thomas 61
Wilamowitz, Ulrich von 150
Wills 8, 120, 164, 168, 174
Witnessing 11–13, 20–1, 26, 28, 43–5, 111,
144–5, 150–1, 180–1, 186, 209–10, 212,
215

Xenophon 155

Zeno 95, 98, 166